Strategy and Human Resource Management

4th edition

MANAGEMENT, WORK AND ORGANISATIONS

Series editors: **Gibson Burrell**, School of Management, University of Leicester, UK
Mick Marchington, Manchester Business School, University of Manchester and Strathclyde Business School, University of Strathclyde, UK
Paul Thompson, Strathclyde Business School, University of Strathclyde, UK

This series of textbooks covers the areas of human resource management, employee relations, organisational behaviour and related business and management fields. Each text has been specially commissioned to be written by leading experts in a clear and accessible way. The books contain serious and challenging material, take an analytical rather than prescriptive approach and are particularly suitable for use by students with no prior specialist knowledge.

The series is relevant for many business and management courses, including MBA and post-experience courses, specialist masters and postgraduate diplomas, professional courses and final-year undergraduate courses. These texts have become essential reading at business and management schools worldwide.

Titles include:

Maurizio Atzeni
WORKERS AND LABOUR IN A GLOBALISED CAPITALISM

Stephen Bach and Ian Kessler
THE MODERNISATION OF THE PUBLIC SERVICES AND EMPLOYEE RELATIONS

Emma Bell
READING MANAGEMENT AND ORGANIZATION IN FILM

Paul Blyton and Peter Turnbull
THE DYNAMICS OF EMPLOYEE RELATIONS (3rd edition)

Paul Blyton, Edmund Heery and Peter Turnbull (editors)
REASSESSING THE EMPLOYMENT RELATIONSHIP

Sharon C. Bolton
EMOTION MANAGEMENT IN THE WORKPLACE

Sharon C. Bolton and Maeve Houlihan (editors)
SEARCHING FOR THE HUMAN IN HUMAN RESOURCE MANAGEMENT

Peter Boxall and John Purcell
STRATEGY AND HUMAN RESOURCE MANAGEMENT (4th edition)

J. Martin Corbett
CRITICAL CASES IN ORGANISATIONAL BEHAVIOUR

Susan Corby, Steve Palmer and Esmond Lindop
RETHINKING REWARD

David Farnham
THE CHANGING FACES OF EMPLOYMENT RELATIONS

Ian Greener
PUBLIC MANAGEMENT (2nd edition)

Keith Grint
LEADERSHIP

Irena Grugulis
SKILLS, TRAINING AND HUMAN RESOURCE DEVELOPMENT

Geraldine Healy, Gill Kirton and Mike Noon (editors)
EQUALITY, INEQUALITIES AND DIVERSITY

Damian Hodgson and Svetlana Cicmil (editors)
MAKING PROJECTS CRITICAL

Marek Korczynski
HUMAN RESOURCE MANAGEMENT IN SERVICE WORK

Karen Legge
HUMAN RESOURCE MANAGEMENT: ANNIVERSARY EDITION

Patricia Lewis and Ruth Simpson (editors)
GENDERING EMOTIONS IN ORGANIZATIONS

Patricia Lewis and Ruth Simpson (editors)
VOICE, VISIBILITY AND THE GENDERING OF ORGANIZATIONS

Alison Pullen, Nic Beech and David Sims (editors)
EXPLORING IDENTITY

Jill Rubery and Damian Grimshaw
THE ORGANISATION OF EMPLOYMENT

Hugh Scullion and Margaret Linehan (editors)
INTERNATIONAL HUMAN RESOURCE MANAGEMENT

John Walton and Claire Valentin (editors)
HUMAN RESOURCE DEVELOPMENT

For more information on titles in the Series please go to **www.palgrave.com/business/mwo**

Series Standing Order

If you would like to receive future titles in this series as they are published, you can make use of our standing order facility. To place a standing order please contact your bookseller or, in case of difficulty, write to us at the address below with your name and address and the name of the series. Please state with which title you wish to begin your standing order.

Customer Services Department, Macmillan Distribution Ltd,
Houndmills, Basingstoke, Hampshire, RG21 6XS, UK

Strategy and Human Resource Management

4th edition

Peter Boxall

and

John Purcell

 palgrave

First published 2016 by
PALGRAVE

Palgrave in the UK is an imprint of Macmillan Publishers Limited, registered in England, company number 785998, of 4 Crinan Street, London, N1 9XW.

Palgrave Macmillan in the US is a division of St Martin's Press LLC, 175 Fifth Avenue, New York, NY 10010.

Palgrave is the global imprint of the above companies and is represented throughout the world.

Palgrave® and Macmillan® are registered trademarks in the United States, the United Kingdom, Europe and other countries.

ISBN 978–1–137–40763–4 paperback

This book is printed on paper suitable for recycling and made from fully managed and sustained forest sources. Logging, pulping and manufacturing processes are expected to conform to the environmental regulations of the country of origin.

A catalogue record for this book is available from the British Library.

A catalog record for this book is available from the Library of Congress.

Printed in China

Contents

List of boxes, figures and tables   viii

Introduction   x

Acknowledgements   xiii

Part 1   Foundations

1   Human resource management: what and why?   **3**
Fundamental characteristics of HRM   3
Strategic goals and tensions in HRM   7
Discerning and describing HR strategies   25
Conclusions   28

2   Strategy and strategic management   **31**
Strategic problems and the strategies of firms   31
Strategy and the life cycle of the firm   41
The process of strategic management   46
Conclusions   53

Part 2   General principles

3   Strategic HRM: 'best fit' or 'best practice'?   **57**
Strategic HRM: the best-fit school   58
Strategic HRM: the best-practice school   72
Conclusions   79

4 Strategic HRM and sustained competitive advantage   **82**
The resource-based view of the firm   82
Competences and dynamic capabilities   90
HR strategy and sustained advantage   96
Conclusions   102

5 Building a workforce: the challenge of interest alignment   **104**
Talent management: building and renewing a workforce   105
Job quality and organisational attractiveness   115
Conclusions   130

6 Management power, employee voice and social legitimacy   **132**
The contested nature and changing contours of employee voice   133
What are the impacts of employee voice systems?   143
Management style in employee relations   148
Conclusions   151

7 Workforce performance and the 'black box' of HRM   **154**
The AMO model of performance   155
Analysing the management process in HRM   161
Conclusions   175

Part 3   Specific contexts

8 HR strategy in manufacturing   **179**
Manufacturing and its impacts on models of HRM   180
Globalisation and HR strategies in manufacturing   191
Lean production and HRM   196
Conclusions   200

9 HR strategy in services   **202**
What's different about services?   202
HR strategy in private sector services   205
HR strategy in public sector services   216
Conclusions   226

10 HR strategy in multidivisional firms   **228**
Structure and control in multidivisional firms   229
The implications of private equity for the multidivisional company   234
Challenges for HR strategy in the multidivisional company   239
Conclusions   249

11 HR strategy in multinational firms   **251**
The growth of multinational firms   251
Multinational strategies, structures and value chains   253
What's different about HR strategy in the multinational firm?   261
Conclusions   271

12 Final thoughts: main themes and next steps   **274**
   The main themes of this book   274
   Developing a 'more strategic approach' to HRM   288
   Conclusions   300

References   302

Author index   333

Subject index   344

List of boxes, figures and tables

Boxes

1.1	Human resource strategy	28
2.1	Human cognitive issues affecting strategic management	48
4.1	Qualities of desirable resources	86
4.2	Hamel and Prahalad's notion of 'core competence'	91
5.1	Supporting conditions for performance-related pay	127
12.1	An example of scenario-based HR planning	295

Figures

1.1	The strategic goals of HRM	17
2.1	Four critical elements in establishing a viable business	35
2.2	Phases of industry evolution	45
3.1	The Harvard 'map of the HRM territory'	59
3.2	Linking HR practices to competitive strategy	69
3.3	The 'best fit' versus 'best practice' debate: two levels of analysis	80
4.1	'HR architecture': a blended model	100
5.1	Mapping the quality of performance and potential in a workforce	108
6.1	Contrasts in, and examples of, employee voice	135
6.2	Voice systems and management style	150
7.1	The AMO model of individual performance	156
7.2	An expanded model of the 'black box' of HRM	173
8.1	High-involvement work systems: envisaged linkages and impacts	190
10.1	Three levels of strategic decision making in Anglo-American multidivisional firms	231

12.1   Drivers of job satisfaction and retention (a hypothetical model
       involving software developers within an expert model of HRM)   291
12.2   A hypothetical performance model (satisfaction with software
       services)   292

Tables

3.1   Pfeffer's seven practices   75
4.1   Types of knowledge   97
5.1   Job facet priorities of British workers   123
8.1   Hourly compensation costs in US dollars for production
      workers in manufacturing, 2012: selected countries   192
9.1   Business dynamics and HR strategies in services   205
12.1   Typology of models of HRM   280

Introduction

The last 30 years witnessed a major growth of interest in strategy and human resource management (HRM). Reacting to the dramatic growth of new technology, of competitive change and of regulatory reform, business leaders, and their counterparts in the public sector, looked for ways to design and implement more successful strategies. Consultancy practices responded to this explosion of interest. So too did the academic field of strategic management, which is now characterised by a range of theoretical schools, by extensive research and by large academic conferences. Business schools have invested enormous resources in the teaching of strategy, both in MBA programmes and in the 'capstone courses' of major undergraduate degrees.

The situation is much the same in HRM. The term first gained prominence in the USA where the most influential textbooks were initially published and where leading journals such as *Human Resource Management and Human Resource Management Review* are based. Outside the USA, the significance of HRM has been recognised in the launch and growth of the *Human Resource Management Journal*, the *International Journal of Human Resource Management* and *Asia Pacific Journal of Human Resources*, among others. Within business schools, and across more traditional academic departments, there has been an explosion of courses and publications concerned with the management of work and people. It may have been fashionable to treat Personnel Management as a 'Cinderella' subject in the 1970s but few universities today treat HRM with quite the same disdain.

The growth of interest in strategic management and HRM has not, however, been accompanied by sufficient concern for integrating these two important fields. This was our argument for writing the first edition of this book and remains our motivation in this fourth edition. Too much of the literature in strategic management continues to disregard the human issues that affect the performance and development of firms. Similarly, too much of the literature in HRM carries on the preoccupation of the personnel literature with individual techniques and fails to understand HR practices within their strategic context. Both bodies of literature have their characteristic weaknesses. On the strategy side, it is the failure to appreciate the ways in which the management of work and people is strategic to organisational success. On the HRM side, it is the failure to look up from the nooks and crannies of currently fashionable practices to study the bigger picture, to perceive the ways in which patterns of HRM relate to broader business problems and need to vary with the organisation's environment.

Strategy and Human Resource Management is not organised around the classical sub-functions of HR practice – selection, appraisal, pay, training and so on – with the word 'strategic' slipped in front. The sub-functional domains of micro-HRM do not dominate the design of chapters as if they were self-contained 'solutions'. Instead, we are concerned with examining how HR strategy impacts an organisation's chances of survival and its relative success, as well as with understanding how it varies across important organisational, industry and societal contexts. In tackling these questions, we are committed to what we call an 'analytical approach' to HRM. This means we try to understand what managers do and why they do it before we offer any sort of prescription for what we think they should do. In an analytical approach, empirical description and theoretical explanation come before policy prescription. This is an approach that is uncompromisingly about research but, wherever possible, we try to bring the story to life with the more interesting illustrations – cases and vignettes – with which we are familiar and, wherever possible, we insert references to valuable internet sites. In the book's companion website, we provide learning-support materials for every chapter.

Our overriding goal is to help readers perceive general principles in strategic HRM while simultaneously appreciating the ways in which HR strategies vary across specific contexts. The need for a dialogue between general principles and specific contexts is the central idea that informs the design of the book. We provide a comprehensive review of the literature for the academic reader and a basis for the practitioner to analyse their specific situation while also developing transferable lessons. The book can be used in MBA teaching and in courses in strategic HRM (at third- and fourth-year level), but it is not suitable for undergraduates with no prior introduction to organisational behaviour, HRM or employment relations in their national system. Those who want a compendium of HR practices should look elsewhere.

For this edition, all theoretical and practical material in the book has been rigorously reviewed and updated. The changes will be apparent from the first chapter to the last. Readers will find our main themes largely intact but many of the arguments have been revised, the selection of key studies has been reviewed, the terminology refined and the links to major events brought up to date. And now we come to a warning. The book has been somewhat reorganised so that the changes from the third to the fourth edition are much greater than those from the second to the third. The essential material in the previous Chapter 9 (on industry life cycles) has been shortened and incorporated into Chapter 2 (which builds our foundations on strategy), and the material on work organisation in the old Chapter 5 has been moved to Chapters 8 and 9 on manufacturing and services. We tackle our general foundations and principles in Parts 1 and 2, much as before, but we have enlarged Part 3 to ensure we cover more effectively the 'mega contexts' of manufacturing, services, multidivisional firms and multinationals. To give better attention to what is different about HR strategy in each of these sectors, they each have their own chapter. As a result, the book has been extended from 11 to 12 chapters with the final one summarising the overall themes and discussing how practitioners can enhance strategic analysis and planning in HRM. However, due to selective culling, the manuscript is 6,500 words shorter than the third edition. We think the revised structure will help readers to more effectively identify the general principles of strategic HRM and understand its distinctive contexts – but we will let you be the judge.

PETER BOXALL
JOHN PURCELL

Acknowledgements

Once again, it has been daunting, but satisfying, to work together on a book that sets out to survey an entire field, the kind of undertaking that is difficult for academics in an era of short-term projects targeted to research-quality assessments. Throughout four editions, we have learnt from and challenged each other, gaining insights, from both theory and experience, that we would never have obtained working alone. Working on this fourth edition at a time of great change in the world of employment and the wider recession has meant much reading and sharp debates, which has been invigorating. Some key people have made the project possible. We are particularly grateful for the support of Professor Greg Whittred, Professor Jilnaught Wong and Professor Nigel Haworth at the University of Auckland Business School who have enabled Peter to remain active in research while serving as an Associate Dean. A range of colleagues, students and practitioners helped us to develop and reshape the views reflected in the book and we are indebted to them all. This time, special thanks go to Professor Jaap Paauwe and Professor Jonathan Winterton for making it possible for Peter to spend his sabbatical in the lively environments of Tilburg University and Toulouse Business School. We are also indebted to Val Jephcott, the administrator of the Industrial Relations Research Unit at Warwick Business School, for the help given to John even after he had retired from a paid academic post at the research unit. But it is often observed that professors do not retire: they just lose their faculties. We thank our publisher, Palgrave Macmillan, for the faith expressed in the commissioning of this fourth edition of our work. We are especially appreciative of the many efforts of Ursula Gavin, Holly Rutter and Alex Antidius Arpoudam on our behalf. As ever, we express our heartfelt thanks to Marijanne and Kate for their unfailing interest in our work and well-being.

PETER BOXALL AND JOHN PURCELL

The authors and publishers are grateful to Professor Michael Beer for permission to reproduce the following copyright material: Figure 3.1 The Harvard 'Map of the HRM Territory'.

part 1
Foundations

1

Human resource management: what and why?

What is human resource management (HRM) and why is it a pervasive activity in organisations? What are managers trying to achieve through engaging in HRM and what kinds of challenges does it pose for them? The aim of this chapter is to address these basic, but critical, questions. We begin by defining the fundamental characteristics of HRM, emphasising the fact that organisations are dependent on the human resources that belong to people. Without ongoing access to people with the kind of talents they need, organisations are simply not viable. We then consider in greater depth the principal goals, or underpinning motives, that characterise management's behaviour in HRM. We examine the reasons why achieving these goals is difficult and why some firms fail at it or have highly variable outcomes. Understanding the importance of these goals, and the strategic tensions associated with them, helps us to appreciate the ways in which HRM makes a strategic impact on organisational performance. Finally, we provide some guidance on how to discern a firm's HR strategy, which is the concept we use to describe the critical choices that managers make in HRM. This chapter will introduce a range of concepts that will be developed further throughout the book.

Fundamental characteristics of HRM

What are human resources?

As the term suggests, HRM is a management activity concerned with 'human resources' but what do we mean when we link the words 'human' and 'resources'? In this book, we define human resources as the characteristics that are intrinsic to human beings, which people can apply to the various tasks and challenges of their lives (Boxall 2013, 2014). Most obviously, human resources include the knowledge, skills and energies that we can use in our daily roles or what Karl Marx (1867) called our 'labour-power' or 'capacity for labour'. Less obviously, human resources include our underpinning or dynamic characteristics, including our physical and emotional health, our intellectual capabilities, and our personalities and motivations. We can, in fact, think of these human characteristics as a set of human assets and liabilities. We have strengths (assets) that we can build on throughout life, using them to create social and economic opportunities for ourselves. But we also have weaknesses (liabilities) that can influence our options and affect the way other people, including recruiters, managers and colleagues, perceive us. This definition means that it is wrong to call people themselves 'human resources', a mistake made in a variety of textbooks and dictionaries. People are *not* human resources. On the contrary, people are independent agents *who possess* human resources, which are the talents they can deploy and develop at work and which they take with them when they leave an organisation.

Whatever our particular blend of strengths and weaknesses, we each have an underlying potential that can be more or less realised in our life. This principle was emphasised by Abraham Maslow (1970) in his classic analysis of human needs, in which 'self-actualisation' was positioned as the ultimate goal. We can apply our human resources to an ongoing process of personal development or may underuse our talents and fail to reach our potential. The latter syndrome was often noted in school reports in less politically correct days when a teacher made a comment about a child such as, 'Has ability but won't use it'. That child may, of course, have been switched off by the school system, or by this teacher in particular, but have found various ways to explore their talents outside of school and when they left it for good. Over the course of our adult lives, we face a lot of choices around how to use our talents. What form of higher education should we take, if any? How far should we go with it? When is a good time to get work experience? Are our particular abilities better fitted to this job opportunity or to another? Which organisation offers us the best scope for personal development? Would contracting to a variety of organisations, or starting our own business, be a better use of our talents?

Individuals, as Inkson (2008) argues, face a challenge of *self-management*. They need to make choices about how to deploy and develop their human resources. And the issue is not solely about how to deploy talents at work. People have interests in out-of-work activities, including friendships and family relationships, and various kinds of activity in their community. How well these concerns are balanced with paid work and with personal career advancement ('work-life balance') is a very major issue in our time. Overuse of our talents in work, and under-investment in our relationships, can lead to late-life regret, a phenomenon encapsulated in that infamous deathbed confession: 'I wish I hadn't spent so much time at the office'. Nowadays, of course, information and communication technologies, including computers and mobile phones, enable many of us to keep working wherever we are.

The styles we adopt to make these choices are very variable. Some individuals are driven by the expectations of others, including parents and friends, at least to begin with, before they accumulate greater understanding of their own likes and dislikes. Some develop a highly specific set of goals for their working lives, including answers to questions like 'Where do I want to be in five or ten years' time?' Many of us do not plan these choices in any formal way, but we learn from our experience as it accumulates. We 'go with the flow', taking an initial step in one direction and then taking up interesting opportunities that come across our path. The key point, however, is that human resources belong to us as individuals and move around with us as our lives unfold. In any society in which slavery has been eliminated, people possess their own human resources and have rights over how they are used.

What is human resource management?

What, then, does management want with human resources? In a nutshell, organisations are dependent on people who have the kind of human resources that will make them successful in their environment. It is only people, working with physical, symbolic and financial resources, who can create a viable business. Managers need to gain access to the human capital, or stock of human talents, that is relevant to the organisation's survival because organisations cannot develop products or services for a market and deliver them reliably unless they recruit and retain the people who have the knowledge, skills and inclination to do so. Furthermore, there is no hope of renewing the business, when it needs to change, unless it has access to individuals with the kind of insight and leadership abilities to make this happen (Boxall and Steeneveld 1999, Teece 2011).

But HRM is not simply about engaging the services of talented individuals. Working with the individuals they have recruited, managers are concerned with developing the organisation's *social* capital and fostering the *overall* performance that it needs. They are involved in creating a network of relationships among these people that combines their talents into the collective outcomes on which the business depends (Nahapiet and Ghoshal 1998, Leana and van Buren 1999). This challenge starts with the entrepreneur or with the 'intrapreneurial' team at the point of founding a business. HRM is an inevitable process that accompanies their efforts in combining a group of individuals into a functioning organisation. It is an essential element in entrepreneurial activity and a driver of organisational growth. The idea that we might need to justify the process of HRM in organisations is, thus, rather absurd. We may well wish to analyse the quality of a firm's approach to HRM and make changes but we inevitably come back to some kind of 'human resourcing' process (Watson 2005). Long-standing firms may go through periods in which they need to lay people off – possibly very large numbers of people – to improve their cost structure, but hardly any business will survive unless it is employing at least some suitably talented people on a regular basis. If everyone is laid off and their final entitlements are paid to them, the process of HRM will cease – but so will the firm.[1]

In order to build the human and social capital the organisation needs, managers adopt policies and practices for organising work and employing people. These policies and practices are the basic materials, or instruments, of HRM. Work policies and practices relate to the structure of work, which can range from low-discretion jobs where individuals have very limited control over what they do through to highly autonomous jobs where individuals largely supervise themselves. They include processes for building teams, where teamwork is considered important, and any associated opportunities to engage in problem-solving and the management of change (for example, through team meetings before shifts or task forces across departments). Employment policies and practices, on the other hand, are concerned with how managers try to hire and manage the people they need to do the organisation's work. They include management activities in recruiting, selecting, deploying, motivating, appraising, training, developing and retaining individual employees. In addition, they include processes for informing, consulting and negotiating with individuals and groups, such as trade unions and works councils, and activities associated with disciplining employees, terminating their contracts and downsizing entire workforces. As this makes apparent, the management of work and people includes both individual and collective dimensions, and it includes decisions that will have variable impacts on the interests of firms and workers. Some processes, such as the growth of employment and promotion opportunities, will typically foster greater cooperation between firms and workers because both parties see their interests being served. On the other hand, processes such as downsizing or negotiations over a reduced

---

[1] Except in the case of 'shell companies', which are defunct but may be revived when someone acquires the rights to the name and decides to use them.

salary budget inevitably bring conflict and require the management of difficult trade-offs between the interests of the firm and those of its employees.

Given this wide remit, it should be obvious that HRM is never the exclusive property of HR specialists. All firms have 'workforce strategies' (Huselid, Becker and Beatty 2005), whether or not they have a specialist HR department or function. Line managers – those who directly supervise employees engaged in the operations of the firm – are intimately involved in HRM, hiring people in their team when others resign and almost always held directly accountable for the performance of that team. In larger organisations, there may be permanent in-house HR specialists contributing specialist skills in such technical aspects of HRM as the design of recruitment and training processes, the maintenance of remuneration and benefit systems, the management of individual problems and grievances, and the conduct of collective employment negotiations. There may also be specialist HR consultants contracted to provide such important services as executive search and team building. All HR specialists, however, are engaged in 'selling' their services to other managers, in working together with other members of the management team to achieve the overall results. While at times they may be required to ensure compliance with employment laws, HR specialists are primarily people who use their knowledge and skills to support the line managers who directly manage the workforce (Legge 1978, O'Brien and Linehan 2014). In this book, the acronym 'HRM' is therefore used to refer to the totality of the firm's management of work and people and not simply to those aspects where HR specialists are involved.

Strategic goals and tensions in HRM

HRM, then, is the process through which management builds the workforce and tries to create the human performances that the organisation needs. This definition, however, only takes us so far. To improve our understanding of what is at stake in HRM, it helps to ask a deeper set of questions about the goals that underpin the process. What sorts of goals characterise the behaviour of managers as they undertake the complex and varied activities that make up human resource management? What, ultimately, do they want to achieve? What would they regard as a good performance? And how difficult is it? What obstacles stand in the way?

These are not necessarily easy questions to address. In asking about management's goals for HRM, we face the problem that these goals are often implicit or left unsaid (Purcell and Ahlstrand 1994, Gratton et al. 1999b). Research shows that it is the larger firms that are more likely to develop some formal or explicit goals for their HRM (Van Wanrooy et al. 2013: 54–5). Even when they do, we need to be careful in taking them at face value. In HRM, such documents can contain aspirational statements about the treatment of people that shroud a more opportunistic or pragmatic reality (Marchington and Grugulis 2000, Legge 2005). Statements of values and broad policies are always open to the interpretations of managers and sometimes their active subversion, as we will explore further in this book. To understand management's purposes, it is better to look at patterns of managerial behaviour in HRM, which tend to be laid down or 'sedimented' at critical moments in an organisation's history (Poole 1986). Goals may not be seriously questioned unless some kind of crisis emerges in the firm's growth or performance that forces reconsideration and restructuring (Snape, Redman and Wilkinson 1993, Colling 1995). Our task, then, is better understood as trying to infer the general intentions or motives underpinning HRM, recognising that we are studying a complex, collective process that is built up historically and inevitably subject to a degree of interpretation, politicking and inconsistent practice. It helps if we start by dividing the goals of HRM into two broad categories: the economic and the socio-political (Boxall 2007).

The economic goals of HRM

Cost-effective labour

HRM is always located in an economic context. The primary problem facing managers is how to secure the economic viability of their firm in the markets in which it competes. Economic viability means that a firm generates a return on investment that its shareholders consider acceptable or that meets the obligations it has to its bankers and other lenders (Cyert and March 1956, Kaysen 1960, Williamson 1964). Shareholders and other finance providers form part of the political coalition of stakeholders that sustains a firm (March 1962, Cyert and March 1963: 42–3). Management needs to ensure it meets their demands for a worthwhile return from the risk they are taking. The consequences of failing to generate an acceptable profit are that managers may be sacked, firms may be sold off, or they may be broken up and reabsorbed into other parts of a larger organisation. The profit motivation is fundamental to understanding how the firm works, including how managers choose their level of investment in HRM (Kaufman and Miller 2011).

For the HRM process to contribute to economic viability, managers need to ensure that the firm has access to the people it needs and that they can be employed in a way that is affordable. In other words, management needs to establish a *cost-effective* system for managing the people the business requires

(Geare 1977, Osterman 1987, Godard 2001). Cost-effectiveness is a dual concept. It incorporates the idea that a firm needs people who are effective, who are skilled at what the firm wants them to do, while also motivating them to perform at a cost (wages, benefits, training, etc.) that the firm can afford to pay. A viable approach to HRM is one that delivers on the grounds of *both* effectiveness *and* cost.

The shape of a viable strategy for HRM, however, varies significantly across the kind of industries and markets in which the firm competes. For example, in the discount retail sector, where standard, low-priced goods are sold in bulk, consumers often shop around for the lowest prices, competition among firms is often intense and even minor cost differences can threaten a firm's viability (Jany-Catrice, Gadrey and Pernod 2005). In such circumstances, stores have some long-term managers and experienced employees to provide a reliable 'backbone' to operations but otherwise do enough in HRM to attract less experienced workers, such as part-time student workers and new migrants, who are paid the kind of wage that is adequate in the retail sector (Siebert and Zubanov 2009). This is typically at, or not much above, the legal minimum wage (Osterman 2001). Managers do not expect most of these workers to stay for the long term but provide a basic setting in which they can gain some working experience and move on. Their business model typically turns on providing sufficient, rather than superior, service standards because customers are more price- than quality-sensitive. As a result, expensive models of HRM, which incorporate more rigorous employee selection, higher pay, and extensive internal employee development, are unusual in this industry (Boxall 2003).

On the other hand, as Godard and Delaney (2000: 488) explain, high-skill, high-commitment HR strategies are more often found in industries where the production system is capital-intensive or where advanced technology is involved. In capital-intensive conditions, the actual level of labour cost will be quite low (often 10 per cent or less of total cost), but workers will have a major effect on how well the expensive technology is utilised (Blauner 1964). It thus pays to remunerate and train them very well, making better use of their skills and ensuring their motivation is kept high. As they find ways of making the equipment meet or even exceed its specifications, the unit costs of labour fall and productivity rises. Thus, in this kind of context, the firm can easily sustain high wage levels. It is more important *not* to alienate this kind of labour – because of the productivity impacts of disruptions to production – than it is to worry about wage levels (Blauner 1964: 136, 180).

In summary, the fundamental economic motive that can be observed in HRM is concerned with making the firm's human capabilities productive at an affordable cost in the market concerned. In effect, managers ask: what HR systems are cost-effective or 'profit-rational' in our specific context? In capitalist societies, the pursuit of cost-effectiveness runs across the management of people in all business organisations and also makes its impact in public sector organisations through their budget constraints and contracting requirements. Cost-effectiveness is a core consideration in the way managers go about HRM.

Organisational flexibility

Cost-effectiveness is not, however, the only economic motive we can observe in HRM. While cost-effective labour is essential to economic viability in any context, change is inevitable and so an element of flexibility is also an issue for managers. Managers have an incentive to adopt some HR practices that will enhance organisational flexibility or the capacity of the firm to change as its environment changes (Osterman 1987, Streeck 1987).

In thinking about the goals that managers pursue in the area of organisational flexibility, it is useful to distinguish between *short-run* responsiveness and *long-run* agility. The former includes managerial attempts to bring about greater numerical flexibility, that is, policies which make it easier to hire and shed labour (Atkinson 1984). Thus, when firms are engaged in cyclical activities, managers may seek to relate their permanent staff numbers to their calculation of the troughs in business demand rather than the relatively unpredictable peaks, seeking to offer overtime and bring in temporary or 'seasonal' staff if, and when, the workload surges. In a variety of industries, the drive to achieve numerical flexibility now includes 'zero-hours contracts', which do not guarantee the worker any set number or regular schedule of working hours. This obviously provides a very high level of flexibility for employers by transferring the risk of fluctuation in the level of work demand onto the employee. There may be 1 to 2 million British workers on such contracts, which have grown since the Global Financial Crisis of 2008–9 and which raise concerns about abuse. Questions centre on whether such contracts are really justified by the nature of the work (does it, in fact, have some degree of regularity that could provide a more secure basis for the employee?) and on those employers who not only offer no guarantee of working hours but, staggeringly, also want workers to work exclusively for them.[2]

Short-run flexibility also involves financial flexibility or attempts to bring greater flexibility into the price of labour (Atkinson 1984). Managers, for example, may seek to pay workers a mix of wages and profit-related bonuses,

---

[2] See, for example, http://www.theguardian.com/uk-news/2014/jun/25/vince-cable-moves-against-zero-hours-contracts, accessed 16/1/15.

with the latter fluctuating in line with the company's financial fortunes. Short-run responsiveness also includes attempts to hire workers who are cross-trained or 'multiskilled', combining roles that have historically been kept in separate job descriptions. Such 'functional flexibility' (Atkinson 1984) helps the firm to maintain a lower headcount but cope better with marginal improvements in product design or production processes.

Long-run agility, on the other hand, is concerned with the question of whether a firm can show the ability to survive in an environment that can change radically (Dyer and Shafer 1999). Does the firm have the capacity to create, or at least cope with, long-run changes in products, costs and technologies? Can it adapt to change as fast as, or faster than, its major rivals? What elements of its HR strategy might need to be flexible to achieve this? While business leaders may aspire to long-run agility, organisational ecologists such as Carroll and Hannan (1995) observe that it is very hard to achieve because core features of organisations are hard to change once laid down in the early stages of establishment and growth.

A key challenge to the agility of firms in recent times has come from the major cost differences between companies with operations in the developed world and those with operations in newly industrialising nations. When companies in lower-cost countries find ways of making the same products at the same quality and delivery benchmarks but do so at much lower prices, established firms operating in high-cost countries either adjust their HR strategies or go out of business. A case in point is one of Britain's most innovative manufacturing firms, Dyson. The firm, an international leader in vacuum cleaner technology, shifted its production facilities to Malaysia in the year 2002. Relocation to Malaysia delivered lower unit costs than was possible in the UK and also ensured proximity to suppliers of key parts, thus improving the firm's location in its supply chain. Several hundred British workers were laid off in the process, and HR strategy now revolves around managing a dual workforce: one in the UK, where research and development (R&D) staff are employed, and one in Malaysia, where the products are assembled.[3] This shift in production facilities and labour forces has made Dyson a more agile firm, enabling it to invest more heavily in R&D and to expand production. The company sees its long-run ability to survive as relying on innovation in its core products or technologies. Making a difficult change in its production and HR strategy has enabled it to focus more effectively on this goal. Agility, then, may mean that the firm needs the capacity to make quite radical changes in HRM.

---

[3] For a summary of the company's history, see http://en.wikipedia.org/wiki/James_Dyson, accessed 16/1/15.

Human resource advantage

The achievement of economic viability, in the current context and as it changes, is clearly a baseline priority for management. However, firms that survive are engaged in an ongoing process of trying to build and defend competitive advantages, which can enhance their profitability (Porter 1980, Hunt 2000). Advantages may be temporary or more sustained. The sort of production switching we have just talked about in the Dyson case is more likely to enhance viability than it is to bring about a sustained advantage. The firms that do it first enjoy some temporary advantages in performance, but their offshoring moves are highly visible and are based on well-known information about cost differences in different countries. As other firms follow suit, profits typically return to normal (Hayes and Pisano 1996). High-tech manufacturing firms, like Dyson, generally seek a more enduring form of advantage through some distinctive feature that is not so easily emulated. Dyson has clearly built up a leadership position that depends on the innovativeness of its products, which stems from the quality of the highly skilled executives and designers who drive this. This is a form of differentiation in the quality of human resource management, a form of 'human resource advantage'.

Human resource advantage can be broken down into two dimensions (Boxall 1996, 1998). The first of these is 'human capital advantage', which a firm enjoys when it employs more talented individuals than its rivals. A human capital advantage rests on the outstanding intellectual, emotional and physical performances of individuals employed in the firm. The second dimension of HRA is 'organisational process' or 'social capital advantage', which occurs in those firms that have developed superior ways of combining the talents of individuals in collaborative activities. It is possible to hire brilliant individuals, and this can bring important breakthroughs for a company, but fail to make best use of their potential as a result of poor organisational processes in teamwork and cross-functional coordination. Thus, more powerful forms of human resource advantage occur when both the human and social capital of an organisation are superior to those of its rivals.

We will analyse and explore the possibility of human resource advantage further in this book. A key argument we will pick up is that the nature and extent of investment in HRM varies from 'elite' to more 'egalitarian' models. In low-skill services, for example, firms typically reserve their greatest investments for their management, marketing and supply chain experts (i.e. their elite) and employ their operating workforce on much less attractive conditions (Boxall 2003). The goal of building human resource advantage in a more extensive way throughout an entire workforce is more likely in high-skill or professional services where firms invest very carefully in the initial recruitment process and in individual employee development in order to ensure that their staff can deliver high-quality, and highly priced, services to their clients.

In summary, the purposes of management in HRM must be understood as fundamentally economic. The need to forge an approach to managing people that will support the firm's economic viability is a critical driver of managerial behaviour. This rests on achieving a cost-effective approach to managing people and some degree of flexibility in how people are employed over time. As the competitive struggle unfolds, however, managers often consider how HRM can support or develop competitive advantage, either through management of an elite core of employees or, in certain conditions, more generally across the workforce.

The socio-political goals of HRM

Social legitimacy

While economic motives are fundamental in HRM, they do not fully account for the strategic behaviour of managers. This is because firms are not unrestricted economic actors. Rather, they operate in societies, in which there are laws that aim to control how managers employ people and in which there are customs, or widely shared expectations, for how people should be treated in workplaces. This was graphically illustrated, for example, in the Global Financial Crisis of 2008–9 when some American and British managers were kidnapped – or 'bossnapped' – in French companies and forced to renegotiate deals involving major redundancies.[4] French workers sought to send the message that Anglo-American assumptions about hiring and firing labour would not be treated so charitably in France. These events were viewed with incomprehension in the USA, where labour contracts are more easily terminated, often requiring no advanced notice or compensation.

The need for managers to adapt to the social environment in which their firms are operating is strongly underlined by sociologists who bring an 'institutional perspective' to the analysis of organisations, examining the ways in which they are influenced by a range of forces in wider society (DiMaggio and Powell 1983, 1991, Paauwe and Boselie 2007). In a major review of this perspective, Scott (2008: 50–9) defines 'three pillars of institutions': the 'regulative', the 'normative' and the 'cultural-cognitive'. Regulative pressures, which include different codes of employment law, are the most obvious. Organisations can be coerced to comply with legal rules if the state deems this

---

[4] See, for example, http://en.wikipedia.org/wiki/Bossnapping, accessed 16/1/15.

necessary and has the power to do so. Normative or moral pressures are also fairly apparent, evidenced in the way that managers come under pressure to conform to prevailing social values and norms around how to treat people in the workplace. For example, in the Anglophone world, the last 50 years have seen a growing movement to foster equal employment opportunity and to eliminate discrimination on such grounds as gender, race, sexual orientation and physical disability, and the largest companies increasingly invest in practices that foster diversity and social inclusion (Kossek and Pichler 2007). Few companies that are large enough to be 'household names' are untouched by this important social trend. To be sure, a lot of this expectation is now embedded in regulation, but much of it is conveyed through norms of behaviour that were less prevalent in earlier times. Finally, there are cultural-cognitive pressures, which include the ways in which people customarily think and behave in a society. Hofstede's (1980, 1983) pioneering work on national culture has emphasised the ways in which people in some societies are more individualistic than they are in others, more comfortable with status and power differences, more prone to avoid uncertainty, and so on. These are more subtle, deep-seated pressures that affect how HRM is conducted.

The key implication is that prevailing notions of legitimate or appropriate behaviour in how people are employed affect the standing of organisations (Suchman 1995, Scott 2008). This is certainly true in societies where labour laws are not simply enacted but also effectively enforced through government agencies and/or trade union action. As Lees (1997) argues, it is therefore important that social legitimacy is recognised as an employer goal in HRM alongside the more market-oriented ones. Not only are there legitimacy issues for firms operating in one society but there are extremely complex legitimacy issues when firms operate in multiple societies (Kostova and Zaheer 1999). In general, then, employers are concerned with ensuring their social legitimacy *while simultaneously* pursuing their goals for economic performance (Boxall 2007). More broadly, of course, the quality of the firm's reputation as an employer is only one aspect of its social legitimacy, which also includes such things as its impacts on the natural environment.

In practice, we see significant variation in the extent to which employers take legitimacy into account in their management of people. At one extreme, there is a group of employers in any society who try to avoid their legal responsibilities. There are sectors of the British economy, for example, such as the restaurant industry, where a significant number of employers do not pay the minimum wage (Edwards and Ram 2006). The majority of employers, however, comply with their responsibilities under employment law and under government regulations for occupational safety and health. Their legitimacy goal is legal compliance. Compliance is the baseline legitimacy goal for employers who wish to avoid prosecution and bad publicity, a risk in any society in which labour laws are efficiently enforced. It is apparent, however, that some firms, at least, operate beyond this baseline. For example, some firms are now actively competing for Equal Employment Opportunity (EEO) awards or for favourable rankings in lists of the best companies to work for or the most family-friendly workplaces.[5] These tend to be larger, better-known firms, but some are also innovative small firms with a strong interest in building their standing as an 'employer of choice'. Some see the achievement of the Investors in People (IiP) standard,[6] based on a commitment to training and development linked to business needs, as a dimension of legitimacy, while for others being recognised for corporate social responsibility, including in employment, is a desirable goal.

Managerial power

As with economic motives, where we see both attempts to stabilise cost-effectiveness in the short run and the need to build flexibility and competitive advantage if firms are to survive into the long run, it is important to think about management's socio-political motives in a dynamic way. All firms can be seen as political systems in which management holds legitimate authority but one in which management decisions are nonetheless subject to legal and moral challenges (Donaldson and Preston 1995). What is management trying to achieve in the politics of the workplace as time goes by? The evidence suggests that management exhibits a fundamental desire to enhance its power as a stakeholder, a tendency that can have both positive and perverse consequences for the organisation.

Gospel (1973) refers to management as having a less openly acknowledged 'security objective' alongside the profit (cost-effectiveness) motive, a goal to maximise managerial control over an uncertain environment including threats to its power base from work groups and trade unions. We can see this in the way the managers of multinational firms tend to favour investment in countries with less demanding labour market regulations (Cooke 2001, 2007b). We can also see it at industry and societal levels, in the tendency of employer federations to lobby, over time, for greater freedom to manage and to resist new employment regulations seen to be diminishing managerial prerogative.

---

[5] See, for example, http://money.cnn.com/magazines/fortune/best-companies/, accessed 16/1/15; http://www.greatplacetowork.co.uk/, accessed 16/1/15.
[6] http://www.investorsinpeople.co.uk/, accessed 16/1/15.

Power, of course, has negative connotations, but we should not rush to such a judgement. An appropriate level of management power is positive. It is needed so that management can coordinate the interests of the diverse stakeholders on whom the organisation depends, an assumption of good governance which has long been recognised (Blau 1964, chapter eight). Most people would acknowledge that there is a natural tendency in positions of authority, or in conditions of risk, to try to ensure that one can act effectively. It is unhelpful to firms if managers are hopelessly checked at every point when they need to make important decisions for the sake of the organisation. Like other organisational actors, managers need some degrees of freedom, or the job is impossible (Clegg and Haugaard 2009, Gohler 2009).

However, there is always the potential for power-seeking behaviour to become perverse, bringing about consequences that are counterproductive for organisational and societal well-being. Economists studying managerial behaviour inside the firm have long emphasised the fact that the interests of shareholders and managers do not perfectly coincide. Williamson (1964), for example, argues that while managers need to generate an acceptable level of profit, their motives also include enlarging their salaries, enhancing their security, and increasing their status, power and prestige. In the branch of organisational economics known as 'agency theory', managers are seen as agents whose interests overlap with, but also diverge from, those of the firm's principals or owners (Jensen and Meckling 1976, Lazear 1999). Managers, like other stakeholders in organisations, can use their power to pursue their own interests, including their personal rewards. Evidence for this perspective is not hard to find. The Global Financial Crisis of 2008–9, for example, gave rise to widespread criticism of the way in which banking executives profited enormously from annual bonus payouts based on short-term performance targets while the long-term health of their organisations was undermined, or fatally compromised, by ill-informed and excessive risk-taking (Stiglitz 2010). Although the worst excesses were in banking, the executive bonus culture has actually been more widespread. It has been encouraged by the growth of private equity firms and 'hedge funds',[7] which have promoted highly leveraged company acquisitions and speculative investments based on predictions of share price movements rather than on more conservative valuations of a company's assets and liabilities. This trend to 'financialisation' (Sisson and Purcell 2010: 91–4) has brought an increasing emphasis on managing managers through pay-for-performance schemes. We are living in an era when

---

[7] See, for example, http://en.wikipedia.org/wiki/Hedge_fund, accessed 16/1/15.

many CEOs and senior managers are employed on 'super-salaries', in which performance-based elements create multimillion pay packets, a trend which continues to fuel concern about the impacts of rising inequality in countries such as the USA and the UK.[8]

Thus, while management is generally concerned about social legitimacy, at least to the extent of legal compliance in societies where there is a risk of legal enforcement, and sometimes well beyond this, we also observe management, as a stakeholder, playing a longer-run political game. The tendency of management is to act, over time, to enhance its power base, something which can have both positive and negative consequences for organisations, for workers and for society at large.

Strategic tensions and problems in HRM

We have identified, then, some fundamental or strategic goals underpinning management's activities in HRM (Figure 1.1). These have been split into economic and socio-political motives because the firm is not simply an unconstrained economic actor; it is an economic entity located in a social context. Firms need a cost-effective approach to HRM in the markets in which they compete, while also needing legitimacy in the societies in which they are located. If managers fail on these two criteria, the firm will generally not survive. Over time, they need to develop some degree of flexibility in their HRM and need to secure enough power to be effective. Managers in firms that survive are concerned with how to build and defend competitive advantages. This implies some thinking about 'human resource advantage', not necessarily for the entire workforce but at least for elite elements in it. Such a

Figure 1.1   The strategic goals of HRM

---

[8] See, for example, http://www.nytimes.com/2014/04/13/business/executive-pay-invasion-of-the-supersalaries.html?_r=0, accessed 16/1/15; http://www.theguardian.com/comment isfree/2014/apr/19/executive-pay-ceos-dont-need-cash, accessed 16/1/15.

discussion naturally arouses the suspicion that the pursuit of these goals is not straightforward. This is indeed the case. The strategic management of work and people in the firm inevitably involves management wrestling with 'strategic tensions', including trade-offs between employer and employee interests (Evans and Genadry 1999). We turn now to a discussion of the key tensions and problems that management faces.

The problem of labour scarcity

The most fundamental tension associated with HRM stems from the fact that firms need to compete in labour markets for the individuals they need (Windolf 1986, Rubery 1994). Managers cannot dictate who will work for them but must compete with others to attract and retain appropriately skilled staff. In all countries where forced or slave labour has been eliminated, workers are free to resign and seek alternative employment. The general severity of labour-supply problems waxes and wanes with the level of economic activity (Kaufman and Miller 2011). Organisations are often inundated with job applicants and have less difficulty recruiting in major recessions when unemployment levels are high, a situation that has persisted in much of southern Europe since the Global Financial Crisis of 2008–9. However, the challenge of recruiting the *quality* of labour they need tends to remain an issue, as is currently emphasised in the literature on the 'global war for talent' (Lanvin and Evans 2013).

There are, in fact, winners and losers in the labour market at firm, industry and societal levels. At the firm level, the labour market tends to be dominated by large, well-recognised and well-resourced organisations, which can pay higher salaries and offer individuals greater avenues for career development. Small firms often struggle to compete with such firms and can remain fragile, tenuous organisations because of it (Storey 1985, Hendry, Arthur and Jones 1995). But labour scarcity can afflict entire industries, in which working conditions are seen as less attractive. In the British trucking industry, for example, there have often been major shortages of drivers because of unattractive conditions: drivers have responsibility for valuable vehicles and dangerous loads, work long hours in stressful driving situations and are often away from home (Marchington, Carroll and Boxall 2003). Many people who hold driving qualifications do not use them, preferring to work in an occupation that will give them a regular life in a settled location. In some industries, problems of labour scarcity are global in their implications. In the health sector, for example, competition for workers is straining the resources of public and private health systems all over the world. In 2013, the

World Health Organisation (WHO) reported a global shortage of 7.2 million health workers and predicted that this would rise to 12.9 million by 2035.[9] As recruiters in rich countries comb the globe for scarce labour, this creates problems for poorer countries. Health services in third-world countries can be denuded of expensively trained health professionals by first-world 'poaching'. Similarly, small countries can find that capable managers are constantly being recruited to more challenging and better paid jobs in larger countries where the big companies offer extensive career opportunities (Gilbert and Boxall 2009). Labour scarcity is therefore a multilayered problem in HRM; it can cause severe problems at organisational, industry and societal levels.

The problem of employee motivation

A second major tension is associated with the motivation of employee behaviour if and when workers are actually hired. The employment contract is an exchange relationship but, unlike the sale and purchase of commodities, it involves an ongoing, unpredictable interaction between the parties. As the pioneering industrial relations writers Sidney Webb and Beatrice Webb (1902: 658) put it, the labour contract is 'indeterminate' or, as Cartier (1994: 182) puts it, 'the contract of employment is inherently incomplete'. As a result, the law of employment gives employers the right to issue what are commonly known as 'lawful and reasonable orders', but herein lies the rub. The simple fact is that employer control of the behaviour of other human beings is always limited and 'management is reliant on employee cooperation' (Keenoy 1992: 95). This means that the employer, like the employee, must exercise some trust, relying on workers to use their judgement in productive ways. For example, no matter how much 'scripting' there is of how to deal with customers in shops, the individual employee still decides whether to be helpful to customers or to be plainly rude in a way that alienates them – something we have all experienced.

While it is true that employers typically have greater economic power and may use it to impose terms on workers (Webb and Webb 1902), we should not imagine that employees are passive or lack power resources, even in low-wage, low-skill conditions. All employees have some power over their own actions, and those with know-how that is critical to production, and who are not easily replaced, have greater power. For example, in Edwards and Ram's (2006: 909) study of a selection of Indian restaurants in Britain, chefs were

---

[9] http://www.who.int/mediacentre/news/releases/2013/health-workforce-shortage/en/, accessed 16/1/15.

'in relatively short supply and the quality of their cooking was critical to the success of the restaurant'. This meant that they were granted greater autonomy in how they ran the kitchen and could sometimes get extended leave to visit their family in India, a concession rarely available to waiters. Workers also gain greater power when they are prepared to act in concert, as is demonstrated in those strikes that shut down operations and impose major costs on employers. It pays, therefore, to think of employment relationships in terms of a 'bargaining model': the parties are 'mutually dependent' and each has some room to negotiate or bargain with the other party over time (Edwards and Ram 2006: 897).

There is a huge body of literature examining the relationships between employer and employee interests in the workplace and their implications for motivation and performance. Researchers in industrial relations and the sociology of work emphasise the fact that there are fundamental conflicts of interest in the workplace (Clegg 1975, Kelly 1998, Blyton and Turnbull 2004). An important perspective is 'labour process' theory (LPT), which analyses the tensions between employer strategies of control and worker strategies of resistance (Braverman 1974, Burawoy 1979, Thompson and Harley 2007). Conflicts over income (e.g. what share of revenue goes to profit and what to wages? what relativities should there be across occupational groups?) and over the control of work (e.g. who makes decisions about work processes? how fair is the workload?) are seen to affect the basis for workplace cooperation. Many scholars emphasise the role of institutions for employee voice in improving the balance of interests. The general argument is that management should work with worker representatives in processes of collective bargaining, information sharing and consultation to enhance fairness and build a work climate characterised by trust and mutual respect. A willingness on management's part to share control is seen as important in developing a stable 'social order' in which both the firm and its workers can work productively and reap the rewards they value (Watson 2005, 2007).

Organisational psychologists also emphasise the impact of fairness or equity concerns on employee motivation, including employee concerns with the justice of their rewards and workplace decision-making processes (Folger and Cropanzano 1998, Folger 2005). The process of building trust is seen to depend on the employer, creating a track record of fairness in HR decisions. In terms of conceptual frameworks, the notion that individuals have a 'psychological contract' with their employer has become increasingly important (Rousseau 1995, Guest 2007). A major gap between what management promises and what management delivers inevitably affects an individual's perception of their psychological contract and thus their level of trust and commitment. Furthermore, an overall sense of fairness and trust can develop across a work site or workforce, creating a collective or social climate that is more or less positive for cooperation (Grant 1999).

Employee motivation, then, is an ongoing concern for individual managers and for management collectively. At their worst, motivational challenges can be expressed in forms of collective action (such as lowered work norms and strikes) or in high levels of individual resistance (such as dysfunctional levels of absenteeism and employee turnover). Such challenges can affect management's legitimacy, depress productivity and threaten the firm's viability.

Change tensions in labour management

The reality of change also creates strategic tensions. The need to establish a stable production system, while also pursuing some degree of organisational flexibility, poses major dilemmas within management strategy (Osterman 1987, Brown and Reich 1997, Adler, Goldoftas and Levine 1999). How much weight should management place on strengthening its production routines to make the firm more efficient and how much weight should be placed on building flexibility for the future (Wright and Snell 1998)?

To illustrate the difficult choices involved, suppose a firm developing a new line of business decides that it wants a high degree of flexibility. It faces a context in which unemployment levels are presently high. In this context, management decides to employ all operating staff in the new business on short-term or temporary employment contracts. This means the firm can shed labour or downsize more easily if it has to. A problem emerges, however, when the labour market improves: many of the more highly productive workers take the opportunity to move to more secure jobs elsewhere (why should they work on a short-term contract when they can obtain a permanent job, one that will help them gain home loans and make their families more secure?). In this labour market context, the firm finds that it fails to recruit and retain as well as its competitors or to reach their level of production quality. Too much emphasis on flexible employment starts to threaten its chances of survival. It will have to think again about how to employ people.

Imagine another firm, which employs all its labour on well-paid, permanent contracts to build a loyal workforce (traditionally called 'labour hoarding'). This works well for quite a time, but the firm's sales are sensitive to consumer discretionary spending and they decline sharply when an economic recession comes along. The firm has products with excellent long-term prospects, but greater flexibility is needed in its staffing structure to ensure it can weather these sorts of short-term variations in demand. It feels forced to make some lay-offs, a process that tarnishes its 'psychological contract' with its employees, and spurs management to think about whether all staff should actually be on permanent contracts.

As these illustrations make apparent, both of these scenarios represent undesirable extremes. Both firms need to consider how to strike a better balance between the short run and the long run. For example, in the Global Financial Crisis of 2008–9, many firms sought to avoid lay-offs by reducing the working week or encouraging employees to take leave on reduced pay in order to retain skills and employee goodwill.[10] Further, as the scenarios make clear, the problem of how to cope with change not only creates dilemmas within management strategy but brings trade-offs with the security interests of workers. In Hyman's (1987: 43) memorable phrase, capitalism is a system in which 'employers require workers to be *both* dependable *and* disposable'. The most resilient firms are those which can evolve a clever balance between stability and flexibility while maintaining employee trust and confidence. This is much easier said than done.

Tension between management power and social legitimacy

As emphasised above, some level of social legitimacy typically matters to managers. Social legitimacy can be thought of as having an inward and an outward face: there needs to be an appropriate 'social order' within the firm, which then connects to the firm's reputation in wider society. An important strategic tension lies in the fact that establishing an appropriate social order depends on management accepting some constraints on its power. Historically, this has not always come willingly from management, and actions by trade unions and the state have often been necessary to enforce it (Clegg 1994, Hannan 1995). In countries such as the UK, France and the USA, the growth of trade unions in the early to mid parts of the 20th century saw the legitimacy challenge spill over from the shop floor onto the streets. These countries, and many others, experienced waves of strikes and social disruption until unions won recognition from employers and gained the right to collective bargaining to improve workplace safety, reduce workloads and lift wages. Collective bargaining enabled workers to 'jointly regulate' their employment conditions with management (Flanders 1970). Unions also turned to national political activity, lobbying political parties and, in many countries, forming their own. As a result, progressive social legislation –

---

[10] See, for example, http://blogs.smh.com.au/business/executivestyle/managementline/ 2009/03/, accessed 16/1/15.

which brings organising rights and minimum conditions to all workers – has largely eliminated this sort of challenge in advanced industrialised countries. There are exceptions, of course. Stubborn management resistance to employee influence is still apparent in a minority of firms (Freeman 2007), something which can require the intervention of labour courts or government mediation services. There is also the fact that there are large low-wage sectors in advanced countries, which are targeted by unions and community coalitions in 'living wage' campaigns (Juravich and Hilgert 1999, Nissen 2000). The existence of low-wage environments still generates political concern throughout the rich countries (Appelbaum, Bernhardt and Murnane 2003).

In addition, public attention is increasingly focused on the ethics of human resource management in global supply chains. In their search for production sites that offer lower costs and greater freedom to manage (Cooke 2001, 2007b), multinational companies can acquire a reputation for engaging labour on exploitative terms or in life-threatening conditions. The ethical issues associated with global sourcing were dramatically illustrated in 2013 when the Rana Plaza, an eight-storey building in Bangladesh containing clothing factories, collapsed.[11] Over 1,000 garment workers died. Subcontractors producing apparel for various international clothing brands were housed in the building and the companies who own the brands have inevitably been linked to the disaster. In the aftermath, some fashion chains have offered compensation, some have signed up to new agreements on factory safety in Bangladesh and others have refused to do either. Improvement in factory standards is likely to occur, but it is not going to be easy to achieve. As industry commentators note, Western consumers are accustomed to buying cheap, good-quality clothes and do so at higher volumes than ever before, raising the question of how to shift both corporate and consumer behaviour.[12]

Key questions in global HRM, then, concern what level of rights should be universally available to workers and respected by companies, whether or not in their own operations or in their supply chains. The International Labour Organization (ILO), established in 1919 and incorporated into the United Nations in 1946, is the tripartite UN agency whose aims are 'to promote rights at work, encourage decent employment opportunities, enhance social protection and strengthen dialogue on work-related issues'.[13] Its Decent Work Agenda includes attempts to ensure that workers everywhere can freely join

---

[11] http://en.wikipedia.org/wiki/2013_Savar_building_collapse, accessed 16/1/15.
[12] See, for example, http://www.theguardian.com/world/2014/apr/19/rana-plaza-bangladesh-one-year-on, accessed 16/1/15.
[13] http://www.ilo.org/global/about-the-ilo/lang--en/index.htm, accessed 16/1/15.

unions and engage in collective bargaining while also aiming to eliminate forced labour, child labour and discrimination in employment (Hughes 2005).

These are critical issues for managers to consider. In principle, when management reaches employment agreements with workers and their organisations, and thus willingly constrains its own power in certain ways, the legitimacy of the employment regime in the firm is usually enhanced. Furthermore, when management in international companies openly embraces the ILO's Decent Work Agenda, including fundamental labour rights, its legitimacy in both its home country and around the world is very likely to be improved. It is readily apparent, however, that there are many firms that try to 'fly under the radar', in which the tension between management power and social legitimacy is being resolved at a much lower level, including firms in which managers breach the minimum wage or create unsafe working conditions and seek to avoid providing channels for employee voice.

Complexity and politics in management

What we have said so far should indicate the kind of complexity that is involved in managing work and people. The fact that we can highlight the sorts of problems firms face in pursuing their HRM goals does not mean that it is easy to solve any of them. Complexity grows as organisations grow and as they become more diverse. Management faces 'cognitive limitations' in developing good strategy. But strategic management is not just mentally hard, it is politically fraught. Never mind the politics between management and labour; some of the worst battles are within the management ranks. Besides the personal power struggles that take place between ambitious managers in organisations, management can be split between disciplines and across levels of the hierarchy. Marketing and operations executives, for example, may clash over how best to provide customer service when there are pressures on company margins (Batt 2007). The desire of marketers to personalise customer service may be resisted by operations managers who are accountable for increasing efficiency, which often implies reducing costs through staff reductions and using technology to standardise how customers will be treated. In large firms, this will then affect the HR specialists because they will have to carry out the lay-offs that deliver the cost reductions. Batt (2004) also provides a vivid illustration of conflict within management across hierarchical levels. She describes how senior management in one company wished to introduce self-managing teams on the grounds that they would enhance productivity but supervisors and middle managers successfully resisted the initiative, which would radically change their roles. Implementation became impossible without their willing cooperation. Such an illustration reinforces the point that change in labour management can be as much about politics and power within management as it is about economic rationality.

Variations in institutional supports and societal resources

Finally, supposing management understands the strategic problems of HRM well enough, is well resourced and is well disposed to handle them, we must recognise that firms are embedded in societies and are not completely in control of their HR strategies. Small firms are clearly very dependent on state support, which includes systems for vocational education and training in their sector, but firms of all sizes are affected by the dominant ways in which societies organise their human resource development. The UK, for example, may have a range of great universities, but in terms of the development of skills for manufacturing, all kinds of British firms – small, large and global – have been at a disadvantage for some time. German firms, by contrast, have enjoyed the benefits of the superior technical training systems associated with their society, which have long been regarded as superior to those developed in the Anglophone countries (Steedman and Wagner 1989, Wever 1995). As Winterton (2007: 327) explains, 'the higher skill level of the German workforce is generally seen as a source of competitive advantage, permitting German firms to focus on higher value-added market niches'. On the other hand, he also explains that German firms do not have it all their own way; firms in the US and the UK often find it easier to make the changes necessary to bring in more flexible ways of working. The slow pace of the German institutional structure, with its layers of industrial negotiation and consultation, can act as a costly drag. Firms in the Anglophone world often take advantage of their more fluid decision-making structures. This helps to make the point that the societal context both constrains and enables firms to perform.

In sum, then, firms are not masters of their own destiny in HRM even if managers perceive the issues well and want to act effectively. Firms are embedded in societies, which affect what managers take for granted in HRM and what they are able to achieve. We will be arguing that management does enjoy a realm of strategic choice to make distinctive decisions in HRM, but the extent of that realm varies: the choices are never entirely in management's hands.

Discerning and describing HR strategies

This discussion of the strategic goals and tensions that managers face in HRM can now be rounded off with some guidance on how we might discern and describe the HR strategy of a particular firm. The concept of HR strategy was first developed by Dyer (1984) to describe an organisation's pattern of strategic choices in HRM. Drawing on his work, we define an organisation's HR strategy as the critical set of economic and socio-political choices that managers make in building and managing a workforce. Managers face strategic questions around how to attract a workforce with the appropriate capabilities at a cost that is affordable to the business and how to manage the people in it to achieve the firm's goals and develop the business over time. Thus, HR strategy is concerned with critical choices associated with constructing and managing an entire workforce. It is not to be confused with a firm's strategy for its specialist HR function, as Huselid, Becker and Beatty (2005) emphasise. It is better to think of HR-function strategy as something that supports the larger workforce or HR strategy. In organisations that have HR specialists, HR-function strategy covers the ways in which executives utilise their HR specialists to help them build and manage their workforce.

How do we discern these strategic choices? Some are more evident than others. Major decisions around where to locate particular kinds of work can be revealing, showing which capabilities managers are seeking, where they are thought to be most effective, and what level of labour cost is seen as 'profit rational'. We illustrated these choices in the case of the British firm Dyson, which relocated its manufacturing to Malaysia but retained its R&D and executive functions in Britain. This set of choices told us about how Dyson was trying to improve its cost-effectiveness and also said something about how Dyson was trying to enhance its long-run agility because restructuring the labour costs associated with the manufacturing process released resources for investment in the innovative processes required to create new products.

In well-known firms, such choices around workforce capabilities, locations and costs can be discussed in the media, as they were in this case. After that point, however, observation from outside the firm becomes more difficult and there are still critical dimensions of the HR strategy we wish to describe. To some extent, we can discern how managers are handling the challenges of social legitimacy from whether their firm is known to recognise unions or support other forms of employee voice, but this does not tell us about how employees see the quality of the voice regime, including the extent to which they can influence the decisions that affect them. Viewing the socio-political dimensions of HRM from the outside has serious limitations because much of the relevant action takes place inside the 'black box' of the firm, where managers are engaged in creating the collective outcomes the business needs.

The notion of the 'black box' is central to this book. This term covers the complex set of attitudes and behaviours inside a firm that make it productive. Managers are involved in shaping the kind of performance climate that they think the firm needs to reach its business goals. As Lepak et al. (2006) explain, a business model may depend on generating a 'climate for innovation' because the strategy is to outperform rivals by creating a stream of new products that customers find highly desirable, as Apple has done with the iPod, iPad and iPhone. Alternatively, management may seek a climate that delivers efficient production or service with little interest in innovation or in the empowerment that might help to generate it (Boxall, Ang and Bartram 2011). Managers may be pursuing some blend of these or, indeed, other types of climate. Understanding these choices, and the tensions they imply, should be part of our description of an organisation's HR strategy. To do a decent job of describing an HR strategy, then, we are going to need to look further than the more visible choices around workforce capabilities and costs and probe into the muddy waters of company cultures and their working climates. The concepts, theories and tools that we need to do so will receive much greater attention as this book unfolds.

In this process, of course, we are going to need to be aware of the way in which the workforce is segmented or made up of different types of employee. Firms rarely adopt a single style of management for all their employee groups (Osterman 1987, Pinfield and Berner 1994). HR strategy is more often a cluster of different *models* of HRM. In manufacturing, for example, HR strategy has historically been based on an 'industrial model' for operating or waged workers, in which work is heavily paced by machinery and in which workers have narrowly defined roles of limited responsibility. Managers and advanced technical specialists, however, typically have more complex responsibilities and are managed in a more trusting, salary-based model of HRM, which incorporates higher remuneration and greater investment in individual development. Similar differences of style can be observed across different kinds of employees in service firms. Questions of social legitimacy and internal political pressures mean that there will usually be overlaps across models of HRM in a firm; for example, there may be common ways of handling leave entitlements and common ways of dealing with personal grievances. However, there are typically substantial differences across models of HRM inside any single organisation, including variations in the kind of climates that management is trying to create.

It is also important to recognise that we have been talking as if the firm is a single business unit. This is the primary level at which strategy, including HR strategy, is defined. Reality, however, is more complicated. Difficulties arise with multidivisional firms that operate across a variety of markets. To what extent are business-unit managers free to adapt HR strategies that suit their unique contexts? How are they impacted by financial and HR policies developed at divisional and corporate levels in these complex firms? Can corporate HR strategy provide some form of 'parenting advantage', which adds value to what business units can achieve without corporate influence? These questions are explored in this book.

A final complication arises with international firms, as many multidivisional firms are. Where firms compete across national boundaries, in what ways do they adapt their HR strategies to local conditions? How is HRM organised when the firm operates in more than one society? This is one of the key concerns of the field of international HRM (Brewster et al. 2011, Dowling, Festing and Eagle 2013), and we will be addressing it in this book. Overall, what we mean by the notion of HR strategy is summarised in Box 1.1.

Box 1.1   Human resource strategy

- Is a term describing the critical set of economic and socio-political choices that managers make in building and managing their workforce
- Is not to be confused with HR-function strategy, which covers decisions around how to use HR specialists to support HR or workforce strategy
- Is usually segmented – while there are overlaps, firms typically have different models of HRM for different employee groups (e.g. different models for operating workers and for managers)
- Like strategy in general, is easiest to define at the business-unit level
- Is more complex in multidivisional firms in which different business units face different markets and in which there are political interactions between the corporate, divisional and business-unit levels
- Is more complex in firms that operate across national boundaries because of the impact of different societal contexts

---

Conclusions

Human resources belong to people, but they are critical for the basic survival and relative success of organisations. Human resource management is the process through which management builds the workforce and tries to create the human performances that the organisation needs. It is concerned with the work and employment policies and practices that will enable the organisation to function. This process engages the energies of both line managers and specialist HR managers (where the latter exist).

This chapter has discussed the strategic goals or motives that underpin the behaviour of managers in HRM. It has argued that both economic and socio-political goals are in play in the management of people. The fundamental economic goal in HRM is concerned with developing a cost-effective way of managing people that supports the firm's financial viability. Managers are driven to ask: what approaches to HRM are 'profit-rational' in our specific business? This goal implies a second one: achieving a degree of flexibility in HRM if the firm is to remain financially viable as the economic context changes. A third economic motive involves seeking ways of supporting or developing competitive advantage through the quality of HRM in the firm (human resource advantage), although this is often pursued for an elite group of employees rather than the entire workforce. These economic goals are accompanied by two socio-political ones: social legitimacy and management power. At the same time as they are seeking economic viability, managers typically think about how to secure legitimacy in the societies in which the firm operates. At a minimum, this means employing labour according to legal requirements and taking important social customs seriously, but, in reality, there are always some firms that do not operate legitimately. In the dynamic picture, we also observe management seeking to enhance its power. Much of this stems from the fact that management needs a secure power base in order to coordinate the stakeholders who contribute to the firm. However, power-seeking can become perverse, as recently illustrated in the controversy over the ways in which management has used its power to inflate its personal rewards in the finance sector – often at the expense of shareholders and the wider community. A key implication of this analysis is that HRM's role in organisations should not be thought of simply in terms of a single, profit-oriented 'bottom line'. This is critical, but firms are economic entities located in a social context, so a good performance in HRM will always be multidimensional.

Pursuing this complex set of goals inevitably involves grappling with strategic tensions. Failure to handle these problems effectively will have strategic impacts on the organisation. Critical tensions include the problem of labour scarcity, which hamstrings firms that are weak in the labour market and which can impact on entire industries and societies. Employee motivation is an inevitable challenge in all firms because employment relationships rely on human discretion and the control of human behaviour is always limited. The need to grapple with change creates a difficulty around balancing short-run with long-run strategy and brings trade-offs between company survival and employee security. Management's pursuit of political power can bring major challenges to the firm's social legitimacy. The cognitive and political issues associated with these problems are a major problem in themselves. And, even where the firm is well resourced and astutely led, there are serious challenges posed by the societal contexts in which firms are embedded. Firms are not autonomous entities. They exist in larger systems that enable, and constrain, their performance.

An organisation's HR strategy, then, is something that can have a major impact on its fortunes, including its chances of survival, its level of profitability and its reputation in wider society. HR strategy is the term we use to describe the critical set of economic and socio-political choices that managers make around how to build their workforce and how to manage it. HR strategy contains internal variation across workforce groups and is more complex in multidivisional and multinational firms. Having established these fundamental concepts around HRM and HR strategy, in the next chapter, we examine in greater depth what we mean by strategy and by the process of strategic management, a process in which HRM is embedded. Together, these first two chapters set out the basic terminology and concerns of the book and complete Part 1. The book is then organised around the idea that we must understand both general principles in HRM (Part 2) and develop an ability to analyse how it varies across specific contexts (Part 3). Part 2 starts with our review of the theoretical debate around ideas of 'best fit' and 'best practice' in HRM (Chapter 3) and leads into an examination of the relationship between HRM and the competitive advantages of firms (Chapter 4). From here, we examine the ways in which firms try to attract people with the human capital they need (Chapter 5), analyse the perennial tension between management power and social legitimacy in HRM (Chapter 6) and build a model of the key variables and linkages inside the 'black box' of HRM (Chapter 7). These chapters are concerned with identifying and explaining general ideas and theories that apply across the field of strategic HRM. In Part 3, we apply these general concepts and principles to a set of critical contexts in which HRM varies. These include the manufacturing sector (Chapter 8), the service sector (Chapter 9), and the contexts of multidivisional (Chapter 10) and multinational firms (Chapter 11). Each of these chapters covers a diverse terrain, and our discussion inevitably oversimplifies the picture, but it is designed to build an appreciation of how context matters in HRM and how practitioners handle it. Chapter 12 summarises the major arguments of the book and finishes with a discussion of how the process of strategic analysis and planning in HRM can be improved.

2

Strategy and strategic management

Like the previous chapter, this one is also concerned with establishing foundational concepts. Its role is to address the questions: what do we mean by the notion of 'strategy', and how do we understand the process of strategic management? Our answer rests on making an important distinction between the strategic problems that firms face in their environment and the strategies they develop to address them. Our definitions emphasise the systemic challenge that strategic management implies. If they are to be successful, the firm's leaders will need to integrate their approach to a range of business functions, including marketing, operations, HRM and finance, all of which can derail the firm's performance if they are not taken seriously. We then discuss the ways in which strategies evolve over the life cycle of firms, including the ways in which people are critical in this process. As the chapter will make clear, strategic management is a risky activity, in which people wrestle with both intellectual and political challenges. This puts a premium on the quality of HRM, including the management of managers.

Strategic problems and the strategies of firms

As many writers have pointed out, the notion of strategy is subject to a confusing variety of interpretations. Much of the early literature in the field of strategic HRM leapt into the fray with little recognition that the notion of strategy needs careful handling. In order to describe what we mean by the word, it helps if we start with the negative. What definitions or conceptions of strategy are not helpful?

Defining strategy: misunderstandings

First, as Henry Mintzberg (1978) argued in a classic paper, it is unhelpful to equate strategy with 'strategic plan'. A strategic plan is a formal document setting out an organisation's goals and initiatives over a defined time period. Strategic plans are characterised by a variety of formats. For example, the time horizons vary. Some firms use three-year plans, others use five-year plans and still others, in industries such as mining, characterised by long-term investments and controversial environmental issues, create plans that run for 25 years or beyond. Other variations include the range of goals targeted, the activities that are planned for and the ways in which the functional areas of the business are integrated with one another. Strategic plans are more likely to be found in large, complex companies which have major problems with coordinating efforts towards common goals (Grant 2010). It is hard to see how any multidivisional firm – facing the task of allocating its capital across business units – could cope without them. It is easy to see why such 'vast, diverse' firms as General Electric developed corporate planning in the 1960s (Whittington 1993: 71). Such complex firms need to engage in strategic planning in order to enhance communication across organisational levels and to negotiate goals in an array of business units located across diverse political environments (Jarzabkowski and Balogun 2009). Strategic plans are also more likely to be found in public sector organisations which are required to disclose their goals and principal activities to politicians and the public. There are also certain industries where formal planning is *de rigueur*. It is virtually impossible, for example, to undertake major construction projects, such as a new hotel or office tower in a city, without formal planning for the architectural, financial, material, labour and environmental implications. Official permission is rarely forthcoming without it.

However, the formality of strategic planning is unusual in small businesses, which often account for as much as half the private sector economy, even in the world's richest countries. Does this mean these firms have no strategy? Certainly not. It is possible to find strategy in every business because it is embedded in the important choices that managers and other employees of the firm make about what to do and how to do it. In other words, when we make the effort, it is possible to discern the firm's strategy in its behaviour, in the significant actions it takes in its environment (Freeman 1995). As will be explained further below, we intend to base our understanding of strategy on the 'strategic choice' perspective. A firm's strategy is the set of strategic choices that is revealed in its actions.

This understanding of strategy means that we should 'treat with a grain of salt' the strategic plans we do find in organisations that use them.

Formal planning documents rarely describe all of the organisation's strategic behaviour or keep track of its 'strategic learning' as major decisions are implemented (Mintzberg 1990). Sometimes they leave out the most critical tensions with which executives are wrestling, which makes them unhelpful documents inside the organisation and potentially misleading to investors. We are not intending to imply, however, that strategic planning is therefore a waste of time. Such planning can be a very valuable activity, as we shall argue in the final chapter of this book. The point we are making here is that strategy is best discerned in the organisation's behaviour or significant actions, not in its formal planning documents.

Second, we need to be careful with the popular distinction between 'strategy' and 'tactics' or between 'strategy' and 'operations'. This is a problem that has crept into management jargon from the military origins of strategy. In classical Greek, 'strategos' is associated with the role of the general, the high-level, orchestrating commander (Bracker 1980). In popular usage, we still tend to associate strategy with the top leader who articulates a vision, or who makes great decisions at a distance from the action, and who lets lower-level staff deliver the results later. A major problem with this imagery is the way it tends to imply that the goals or ends we decide on are much more important than the tactics, or means, that we use to reach them.

In reality, this is a dangerous way of thinking because reliable delivery on the ground, in credible, day-to-day operations, is essential to the success of any business (Kaplan and Norton 2001). Operational mistakes can be fateful for an organisation or can generate major losses. A case in point is what happened to security arrangements during the London Olympics of 2012. The private security firm responsible for the Games' security, G4S, did not recruit sufficient numbers of guards in time, and the government deployed 3,500 members of the armed forces to meet the shortfall.[1] In the end, G4S made a loss of £88 million on the security contract rather than a profit of £10 million.[2] This kind of example underlines the fact that both our goals or desired ends (what we intend to achieve) and our means (how we intend to go about it) are critical to our success. Underestimating what it will take to deliver a product or service is a very risky strategy.

In business, then, successful leaders take care with both ends and means. They do not diminish the importance of the latter. This is a reason why, in some enduring organisations, only those who have worked their way up from

---

[1] See http://www.theguardian.com/uk/2012/jul/18/g4s-may-lose-management-fee, accessed 16/1/15.
[2] See http://www.theguardian.com/business/2013/feb/12/g4s-olympic-security-contract-losses, accessed 16/1/15.

the fundamental roles at the base of the organisation can ever hold the top management posts (Pascale 1985). Historically, many of the largest firms have structured their internal management development programmes so that new recruits with management potential are required to spend time learning what matters to the firm's customers, suppliers and employees. With a suitable apprenticeship in the 'engine room' of the firm, they get a chance to learn what is critical in the fundamental disciplines that make the business successful.

In adopting this perspective, some may think we are debasing the currency of strategy. Where do we draw the line between the strategic and the non-strategic? It must be emphasised that this is a difficult thing to discern because the 'strategic work' of managers takes place in complex and uncertain environments (Spender 2014). Strategic issues shift over time and take on different characteristics in different situations. Take the internet, for example. Twenty years ago, it seemed that retailers, particularly the small ones, could ignore its implications for sales and distribution processes. Now hardly anyone in retail can afford to be complacent about it, large or small: a retailer's web pages help potential customers to locate its products, search for items in the stock and make purchases online. Failure to use the internet can now be devastating for a retail business.

It seems we need some way of discerning where the strategic issues lie. We need some basis for distinguishing between the critical aspects of running a firm successfully and those that are of lesser significance. In the sections that follow, we will provide a way of thinking about this.

Establishing a viable business

We are now in a position to move from the negative to the positive. In our view, strategy is best defined by making a distinction between the 'strategic problems' firms encounter in their environment and the strategies their managers adopt to address them (Boxall 1998: 266). It helps to think this through in two steps. The initial strategic problem for any management team is that of identifying a market opportunity and establishing a viable way of meeting it. The business will need what Hamel and Prahalad (1994: 226–7) call 'table stakes': the 'minimum set of capabilities simply to participate in a particular industry'. They give the example of the package-delivery industry and note that all firms require a team of trained drivers. They restrict their example to the need for capable drivers and do not spell out the fuller consequences. However, it is clear that a viable business in this industry will also need access to a fleet of suitable vehicles, some kind of access to office, parking and storage facilities, and the kind of sales and information system that can win customers and link their needs with drivers. All of this matters to viability in the package-delivery industry. Decisions about 'table stakes', then, are strategic: they are make-or-break factors. If the firm's leaders get the system of these choices right, or right enough, the firm will be viable. If they miss a key piece out, the firm will fail, usually quickly (Reynolds 1987). In other words, when we use the word 'strategic' to describe something, we mean that it is something that is critical to the firm's survival. It will be fatal if we get it wrong.

Figure 2.1 depicts the four essential elements of any business. These are the four sets of factors that need to be perceived and managed if the firm is to demonstrate its 'table stakes' and emerge as a credible business. One element is concerned with marketing. The firm's managers need to identify a market, or a market segment, and develop products or services that can potentially meet a profitable set of customer needs (e.g. Hunt 2000, Teece 2011). It will fail if it simply produces something that no one wants to buy or that they might desire but cannot afford to buy. It also needs a stable production or operational system, a credible way of making the product or providing the service that it promises to its customers (e.g. Das and Narasimhan 2001, Lovelock, Patterson and Walker 2007). Thus, suitable production technologies or productive know-how, built into reliable processes, are critical to a firm's survival. Production technology is integral to manufacturing while productive know-how is vital to the delivery of services. In most industries, information and communication technology (ICT) has become an essential aspect of the operating or production system. ICT is now heavily embedded in business processes, as in the example of package-delivery firms, which have electronic track-and-trace systems. Electronic communication is essential to the networked supply chains

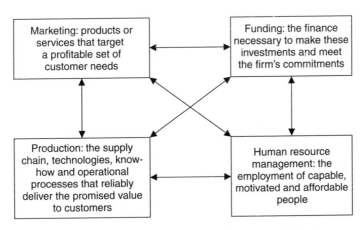

Figure 2.1 Four critical elements in establishing a viable business

that have become part and parcel of modern manufacturing and many service industries. But there will be no production or operational performance without the employment of people who provide some level of stability to the firm's operations (e.g. Rubery 1994, Watson 2005). The functions of production and HRM are heavily interdependent. Even where a firm is heavily involved in robot-controlled processes or in service delivery through highly automated processes, it will need the managers and other employees who have the skills that are necessary to implement these productive technologies and make them work reliably. Finally, the firm's leaders need an understanding of the pattern of revenues and costs that the business will create and the funding to meet its commitments to suppliers, employees and others (e.g. Alpander, Carter and Forsgren 1990, Teece 2011). A firm's leaders may have great ideas, but unless they have the finance to back the venture, including throughout the period before it generates its own positive cash flow, they lack the complete set of 'table stakes' to enter, and stay alive, in the game.

To survive, then, each firm must develop a system of interdependent activities that fits its specific context (Porter and Siggelkow 2008). As an illustration, take the case of a company launching a new high-street or main-street bank. As Freeman (1995: 221) emphasises, much of a firm's strategy is formed in a 'package' when the original choice of industry is made. A bank has to act like a bank: it comes with the territory. To be credible at all, it must have a similar profile of products or services to competing banks. It must also have the premises and the technologies that will help it to process deposits and facilitate lending, plus the skilled staff who can make its services work, both during normal operating hours and throughout the 24/7 banking timetable that internet banking enables. Finally, it needs the funds, including the minimum level of capital reserves stipulated in a country's banking regulations, that will underpin these investments. Failure to maintain these financial requirements meant that many banks collapsed in the Global Financial Crisis of 2008–9. In the USA, the Federal Deposit Insurance Corporation maintains a list of bank failures, which shows that 140 banks failed in 2009.[3] This illustration should underline the point that all four of the critical elements of viability that we have identified are essential: a failure in one part will compromise all the others.

While Figure 2.1 naturally oversimplifies the ambiguities and complexities that are involved in the problem of viability, we use it to emphasise the fact that there is no solution without integrating these four functions. Each one is important and this includes human resource management. Capable, motivated and affordable human beings are strategic to the success of every firm.

---

[3] http://www.fdic.gov/bank/historical/bank/2009/index.html, accessed 16/1/15.

It is only people that pose the questions, 'What goals are appropriate for our business?' and 'What resources are relevant to our goals?', and take an interest in making the answers a reality. Starting with the entrepreneurs who establish the firm, a suitable way of attracting and motivating the people the organisation needs is one of the critical elements in business success. It is the role of HRM to ensure the firm engages the people who have the human resources it needs, including the insight to read its environment and manage its activities. HRM is part of what is essential for the viability of any business.

The problem of establishing viability, then, is the most fundamental strategic problem facing the firm. It involves an interactive set of concerns relating to marketing, production, HRM and finance. There are critical choices about goals and means in each of these functions, and in how they fit together, which make or break a business. A viable 'business model', which is a term increasingly used in strategic management, is one that puts these pieces together in a profitable way (e.g. Teece 2011: 24–6).

Struggling for competitive advantages

While the task of establishing the baseline viability of the firm is the fundamental strategic problem, it does not lead to an 'equilibrium', as if the job is done and we can take a holiday. As Hunt (2000: 138) explains, competition is a 'constant struggle among firms for comparative advantages in resources that will yield marketplace positions of competitive advantage'. In this process, a firm that builds a relatively consistent pattern of superior returns for its shareholders is said to have developed some form of 'sustained competitive advantage' (Porter 1980, 1985). Chief executives are often incentivised for this outcome: they may, for example, be promised certain bonus sums if the firm's profitability significantly exceeds the industry average or if its share price beats the average of its rivals over a certain time-frame. Their goal is typically to achieve 'superior financial performance', bringing greater rewards to the firm's owners and executives (Hunt 2000).

How long such superior performance can be sustained is, however, variable. Many advantages are simply temporary. They involve spotting and benefiting from a profit-making opportunity before others notice it. But it generally doesn't take long for imitative forces to set in. There simply have to be serious rivals – as there are in most markets – who observe that someone has achieved an unusual level of profitability and seek to compete it away (Porter 1980). It is better to think of 'barriers to imitation' as having different heights and different rates of decay (Reed and DeFillippi 1990). And, as Barney (1991) reminds us, there is also the possibility of 'Schumpeterian shocks'.

This refers to the great Austrian economist Joseph Schumpeter's view that capitalism involves 'gales of creative destruction' (Schumpeter 1950: 84). These are major innovations in products or processes which can destroy whole firms and the industries they inhabit. As he pointed out, this is a lot tougher than price-based competition. A very contemporary example is the way in which digital cameras and the growth of smartphones have decimated the film-processing industry with kick-on effects to the retailers who used to sell and service cameras.[4]

The question of how to achieve competitive advantage is the dominant concern in the strategic management literature. Following theorists like Porter (1980, 1985, 1991), strategy textbooks typically focus on competitive advantage as the dependent variable of interest in the whole subject, stressing the ways in which firms can make themselves profitably different from others. This is a very important concern, which will be discussed in greater depth in this book, but we use the concept with an awareness that firms are never entirely different from others. They need to meet certain baseline conditions in the industries and societies in which they are based, which means they need, and tend to retain, similarities to other firms (DiMaggio and Powell 1983, Carroll and Hannan 1995). In saying, then, that firms need to find competitive advantages if they are to survive over the long run, we are not wanting to imply that this will make them completely different from their rivals. Firms that survive for long periods evolve a blend of similar and distinctive traits.

Let's look at firms in the low-cost airline industry, for example. In terms of competitive strategy, they follow a very similar formula: 'cheap airlines' focus on the short-haul market (including the lucrative tourist destinations), tend to use one or two types of airplane to reduce maintenance costs, carry higher loads of passengers, reduce turn-around times, offer fewer of the staffing entitlements common in 'legacy airlines', charge for optional services and foster internet booking enormously.[5] All of this helps to reduce operating costs and raise productivity, supporting the low-pricing strategy, and makes these low-cost airlines similar to each other and discernibly different from 'full-service carriers' or 'legacy airlines'. However, there can still be differences in their strategies: for example, in the extent to which they use primary or secondary airports and in their approach to HRM. Research by Gitell and Bamber (2010) and Harvey and Turnbull (2010) in this industry points to markedly different approaches to managing people between 'high-road' and 'low-road' models of

---

[4] http://www.bbc.com/news/magazine-16483509, accessed 26/2/15.
[5] See, for example, http://www.guardian.co.uk/business/2006/oct/06/theairlineindustry.travelnews2, accessed 12/3/14.

HRM. Although such contrasts can be oversimplified, in the former, company executives see their business model of cost reduction as consistent with fostering individual commitment and working in a cooperative, 'mutual-gains' approach with unions. This means working with employees to find ways of reducing non-labour costs while enhancing service performance, something exemplified in the case of Southwest Airlines (Gitell and Bamber 2010). In the low-road model, executives are not convinced that such 'touchy-feely' practices (Gitell and Bamber 2010: 176) will support cost reduction. They practise a more contingent approach to employee interests and aim to remain union-free, something that can help to enhance flexibility when downturns come, which they regularly do (Blyton and Turnbull 2004, Harvey and Turnbull 2010: 231). As this example suggests, one can expect to find a blend of similarity and difference in a detailed analysis of organisations in any industry.

The strategies of firms

In this context, the *strategies* of firms are their particular attempts to engage with the strategic problems in their environment. They are the ways in which the managers of firms understand their goals and develop resources – both human and non-human – to reach them. Some strategies are better than others in the context concerned: some address the problem of viability extremely well while others are simply disastrous – with every shade of effectiveness in between. The very best strategies are those that lay a basis for sustained competitive advantage. When key requirements for viability are not addressed by a firm's strategy, either its leaders learn quickly where they are failing or the firm will fold up. In this sense, all firms have strategies but some have strategies that are much smarter than those of other firms. The fact that a firm has a strategy does not mean that it is successful. It simply means that it has a discernible way of engaging with its environment.

As noted earlier, we should not make the mistake of equating the strategies of firms with formal strategic plans. Following the 'strategic choice' perspective (Child 1972), it is better if we understand the strategies of firms as *sets of strategic choices*, some of which may stem from planning exercises and set-piece debates in senior management, and some of which emerge in a stream of action. The latter, called 'emergent strategy' by Mintzberg (1978), is an inevitable feature of strategy. Once a firm commits to a particular strategy, such as a decision to enter the Chinese market, it is inevitable that the process of carrying out that commitment will involve learning that will shape the strategy over time. Resource commitments of this kind provide a structure or frame within which strategy evolves.

And, as implied by Figure 2.1, in defining a firm's strategy as a set of strategic choices, we are saying that it includes critical choices about ends *and* means. A firm's strategy contains 'outward' and 'inward' elements. Firms face the problem of choosing suitable goals in markets and the problem of organising appropriate resources to meet them. In effect, our 'strategic choice' definition draws on a 'configurational' or 'gestalt' perspective (Miller 1981, Meyer, Tsui and Hinings 1993, Veliyath and Srinavasan 1995). To be successful, firms need an effective *system* of choices involving all the key dimensions of the business: marketing, production, human resource management and finance.

This definition means we do not use the terms 'business strategy' and 'competitive strategy' interchangeably (Boxall 1996). As the word implies, *business* strategy is the strategy for the whole of the business, for all the critical functions it needs and how they should relate to each other. A business is a system, not a single component. Competitive strategy is concerned with the marketing aspect or dimension of the business strategy: with what customers are targeted, with which products or services and with how the firm positions itself in relation to competitors for these customers. It is an aspect that interacts with, and evolves with, other aspects of the business strategy over time. This is not an attempt to downplay competitive strategy. There is no doubt that decisions about market positioning are extremely important. However, they constitute only one element of a business strategy, which must be effectively related to the other essential parts if the business is to be successful.

Our discussion so far implies that business strategy is composed of a cluster of strategies covering the critical functions of the business: marketing, production or operations, human resource management and finance. Another way of putting this, using stakeholder theory, is to say that business strategy includes key choices involving all the stakeholder groups: it covers critical aspects of the firm's relations with investors, customers, suppliers, employees and regulators (Hill and Jones 1992, Donaldson and Preston 1995). Business strategy is the system of the firm's important relationships, a system that could be well integrated around common concerns or which might have various weak links and 'foul-ups'. As noted before, there is nothing in this definition to say that a firm's strategy is particularly clever.

A key issue associated with the strategic choice perspective is the question of what we are implying about the *extent of choice* available to firms. It is widely accepted in the strategy literature that firms in some contexts have greater 'degrees of freedom' than others enjoy (Porter 1980, 1985, Nelson 1991). Some environments are more benign – more 'munificent' – than others (Pfeffer and Salancik 1978). Some firms are heavily constrained by competitive forces pushing them towards intense margin-based competition (something suppliers of supermarkets regularly complain about) while others enjoy a much more dominant position (companies like Microsoft come readily to mind). Consistent with John Child's (1997) re-formulation of the strategic choice perspective, we believe it is important to steer a path between 'hyper-determinism', on the one hand, and 'hyper-voluntarism', on the other. That is, firms are neither fully constrained by their environment nor fully able to create it. Adopting a strategic choice perspective means that we see firms as experiencing a varying blend of constraint and choice somewhere in between these two extremes. The 'choice' in 'strategic choice' is real but its extent is variable.

Before moving on, we should note that this definition of strategy is based at the business-unit level. This level is, in fact, the most logical one at which to define strategy because different business units are organised around markets or segments of markets which require different goals and clusters of resources (Porter 1980, Ghemawat and Costa 1993). Theory and analysis in strategy stems, almost entirely, from the business-unit level (Porter 1985, Kaplan and Norton 1996). However, we should note that more complex frameworks are needed to encompass corporate strategy in multidivisional and multinational firms. Questions about 'parenting advantage'– about which businesses to buy, which to invest in, which to 'milk' for profit, which to divest and when – are vital in multidivisional firms. At this stage, we will not introduce this level of complexity but we will examine the different ways multidivisional firms make these choices in Chapter 10, and Chapter 11 will look at the added complexity of strategic choice in multinational companies.

Strategy and the life cycle of the firm

A firm's strategy, then, is a system of strategic choices, which includes critical elements related to HRM. But how do such strategies emerge and what happens to them as circumstances change? To deepen our understanding of strategy, it helps to examine the life cycle of firms, beginning with their birth in the initial phases of industry development.

Industries emerge at particular points in time and evolve through periods of crisis – in which there are winners and losers – and periods of relatively stable growth (Schumpeter 1950, Miller and Friesen 1980, Tushman, Newman and Romanelli 1986). This understanding of industry evolution is analogous to the well-known biological concept of 'punctuated equilibrium': the idea that the life forms we find around us are not simply the product of incredibly long periods of time, as originally argued by Charles Darwin, but result from alternating periods of intense change and periods of gradual adaptation (Gersick 1991).

Phases of industry evolution

At the outset of industry formation, pioneering firms introduce product or service innovations that create new competitive space: in other words, they develop a new offering that provides a better solution to an existing need that customers have or they invent something that customers now want to have. This is the 'establishment context' or the founding stage of the firm. Strategic management research indicates that key decisions taken at founding have profound consequences, establishing a pattern of behaviour that is difficult (though not impossible) to change (Freeman and Boeker 1984, Boeker 1989, Eisenhart and Schoonhovern 1990).

Firms are established by entrepreneurs or by 'intrapreneurial' teams in existing organisations (Schnaars 1994, Freeman 1995, Mueller 1997). They are founded by people who 'sense, shape and seize' opportunities to create new sources of value (Teece 2011: 9–24). These are the 'pioneers', whose activities typically create a group of 'followers' who perceive that new value is being created and join the industry as it establishes. As we have argued, one of the key challenges for both groups, along with finding the money to meet their development costs, is to hire a group of people around them who will make their vision a reality, people who have the productive talents needed to make the business a success and who will work effectively for the rewards being offered. The resource-based view of the firm, which will be discussed in Chapter 4, argues that pioneers can build competitive strength through better timing and learning, moving more quickly up the 'experience curve'. This means that those following them tend to perform better if they are 'fast followers', capitalising on the innovations developed by the leaders while astutely avoiding some of the mistakes that leaders inevitably make.

All industries, in effect, demonstrate a dynamic interplay between innovation and imitation (Schnaars 1994). Over the long haul, resilient firms exhibit an astute blend of the two processes. The microcomputer industry provides an interesting example of this. The legendary innovators, Apple Computer, and about a dozen other firms, entered the industry in 1976 (Carroll and Hannan 1995). Apple produced the first personal computer that could display colour graphics and which could operate with floppy disks. IBM, the industry behemoth, entered five years later, in 1981. For quite a while, Apple enjoyed the fruits of successful leadership through its various innovations (including the ability of Apple 11 to run spreadsheeting software) but IBM showed an extraordinary ability to execute an astute 'fast follower' strategy (Utterback 1994, Carroll and Hannan 1995).

The mature context arrives when the industry settles into a period of stable growth based around one or two 'dominant designs' for products or services and the organisations that provide them (Abernathy and Utterback 1978, Teece 2011). The development of a dominant design enables firms to move quickly up what technology strategists call the S-curve (Foster 1986, Utterback 1994, Henderson 1995). High levels of effort on research and product development achieve slow progress to begin with but breakthroughs associated with the dominant design create the basis for rapid movement up the curve. Ultimately, the potential of existing technology reaches some kind of performance limit as the curve levels out.

In the case of personal computers, the IBM PC brought together the defining features that shaped the industry standard: 'a TV monitor, standard disk drive, QWERTY keyboard, the Intel 8088 chip, open architecture, and MS DOS operating system' (Utterback 1994: 25). Dominant designs represent the strategic configurations that have proved more successful than rival models of strategic management in the establishment phase. As Mueller (1997: 827–8) puts it:

> At some point the market begins to select its favourite model designs, producers begin to concentrate upon the best production techniques. Those firms that have selected the 'right' product designs or production processes survive, the others depart. Following this 'shake-out' period, the industry stabilizes and enters a mature phase in which the number of sellers and industry concentration do not change dramatically.

In the mature context, those who remain credible members of the industry enter a period of relative stability in which the emphasis is on continuous improvement within the prevailing business paradigm. Growth beyond the establishment phase into the mature context typically ushers in more bureaucratic styles of management with the organisation inevitably developing a hierarchy and a set of routines (e.g. Teece 2011: 34–8). With this process, new leaders are often hired. Entrepreneurs may give way to 'professional managers' who are more accustomed to managing large organisations. The challenges of size, increasing workforce complexity, the need to comply with various regulations and greater visibility to the public mean that the firm adopts more formalised procedures and policies. Reliance on the implicit philosophies and informal practices of the small, entrepreneurial firm becomes much less realistic but the trend to bureaucratisation may antagonise those who revelled in the informality and adrenalin-pumping riskiness of the firm's founding years. These individuals may experience a sense of loss, a sense that the company will never again be driven by the same creativity and sense of fun. Thus, growth can generate a tension around the desirability of bureaucratisation: on the one hand, it is needed to manage size and complexity and, on the other, it threatens the intimacy and flexibility of earlier times.

Throughout this phase, firms come to vary in their profitability and in their readiness for change. Stable growth is punctuated by the next crisis, which calls for renewal or leads to decline. Renewal crises may be the result of a new round of technological or organisational innovation within the sector – not necessarily by the original pioneers – or may be introduced by a general threat external to all firms – such as a national or global economic recession, the decline of import protection or a technological revolution in a different field that has dramatic implications across industry boundaries. In the case of technological challenges, particular technologies tend to reach limits (the flat top of the S-curve) and firms must move to new technologies (with their own S-curves) or fail if they cling to an obsolete technology (Foster 1986).

The renewal context disturbs the continuities built up over the establishment and mature phases, threatening to turn previous strengths into weaknesses. It is very hard to change the 'core features' of organisations – such as their fundamental mission, their basic technologies and their marketing strategies – so the difficulty of change in the renewal context should never be underestimated (Carroll and Hannan 1995: 26–8). The firm needs leaders who can see which of its competences will retain their relevance in the future while perceiving which ones have already become liabilities. Where, in effect, should the firm consolidate its learning and what should it 'unlearn' (Miller and Friesen 1980, Leonard-Barton 1992, 1998, Snell, Youndt and Wright 1996)? And when, and in what order, should it make the desirable changes: how should it shape its 'strategic staircase' (Baden-Fuller and Stopford 1994)? Senior management faces a complex problem in discerning the kind, extent and timing of the change that is needed to enable the firm to survive. Again, this may mean a change of leadership, ushering in 'turnaround managers' with reputations for handling these tough, highly politicised decisions.

Two kinds of mature firms manage to survive (Baden-Fuller 1995). One is the firm that succeeds in dominating the direction of industry change: the ultimate level of economic achievement for any firm. The other is the firm that manages to adapt to the direction of change. This kind of firm incurs serious costs of adjustment but retains its viability by making the necessary changes without insolvency or loss of investor confidence. It imitates key changes by the new innovators quickly enough to stay afloat. All other firms fail. New entrants may, of course, appear at this point and may hold a winning advantage if they can add new sources of value and behave as nimble entrepreneurial firms which outmanoeuvre the more inertial mature organisations around them.

Successful weathering of the renewal crisis ushers in another opportunity for stable growth. In effect, the cycle of stability and crisis continues for as long as the industry remains relevant to a profitable set of customer needs. If it does not, the industry enters terminal decline and firms must find something else to do or disappear altogether from the corporate landscape. With the advent of free internet-based news services, the daily and weekly newspapers have been facing just such a challenge in the early twenty-first century. Their business model, which relies on a mix of advertising and a high volume of paying subscribers, is now heavily compromised. Many have closed, others are making major losses and some are consolidating their local market as their rivals collapse.[6]

The framework shown in Figure 2.2 has been drawn to encompass both goods and service industries. The S-curve is essentially a concept that relates to manufacturing or to service industries which depend heavily on manufactured technologies for customer service (such as air travel which depends on aircraft technology as well as computerised reservation and passenger management systems). However, all industries – service, manufacturing, public sector, not-for-profit – can be thought of as facing alternating periods of change and stability. Change need not stem from technological breakthroughs: it may stem from ecological, social, cultural or political change as well as general economic trends, such as the Global Financial Crisis of 2008–9.

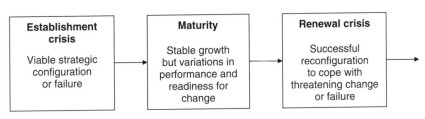

Figure 2.2   Phases of industry evolution

---

[6] See, for example, http://www.digitaljournal.com/article/281092, accessed 16/1/15.

It is also important to note that Figure 2.2 does not imply that all industries change at the same rate across the contexts of establishment, maturity and renewal. Some, like the profession of law, in which precedent and personal service are so engrained, seem to change only in a slow, stately manner. New information technologies have been adopted in law offices but the fundamental nature of legal research and representation has changed very little over the last 100 years or more. Others, such as consumer electronics, seem characterised by what some consultants call 'permanent white water'.

Williams (1992) distinguishes between slow-cycle, standard-cycle and fast-cycle industries. One might usefully imagine a dental practice. The dentistry itself (extraction of teeth, filings, etc.) is an example of a slow-cycle industry. Little has changed in the fundamental nature of dental work for a long period of time. On the other hand, the toothpaste used by the dentist and his/her clients is an example of a standard-cycle industry. The product is mature, controlled by huge oligopolists, and advertising budgets jostle to hold and enlarge market share. Finally, the accounting and client management software on the computer in the dentist's office is an example of a fast-cycle industry. New upgrades and new versions are almost constantly available. Despite variations in rates of change, the three-phase model of industry evolution – establishment, maturity and renewal/decline – is well supported by research in industrial economics (Mueller 1997) and provides a useful basis for thinking about the way that strategic problems, and the strategies of firms, evolve over time.

The process of strategic management

As this discussion implies, strategic management is best defined as the process of strategy-making: of forming and, if the firm survives, of re-forming its strategy as the environment changes. And, as we have already indicated, this may involve elements of formal planning, including the application of analytical techniques such as industry analysis, which examines the competitive forces firms face in their industry (Porter 1980, 1985). It may involve set-piece debates among directors and executives, framed around policy papers and financial proposals. It may also involve *force majeure* if key power brokers – the 'dominant coalition' (Child, 1972, 1997) – impose their will where they have the ability to do so. It will also, as Mintzberg emphasises (1978, 1990, 1994), inevitably involve a learning process as the managers of firms find out what works well in practice for them – or, we might add, what works better for their rivals.

This description of the strategic management process implies that it is hard to do it well. Following Eisenhardt and Zbaracki (1992) and Child (1997), we see strategic decision-making as difficult in two key ways that need exploring in greater depth: it is mentally or 'cognitively' tough, and it is politically fraught.

Strategic management and human cognition

'Human cognition' is a psychological term for thinking processes, for our ability to process information and make decisions. Research on cognition recognises the validity of Herbert Simon's (1947) classic observation that human beings are subject to 'bounded rationality'. We cannot know everything about our environment, nor can we easily manipulate more than a handful of key ideas in a problem-solving situation: we are limited in the number of variables we can actively 'work on' as we wrestle with an environment that is much more complex than that. Our search for information is 'incomplete, often inadequate, based on uncertain information and partial ignorance, and usually terminated with the discovery of satisfactory, not optimal courses of action' (Simon 1985: 295).

Following Simon (1947), theory in strategic management does not typically employ the assumptions of 'homo economicus': that tradition within economics which keeps alive a view of economic agents acting with all the information they need and with no debilitating debates or frustrating compromises over the firm's desirable direction or internal organisation (see, for example, Hunt 2000). As many academics have quipped, this view of business behaviour is largely unjustified by the facts but it makes the maths easier. Certainly, whoever thought of it first had no familiarity with the management of organisations.

On a practical level, management can ill afford to assume it holds perfect knowledge or has outstanding problem-solving abilities. Research shows that human performance becomes increasingly variable in jobs of high complexity (Hunter, Schmidt and Judiesch 1990). The work of strategic management, of finding a desirable path for the firm and managing its resources accordingly, is complex work that takes place in an environment of risk and uncertainty (Spender 2014). As we have emphasised, it involves *systemic* factors – the problem of thinking not only within 'silos' but of identifying and linking a range of critical elements across the business. Box 2.1, drawn from various sources (Belbin 1981, Isenberg 1984, Simon 1985, Barr, Stimpert and Huff 1992, Eisenhardt and Zbaracki 1992, Hambrick 1995), summarises some of the main findings of research on the cognitive problems of decision-making in firms. The overall effect of this research should induce some humility in the face of complex decisions. In respect of strategic decisions, it is much better to be 'often in doubt but seldom wrong' than 'seldom in doubt and often wrong'.

Box 2.1   Human cognitive issues affecting strategic management

1. We have reasons or goals for our actions but some of them are not very smart by other people's standards. Our powers of reasoning and our understanding of the world vary considerably.

2. We often have to act without knowing everything we'd like to: complexity and uncertainty are facts of life, especially in strategic management. We do not know the future. Managers rely on 'mental models' which simplify and may distort the changing nature of their environment.

3. We often commit emotionally to a failing course of action and 'throw good money after bad'. People do not generally like to lose face.

4. We tend to search for confirming rather than disconfirming evidence to support our views (which is a common trap in employee selection, for example).

5. In problem-solving, we often leap to a favourite or preferred solution without disciplining ourselves to diagnose the problem more deeply, mapping causes and consequences, generating real alternatives and remaining truly open to the criticisms and refinements offered by others. Existing 'mental models' (about major cause–effect relationships in our world) tend to limit the range of our thinking about solutions to new problems.

6. No single executive in a large business is likely to have all the answers to complex, ambiguous problems: strategic management in large organisations needs teams of people with complementary strengths and styles.

7. Even if the need for management teamwork is recognised, knowledge of how things are done, and of how the firm might best respond to competitor threats or new technology, is dispersed throughout the firm, not held exclusively by far-sighted or 'heroic' executives.

8. The management process tends to repeat yesterday's success formula. It can take a long time to change the focus on 'what worked before' in a business. This opens up profitable opportunities for firms whose people can think differently. One firm's mindset or 'strong culture' is another firm's competitive opportunity.

Barr, Stimpert and Huff (1992) provide an interesting illustration of the cognitive problems of strategic management. They examine the quality of strategic decision-making in two US railway companies in the 1950s, a time when rail faced growing competition from other transport modes, particularly the trucking industry. Between 1949 and 1973, the number of major railway companies roughly halved (down from 135 to 69). Barr et al. examined the efforts of two companies, the Chicago and North Western (C&NW) and the Chicago, Rock Island and Pacific (Rock Island), to handle this threatening environment. C&NW survived but Rock Island went bankrupt in the mid-1970s. Barr et al.'s analysis of 50 letters to shareholders written by the directors of these companies is revealing. As the environment began to turn against the rail companies in the 1950s, both companies blamed *external* factors for their poor performance – such as the weather, government programmes and regulation. By about 1956, however, management at C&NW began to change its mental model, focusing efforts on *internal* factors (associated with costs and productivity) that management could control more effectively. This set in train (so to speak) a progressive learning process in which management strategies were improved by trial-and-error. This kind of shift in mental model did not occur at Rock Island until 1964, when an abrupt change of thinking occurred, by which time it was too late.

Barr et al. suggest that Rock Island's directors may have been caught in a 'success trap'. Having been prosperous for many years, they tended to dismiss the need for change even though the post-war environment was steadily moving against rail transport. This study is interesting because it demonstrates the way in which a dysfunctional mental model – one in which notions of cause-and-effect are well wide of the mark – can persist among the members of a senior management team. Not only was the environment clearly difficult but there were other firms – such as CN&W – that were handling it better.

Strategic management and organisational politics

Cases such as the demise of the Rock Island railway point to the role of cognitive strengths and weaknesses in strategic decision-making. There is no doubt that cognition – cleverness – counts for a lot in company success. Most of the research on human cognition, however, overlooks the fact that strategic decision-making is not simply about dealing with complex mental challenges in threatening environments. More than this is involved: politics matter, particularly in larger organisations. Strategic management is about steering a course in a politically constituted organisation (Child 1972, 1997, Eisenhardt and Zbaracki 1992).

The point is well made in Child and Smith's (1987) study of Cadbury's attempts to transform itself in the 1960s and 1970s. Facing the concentration and growth of retailer power and rising oligopolistic competition in a saturated home market, Cadbury needed strategic renewal. It needed to move away from some key elements of 'Cadburyism' – including a huge range of products and some key HR policies such as life-time commitment – towards a more efficient model of manufacturing with better technology and fewer but more flexible workers. The leaders who made this change happen were people who handled the cognitive problems well. They cleverly perceived which parts of 'Cadburyism' needed to change and which ought to be enduring. However, as Child and Smith (1987: 588) explain, they also had the power to influence events, the political position and credibility needed within the firm to effect change: 'The Cadbury transformation relied on the exercise of power as well as on the persuasive force of vision and its attendant symbols'.

Because firms are coalitions of stakeholder groups (Cyert and March 1963), we must expect that any major initiative involves *political* management, particularly where investors must be persuaded to support the initiative or where employee groups are being asked to make changes that threaten their interests, as was the case in the Cadbury transformation. This is one of the straightforward implications of the stakeholder theory of the firm (Hill and Jones 1992, Donaldson and Preston 1995) and of 'resource-dependence' theory (Pfeffer and Salancik 1978). In a nutshell, firms are beholden to stockholders (who supply financial capital) but they are also dependent on any stakeholder group (such as suppliers and key customers) that contributes resources that are valuable to the firm. Those who provide labour are powerful in this sense. Workers – employees and contractors – do not need 'equal power' to have influence with management, they simply need the power to affect performance in some significant way. This is almost invariably the case. Dealing with the power of workers is one of the most visible of the power dynamics in firms. It often hits the media when strikes or lockouts are involved. Less eye catching is the loss of employees with scarce know-how and influential networks, who exercise their labour-market power by resigning from the firm. Loss of such 'key value generators', either individually or in teams, can have devastating impacts.

Much of the political difficulty of strategic management occurs within the management structure itself. Organisations offer managers opportunities for personal enrichment (Williamson 1964). The large enterprises of our time – the *Fortune 500* companies and the like – provide management 'careerists' (Rousseau 1995) with a huge domain for self-serving behaviour.

Intra-management political problems are of two main types. On the more 'macro' level, departments acquire power when they are central to the fundamental strategy on which a business is founded (Boeker 1989). Managers who head the historically strong departments often fight change even when the larger picture indicates that strategic change is now needed. For example, a firm in which production has historically led the way may well suffer from serious managerial in-fighting if the marketing department grows in significance and starts to challenge production's power base.

On the more 'micro' level, individual managers have personal reasons to advance their own interests irrespective of whether they are located in a powerful department. Perhaps the most significant problem presented by the lure of rewards is the way consideration for one's personal future often encourages managers to keep quiet about problems, to filter the bad news. Alternatively, individuals may try to fix blame onto their supervisors, subordinates or peers as a way of displacing attention from their own performance (Longenecker, Sims and Gioia 1987).

When most managers in a team are afraid of introducing conflicting opinion, the organisation can suffer from what Irving Janis (1972) calls 'groupthink', a syndrome where executives close down debate prematurely and take decisions with negative consequences. The decision by the US cabinet to invade Cuba at the Bay of Pigs in April 1961 is one of Janis's famous examples. Barbara Tuchman (1996: 302–3), in her classic study of flawed decision-making in a selection of great historical events, *The March of Folly: From Troy to Vietnam*, finds many cases of the tendency:

> Adjustment is painful. For the ruler it is easier, once he [sic] has entered a policy box, to stay inside. For the lesser official it is better, for the sake of his [sic] position, not to make waves, not to press evidence that the chief will find painful to accept. Psychologists call the process of screening out discordant information 'cognitive dissonance'.... Cognitive dissonance is the tendency 'to suppress, gloss over, water down or "waffle" issues that would produce conflict or "psychological pain" within an organization.' It causes alternatives to be 'deselected since even thinking about them entails conflicts.' In the relations of subordinate to superior ..., its object is the development of policies that upset no one.

The tendency to look after oneself is recognised by those branches of organisational economics, such as agency theory, which acknowledge that managerial interests can diverge from those of shareholders (McMillan 1992, Rowlinson 1997). Our point here is that the politics of executive ambition adds complexity to the broader stakeholder-based politics we find in organisations and makes the process of strategic management more complex.

HRM and the strategic management process

Given the cognitive and political challenges in strategic management, it should be clear that the quality of a firm's HRM can make a major difference to the quality of its strategic management. Strategy does not emerge out of nowhere. Strategy exists because people think it up and make it happen. As a general rule, the greater the uncertainty involved in work, the more important it is to hire or develop people of high ability, with a well-rounded intellectual and emotional profile, who have a capacity to think critically and flexibly. This is particularly true at the apex of organisations because the performance of companies tends to reflect the quality of their 'upper echelons' (Hambrick 1987, 1995, Norburn and Birley 1988). Failure to recruit and retain suitable managers will hamstring company performance.

There is lots of evidence that company directors and chief executives act on this common-sense principle. The enormous resources they invest in executive search ('headhunting') testify to the significance they place on hiring the best leaders they can. In 2013, the worldwide revenues of executive search firms were estimated at more than US\$10 billion.[7] On top of this, there are all the resources invested inside companies that handle their own recruitment. Added to the investment in recruitment is another enormous investment in employee development, incorporating executive education, such as MBA programmes, in-house training and one-to-one coaching.

There is also evidence that senior HR specialists orient their jobs to focus on critical activities associated with managing managers. In a study of human resource directors in the largest New Zealand corporates, Hunt and Boxall (1998) found a strong emphasis in their work priorities on developing executive capability and performance. In line with findings in the UK (Marginson et al. 1988), the primary concern of most of the senior HR specialists in the study was the management of managers, including recruitment, remuneration, development, succession planning and termination. One stated that they 'worked constantly' with the CEO of the company: 'looking at managers, identifying strengths and weaknesses, seeing who will go further and who needs to go' (Hunt and Boxall 1998: 772–3).

But we should not think that the strategic management process will improve solely as a result of selecting or developing key individuals. Team processes are also vital to performance (e.g. Burch and Anderson 2004) and team-building activities are widely observed in management development. One of the most celebrated frameworks is associated with the work

---

[7] https://members.aesc.org/eweb/upload/Q3_2014_AESC_State_of_the_Industry_Report.pdf, accessed 16/1/15.

of Belbin (1981, 1993). Belbin's model of team roles has been used to analyse the strengths and weaknesses of many senior management teams. According to this theory, it is a mistake to construct management teams simply based on the functional expertise of individuals (i.e. their abilities in marketing, finance, operations, ICT or HRM). Belbin argues that the most effective management teams enjoy a healthy mix of complementary *teamwork* styles (i.e. how people characteristically behave during team activities). In its original formulation, highly performing teams include at least one clever and highly creative individual (originally called a 'plant'), are chaired by someone who knows how to use the talents of others and contain a spread of other useful styles (e.g. a 'monitor-evaluator' to provide some dispassionate intellectual appraisal of the plant's ideas, and a 'completer-finisher' who will ensure sound organisation and follow-through) (Belbin 1981: 93–9). Frameworks such as this offer ways of helping individuals to become aware of the way they typically interact with others in teams and can help them develop new strengths in group work.

Clearly, the development of better teamwork in management, and the development of a workplace culture that supports strategic renewal, depends more than anything on the leadership of the chief executive. The CEO plays a critical role in setting the style of participation within the senior management team and, through them, throughout the organisation. He or she can decide that team-building processes are important or can ignore the issue. He or she can foster wider involvement in decision-making or restrict key decisions to a select few, who may not be well informed about what is happening in the business. Even when a company has built a more a participative culture, every time a new chief executive is appointed there is potential for decision-making to revert to a closely held style. Business organisations are not constituted as democracies. Disproportionate power keeps reverting into the hands of senior management. This should remind us how central executive appointments are to the long-term success of the firm. Such appointments are clearly strategic choices. But so is much more in HRM, as we shall see.

Conclusions

As common sense tells us, the word 'strategic' implies something that is seriously consequential for the future of the firm. Strategic choices are those that are fateful for a firm's survival or, if it does survive, that explain major variations in its performance compared to its rivals. The fundamental strategic problem is that of choosing a market or market segment and establishing a viable business in it. To be a credible player, a firm needs 'table stakes': a set of resources appropriate to the specific context in which it wishes to operate. Along with a suitable approach to marketing, to production or operations management, and to finance, this means that firms need a cost-effective approach to HRM. Without certain kinds of capable, motivated and affordable people, firms are simply not viable.

Across the phases of industry development, firms are engaged in an ongoing struggle to build and defend competitive advantages. Some of these are temporary while others are more enduring. Those that build a relatively consistent pattern of superior returns for their shareholders have developed some form of sustained competitive advantage. This does not mean, however, that they will be completely different from their rivals because all firms develop features characteristic of their industry and the societies in which they have evolved.

Strategies are the ways in which the managers of firms understand their goals and develop resources – both human and non-human – to reach them. Some aspects of strategy may be formally planned, but it is inevitable that much of a firm's strategy emerges in a stream of action over time. Strategic learning occurs when firms make commitments, such as launching a new product or opening a new branch in a foreign country. How well a strategy is conceived and implemented is very variable. Observing that firms make strategic choices does not mean that they are successful in their environment. Many, if not most, firms fail in the founding phase of an industry while others fail when a crisis comes along that demands organisational renewal.

Strategic management, therefore, is a risky process, fraught with difficulty, both intellectually and politically. It takes place in a complex, uncertain environment in which strategic issues emerge and vary over time. Improving the process of strategic management has everything to do with people: with who is attracted to the firm, with how they learn to work together and with the organisational culture they create over time. It not only involves making some critical decisions about 'talent', about the recruitment, development and retention of key people, but it also involves astute forms of teamwork and cross-functional cooperation, both within the management team and throughout the organisation. This means that human resource management is very much involved, and it is something that bears close study if we are concerned about the quality of strategic management.

part 2

General principles

3

Strategic HRM: 'best fit' or 'best practice'?

Part 1 of this book established some fundamentals about the nature of strategy and the role of HRM in it. It emphasised the fact that managers cannot create a viable business without engaging a group of capable, motivated and affordable people, people who possess the kind of human resources that will build the business. Furthermore, in the long-run struggle for competitive advantages, managers depend heavily on the quality of the human talents they can access and how well these are brought together in the firm's culture. Failing to deal effectively with such strategic issues as labour scarcity, employee motivation and change management will imperil the firm. We now wish to analyse the strategic role of HRM in greater depth. Here, in the five chapters of Part 2, we will be examining a set of general principles, or major concerns, that underpin the theory of strategic HRM. Then, in Part 3, we will be applying these principles across the manufacturing and service sectors and examining them in the complex contexts of multidivisional and multinational firms.

In this chapter, we begin the 'theoretical story' of strategic HRM by reviewing the debate around how HRM should be integrated with strategic management. Perhaps one message – more than any other – is communicated in job advertisements for HR managers: the successful candidate will be someone who can *integrate* HRM with the business, someone who can demonstrate a 'business savvy' approach to HR strategy. This challenge is widely endorsed by executives in prominent firms. But how are they thinking about it? And how are managers, including HR specialists, going about it in reality? Could the task be interpreted in quite different ways?

This has been a critical issue in the theory of strategic HRM, and our task in this chapter is to consider the main ways in which it has been approached.

One approach, the 'best fit' school, is associated with the contingency perspective that is central to the theory of strategic management generally. It argues that managers must adapt their HR strategies to other elements of the firm's strategy and to its wider environment. In other words, what constitutes a good HR strategy will depend on what works for the business in its specific context. But this is not necessarily straightforward. It invites a string of questions about which are the most critical variables in the firm's context and how they are best connected. The other approach advocates 'best practice', a form of theoretical universalism, which downplays the role of context. It argues that all firms will be better off if they identify and adopt those HR practices which are shown to be 'best' for organising work and managing people. This is not straightforward either: it begs questions about how best-practice models are defined and about whose interests are best served by them. This chapter subjects these two approaches to close scrutiny. We examine in each case what the research and theoretical critiques have to say, and we reach an assessment of the relative merits of each approach.

Strategic HRM: the best-fit school

The best-fit school of strategic HRM argues that the variety we see in HRM in the real world implies that managers tailor their HR practices to their specific context. Furthermore, they are wise to do so: firms underperform and may fail if they do not adapt to their environment or if managers do a poor job of integrating the different parts of the business effectively. The best-fit literature contains both broad analytical models and more specific theories. In this section, we will outline these and consider the research evidence and conceptual critiques.

Best fit: broad analytical frameworks

In the late 1980s and early 1990s, the Harvard framework (Beer et al. 1984) provided one of the first major statements in the HRM canon on the issue of how managers should make strategic choices in HRM (Figure 3.1) (Poole 1990, Boxall 1992). In this analytical framework, managers in firms are encouraged to set their own priorities in HRM based on a consideration of stakeholder interests and situational factors. HR outcomes, in turn, are seen as having longer-term impacts on organisational effectiveness and on individual and societal well-being.

In terms of our understanding of HR strategy, the most important chapter in the Harvard text was the last one in which the authors sought to integrate

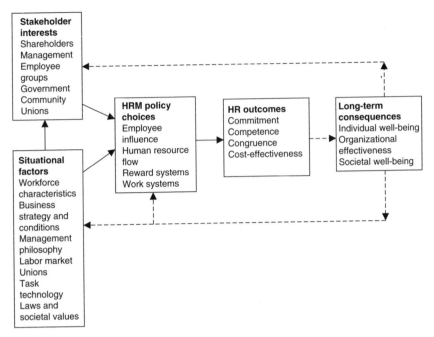

Figure 3.1 The Harvard 'map of the HRM territory'
Source: Beer et al. (1984).

the huge range of HR choices that might be adopted by considering the differences between 'bureaucratic', 'market' and 'clan' models of HRM, a set of
categories that draws on the work of Ouchi (1980). The bureaucratic model
is seen as concerned with 'control and efficiency', using traditional authority
and such staples of personnel management as job descriptions and job evaluation to provide order and equity (Beer et al. 1984: 179). This HRM approach
is regarded as relevant to markets with stable technology and employment
levels. The market HRM approach, on the other hand, aims to treat employees
more like sub-contractors, fostering short-term exchanges and performance-
related pay systems. This is seen as relevant to fast-changing environments
such as high-fashion merchandising, advertising and professional sports
(ibid.: 180). Finally, clan HRM systems are seen as building more diffuse
kinship links, fostering shared values, teamwork and strong commitment in
organisations seeking 'long-term adaptability' (ibid.: 181). This is seen as relevant to firms pursuing quality and innovation. Combining aspects of two
or even three models is seen as useful when facing complex environments
(ibid.: 184).

The clear implication of the Harvard framework is that HR strategies can,
and should, vary based on contextual factors and that firms should aim to

develop a relatively consistent style. Beer et al. (1984: 178, 184) argue that 'HRM policies need to fit with business strategy' and with 'situational constraints' while also envisaging a role for management values (ibid.: 190–1). The goal of fit with broader business strategy and with the environment of the business, followed by internal consistency in HR choices, was argued to be the essential purpose of HRM.

The Harvard framework was followed by a range of similar models. In Dyer and Holder's (1988) framework, management is advised to aim for 'consistency between HR goals ... and the underlying business strategy and relevant environmental conditions' (with the latter, like the Harvard framework, including influences such as labour law, unions, labour markets, technology and management values). In Baron and Kreps's (1999) framework, managers are advised to consider the impact of 'five forces' on HR policy choices: the external environment (social, political, legal and economic), the workforce, the organisation's culture, its strategy and the technology of production and organisation of work. This advice is not offered in a simple, deterministic fashion: managers still have choices (such as where to locate plants in manufacturing) but once some choices are made, certain environmental consequences do follow: so, if you locate in the USA, rather than Honduras, US laws, culture and labour markets inevitably come into play. The goal of achieving internal consistency in whatever model of HRM is adopted – otherwise known as 'internal' or 'horizontal' fit – is then strongly emphasised by Baron and Kreps (1999).

Like the Harvard authors, if not more emphatically, Dyer and Holder (1988) and Baron and Kreps (1999) argue for a contingent understanding of HR strategy or the necessity of moulding HRM to the firm's particular context. Dyer and Holder (1988: 31) conclude that 'the inescapable conclusion is that what is best, depends'. Baron and Kreps (1999: 33) assert that 'in HRM, there is no one size that fits every situation' and argue that no model should be adopted unless the benefits outweigh the costs. None of these frameworks is inherently anti-union or takes the view that HRM is restricted to one style. The message in terms of HR strategy is one of fit or adaptation to the firm's broader business goals and its environmental context.

'Best fit': research and critique

The broad frameworks just described have been important as analytical models that help managers to identify options and make choices in their own environments. In terms of theoretical development, however, progress depends on picking particular variables in these frameworks and subjecting them to formal research, typically through surveys and/or case studies. We must examine these studies if we are to be rigorous in any debate between best fit and best practice. There is an enormous body of research we could call on here, and it does not sit solely within the HRM field. There is a range of studies in related fields such as comparative industrial relations, international business, strategy and operations management. To help organise the evidence, we will look at research on three analytical levels – society, industry and organisation. Such a structure can be useful for undertaking a review of contingencies that might affect HRM in a company.

Societal fit

Societal fit is about the question of whether organisations adapt to the characteristics of the societies in which they are located and whether they are wise to do so. We should recall here the discussion of the goals of HRM in Chapter 1. As explained there, firms that wish to be socially legitimate need to comply with the labour laws of the countries in which they have operations, something which is emphasised in the institutional perspective in organisational studies (e.g. DiMaggio and Powell 1983, Scott 2008). In reality, compliance with labour law is variable, with some firms seeking to avoid their legal responsibilities in any society. However, the evidence suggests that different labour regulations, including laws on union recognition, collective bargaining and workplace consultation, do account for major variation in HR practices across countries, vindicating the institutional perspective (e.g. Gooderham, Nordhaug and Ringdal 1999, Paauwe and Boselie 2003). An obvious contrast is between countries in the Anglo-American world and those European countries in which unions are recognised as 'social partners'. In the latter, employees have much stronger statutory rights to collective bargaining and workplace consultation (e.g. Gooderham et al. 2004). The overall point is that the behaviour of firms *is* heavily shaped by labour law, and all firms *ought* to comply with it if they wish to be responsible corporate citizens.

However, societal fit in HRM relates to a range of economic and social factors that extend well beyond the law. It also includes adaptation to national economic conditions, including the relative difficulty of recruiting suitable labour in local labour markets. Research shows that when economic growth in a country is strong and labour markets are tight, firms adjust their employment practices: managers tend to respond with more generous pay offers and more motivating conditions (e.g. Jackson and Schuler 1995, Kaufman 2010). The converse is true when economic growth is slow or negative, as in the Global Financial Crisis of 2008–9. In these conditions, firms 'hold the whip hand' in negotiations over pay and conditions. Even if they don't shed labour, managers often institute a hiring freeze and cut back on overtime work. While this recession was global, the effects were variable across countries: the negative impact on people was much greater in the USA and the UK than in Australia, for example, where unemployment rates remained lower.[1]

Alongside this critical economic factor, there is the issue of differences across countries in cultural norms, in the ways people instinctively behave. There is now a major body of literature in international business stemming from Hofstede's (1980) classic study of a databank of 116,000 employee attitude questionnaires collected in IBM's international subsidiaries over the period from 1967 to 1973. Hofstede (1983: 76) defined culture as 'collective mental programming ... the conditioning we share with other members of our nation, region or group but not with members of other nations, regions or groups'. Hofstede's study distinguishes cultures that are high on 'individualism', in which people focus on their own self-interests and perhaps those of their immediate family, from those that are high on 'collectivism', in which people are much more concerned with the collective welfare of their wider family groups and communities. He also distinguishes societies low in 'power distance', in which employees prefer egalitarian types of decision-making and are relatively comfortable questioning the boss, from those high in power distance in which people are more approving of social inequalities and more readily accepting of directive styles of leadership. On top of this, there are differences across cultures in the extent to which people cope positively with novel and unusual situations ('uncertainty avoidance') and in attitudes to gender roles. Cultures with sharp distinctions between male and female roles and in which competitiveness is highly valued are more 'masculine' while, in more 'feminine' cultures, both sexes show stronger nurturing values. Another dimension, added later, concerns 'long-term versus short-term orientation' in a culture, with Asian cultures typically taking a more patient, long-term attitude to life and business (Hofstede and Bond 1988).

The vast majority of evidence suggests that these sorts of differences in cultural attitudes do find their way into HR practices. In a major review of international HRM, Aycan (2005) describes a wide range of research showing that practices in such areas as selection, performance appraisal and pay are affected by such dimensions as the extent to which individualism is fostered over collectivism and the extent to which it is considered legitimate to challenge authority. In Anglo-Saxon and in Dutch cultural contexts, for example, it is common to consider people as individuals who can be selected,

---

[1] See http://en.wikipedia.org/wiki/Late-2000s_recession, accessed 16/1/15.

evaluated, rewarded and dispensed with on their individual merits, but such assumptions risk failure in more collectivist cultures where an overemphasis on individuals can threaten group harmony and challenge important status differences. This makes some common Anglo HR practices, such as individually based performance-related pay, dangerous cultural exports. In another highly cited study similar to Hofstede's work, *Riding the Waves of Culture*, Trompenaars and Hampden-Turner (1997: 4–5) comment:

> Pay-for-performance ... can work out well in the USA, the Netherlands and the UK. In more communitarian cultures like France, Germany and large parts of Asia it may not be so successful, at least not the Anglo-Saxon version of pay-for-performance. Employees may not accept that individual members of the group should excel in a way that reveals the shortcomings of other members. Their definition of an 'outstanding individual' is one who benefits those closest to him or her...

Various studies in the international business literature suggest that organisations are more effective when managers work with the grain of these cultural differences rather than against them. For example, Newman and Nollen (1996), in a quantitative study of 176 work units in one US company operating in 18 European and Asian countries, find that higher financial performance is associated with those units where management practices are more congruent with the local culture. Similarly, but in an in-depth case study of two Russian companies, Michailova (2002: 183) finds that the attempts of expatriate American managers to foster employee empowerment, often regarded as an enlightened management principle in US organisations, can be dysfunctional in Russia: Russian employees, who are more accustomed to directive and paternalistic leadership styles, can perceive participation in decision-making as 'avoidance of responsibility and lack of professionalism or as a burden that brings more work to the lower level'.

These sorts of studies do not imply that multinational firms completely adapt to local conditions. Rather, the evidence suggests that they *substantially* adapt to national institutions and cultural norms while still seeking to take advantage of their proprietary technologies (Cooke 2007a) or their service know-how (Gamble 2010). This process is well illustrated in a study by Doeringer, Lorenz and Terkla (2003) of the HR practices of Japanese multinationals with transplants in the USA, the UK and France. These plants are required to meet Japanese productivity benchmarks and usually have Japanese managers appointed to them to monitor local management. Examination of the ways they have sought to organise work and employment over the last 20 to 30 years provides a kind of 'natural experiment' on the interaction between HRM and societal institutions and cultural norms. Doeringer,

Lorenz and Terkla (2003: 271) conclude that there is 'almost no evidence' of Japanese management practices 'being transferred intact to Japanese transplants'. What they do show, however, is that *work* processes associated with Japanese quality-oriented production systems (such as problem-solving in quality circles, teamworking and worker responsibility for quality) are much more likely to have been diffused than *employment* practices associated with pay, skill, promotion systems and the like. This makes a lot of sense: the transplants need work processes that are consistent with the economics of their production systems but can be more flexible in relation to employment practices. The latter are much more driven by national laws, by local labour markets, by union contracts and by deep-set social attitudes. In the UK, for example, Japanese firms have learnt to work with a higher level of unionisation than they find in the USA, and they have been found to adapt to British attitudes to bonus systems (which often favour simpler and 'less subjective' systems to those found in Japan) and to the status differences in British society between technicians and production workers. In France, among other things, Japanese firms have learnt to accept that supervisors will typically be appointed directly to a position of responsibility based on their personal achievements in France's national system of educational qualifications and without any prior experience (for an excellent overview of national differences in approaches to vocational education and training, see Winterton 2007). The French elite model of education, with all its hierarchical rungs, is not easily sidestepped. This contrasts sharply with the Japanese practice of promoting from within based on extensive shopfloor experience.

In other studies, even less of the Japanese approach to work and employment is found to be diffused across countries. A compelling example is Wilkinson et al.'s (2001) case study of two Japanese-owned multinationals operating in Malaysia, which draws on Kenney et al.'s (1998) distinction between 'learning factories' and 'reproduction factories'. The Japanese firms in this study use their Japanese plants to foster their product innovation and to iron out the bugs in the production system (i.e. these plants are the 'learning factories'). Once problem-solving by highly trained and well-paid Japanese workers has played its part, they then mass produce the standardised products in Malaysian plants (their 'reproduction factories'). In the latter, less skilled and lower paid workers assemble what are essentially pre-designed and quality-engineered products. A subsequent study by Morris, Wilkinson and Gamble (2009) of Japanese and Korean firms operating factories in China finds the same phenomenon there, as does Shibata's (2008) study of Japanese transplants in Thailand. Such studies challenge the assumption that multinational companies *want* to export their HR practices around the globe.

As Edwards and Kuruvilla (2005) argue, much of the literature in international HRM makes the faulty assumption that multinational firms somehow want to export the way they manage people from the richer countries to the less developed ones. As they argue, research on the 'international division of labour' often reveals the reverse: many firms go offshore to take advantage of lower labour costs and less demanding labour regulations (see also Cooke 2007b). They are not seeking to export their high-cost models of HRM but to escape them, as we shall explain further in Chapter 8.

Where, then, have we come to? The studies we have discussed help us to see that national boundaries are not impermeable barriers in HRM: multinational firms search out ways of making money through transferring their financial capital and, often, the core elements of their production systems across them. On the other hand, once they land in a country, they face the human elements of running a business that are essentially local (Hofstede and Bond 1988). Firms arriving in a new country come into contact with national labour laws, with local labour markets, with people carrying different cultural expectations, and with specific systems for trade union recognition and for vocational education and training. All of these labour factors help to *localise* HR practices, ensuring that in each country a large measure of adaptation to the legitimate and customary employment practices takes place. Furthermore, multinationals are often heading to these countries precisely because they offer lower-cost models of HRM. They know that reducing their reliance on the high-cost labour markets in their home country will increase their survival chances.

Industry fit

While societal fit emphasises the way national features affect HRM, the notion of industry fit encapsulates the relationship between firms and the factors that are specific to their particular industry. Again, the question is: do firms adapt to their industry contexts and are they wise to do so? The industry is a critical level of analysis in strategic management, as long emphasised by Michael Porter (1980), and as affirmed by strategy researchers who have uncovered 'industry recipes' in the ways firms strategise (Spender 1989). The existence of industry recipes shows that firms tend to imitate what is seen to work in their industry, or in the segment within the industry in which they actually compete, and this includes approaches to managing people.

Industry, however, is a rather complex or 'fuzzy' variable (McGee 2003: 276). When we say 'industry', we are, in fact, thinking about various levels at which differences in management behaviour can occur: differences between broad sectors, differences between industries within sectors, and differences within industries across customer segments or 'strategic groups'. The highest level is the broad sector in which HRM takes place: no one needs much convincing that there are major differences between the private sector, in which firms need to make profits to survive, and the public sector, something which is readily confirmed by major studies and reviews (e.g. Kalleberg et al. 2006). Public sector HRM is not profit driven but it is subject to the directives of governments, which vary as economic conditions and political agendas change. Public sector organisations are typically larger and more bureaucratic than private sector ones, as well as being much more highly unionised (Freeman, Boxall and Haynes 2007). Not only are public sector managers more constrained by their political masters, but they must learn to live with more prescriptive employment contracts that restrict their discretion in HRM, and may face conflict-laden collective negotiations whenever they seek to make change.

Then, within these broad sectors, there are further important differences. HRM in the private sector varies between manufacturing and services and varies markedly within each domain (e.g. Cooke 2014). Within manufacturing, as a general rule, the greater the investment in production technology required in the industry, the greater will be the incentive to invest in the people who work with it. For example, Snell and Dean's (1992) study of 512 US metal manufacturing plants shows that heavier investments in individual employees, including more extensive screening and training practices, are associated with plants using advanced manufacturing technologies (AMT) such as computer-integrated manufacturing systems. The value of such investments, however, is likely to be questioned by managers when the industry they are operating in is characterised by a stable, low-technology environment (Kintana, Alonso, Olaverri 2006, Fabling and Grimes 2010). As we shall explain in Chapter 8, labour intensive, low-tech manufacturing is much more likely to be associated with pressures to outsource production to low-wage countries.

We see similar patterns within services, which we will be examining in Chapter 9. The service sector encompasses a range of industries from those that are expensive and esoteric, such as professional and consulting services, through to those that are low cost and routine, including retail, fast-food and cleaning services (e.g. Katz and Darbishire 2000, Appelbaum, Bernhardt and Murnane 2003, Batt 2007). The general observation in service industries is that the greater the knowledge required to deliver the service, or the higher the quality of the service, the higher will be the price of it and the greater will be the investment in recruiting, paying and developing the people who deliver it (Boxall 2003, Fabling and Grimes 2010). High-investment models of HRM are cost-effective in those service industries where customers will pay the premium prices that make the firm's high-cost labour sustainable.

Let us now take this down to the strategic-group level. Industries are not uniform: they consist of clusters of firms, operating in different parts of the industry (Porter 1980, Peteraf and Shanley 1997). Mobility barriers between these 'strategic groups' make it costly for firms in other parts of the industry to challenge them. Take, for example, the hotel industry in which there are firms targeting wealthy travellers (4-star and 5-star hotels), those targeting mid-range travellers who do not need the full amenities of an elite hotel (3-star and 2-star hotels), and those targeting the low-cost traveller (1-star hotels and backpacker hostels). These can be seen as distinct strategic groups of firms with major investments required to move from one category to another. Barring a war, a terrorism incident or a natural disaster, it is laughable to think that backpacker hostels actually compete with the higher-quality strategic groups in hotels, although all are notionally in the 'hospitality industry'. Not only do the mobility barriers between groups include investments in facilities but studies show that those firms at the luxury end of the hotel industry invest more heavily in their staff in order to deliver superior customer service (Lashley 1998, Knox and Walsh 2005, Sun, Aryee and Law 2007). Strategic-group effects can also be seen in studies of rest homes (Eaton 2000, Hunter 2000) where HR investments (in training, pay, career structures and staffing levels) are greater in firms that target higher-value niches (more expensive rest homes with better facilities and a higher level of nursing care). Thus, HR investments vary not only between industries but tend to vary enormously within any industry in which there are major quality differences.

Overall, then, research confirms that industry characteristics make a major impact on the ways firms manage work and people. At the highest level, there are broad differences between private sector and public sector HRM. There are then major variations across industries within each sector and, on top of this, contrasts between customer segments or strategic groups within industries. Not only do we see major differences in HRM across these categories but the process of adapting to the economic realities in one's industry niche is important for competitive survival. It seems, again, that firms adapt to their context, and they are wise to do so.

Organisational fit

The process of cascading down the layers of industry fit leads us inevitably to our last type of fit: organisational fit. The issue here is whether managers can, and should, mould their HR strategies to fit in with other critical features of their particular business, including its wider strategy and its structural features. Most contingency research starts by looking at the correlation between two variables. A simple example is the relationship between organisational size and HRM. In a major review of studies on contextual influences in HRM, Jackson and Schuler (1995) show that larger organisations are more likely to have due-process procedures, use more complex staffing and training practices and have more developed 'internal labour markets' (i.e. a structure of more specialised jobs and more extensive career hierarchies which provide greater scope to promote and develop people from within), among other features. In effect, managers of larger firms adopt more formalised practices to manage larger numbers of people, which is consistent with the observation that organisational structures and HR practices change as firms move from the entrepreneurial phase to the mature phase of the organisational life-cycle (Baird and Meshoulam 1988).

Among the most influential models of organisational fit in HRM are those that have argued that the key issue in organisational fit concerns the link between competitive strategy and HR strategy. In this line of thinking, it is seen as critical to bring HR strategy into line with the firm's desired market position (sometimes called 'external' or 'vertical' fit): in other words, management should do what it takes in HRM to enable the firm to meet the customer needs it is targeting. We should make two clarifying points about this idea. First, theorists are usually talking about matching HR practices to the competitive strategy of a particular business unit which operates in a particular industry. This should not be confused with the more complex question of how to develop HR strategy in a multidivisional organisation in which the parent company presides over diverse divisions and business units, something we discuss in Chapter 10. Second, theorists are generally talking about how management should manage core operating workers: those most intimately involved in making the product or providing the service.

The most heavily cited work on this kind of fit in strategic HRM is associated with a model developed by Schuler and Jackson (1987) who argue that HR practices should be designed to reinforce the behavioural implications of the various competitive strategies defined by Porter (1980, 1985). A giant in the strategy field, Porter (1980, 1985) advises firms to specialise carefully in competitive strategy. In his view, firms should choose between cost leadership (achieving lowest unit costs in the industry), differentiation (e.g. based on superior quality or service) or focus (a 'niche play' in cost or differentiation). They should avoid getting 'stuck in the middle' or caught in a strategic posture which is mixed – neither fish nor fowl, one might say.

Schuler and Jackson (1987) use Porter's framework to argue that performance will improve when the HR practices in a business mutually reinforce competitive strategy (Figure 3.2 teases out the line of thinking). To arrive at a

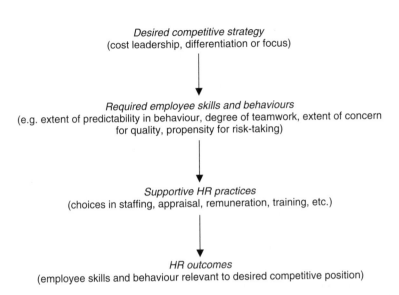

Desired competitive strategy
(cost leadership, differentiation or focus)

Required employee skills and behaviours
(e.g. extent of predictability in behaviour, degree of teamwork, extent of concern
for quality, propensity for risk-taking)

Supportive HR practices
(choices in staffing, appraisal, remuneration, training, etc.)

HR outcomes
(employee skills and behaviour relevant to desired competitive position)

Figure 3.2   Linking HR practices to competitive strategy
Source: Based on Schuler and Jackson (1987).

desirable set of HR practices, they argue that different competitive strategies imply different kinds of employee behaviour. If, for example, management chooses a competitive strategy of differentiation through continuous product innovation, this would call for high levels of creative, risk-oriented and cooperative behaviour. The company's HR practices would therefore need to emphasise '... selecting highly skilled individuals, giving employees more discretion, using minimal controls, making greater investment in human resources, providing more resources for experimentation, allowing and even rewarding occasional failure, and appraising performance for its long-run implications' (Schuler and Jackson 1987: 210). On the other hand, if management wants to pursue cost leadership (i.e. to attain lowest unit costs in the sector), the model implies designing jobs which are fairly repetitive, reducing employee numbers and wage levels, training workers as little as is practical, and rewarding short-term results.

Although competitive posture is complex and two-dimensional typologies, such as Porter's, can oversimplify it (Murray 1988, Miller 1992, Cronshaw, Davis and Kay 1994), the fundamental idea is that business performance will be better when there is alignment between competitive strategy and the management of the core workforce. In evaluating such a claim, we come back to our two questions: do managers relate their HR practices to this contingent variable and are they wise to do so? There have only been a few studies that have carefully tested the argument put forward by Schuler and Jackson (1987) across a cross-industry sample of firms. One of the few that does so is Michie and Sheehan's (2005) analysis of 362 British firms across the manufacturing and service sectors. This study had a range of methodological strengths: it used objective rather than opinion-based measures of performance, averaging these over a 3-year period, it provided good descriptions for managerial respondents of what it meant by cost-, innovator- and quality-based strategies, it did this at the establishment level of the firm rather than at the more amorphous corporate level, and it included indicators of both HR practices and the approach being taken towards flexibility in employment. On this methodological basis, Michie and Sheehan (2005) find that choices in HRM are more supportive of organisational performance when they are related to competitive strategy. It is the firms adopting a 'high-road' approach to innovation or quality that gain from a high level of investment in employees rather than those adopting a cost-cutting strategy. On economic grounds, the latter are better off investing much less in HRM. This is a strong endorsement of the contingency perspective. Similar studies that include performance data and endorse a contingency perspective on the strategy-HRM linkage include Chênevert and Tremblay's (2009) and Chadwick et al.'s (2013) analyses of Canadian firms.

It is also worth looking at studies that examine the relationship between competitive positioning and HRM at the industry level. One such is Batt's (2000) analysis of HR strategy in call centres in the US telecommunications industry. She examines firms in four different segments of this industry, which vary in terms of the complexity and value of the interaction between customers and employees. At the low end, there are low-margin interactions of short duration, typically with predetermined scripts and with strong technological monitoring of call-centre workers. At the high end, there are high-margin, low-volume interactions relying more on employee skill and discretion where technology is more of an enabler than a monitor. One statistic alone is telling: at the low-margin end, operators deal with an average of 465 customers per day, in the two mid-range segments they deal with 100 and 64, and at the top end they deal with an average of 32 (Batt 2000: 550). What Batt (2000) demonstrates is that there are significant differences in the contours of HR strategy across these market segments: skill requirements, the degree of discretion allowed to employees and pay levels are all higher among firms competing at the high-margin end of the call-centre market. While there is no information on business performance in this study, it is clear that managers in these firms have adopted more expensive models of HRM where the market being served generates higher value per customer.

Studies of specific service industries like this one on call centres, and those on hotels and rest homes referred to earlier, generally support the notion that managers try to relate their HR strategies to their competitive positioning in services, with higher-quality or knowledge-intensive services implying greater investment in employees. This is a principle we will examine in greater detail in Chapter 9. The picture in manufacturing, however, is likely to be somewhat different because contemporary manufacturing technologies can make it possible for firms to be simultaneously pursuing quality improvements *and* cost reductions, along with improvements in such other performance indicators as delivery time and product flexibility (e.g. Jayaram, Droge and Vickery 1999, Das and Narasimhan 2001). Zatzick, Moliterno and Fang (2012), for example, find that implementing the techniques of total quality management (TQM) enhances the performance of firms pursuing cost leadership. To understand how HRM fits into business models in manufacturing, we need to look not only at a firm's competitive goals but also at the relationship between its operating strategy and its HR practices (Purcell 1999). When the operating strategy is built around expensive investments in technology, which requires highly skilled handling, managers are likely to spend money building employee competencies and fostering employee commitment (Steedman and Wagner 1989, Godard 1991, Kaufman and Miller 2011). This is likely to be important *even if* one of their competitive goals is to achieve the lowest unit costs in the industry.

This line of analysis actually leads to a more powerful point about the nature of 'organisational fit' in firms. Rather than simply looking at how two variables or functions are related, we need to understand, as best we can, the overall configuration or system of variables in a successful business. Organisational fit involves relationships among *all* the parts of a particular business, including its marketing, operations, HRM and finance. In other words, the contingency perspective leads us naturally to a more holistic understanding of strategy in which contingencies operate in multiple directions. The configurational or 'gestalt' perspective is recognised in the HRM literature (e.g. Delery and Doty 1996, Michie and Sheehan 2005) but it is developed much more strongly by strategy theorists such as Porter and Siggelkow (2008) who understand businesses as interlocking sets of activities. Similarly, Teece (2011: 40–2) argues that successful firms depend on developing complementary or 'co-specialised' assets, which are well adapted to their context and thus difficult for others to imitate. There are major methodological challenges involved in configurational research, but the challenge is something we must increasingly take up (Short, Payne and Ketchen 2008, Chênevert and Tremblay 2009).

In conclusion, then, we have looked at the case for best fit on three levels: the societal, the industry and the organisational. These three levels of analysis, each rather complex, demonstrate the overwhelming impact of context on HRM. In arguing a case for the wisdom of adapting HRM in an organisation to its particular context, one could simply pick out one of two killer blows: employment law, for example. Most firms in the Anglophone world respect the employment laws of the societies in which they operate and, because social legitimacy is an important goal in HRM, all firms would be wise to do so. A case for best fit in HRM could be argued on this simple point alone. The case only becomes more compelling as we look at other contextual factors, such as local labour market conditions, varying cultural norms, and unique industry characteristics. And then, when we peer inside the organisation itself, we see the importance of relating a range of variables to one another if the business, which is a complex system of interrelated activities, is to succeed.

Strategic HRM: the best-practice school

Given the importance of contingency thinking in the theory of strategy, one might think it strange that a school which argues for the application of best practices across contexts could survive in the management literature. But let's try to understand it first. What does the best-practice school assert? In best-practice thinking, a universal prescription is preferred over a contingency one. The staunchest advocates of best practice in HRM argue that all firms will see performance improvements if they implement practices that have been shown to be best. This brings quite a different understanding of the problem of integrating HR strategy with the rest of business strategy. Integration with strategic management, in this conception, is about top management recognising, measuring and rewarding best practice, assisted by HR specialists who are experts on what ought to be considered best.

Initial difficulties: best for whom?

At the outset, we face an initial difficulty with this school of thought: a lot of writing on best practice moves quickly into prescription without making its basic assumptions explicit. A lot of best-practice writing is a form of advocacy rather than a form of theory. In a classic critique of the best-practice genre in what was then personnel management, Legge (1978) asked the question: *for whom* is a 'best practice' best? *Whose* goals or interests are being served? If a 'best practice' serves both shareholder and employee interests, we can hardly object to it, although consumers and environmentalists might still object to some practices (e.g. when a firm is making high profits and paying high wages but prices are extortionate or the firm is a bad polluter). Similarly, if we agree that some practice is bad for both parties, it should be avoided. But what if a practice is good for corporate returns but bad for workers? This is often the case with downsizing, as the Global Financial Crisis vividly demonstrated: sharemarkets seem to rate companies more highly for doing it, a cold comfort for the workers laid off and for those left behind whose workload may just have become more stressful. When this kind of trade-off emerges, what sort of voice do workers get in deciding the issue? Are their interests recognised? As Marchington and Grugulis (2000) demonstrate, best-practice models typically overlook these sorts of tensions. Models developed in the USA, where managers are often opposed to union representation, do not typically mention or advocate the sort of strong employee voice institutions seen in Europe, which can help to protect employee interests when trade-offs occur. In effect, they tend to reflect what is politically acceptable in their own context.

Furthermore, it is not simply corporate and employee interests that can be opposed. As discussed in Chapter 1, managers have their own interests. So what if a practice is good for executives but not good for either shareholders or waged workers? This is the problem with many exit packages used for senior executives 'let go' because of disappointing performance: *they* benefit but the company and its other employees typically lose out. In fact, the whole area of executive remuneration – staying or going – has become highly controversial, including in the USA. As Kochan (2007: 604) explains, American 'CEO pay relative to the average worker (has) exploded from a ratio of 40:1 in the 1960s and 1970s to over 400:1 today'.[2] This long-term trend may be best for senior executives but many others, both within the USA and looking at US practices from the outside, regard this trend in American HR practice as socially undesirable.

How, then, are we going to proceed with a discussion of 'best practice' in the light of the problem of interest conflicts? Given that explicit assumptions are largely lacking in much of this literature, we need to consider implicit ones. In our view, the most common implicit assumption in the best-practice literature is that 'best practices' as those that enhance shareholder value. We think, however, that a useful test of any best-practice claim is the extent to which it also serves employee and community interests. One would not expect to see a perfect alignment of interests but it is likely that the most

---

[2] For the recent US and international comparisons, see http://www.theglobalist.com/just-facts-ceos-rest-us/, accessed 16/1/15.

sustainable models of HRM over the long run are those that enjoy high levels of legitimacy among people within the firm and in wider society. On the basis of this caveat, we step gingerly forward.

Micro foundations and macro models

Despite their tendency to gloss over basic assumptions, studies of *individual* best practices within the major categories of micro HRM – such as selection, training and appraisal – do have a very long tradition in Western psychology and management studies. During the two World Wars, for example, a lot of British and American energy went into improving practices for officer selection and also into the training and motivation of (non-combatant) production workers (Eysenck 1953, Eilbert 1959, Crichton 1968). The academic discipline of Industrial Psychology gained momentum as psychologists studied the prediction and development of human performance. In the area of employee selection, for example, they usefully compared different practices for selecting individual employees (such as ability tests, personality inventories, 'biodata' obtained through application forms or from an individual's curriculum vitae (CV) or résumé, references and various types of interviews), assessing their validity in terms of subsequent performance (usually as rated by supervisors).

Based on this tradition of work, some micro aspects of best practice *are* widely acknowledged by researchers and practitioners (Delery and Doty 1996: 806, Youndt et al. 1996: 838). In the selection area, hardly anyone would advocate unstructured interviewing over interviews designed around job-relevant factors (i.e. those related to the skills and aptitudes needed in the job). Similarly, no one would advocate input-based performance appraisal for senior executives (such as measures of timekeeping) over processes that examine results achieved (such as profit generated and growth in market share) or the kind of leadership behaviour demonstrated in working with colleagues and clients. The selection and performance appraisal fields are two areas where we can point to an extensive body of research that assists management to carry out these processes more effectively. While there are still major debates and a raft of problems (e.g. Schmitt and Kim 2007, Latham, Sulsky and MacDonald 2007), there is quite a lot of agreement on what constitutes 'bad' or 'stupid' practice, on the one hand, and 'sensible' practice, on the other, when we talk about practices in selection and performance appraisal.

At least, this is a fair generalisation *within* our specific cultural mind-set. We are talking here about selection and appraisal within a Western cultural frame of reference, dominated by US and British research. In this cultural tradition, we are generally comfortable with the idea that management should try to predict, appraise and reward individual performance, as noted in our discussion of research on best fit. In fact, a lot of high-performing employees will be upset and disloyal if their individual merit is not recognised (Trevor, Gerhart and Boudreau 1997). The sort of research discussed earlier helps us to remember, however, that such a high emphasis on individualism may be considered counter-cultural or subversive in societies which place a heavier emphasis on group identification and interpersonal humility. As a result of this, many psychologists nowadays, including those writing in the *Journal of Cross-Cultural Psychology*, will openly acknowledge that cultural factors are important (e.g. Smith 2004). It is decidedly helpful when industrial psychologists identify themselves as working on HRM within a particular cultural domain (e.g. Warr 2007: 283–8).

The interesting and difficult question we face in a book about strategic HRM is whether best-practice thinking can work on a more macro level, on the level of HR systems for a major workforce group or, more ambitiously, on the level of an HR strategy for an entire workforce. There are, in fact, writers who have tried to offer models at this higher level. In the USA, one model that has attracted a high profile is associated with Pfeffer's (1998) seven practices 'for building profits by putting people first', shown in Table 3.1.

What comes through Pfeffer's list is a desire to carefully hire and develop talented people, organising them into highly cooperative teams, and employing them in a way that builds their commitment over the long run (through high pay, employment security and as much egalitarianism and openness as possible). Recruiting and retaining talented, team-oriented, highly motivated people is seen to lay a basis for superior business performance or competitive advantage.

This is a popular model but there are various others, using somewhat different labels, such as 'high performance work systems', a term which has grown in importance since the early 1990s. Such models typically depend on an HR

Table 3.1   Pfeffer's seven practices

1. Employment security
2. Selective hiring
3. Self-managed teams or teamworking
4. High pay contingent on company performance
5. Extensive training
6. Reduction of status differences
7. Sharing information

Source: Pfeffer (1998).

researcher justifying a selection of formal HR practices based on the micro-HRM research we have mentioned or appealing to a prior academic authority whose list has been used in a published study. A major difficulty, however, is the extensive diversity in the lists of practices that make up such systems with variation in the number and nature of items included (Dyer and Reeves 1995, Becker and Gerhart 1996, Combs et al. 2006). Troublesome items, for example, include such things as performance appraisal and performance-related pay. These are better understood as complex sets of activities rather than as single HR practices. They are implemented in diverse ways and can have a wide range of effects, including the very perverse impacts associated with short-term bonus systems in the banking industry. Without understanding what management is seeking in a specific context, and how well managers are going about it, deeming something a best practice in HRM is a very dubious approach (Purcell 1999, Boxall and Macky 2009).

What does the research say?

Despite these definitional and theoretical questions, studies of best-practice systems have generated widespread interest. In one of the most influential papers ever written in HRM, Huselid (1995: 645) identified 13 'high performance work practices (HPWPs)', drawing partly on a set of items considered to represent 'sophistication' in HRM by Delaney, Lewin and Ichniowski (1989). His suite of practices included items on the extent to which firms use information sharing, job analysis, promotion from within, attitude surveys, quality-of-work-life programmes, group incentives such as profit sharing, training, grievance procedures, employment tests, individual performance-based pay, formal appraisals, promotion on merit, and the extent to which firms are selective in employee recruitment. He then surveyed HR specialists in 968 US firms on the extent to which their firms used this set of practices and asked them to estimate the proportion of the firm's sales stemming from particular competitive strategies (using Porter's (1985) categories of cost leadership, differentiation and focus), and describe the practices used to link HRM with strategy. These variables were then related to publicly available information on the firms' financial performance. His regression analyses showed that greater use of the nominated HR practices was associated with lower employee turnover, better productivity and higher profit. These results held irrespective of the HR specialists' assessments of competitive strategy or strategy–HRM linkages. While a lack of longitudinal data was recognised as a weakness, and the validity of the measures generated criticism (e.g. Purcell 1999), this study was interpreted by many HR specialists as offering a strong case for a comprehensive best-practice model of HRM. A subsequent meta-analysis (a study of the bivariate correlations in previous studies) found that 'HPWPs materially affect organizational performance' although the studies included did not provide enough data to assess the impact of strategy on HRM (Combs et al. 2006: 515, 523).

The questions we must address are whether managers actually follow the kind of advice offered by general models of best-practice or high-performance systems and, if not, whether they would be wise to do so. Studies of the actual distribution of HR practices of firms overwhelmingly say 'no' to the first of these questions. There are always individual cases of firms adopting a major suite of 'best practices' but research on the diffusion of management practices shows that they are very much in the minority (e.g. Godard 2004, Fabling and Grimes 2010). This is as true in the USA as anywhere else. For example, after reviewing a range of studies and conducting an analysis of a national survey of US employers, Blasi and Kruse (2006: 572) conclude that 'the combination of many HPW practices is clearly a negligible phenomenon'. There is significant diversity in the HR strategies that managers actually evolve over time. In a comprehensive study of 599 US organisations, Toh, Morgeson and Campion (2008) identify five major HRM models that vary in terms of the emphasis managers place on cost control, the approach they take to pay systems and levels, and the extent to which they invest in employee development and foster employee commitment. Their analysis shows that the HRM models of firms are related to managerial values (such as the extent to which they foster innovation over stability), to the type of organisational structure (such as the extent to which work roles are standardised), and to whether they are unionised. There are no performance variables in the study, and this is simply an initial selection of relevant contextual variables, but Toh, Morgeson and Campion's (2008: 874) findings show that 'HR bundles are adopted that fit with the context in which the organizations are embedded'. They conclude with the advice that 'any prescriptions for a set of universal HR "best practices" must be informed by the contextual factors that surround their use' (ibid.: 877).

The strongest critique of the wisdom of following the advice of the best-practice school of HRM has been mounted by Bruce Kaufman (2010) who deploys economic theory to explain why managers do not take it seriously. Economic theory emphasises the way in which the benefits of any management practice need to be weighed against its costs. Kaufman's (2010) argument is that Huselid's (1995) model of strategic HRM is 'mis-specified'. Rather than seeking to measure the link from HR practices to performance, we should start from the premise that firms are profit seekers and try to explain how profit-motivated managers choose their level of investment in HRM. Measuring the HR expenditure of a sample of 381 US firms, he demonstrates the way in which the 'demand for HRM' is shaped by the specific contingencies of firms (Kaufman and Miller 2011). For example, it is the firms paying higher wages that spend more money *per capita* on their HR functions, as do those that have made a substantial investment in costly technology, which needs to be operated effectively. Such findings point to the economic calculus behind managerial choices in HRM and challenge the idea that all firms would benefit from implementing as many 'best practices' as possible (for a similar critique, see Godard 2004).

There are actually both economic and socio-political grounds for doubting the wisdom of best-practice models. Simply on the fact of societal regulation of labour markets, discussed in Chapter 1 and above, we must discount the idea that there can be universally valid lists of best practice. Similarly, as Hofstede (1980), Trompenaars and Hampden-Turner (1997) and many others remind us, there really is a problem with trying to specify a set of cross-culturally best HR practices because there are significant differences across countries in cultural values. Even if we are talking about the same practice, such as selection interviewing, the application of it can vary very significantly. In New Zealand, for example, where government policy supports biculturalism (English and Māori are both official languages), it is not uncommon for Māori job applicants to request a *whanau* (family, kinship-supported) interview. In such an interview, family members and close friends speak to the merits of the job applicant because it is considered culturally offensive to indulge in self-praise or 'blow your own trumpet'. This is still a selection interview but it is not what American or British writers think of when they use the term.

We would be wise, then, to dispense with the idea that there can be lengthy lists of HR practices that are universally relevant or valuable to firms. A more appropriate line of thinking is to accept that there will always be variations in how HRM is organised and look to systems or configurations of HR practices that have a kind of 'functional equivalence' or 'equifinality' (Delery and Doty 1996). In other words, it is possible to envisage HR strategies that are designed to serve similar ends, or which are based on some common principles, but recognise variety in the practices that are used to reach them in a particular context. This is illustrated in Ichniowski and Shaw's (1999) study of US and Japanese plants in the steel industry, which shows that US plants that have achieved similar operational performance to Japanese ones have done so through adopting the principles of employee-driven problem-solving seen in Japanese plants while customising their employment practices.

Selection tests and pay systems, for example, have been made compatible with local US laws and cultural norms. In another example, Tayeb (1995: 600) underlines the astute capacity of Japanese managers in Britain to implement their core philosophies on 'quality and built-in control ... and harmonious employee-management relationships' while adjusting sensitively to 'British employees' cultural attitudes and values'. In a high-tech firm she studied, Japanese managers did not require 'the famous morning rituals performed in many Japanese companies ... nor did they experiment with ... plant-based unions' (ibid.: 600).

Such studies indicate the way in which the debate about best practice needs to evolve: away from the idea that we can have exact replicas of 'best practices' across contexts towards studies of HRM models that include some common principles but show intelligent adaptation of practices to the specific context. This approach is likely to be particularly useful at the industry level, or at the level of strategic groups within industries, where production systems face common challenges.

Conclusions

In the light of all this, where do things stand in the debate between best fit and best practice? If we want to identify a winner, it is obviously a clear win to the best-fit camp on the evidence of what firms actually do, which makes life very difficult for the more extreme advocates of best practice. It demonstrates that models of HRM are inevitably influenced by context, including a range of economic and socio-political factors. And it also shows that there are very good reasons for adaptation to context, including the needs to fit in with social values and to adapt to industry characteristics. Does this fact invalidate all best-practice thinking? Should the best-practice people pack up their tents and go home?

We think there are three ways in which it is possible to take some value out of the best-practice approach rather than discarding it completely. First, as we explained above, there are aspects of best practice in the micro domains of HRM that are valuable, provided we recognise their contextual limits. When companies commit to a selection process, for example, they are well advised to avoid invalid predictors of performance, including asking candidates questions that don't relate to how they would do the job. Similarly, if they commit to performance appraisal, they are well advised to work hard on dealing with the 'rating errors' that, research shows, will inevitably rear their ugly heads (Latham, Sulsky and MacDonald 2007). However, all of this takes place within a cultural and legal context. The relevant best-practice prescriptions in these domains have been developed in an individualist Anglo-American frame of reference and should have regard to Anglo-American laws on discrimination and equal opportunity (e.g. Kossek and Pichler 2007).

Second, when we come to study specific industries, it is clearly possible to identify HR strategies that embody a set of principles while fostering astute local adaptations in different production sites around the world. The research we cited, by Doeringer, Lorenz and Terkla (2003) and by Ichniowski and Shaw (1999), among others, shows the way in which management might emulate a core set of principles while adapting effectively to the specific context. There is a role for identifying better HRM models within particular industry contexts as these evolve, bearing in mind that such models will more likely be based on 'equifinality' (aiming to achieve similar performance outcomes) than on exact lists of practices.

The second point leads us to a third, more general one. Following Becker and Gerhart (1996), we think there is scope to identify some general principles in HRM and, in fact, this section of our book is dedicated to this task. Building on the arguments in this chapter, it is helpful to make an analytical distinction between the surface level of HR policy and practices in a firm and an underpinning level of HR principles (Figure 3.3). This is not a perfect distinction but it helps to reconcile the tension between best fit and best practice in strategic HRM. We are most unlikely to find that any theorist's selection of best practices (the surface layer) will have universal relevance because context always matters. It is, however, possible to argue that at the level of the underpinning layer there are some desirable principles which, if applied, will bring about more effective management of people. In effect, it is possible to argue that, 'ceteris paribus' (other things being equal), all firms are better off when they pursue certain principles in HRM (Youndt et al. 1996: 837, Edwards and Wright 2001).

Surface layer: HR policies and practices – heavily influenced by diverse contexts (economic and socio-political)

Underpinning layer: general principles of HRM

Figure 3.3   The 'best fit' versus 'best practice' debate: two levels of analysis

What sort of principles do we have in mind? We have, in effect, already been arguing in this book for certain principles that underpin the field of HRM. At the most basic level, there is the principle that all firms rely on an adequate 'human resourcing process' (Watson 2005) if they are to be viable. In other words, a reasonably competent approach to HRM is a necessary condition for organisational performance, which is the conclusion that we think can legitimately be drawn from the large number of studies finding a link between some respondent's perceptions of their organisation's HR practices and its outcomes. Second, we have claimed that a good performance in HRM involves dealing with multiple goals. There are multiple 'bottom lines' in HRM, not just one, and these include a range of economic and socio-political goals. How managers handle the tensions among these goals makes a significant impact on the firm's chances of survival and its relative success. Third, this chapter has underlined the fact that managers can be observed adapting their HRM to their specific context, and it has argued that there are good reasons why they do so. While HRM always affects performance, the choice of which practices to adopt, including which will be cost-effective and socially legitimate, is grounded in a specific situation. This principle is what we like to call the 'law of context' in HRM. We will now proceed to discuss further principles in the chapters that follow in this part, principles concerned with the ways in which HRM affects competitive advantage, with the importance of alignment between organisational and employee interests, with the role of employee voice in building social legitimacy and with the building of productive climates inside the 'black box' of working environments.

4

Strategic HRM and sustained competitive advantage

In this part of the book, we are concerned with general principles of strategic HRM. As Chapter 3 made clear, contingency theory is important in this regard, especially when we locate HR strategy within a more holistic or systemic understanding of business strategy in which the various management disciplines, including marketing, HRM, operations and finance, need to be integrated. This chapter now goes further with the question of how to relate HR strategy to the broader business strategy. Here we are interested in the role of HRM within the driving concern of the strategy literature: how to generate and protect competitive advantage. How might a firm develop, interrelate and manipulate its resources to become the kind of firm that generates enviable levels of financial performance and that does so despite the best efforts of other firms to undermine it? This discussion relies on a core body of theory in strategic management: the resource-based view (RBV) of the firm and the analysis of dynamic capabilities. Anchoring our discussion in this theory, we are then able to consider the ways in which HRM may help firms to build sustained advantages.

The resource-based view of the firm

The resource-based view of the firm is usually sourced to a remarkable book by a University of London Professor of Economics, Edith Penrose (1959). At the time, texts on the economics of the firm were dominated by discussion of 'equilibrium' conditions under different forms of competition. The main focus of these texts was on the relative merits of different types of market, including 'perfect competition', oligopoly and monopoly. While valuable in debates about market regulation, the traditional analysis ignored very important issues inside the 'black box' of the firm's operations, leaving the study of entrepreneurship and business management in a very rudimentary state within the discipline of Economics.

Arguing that her interest was different from that of the standard texts on the economics of the firm, Penrose set out to build a theory of the growth of firms. She made the basic, but critical, observation that the firm is 'an administrative organization and a collection of productive resources', distinguishing between 'physical' and 'human resources' (Penrose 1959: 31, 24).[1] Her understanding of the quality of the firm's resources placed heavy emphasis on the knowledge and experience of the management team and their subjective interpretation (or 'images') of the firm's environment (showing an early grasp of the kind of cognitive problems of strategic management we discussed in Chapter 2). Her analysis proceeded from what has become a fundamental premiss in the theory of business strategy: firms are 'heterogeneous' (Penrose 1959: 74–8). As Nelson (1991: 61) puts it, competition ('perfect' or otherwise) never entirely eliminates 'differences among firms in the same line of business' and these differences account for major performance variations.

Penrose's ideas lay dormant for some time. Her work was not brought within the mainstream of strategic management theory until it was promoted by Wernerfelt (1984) and then by a string of other strategy writers from the late 1980s (e.g. Dierickx and Cool 1989, Barney 1991, Mahoney and Pandian 1992). The result has been an explosion of interest in the resource-based perspective, focusing on the ways in which firms might build unique clusters or 'bundles' of resources that generate enviable levels of performance. Reviews of the strategic management literature now routinely recognise the RBV as a major body of thought concerned with explaining sources of competitive advantage (e.g. Newbert 2007, Lockett, Thompson and Morgenstern 2009).

In effect, the growth of the RBV has provided a counterweight to the marketing-oriented models of strategic management that were dominant in the strategy textbooks of the 1980s. The best known of these models was associated with the works of Michael Porter (1980, 1985), discussed in the context of best-fit theory in Chapter 3. These models place greatest emphasis on critical choices associated with competitive strategy – primarily, choices about which industry to enter and which competitive position to seek in it.

---

[1] In passing, we might note that Penrose was one of the first theorists to adopt the 'human resources' terminology.

In so doing, these models make some fairly heroic assumptions (Boxall 1992, 1996). For example, they assume that the firm already has a clever leadership team which can make these sorts of choices effectively. They assume that the human resource issues that arise when particular paths are chosen, such as hiring and motivating a capable workforce, are straightforward. They assume that culture change, when it might be needed to shift direction, is also unproblematic. In contrast, it is exactly these sorts of people issues that the resource-based view regards as strategic. In the RBV, the quality of the management process and of the firm's workplace culture are seen as major factors that explain enduring differences in business performance (e.g. Barney 1991, 2000).

It can, however, be argued that the RBV is itself imbalanced. In a response to criticism from resource-based theorists, Michael Porter argues that 'resources are not valuable in and of themselves, but because they allow firms to perform activities that create advantages in particular markets' (Porter 1991: 108). Similarly, Miller and Shamsie (1996: 520) argue that the RBV needs 'to consider the contexts within which various kinds of resources will have the best influence on performance'. In a study of the Hollywood film studios from 1936 to 1965, they demonstrate how knowledge-based resources (such as the creative skills of key writers and cinematographers, and big budget coordinating abilities) were more valuable to the studios in the relatively uncertain and turbulent environment of the 1950s when the advent of television seriously affected movie-going habits. On the other hand, in the more stable conditions of the late 1930s and the 1940s (movie-going was very popular before and during the Second World War[2]), property-based resources (such as networks of theatres and long-term, exclusive contracts with particular actors) were more valuable for studio performance. In other words, the human talents that helped the studios to 'think and act outside the square' were more valuable when the context was less predictable.

Wernerfelt (1984: 173) did recognise the interplay of resources and markets when he said there is a 'duality between products and resources'. In effect, the strategic problem has both internal (resource) and external (market) dimensions. These dimensions – what Baden-Fuller (1995) calls the 'inside-out' and the 'outside-in' perspectives on the strategic problem – are interactive over time. The point is well made. One should not get carried away with either external or internal perspectives on a firm's strategy: both are necessary. It seems safe, however, to suggest that what

---

[2] For example, some 90 million Americans went to the movies every week during World War II. See http://en.wikipedia.org/wiki/Cinema_of_the_United_States, accessed 16/1/15.

the resource-based perspective has achieved is a re-balancing of the literature on strategy, reminding people of the strategic significance of internal
resources and their development over time.

Resources and barriers to imitation

What, then, are the basic definitions and concepts associated with the RBV?
In the resource-based perspective, resources are not simply understood as
assets in the formal accounting sense (which can be disclosed on a balance
sheet) but include any feature of the firm with value-creating properties
(Hunt 1995: 322). This means that aspects of the business that are not actually
owned by it, such as the talents and interactions of the people who work in it,
are not ignored but come within the realm of analytical interest. Wernerfelt
(1984: 172) defined resources in the following way:

> By a resource is meant anything which could be thought of as a strength or weak-
> ness of a given firm. More formally, a firm's resources at a given time could be
> defined as those (tangible and intangible) assets which are tied semipermanently to
> the firm. Examples of resources are: brand names, in-house knowledge of technol-
> ogy, employment of skilled personnel, trade contacts, machinery, efficient proce-
> dures, capital etc.

In an interesting study of chief executive opinion about the value of different kinds of resource, Hall (1993) found that CEOs rated the quality of
employee know-how and their firm's reputation with customers as their
most strategic assets. It is easy to see why the RBV is so attractive to human
resource specialists – here at last is a body of thought within strategic management in which human issues figure prominently.

Clusters of resources, understood in this broader way, can be sources
of competitive advantage. Barney (1991, 2000), one of the most influential
theorists in the RBV school, distinguishes between a competitive advantage
which a firm presently enjoys, but which others will be able to copy, and
sustained competitive advantage, a characteristic which rivals find themselves unable to compete away, despite their best efforts. In his conception,
resources are valuable when they enable the firm to take advantage of market opportunities or deal particularly well with market threats in a way that
competitors are not currently able to. The task is to manage these valuable
resources in such a way that rivals are frustrated in their efforts to imitate
or out-flank them.

Using some fairly awkward terminology, RBV theorists are interested in the
conditions that make desirable resources 'inimitable' and 'non-substitutable'
(Barney 1991). What can be done to ensure others do not simply imitate or

copy a firm's strengths or find ways of substituting for them that achieve the same ends? The key characteristics of desirable resources, then, are that they are valuable and inimitable (with inimitability covering both direct and indirect forms of copying) (Hoopes, Madsen and Walker 2003).

It is important, however, to add 'appropriability' to this list of traits, as a number of authors have emphasised (e.g. Kamoche 1996, Coff 1997, 1999). Not only must the firm be able to generate and defend its sources of advantage, but the RBV assumes that the firm is able to capture the benefits for its shareholders. This is easier said than done because the firm is a network of stakeholders, some of whom, such as senior executives, have access to the kind of information and power that can enlarge their share of the firm's bounty. The risk for shareholders is that the firm performs very well but they see little of it. Qualities of desirable resources are shown in Box 4.1.

Box 4.1   Qualities of desirable resources

- Valuable: capable of delivering superior competitive results
- Inimitable: very hard to imitate or copy, either directly or indirectly
- Appropriable: capable of capture to the benefit of the firm's shareholders

---

Having defined these sorts of desirable traits, Barney (1991) notes that such resources are not immune to 'Schumpeterian shocks'. The great Austrian economist, Joseph Schumpeter, referred to the propensity for capitalism to generate 'gales of creative destruction' – radical breakthroughs which disturb technologies or basic concepts of business (Schumpeter 1950). In the transportation sector, for example, inventions such as railroads, automobiles and airplanes each had enormous impacts on the ways of providing transport that preceded them. Our current era is one in which computerisation, mobile telecommunications and the internet have been making a critical impact across various industries, enabling some new styles of business while destroying others. The vast majority of firms cannot insulate themselves from such radical trends but there is scope for firms to differentiate themselves in ways which are relatively sustainable in a *given* competitive context.

The issue is one of how management might build valuable, firm-specific characteristics and 'barriers to imitation' (Reed and deFillippi 1990, Rumelt 1997), which make it hard for others to copy or invalidate what the successful firm is doing. What, then, are the key barriers to imitation noted by resource-based theorists?

Unique timing and learning

Models proposed in the RBV typically place emphasis on the way that historical learning acts as a barrier to newcomers and slower rivals. Theorists cite the value to firms of 'unique historical conditions' (Barney 1991: 107), 'first-mover advantages' (Wernerfelt 1984: 173) and 'path dependency' (Leonard-Barton 1998: 35). They argue that valuable, specialised resources (sometimes called 'asset specificity') are developed over time through opportunities that do not repeat themselves (or not in quite the same way). Competitive success does not come simply from making choices in the present (as positioning models of strategic management seem to imply) but stems from building up distinctive capabilities at critical junctures and over considerable periods of time (Teece 2011).

In simple terms, RBV theorists argue that a sense of time and place matters: if you are not there at the time things are happening, you cannot expect to be successful. Others will take up the unique learning opportunity. As Woody Allen once quipped, 'eighty percent of success is just showing up'. Shakespeare expressed the same sentiment in a famous line from *Julius Caesar*: 'there is a tide in the affairs of men, which taken at the flood, leads on to fortune'. In other words, you have to be there when the tide is turning and seize your opportunity at the best moment. This could be at a time when a new technology is being developed, a new market is being opened up or a new management methodology is being developed. If you are there at such moments, you can build business experience, including important connections and complex know-how ahead of others. There is now good evidence, for example, using a data set that spans a 24-year period, that those British firms that first learnt to integrate the HR and operational practices needed to support 'lean manufacturing' have outperformed later adopters in terms of productivity (de Menezes, Wood and Gelade 2010).

The special value of timing and learning is widely understood in the business community. The difficulty of securing a firm's presence in an area where it has no experience is often a reason for takeovers. Directors of firms often feel they cannot make a mark in a new industry (or a new region) without buying an established player who has built up the necessary client base, employee skills and operating systems. The international accounting firms very often expanded this way in the 1970s and 1980s, taking over much smaller, but well regarded, firms around the world. The small firms thus absorbed provided important political connections, a pool of appropriately qualified staff and a well-established client base. Naturally, the owners of these firms also benefited enormously from the historical learning of the international firm, gaining access, for example, to special audit techniques, management consulting methodologies and training systems developed at considerable expense elsewhere.

Social complexity

The phenomenon of historical learning or 'path dependence' is intimately linked to a second barrier to imitation – 'social complexity' (Barney 1991, Wright, McMahan and McWilliams 1994). As firms grow, they inevitably become characterised by complex patterns of teamwork and coordination, both inside and outside the firm. Successful firms have strong clusters of human and social capital (Lovas and Ghoshal 2000). Productive work communities, like outstanding schools and universities, take time to build and are inherently complex systems. The network of these internal and external connections is a kind of natural barrier to imitation by rivals, a prime reason why firms in some industries try to recruit an entire team of employees. Loss of all or most of an outstanding team of staff can decimate an organisation's reputation. Something like this happened in 1957 when eight scientists and engineers working on the development of the silicon chip resigned from the Shockley Semiconductor Laboratory, a research and development company led by the Nobel laureate physicist, Bill Shockley: 'Their mass departure cut the productive heart out of the laboratory, leaving behind a carcass of men working ... on the four-layer diode project plus a bunch of aimless technicians and secretaries' (Riordan and Hoddeson 1997: 252). The group left to form Fairchild Semiconductor. The rest, as they say, is history.[3]

Mueller's (1996) discussion of 'resource mobility barriers' is one that places strong emphasis on socially complex attributes of firms. Mueller (1996: 774) argues that sustained advantage stems from hard-to-imitate routines deeply embedded in a firm's 'social architecture'. By contrast, he sees little enduring value accruing to the firm from top management's codified policy positions (which are easily imitated because of their public visibility). Indeed, he implies that little value is created by those senior managers who are highly mobile:

> Corporate prosperity not seldom rests in the social architecture that has emerged incrementally over time, and might often predate the tenure of current senior management. ... The social architecture is created and re-created not only or even primarily at senior management levels in the organization, but at other levels too, including at workgroup level on the shopfloor (Mueller 1996: 771, 777).

---

[3] For key events in the company's history, see http://www.fairchildsemi.com/about-fairchild/history/#, accessed 16/1/15.

According to Mueller, outstanding organisational value is more likely to come from persistent, patient management processes that, over time, encourage skill formation and powerful forms of cooperation deep within the firm. A key factor here must be the quality of the motivational incentives inside firms that foster skill-building and cooperation. As Gottschalg and Zollo (2007) argue, many forms of competitive advantage depend on strong interest alignment between companies and critical groups of employees, as we shall argue in the next chapter.

Causal ambiguity

A third type of resource barrier noted in the RBV literature – causal ambiguity – is more controversial. As with social complexity, ambiguity about the cause/effect relationships involved in the firm's performance is an inevitable outcome of firm growth (Reed and deFillippi 1990, Barney 1991). It can take some time to figure why an established firm has become successful and to discern how successful it really is. There is no doubt that firms wanting to acquire other firms should be very careful in the 'due diligence' process that precedes (or ought to precede) the purchase of another business. There are inevitably elements of ambiguity about a firm's performance, as there are about the performance of individuals and teams.

Having said this, it is likely that causal ambiguity is overrated as a barrier to imitation (McWilliams and Smart 1995). Human rationality is always bounded, as was noted in Chapter 2, but if one pushes the notion of causal ambiguity too far, management is virtually meaningless, as is theory (Priem and Butler 2001). The 'paradox of causal ambiguity' has been explored by a study in two US industries: textiles and hospitals (King and Zeithaml 2001). This study examined the way senior and middle managers perceive the competences of their organisations and their links to competitive advantage. Interestingly, the study was one in which chief executives were very keen to participate (which is quite unusual given 'survey fatigue' among managers). It involved finding out how other members of their senior team and a cross-section of middle managers understood the firm's resources and their impacts. CEOs were interviewed and the other managers selected in the 17 firms were surveyed. The study contains evidence that high-performing firms benefit from building consensus across management levels about the resources that enable them to out-perform rivals. Understanding of the key competences and the most important links among them *ought* to be high. This does not mean, however, that all the micro aspects of particular competences will be transparent because there is always some degree of ambiguity embedded in organisational culture and in employee know-how. As we explore further below, 'tacit knowledge' is always present in organisations.

The findings of this study are consistent with the arguments of advocates of the 'balanced scorecard' (Kaplan and Norton 1996) who claim that, given enough effort, it must be possible within business units to evolve a broad theory of how the business works or might work better. Not only this, but the benefits of having agreement about where we are going and how we can get there must be more valuable than confusion and working at cross-purposes! It seems, then, that while causal ambiguity will always be present to some degree, it is likely to be a less important barrier to imitation than the processes of historical learning and social interaction that characterise established firms.

Competences and dynamic capabilities

If we accept, then, that the role of management is critical, what is it that managers should be doing to create competitive advantage? One of the more popular answers to this question is associated with the work of Hamel and Prahalad (1993, 1994). They argue that competitive advantage, over the long run, stems from building 'core competencies' in a firm which are superior to those of rivals. Their notion of core competence is very close to the concept of 'distinctive competence' discussed in the older strategy texts as something that the firm does particularly well. Their definitions of the term (shown in Box 4.2) place strong emphasis on analysing a firm's collective skills: skills found in the complex teamwork embedded in the firm.

The writings of Hamel and Prahalad have implications for leaders of multidivisional firms. CEOs and directors of these firms are encouraged to identify the underlying clusters of know-how in their companies that transcend the artificial divisions of 'strategic business units' – or which might do so, if they were appropriately managed. Sony's 'unrelenting pursuit of leadership in miniaturization' – manifesting itself in various products over time – is one of Hamel and Prahalad's standard examples (Hamel and Prahalad 1994: 119). Another example, offered by Goold, Campbell and Alexander (1994) is that of Canon which sought to integrate development engineers in different strands of the business to exploit fibre-optic technology. Hamel and Prahalad (1994) argue that companies whose managers make the effort to understand their core competences (and envision the core competences they ought to build) are much less likely to get left with outdated products or miss important new applications of a knowledge base. In effect, their work is an argument for developing a 'knowledge-based', rather than a product-based, understanding of the firm. This might be a simple distinction to make but it suggests quite a profound change in the way corporate directors review company strengths and analyse their strategic opportunities.

Box 4.2   Hamel and Prahalad's notion of 'core competence'

A 'core competence':

- is a bundle of skills and technologies that enables a company to provide particular benefits to customers;
- is not product-specific;
- represents ... the sum of learning across individual skill sets and individual organisational units;
- must ... be competitively unique;
- is not an 'asset' in the accounting sense of the word; and
- represents a 'broad opportunity arena' or 'gateway to the future'.

Source: Excerpted from Hamel and Prahalad (1994: 217–28).

A similar analysis is advanced by Leonard-Barton (1998) who uses the word 'capability', instead of 'competence', but is concerned with the same idea. Her framework helps executives to identify the distinctive or 'core capabilities' underpinning their products or services. Core capabilities are 'knowledge sets' composed of four dimensions: the 'content' dimensions which include the relevant employee skills and knowledge and technical systems, as well as the 'process' dimensions which include managerial systems, values and norms. Her framework is helpful in terms of spelling out the HR implications. This is because managerial systems include the critical HR practices needed to recruit, develop and motivate employees with the relevant skills and aptitudes (Leonard-Barton 1998: 19). Employee development and incentive systems are a key part of her notion of core capability. She also emphasises the interlocking, systemic nature of the four dimensions and the resulting tendency of core capabilities to become 'core rigidities' over time, unless firms learn to practise continuous renewal. According to Leonard-Barton (1998: 30), every strength is simultaneously a weakness. The recognition that firms can have weaknesses or 'distinctive inadequacies' is an aspect of the RBV that ought to be given greater attention (West and DeCastro 2001). Some weaknesses can result from having 'too much of a good thing', as Leonard-Barton implies, while others can simply be 'bad things' (such as not developing sufficient skills in environmental analysis and change management).

In outlining her model of how firms might develop outstanding capabilities, Leonard-Barton (1998: 5–16) discusses the interesting case of Chaparral Steel, then a very successful US 'minimill'. While only the tenth largest steel producer in the USA at the time of this study, Chaparral enjoyed a reputation as a world leader in productivity:

> [I]n 1990, its 1.5 person-hours per rolled ton of steel compared to a US average of 5.3, a Japanese average of 5.6, and a German average of 5.7. Chaparral was the first American steel company (and only the second company outside of Japan at the time) to be awarded the right to use the Japanese Industrial Standard certification on its general structural steel products (Leonard-Barton 1998: 6).

With strong values and incentives supporting the creation of new knowledge, Chaparral employees pushed the company's equipment well beyond its original specifications:

> The rolling mill equipment its vendor believed (was) limited to 8-inch slabs is turning out 14-inch slabs, and the vendor has tried to buy back the redesign. The two electric arc furnaces, designed originally to melt annual rates of 250,000 and 500,000 tons of scrap metal, now produce over 600,000 and 1 million tons, respectively (Leonard-Barton 1998: 11).

Leonard-Barton explains how Chaparral achieved these results through building an 'interdependent system' of employee skills and technical systems supported by HR policies, practices and cultural values:

> Chaparral's skills, physical systems, learning activities, values and managerial philosophies and practices are obviously highly interdependent. Competitively advantageous equipment can be designed and constantly improved *only* if the workforce is highly skilled. Continuous education is attractive *only* if employees are carefully selected for their willingness to learn. Sending workers throughout the world to garner ideas is cost-effective *only* if they are empowered to apply what they have learned to production problems (Leonard-Barton 1998: 15–16, italics in the original).

Leonard-Barton's model, then, places emphasis on the fact that cleverly developed systems of this kind – where the parts do reinforce each other in powerful ways – are very hard to imitate. This was certainly the view within Chaparral. Leonard-Barton (1998: 7) notes that the CEO was happy to give visitors a full plant tour, showing them almost 'everything and … giving away nothing because they cannot take it home with them'. This kind of story lends some support to the argument made earlier that even if we have a good understanding of why a firm is successful (low 'causal ambiguity'), the unique path that company has travelled and the social complexity this brings remain significant barriers to imitation.

'Table stakes' and idiosyncratic competences

While sources of differentiation are very important in the RBV, it is worth injecting a note of caution here. A problem with some writing in the RBV is the tendency of authors to focus only on sources of idiosyncrasy, thus exaggerating differences between firms in the same industry. As we have been arguing in this book, all viable firms in an industry need some similar resources in order to establish their identity in the minds of customers and to help secure legitimacy in broader society. For example, retail banks must act like retail banks (having the requisite information technology and the typical range of services, such as the capacity for speedy cash withdrawals through ATMs and a suite of account services through internet and phone banking). They must inspire confidence in the banking public and satisfy investors and regulators that they can behave as responsible repositories and lenders of funds. Without these baseline features, banks lack recognition in their industry and legitimacy in their wider society, as was graphically illustrated in the failures of many banks in the Global Financial Crisis of 2008–9.

Some writers in the RBV are so focused on the firm that they do not recognise these wider connections. However, it is a strength of the frameworks outlined here that the authors do see the importance of 'table stakes' (Hamel and Prahalad 1994) or 'enabling capabilities' (Leonard-Barton 1998). These are features of the business which enable participation in the industry but which do not make the firm distinctive or account for superior performance.

Leonard-Barton (1998) makes useful distinctions among three kinds of capabilities: core (which are superior and cannot be easily imitated), supplemental (which add value to core capabilities but can be easily copied) and enabling (which are necessary conditions of being in the industry). Both Leonard-Barton (1998) and Hamel and Prahalad (1994) note the potential for one company's distinctive or core capability (such as outstanding quality) to be emulated over a period of time by other firms. It then becomes part of the 'table stakes' in the industry and firms that seek superior performance must search for other ways to differentiate themselves. Hamel and Prahalad (1994: 232) note this dynamic in a case many of us can attest to – that of automobile manufacturing:

> ... in the 1970s and 1980s quality, as measured by defects per vehicle, was undoubtedly a core competence for Japanese car companies. Superior reliability was an important value element for customers and a genuine differentiator for Japanese car producers. It took more than a decade for Western car companies to close the quality gap with their Japanese competitors, but by the mid-1990s quality, in terms of initial defects per vehicle, (became) a prerequisite for every car maker. There is

a dynamic at work here that is common to other industries. Over long periods of time, what was once a core competence may become a base-line capability.

From an HR perspective, 'table stakes' or 'enabling capabilities' include the minimum HR investments required by each firm to play the competitive game (Boxall and Steeneveld 1999). The types of HR investment needed inevitably vary by industry or, more accurately, strategic groups or customer segments within industries, as we explained in Chapter 3. The key point is that viable firms in a particular industry are *partially* rather than totally idiosyncratic. Valuable resources, then, include some elements in common with other firms in the industry and some differences.

The dynamic capabilities framework

Standing back from the commentary so far, it should be clear that knowledge and organisational learning play a key role in resource-based models of the firm. For Hamel and Prahalad (1994), building a focus on knowledge management is much more important than the historical focus of Western firms on product management. For Leonard-Barton (1998), understanding the 'wellsprings of knowledge' is the key issue in the long-run renewal of the firm. An influential body of work in this respect is associated with David Teece who has built the 'dynamic capabilities framework', discussed in some highly cited journal articles (e.g. Teece, Pisano and Shuen 1997) and now consolidated into a book (Teece 2011). His analysis deals with the problem that much of resource-based theory is built on a static view of the firm. It tells us that firms depend on certain configurations of resources but not how these resources are developed over time to achieve sustainable competitive advantage. We need an analysis of why some firms are better at learning and at keeping up with the game.

Teece (2011: 206) defines dynamic capabilities as 'the ability to sense and then seize new opportunities, and to reconfigure and protect knowledge assets, competencies and complementary assets so as to achieve sustained competitive advantage'. Sensing is the capacity to read external markets, to understand the firm's internal capacities and to perceive opportunities to create new products and services. Teece (2011: 13) places emphasis on the importance of knowing what is happening in a firm's 'ecosystem', which includes its customers, suppliers and 'complementors' (those organisations whose services or products help to facilitate the business in question, as in the way that airport expansion supports the growth of low-cost airlines). Sensing and seizing involves dealing with the serious intellectual and political problems of strategic management we discussed in Chapter 2. Seizing implies the ability to make astute investment choices in conditions of uncertainty, to then bring resources together in the right kind of combinations and to take the offering to market through a profitable business model. This is a tall order, a rare set of skills. However, smart opportunities will not be seized if managers persist with underperforming projects because they benefit from them. Teece (2011: 19–20) sees a natural tendency in firms to favour incremental adjustment over more radical types of 'competency-destroying innovation'.

Such a framework underlines the importance of the configurational perspective on organisational fit we discussed in the previous chapter: 'the essence of the investment decision … is that it involves estimating interdependent future revenue streams and cost trajectories, and understanding a panoply of continuous and interrelated cospecialized investment issues' (Teece 2011: 22). The firm relies on interdependencies among its assets and business partners, and top management needs the ability to perceive and configure these linkages and then reconfigure them as change occurs. Much of Teece's (2011) analysis deals with the growing importance of intangibles, such as knowledge and skills, in creating value for firms. His argument is that the liberalisation of trade and finance since the 1960s and the spread of ICT have opened up international markets, including for small firms that can sell more effectively across borders through the internet, and exposed all firms to more intensive competition. In this context, it is hard to build an advantage unless the firm has some special knowledge denied to others and maintains its rate of learning. As a result, the firms that survive over the long run have leaders with outstanding entrepreneurial abilities.

This is clearly a framework that places emphasis on human resources but not on the idea that *all* human resources are valuable. Some workforces lack unique qualities and are replicable in other places, where costs are lower, or can be substituted with technology. What Teece (2011) is primarily building is a theory of why management, particularly *entrepreneurial* management, matters. He is stressing the critical role of the rare skills found in the management teams of firms with sustainable competitive advantage. This is a lesson for all firms, which will not survive over the long run without at least someone, or some leadership team, that has special insight into how value can be created in their market and skills in combining resources into a profitable operation. But Teece (2011: 217–18, 224–8) also argues that the opening up of competition in a digital world has placed a premium on the services of exceptionally talented workers, the 'literati and numerati' of knowledge-intensive organisations. He stresses the value of distributed, less hierarchical forms of leadership in getting the best out of such workers and enhancing their identification with a particular organisation, including through 'virtuoso teams' in which outstanding individual talents are cleverly accommodated. As this suggests, Teece's theory of dynamic capabilities, as with the resource-based view on which it is based, leads inevitably into the question of how human resources impact on competitive advantage.

HR strategy and sustained advantage

At the most elementary level, the resource-based view, and the dynamic capability perspective, provide a conceptual basis, if we were ever in any doubt about the matter, for asserting that human resources can be competitively valuable. Taxonomies of valuable resources always incorporate an important category for 'human capital' (Barney 1991, 2000) or 'employee know-how' (Hall 1993) and resource-based theorists stress the value of the complex interrelationships between human resources and other resources: physical, financial, legal, informational and so on (e.g. Penrose 1959, Grant 1991). This much is self-evident: as we emphasised in Chapter 2, a firm is a system of interconnected parts and human resource management forms a necessary, though not a sufficient, part of this system.

But this does not get us very far. The key questions raised by the RBV are twofold: *what* is it that can be valuable about human resources and *how* might a firm develop and defend these sources of value? Identifying what is most valuable and protecting it with 'barriers to imitation' is at the heart of resource-based thinking. It helps to remember that the value of human resources can range from forms of human and social capital that are competitively superior, enabling a firm to build and sustain advantages, through to those which are inferior, which actually undermine competitive performance. Outdated skills, excessive levels of employee turnover and conflict-prone industrial relations are examples of the latter. In between, there are human resources that are competitively neutral. All firms need to hire people who have relevant human resources in order simply to survive or attain 'competitive parity' (Hunt 2000).

At a deeper level, then, what has value in HRM? We can certainly rule out the value of formal policy positions in HRM (what top management says the firm should do in managing work and people). These can simply be run off a photocopier or downloaded from the internet. As Mueller (1996) argues, it is hard to see any distinctive and inimitable value in policy positions *per se*. Formal policy statements are, at best, competitively neutral. Furthermore, because they are a set of promises, they actually carry a level of risk: they can turn 'bad' in terms of value. If there are major disconnections between senior management's espoused HR policies and the actual HR practices enacted by line managers, this can be a source of competitive *dis*advantage (Purcell 1999). There is always a danger that gaps between managerial rhetorics and workplace reality will destroy competitive value through undermining employee trust and commitment (Legge 1995, 2005, Grant 1999), as we shall explain further in Chapters 6 and 7.

Since people vary in their capabilities and cannot work for all firms at once, Wright, McMahan and McWilliams (1994) argue that we are more likely to find value residing in the human resources possessed by the workforce. Human capital is the quality of the individual human talent recruited to the firm and retained in it. All firms need certain kinds of individual talent relevant to implementing the organisation's mission and, if they wish to survive over the long run, capable of helping the organisation to adapt to change or, better still, lead it (Boxall and Steeneveld 1999, Teece 2011). Firms that recruit and retain exceptional individuals have the possibility of generating 'human capital advantage' (Boxall 1996, 1998).

Why can individuals be so valuable? The answer lies in Polanyi's (1962) classic distinction between 'tacit' and 'explicit' (or 'articulated') knowledge. Tacit knowledge is 'nonverbalized or even nonverbalizable, intuitive' while explicit or articulated knowledge is 'specified either verbally or in writing, computer programs, patents, drawings or the like' (Hedlund 1994: 75). Table 4.1 illustrates this distinction with examples across four levels of analysis, starting with the individual and moving up to the 'inter-organisational' domain. The distinction helps to explain why firms are vulnerable to certain kinds of labour turnover (Coff 1997, 1999). They can never entirely capture what individuals know. Some of what and whom we know – including many of our best skills – cannot be reduced to writing or to formulas. When we leave the firm, we take our job know-how and networking knowledge with

Table 4.1 Types of knowledge

Type	Individual	Group	Organisation	Inter-organisational domain
Explicit knowledge	Knowledge of historical facts	A formal report of a consultancy project	Company annual report	A sub-contractor's standard operating procedures
Tacit knowledge	An individual's ability to empathise	Norms of behaviour in a team	The social climate in a workplace	Attitudes of potential recruits to a company

Source: Based on Hedlund (1994: 75).

us. No two individuals are exactly alike and the differences are particularly noticeable in high-skill jobs: as job complexity increases, so does the range of human performance (Hunter, Schmidt and Judiesch 1990). When whole teams of highly talented individuals leave, as was noted earlier in a case from the semiconductor industry, the effect can be devastating.

Moreover, individual human capital is embedded in a social context. The quality of social capital – of human relationships in the firm and with its environment – plays a major role in whether or not firms make outstanding returns from their human capital (e.g. Nahapiet and Ghoshal 1998, Swart and Kinnie 2003). In other words, firms need 'organisational process' or 'social capital' advantages if they are to realise the potential of human capital (Boxall 1996, 1998). This type of advantage is a function of historically evolved, complex processes such as team-based learning and high levels of trust and cooperation, both between management and labour and among co-workers, processes which are very difficult to imitate. Both human capital and social capital can generate exceptional value but they are likely to do so much more powerfully when they reinforce each other. Kay (1993) refers to this as the 'passing game', nicely indicating that teams may have highly talented individuals but their capacity and willingness to play together is vital if they are to achieve outstanding results. Thus, we can say that human resource advantage (HRA) is a product of highly talented people (human capital advantage) and an exceptional working environment (organisational process advantage). In mathematical notation,

$$HRA = f(HCA, OPA)$$

But does the resource-based view imply that all employee groups in a firm generate outstanding value? The answer is no, as noted in our discussion of dynamic capabilities. Rather, it suggests that there are some critical, 'core' workers in all firms, while other individuals are less critical or more peripheral (Purcell 1999). As we explained in Chapter 1, some forms of human resource advantage depend more on an elite group of employees than they do on excellence throughout the workforce. Lepak and Snell (1999, 2007) have picked up on this aspect of the RBV, and related economic theories, in developing what they call an 'HR architectural perspective'. Their analysis rests on two dimensions: the extent to which the particular form of human capital represents a valuable resource for the firm and the extent to which it is unique or firm specific. Lepak and Snell argue that firms need a commitment-oriented HR system for employees whose skills are critical to a firm's core or distinctive capabilities. Firms should invest heavily in the motivation, empowerment and development of those who hold vital knowledge. Thus, when workers are perceived as especially valuable to the firm's strategy, the question of how to defend them turns on adopting HRM models which enhance their motivation and retention in the firm. However, firms can adopt a more productivity-based approach to those, such as accounting staff, whose work is valuable in the labour market but not unique. This means hiring people who can be productive quickly and rewarding them on a more short-term, results-oriented basis. Those whose skills are low in value and generic are prime candidates for contracting out while individuals whose skills may be 'unique in some way but not directly instrumental for creating customer value' (Lepak and Snell 1999: 40), such as a firm's attorneys, are likely to be engaged in some form of longer-term alliance.

This kind of framework offers a way of helping managers to distinguish which types of HRM model are appropriate for which kinds of human capital. Implementing it is not always easy, however. The debate around who should be considered 'core' in a particular firm has both cognitive and political elements. In reality, managers make different interpretations, as illustrated in the bottled gas market in the UK in the mid-1990s (Purcell 1996). British Oxygen was a long established player in the market with a dominant share. Air Products was a relatively new entrant but with lots of experience in the USA. In 1992, British Oxygen needed to improve delivery, cut costs and get customers to trade up where possible. They had a large distribution fleet. Painful negotiations with the drivers' union led to new hours of working, wider job responsibilities including customer relations, more training and cab-based information technology. Drivers became seen as key staff in direct contact with customers. At the same time, Air Products decided to outsource distribution to a specialist haulage contractor. There was no expectation here that drivers would know anything about gas beyond safety considerations. In the case of British Oxygen, drivers were considered a core part of the firm because they always had been, not because they had typically shown distinctive organisational knowledge or skills. Indeed, this knowledge of the customer and the level of skill relating to gas systems had to be developed once the decision was made to give them customer relations' responsibilities.

Another framework for deciding who is in the core has been developed by Baron and Kreps (1999), for whom one criterion is the extent to which an individual's tasks are critically important for the firm's performance. Here, they are on the same ground as Lepak and Snell (1999) with their emphasis on the strategic value of the individual's contribution to the firm. However, Baron and Kreps's second criterion is not the uniqueness of the skill involved but 'the degree to which the activity displays high technical or social interdependence with tasks done by regular employees' (Baron and Kreps 1999: 460). The extent of interdependence between employee groups in the

		Low ← Interdependence → High	
Types of skill/knowledge	Firm-specific	Networked capabilities Valued contractors in the supply chain or expert advisors in the business network *Long-run, trust-based contracts for services*	Core capabilities Managerial and production teams with interdependent knowledge and skills *Commitment-oriented HRM inside the firm*
	Generic	Supplementary capabilities Lower-skilled and temporary employees *Short-run, cost-oriented HRM, including outsourcing*	Enabling capabilities Specialist staff who provide high-skilled support in-house *Commitment-oriented HRM inside the firm or a well-paid but less secure contract?*

Low	**Interdependence**	High

Figure 4.1 'HR architecture': a blended model

Source: Based on Lepak and Snell (2007), Baron and Kreps (1999) and Leonard-Barton (1998).

work unit is an important variable that managers should consider before any kind of restructuring. We share this concern, and in Figure 4.1 we have depicted a blended version of these models, along with some ideas about capabilities, to help readers visualise what is being argued.

Whichever framework is used, a risk for managers is the fact that the firm is both an economic *and* a social entity. If managers approach the question of differentiation in HR strategy solely as a financial issue, they can disrupt the sense of fairness in the firm. Those multinational firms in which senior management wants to create a sense of shared community need to bear this in mind. For example, in 2005, an American company in the UK established an employee forum for the first time. One of the first items raised was the fact that management and professional staff were given free health insurance but other employees were not. This was deemed unfair, at odds with the company's aspiration to be 'an employer of choice' and its emphasis on 'togetherness' (i.e. social interdependency). Free health insurance was subsequently extended to all employees, a cost that the firm chose to pick up. This is a form of 'harmonisation' of employment conditions, which can help to create the sense that we are all working for the same team, but we should note that it rarely, if ever, extends to a full democratisation of employee conditions. In nearly all firms, as in this one, the more senior people will still have higher salaries, greater discretion in their work and better support for their career development.

Issues of cost-effectiveness therefore remain in play, and these are often dealt with through corporate decisions to outsource parts of the business. Where manufacturing has a large degree of 'modularity' to it (Teece 2011), as in the case of the supply chains in the automobile and computer industries, discrete sets of activities are frequently located on separate sites, which helps managers to deal with the social tensions that may arise when all the work is concentrated on a single site. Outsourced sites, especially those offshored to distant low-cost countries, can become 'out of sight and out of mind' once people have adjusted to the initial shock. In Chapter 1, we considered the case of the British manufacturer, Dyson, which, like many others, has off-shored its assembly operations to a more cost-effective location. The intention in these situations may be to treat these workers as core employees but management is doing so within a much lower cost structure or is using either a sub-contractor or an alliance partner who does this. The critical core in the firm is thus defined more parsimoniously.

However it is conceived, the development of a core of critical employees depends on a clever HR strategy that aligns the interests of these people with those of the firm and that brings out the best in their talents as they work collectively in it. In any industry, there are likely to be particular firms which have built 'human resource advantage' in this way. The case of Chaparral Steel, discussed above, certainly implied that it had built an extensive kind of human resource advantage throughout the workforce, which underpinned outstanding performance in its industry, at least for a significant period of time.[4] As Leonard-Barton (1998) stressed, the firm's approach to managing its staff was very well integrated with investments in employee skill development, in incentives to perform and in opportunities to influence decision-making being strongly connected. Reinforcing these linkages led to outstanding rates of learning throughout the workforce, making their achievements hard to emulate. On the other hand, many forms of competitive advantage hinge more on non-human resources. There are, for example, multidivisional companies achieving high levels of success through skilful financial strategies, making clever use of large amounts of financial capital, as we will explain in Chapter 10. There is no doubt that this depends on the expertise and networks of an elite group of highly skilled executives and specialists but it is not likely to require superior human resources throughout all parts of the company or all of its business units, some of which are only

---

[4] Since Leonard-Barton's (1998) study, Chaparral Steel became the second largest producer of structural steel products in the USA and was bought in 2007 by Gerdau Ameristeel Corporation for $4.2 billion or $86 per share: http://www.bloomberg.com/apps/news?pid=newsarchive&sid=aP4iRhmtbjmY&refer=home, accessed 16/1/15.

held temporarily and then spun off to other owners. Some element of human resource advantage is clearly desirable for all companies in the long run but the location and extent of this special resource is variable.

Before moving on, let us recall again that there is a problem with thinking about resources only at the level of the firm. Clusters of valuable resources occur at both industry and societal levels. Industry clusters can benefit all firms through providing a skilled labour pool and networking connections across the supply chain, one of the reasons why Dyson found it attractive to locate in Malaysia, as noted in Chapter 1. In addition, countries provide variable resources of infrastructure, economic systems, social order and so on. Some firms have a 'head start' in international competition because they are located in societies which have much better educational and technical infrastructure than others (Porter 1990, Boxall 1995). American, Japanese, German, British and French firms, for example, are all assisted by the existence of long-established traditions of excellence in higher education which enhance the knowledge-creating capacities of business organisations. The point here is that the potential to develop competitive advantage through human resources does not lie solely in the hands of managers within individual firms.

Conclusions

The resource-based view and the dynamic capabilities framework provide important perspectives for understanding how firms might build competitive advantage. Strategy researchers working with them are interested in the ways in which firms can develop valuable resources and erect barriers to imitation of them, so that a superior performance is maintained despite the best efforts of other firms to copy or outflank it. Shareholders benefit when they enjoy better returns from these resources, meaning that the returns are not entirely appropriated by the bargaining activities of well-placed managers and other critical employees.

Resources are valuable when they enable a firm to be successful in its chosen markets, helping it either to grasp competitive opportunities or to counter threats. This includes much more than the sort of assets, such as property and cash, that are easily valued in a company's accounts: it includes the more intangible, less easily valued resources such as a firm's reputation with its customers, its unique production know-how and the quality of its employees' skills and commitment. RBV theory argues that such resources are built up through astute timing and learning and accumulate in the social complexity that grows as teams of people work together. These can be strong barriers to imitation by other firms, although all resources can be undermined through major, 'Schumpeterian' shocks to an industry or economy. Some element of causal ambiguity is always going to be present in a firm, and can also be a barrier to imitation, but if ambiguity implies confusion and a lack of managerial consensus about how to improve the business, this is usually a bad thing for company performance.

The resource and capability perspectives on strategic management present an account of the firm's fortunes that is richly laced with *human* resource issues. This is seen in the emphasis on identifying the firm's core or distinctive competences, and the role of the workforce's skills in these. It is seen in the interest in knowledge management and organisational learning. A firm's human resource strategy is needed to support its competitive survival but it can also help to add exceptional value or, conversely, help to destroy it. There is little value to be had in formal HR policies or in highly mobile, 'hit-and-run' managers. In fact, major disjunctures between managerial promises and realities in HRM can undermine employee trust and commitment, contributing to competitive *dis*advantage. A heritage of conflict-prone industrial relations almost always destroys value through alienating customers. On the positive side, a key question is how to enhance the motivation and development of those individuals whose human capital is core to the firm's mission and renewal. Defining who is 'core' is not easy, however. Is it the whole workforce, certain parts of it or a much smaller elite? Firms vary on this critical question, and in answering it, there are technical and social interdependencies that benefit from careful handling. Managers can find it easier to deal with these when their operations can be 'modularised' and distributed to where they are most cost-effective. A second key question is how to build the kind of organisational processes or social capital that enable individuals to function effectively or, better still, exceptionally well. What kind of attitudinal and behavioural climates will bring out the best in a collection of individuals, and an array of teams, helping them to achieve the firm's goals? The reader will not be surprised that we regard these questions as extremely important. We take them further in the chapters that follow, looking first at the human-capital question of how to align organisational and employee interests in employment relationships.

5

Building a workforce: the challenge of interest alignment

As Chapter 1 explained, all firms are dependent on gaining access to people with the kind of human capital or talent they need. A fundamental issue for managers in any firm is how to build and maintain a workforce of an appropriate quantity and quality. In this chapter, we ask: what are the strategic challenges that managers face in attracting and retaining a workforce? Why are some firms more successful in employing the people they need than others? These questions are increasingly discussed under the rubric of 'talent management', which is one of the critical concerns of strategic HRM even when labour markets contain major surpluses of job seekers (Collings and Mellahi 2009, Lanvin and Evans 2013). Understanding issues around the attraction and retention of people is a vital precursor to understanding how successful firms are in creating the kind of workforce performances they need, which we will take forward in the next two chapters.

The fundamental principle of HRM at the heart of this chapter is the principle of interest alignment. Constructing and maintaining a workforce depends on aligning the interests of the firm with those of workers, at least to a level that will enable sufficient numbers of people to be recruited and retained. Stronger forms of alignment can help firms to build 'human capital advantages'. This means we need an understanding of the employment relationship from the worker's perspective and not simply from management's. The chapter, then, is organised around a relationship analysis. We begin with the management viewpoint, looking at strategic issues in building and maintaining a workforce of appropriate quantity and quality. We then turn the tables and look at talent management from the employee perspective. What makes a job and an organisation attractive? What are the drivers of employee well-being and commitment? The analysis is designed to help us understand why some firms are better at aligning their interests with those of workers than are their rivals.

Talent management: building and renewing a workforce

We use the term 'talent management' to describe the ways in which managers try to construct and renew the kind of workforce their organisation needs. Managers are involved in decisions around how to attract people with appropriate forms of human capital into the firm, how to develop people from within and how to restructure the workforce as the economic and socio-political context changes. Decisions about the quantity and quality of the workforce have major impacts on the outcomes of HRM. In terms of quantity, both under-staffing and over-staffing are dangerous in terms of their economic consequences. In terms of quality, a poor mix of human capabilities will seriously compromise the firm's performance.

Labour shortages and talent inflows

Talent shortages are a direct threat to an organisation's effectiveness and reputation. A failure to recruit and retain sufficient numbers of suitably qualified people compromises the firm's ability to meet its customers' needs and constrains its ability to grow. This means that profit opportunities are missed or that profits are much less than management desires. We illustrated this in Chapter 2 in the case of the London Olympics of 2012 when security personnel were in limited supply, and we also illustrated its critical importance to the health sector in Chapter 1. Ensuring an adequate supply of qualified health workers has become a worldwide issue as the world's health needs have grown and as medical science has developed a raft of new drugs and procedures. Retention of expensively trained staff in the health sector has become an enormous concern. Many countries have now established health workforce planning units to assist the industry to balance workforce supply and demand. A recent review evaluates the modelling of health workforces in 18 OECD countries (Ono, Lafortune and Schoenstein 2013). This is one industry where the problem of labour scarcity means that workforce planning is now widely embraced. As a general observation, systematic assessment of the size of the workforce needed to enable the organisation to function, and planning for how to meet these needs, becomes a more critical management activity whenever managers learn that the organisation's labour market is problematic or highly competitive.

Problems of labour shortages are primarily dealt with through recruitment and selection, which are concerned with the in-flow of talent and are sometimes called the 'buy' option in human capital. Recruitment strategies include attempts to make the organisation an interesting place to work and attempts to reach larger and better pools of candidates (e.g. Taylor and Collins 2000, Orlitzky 2007). Their importance is captured in the growth of interest in 'employer branding', which 'considers current and potential employees as branding targets' (Edwards 2010: 6). Firms that adopt this notion may develop an 'employment value proposition' (EVP), akin to the marketing notion of a 'customer value proposition'. This is an attempt to convey why the organisation is an attractive place to work in terms of the rewards and career opportunities it can offer. Multinational firms, including the world's elite professional service firms, are among the biggest investors in employer branding, as evidenced in their heavy presence at graduate recruitment fairs and their investment in internet-based recruitment.

In reality, what organisations can offer potential employees is hugely variable and a substantive approach to employer branding depends on understanding the mix of strengths and weaknesses that the firm *actually* exhibits as an employer. Large, well-known and financially successful firms are generally at an advantage in the labour market, although not all of them sell their strengths in a proactive way (Windolf 1986, Edwards 2010). At the other extreme, some firms operate in industries with an attractiveness problem. This can arise where jobs are geographically remote or physically dangerous, as in much of the mining sector, or where work is insecure or poorly paid, as in much of the retail sector. Many small firms face an up-hill battle to get recognition from more highly qualified workers because they lack the scale or scope of activities that suggests there will be room for advancement. Firms with an attractiveness problem in the labour market need to consider how they will deal with these weaknesses. A common approach in mining, for example, is to compensate for the danger and social isolation with very high wages, as seen in the Australian mining industry.[1] But some firms can't do this, including many small firms, where owners need to come up with flexible but less costly ways of adjusting to the needs of the key individuals on whom the business depends (e.g. Marchington, Carroll and Boxall 2003, Edwards and Ram 2006).

---

[1] See, for example, http://iminco.net/mining-job-wages-much-can-earn-miner/, accessed 19/1/15.

Labour surpluses and organisational viability

On the other side of the coin, over-staffing an organisation is also a strategic threat because it, too, can directly cut into the firm's profitability and affect its financial viability. Many organisations found themselves with a talent surplus during the Global Financial Crisis of 2008–9 and were forced, sooner or later, to downsize or make other forms of adjustment (van Wanrooy et al. 2013: 25–47). Downsizing, of course, comes at a risk in terms of organisational attractiveness because it affects employee perceptions of employment security and of management competence. As explained in Chapter 1, organisations in which managers can anticipate major fluctuations in work demand may try to reduce the economic and reputational risks by ensuring they have strategies for organisational flexibility in place. One way is to limit permanent positions to a fixed percentage of the total staffing budget (e.g. 70 to 80 per cent). Another is to outsource non-core functions wherever possible. Yet another approach involves ensuring that employment contracts allow for shortened work weeks if revenues are falling. Some industries, of course, have long traditions of flexibility in staffing practices. Use of casual workers is commonplace in the retail sector, which experiences major seasonality, and firms in large-scale construction and the creative sector, such as in movie production, often maintain only a small core of permanent staff. They scale-up their workforce through a large network of self-employed contractors, and temps from labour-hire agencies, who are only employed when a major project is secured. In various industries, the practice of offering zero-hours' contracts is a growing, but controversial way, of creating greater staffing flexibility, as explained in Chapter 1. A key point we wish to underline here is that employers do not have an absolute commitment to permanent, standard types of employment for all types of worker (e.g. Atkinson 1984, Boxall 2013). Over-staffing presents major risks to employers, who are therefore inclined to vary their commitment to individuals according to the value of the skills they offer and how easily they are replaced.

The quality of human talent

These problems with the size or quantity of the workforce are not, of course, the only strategic issue, serious though they are. The quality of the talent in a workforce is also decisive for its success. One way of depicting the quality of the workforce is illustrated in Figure 5.1, which we have evolved from Odiorne's (1985) 'human resources portfolio'. This categorises the workforce according to the current performance and long-run potential of the individuals in it.

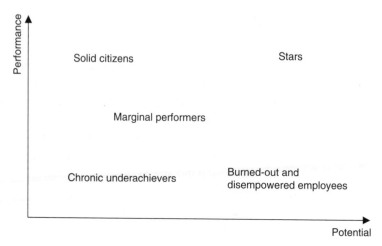

Figure 5.1 Mapping the quality of performance and potential in a workforce

The implicit argument behind Figure 5.1 is that all firms need some blend of people who are 'stars' and 'solid citizens'. Star employees have the sort of productive qualities that add exceptional value, have high potential and are highly motivated to perform. Collectively, they help organisations innovate and forge a competitive future. The need to recruit or develop people of high ability is particularly important where higher levels of discretion or specialised blends of skills are required in the work. As job complexity increases, so does the range of human performance (Eysenck 1953, Hunter, Schmidt and Judiesch 1990). Thus, as people move up from jobs of low complexity to those where greater ambiguity is involved, differences in skills and judgement become more pronounced and are more consequential for the organisation. The phenomenon of individual variation in performance, and in long-run potential, puts a premium on the quality of selection decision-making. That this is widely realised is reflected in the size of the industry devoted to employee search and selection.[2] The elite end of this market is concerned with executive search where assignments involve extensive analysis of suitable candidates and consume large sums of money and time (Hamori, Bonet and Cappelli 2011).

But stars are rarely the majority. People who have the qualities of 'solid citizens' are also vital in a well-balanced workforce: they have the

---

[2] In 2014, over 96,000 people were employed in the UK's recruitment industry, which generated an annual sales turnover of £28.7 billion. See http://www.telegraph.co.uk/finance/jobs/11191471/Recruitment-industry-now-bigger-than-its-pre-crisis-peak.html, accessed 19/1/15.

knowledge and skills to make things happen reliably once the firm's direction has been decided and they exhibit a healthy level of engagement. Their collective impact enables firms to build efficient operations and deliver on promises to customers, so people with this profile are essential to a firm's viability. Solid citizens do not, however, have the same intellectual or creative potential as stars.

The other categories depicted in Figure 5.1 reflect problems in workforce quality. Marginal performers get close to a good performance but have problems with their skills or their motivation or with both. Those whose skills are currently inadequate, but who are highly motivated, can be turned into solid citizens (and sometimes into stars) if these skill deficits are addressed. The more troubling kind of marginal performer has all the skills needed but shows problems in motivation, leading to a variable or inconsistent performance. Chronic underachievers (sometimes called 'deadwood') fall well short of the demands of their job, perhaps because they have misrepresented their abilities at recruitment or because they are carrying serious cognitive and/or emotional weaknesses that undermine their contribution. They may be an example of the 'Peter Principle', which observes that virtually any individual can be promoted to a level at which they become incompetent (Peter and Hull 1969).

Burned-out employees are those who are suffering the health consequences of excessive pressure or emotional exhaustion (Maslach and Jackson 1984), a frequent phenomenon in the 'caring professions', and something that can be a characteristic of stars who have overextended themselves and lost balance. The disempowered are those who could perform more effectively if they were appropriately enabled through better authority, resources or support. This category helps to make the point that the quality of human capital in a firm is not just down to what individuals bring to the table but is an interaction with the working environment. People with high potential who are not adequately enabled by management will only achieve so much.

The sort of model depicted in Figure 5.1 is useful in depicting the range of human performances and potential contributions that exist in any organisation. However, it is an oversimplified representation of human talent (in which there are various shades of grey) and is a static representation or snapshot at a point in time. Lying behind it is a range of dynamic issues that can affect the quality of a workforce. If they want to improve the quality of their workforce, managers have much to gain from analysing these issues. One, for example, is associated with internal flows or the rate of employee mobility upwards and across positions in an organisation. Too little movement or mobility in an organisation can create a 'talent blockage', which encourages star employees to go elsewhere to advance their learning and progress their careers. This is what makes stagnant and retrenching organisations undesirable to many people.

Yet another problem is the 'talent ghetto', where individuals are only developed within their specialisation, which then becomes a dead end because they lack the breadth to take on broader business responsibilities. An HR specialist, for example, who has never worked outside the HR function is unlikely to be appointed to a role in general management, which requires a much broader understanding of the business, including its revenue and cost drivers. A safer way of developing managerial potential is to create 'talent spirals' where individuals are developed in depth within a function but also in breadth across a range of functions. This, for example, would enable HR specialists to move laterally into operating roles, after which they would then become more promotable. The same applies to specialists in any kind of function who may be rotated into other roles to enhance their breadth and long-run scope for advancement. In multinational firms, talent spirals can extend to assignments or positions across a range of countries, making individuals not only cross-functional but also cosmopolitan managers. As this implies, such firms are often among the most interesting employers for people seeking a more challenging and expansive career.

Another issue is how managers address chronic performance problems that have been left unresolved for a long time, possibly because they have become politically fraught or 'toxic'. These are particularly problematic when poor performers are located in what Cascio and Boudreau (2010) call 'pivotal positions', those that can make a strategic impact on the firm's performance. Huselid, Becker and Beatty (2005: 1) comment that 'it's surprising how few companies systematically identify their strategic A positions – and then focus on the A players who should fill them'. Ensuring that the more strategic roles in an organisation are clearly identified and that they are occupied by people who are good performers is a major way of enhancing the impact of human capital (Collings and Mellahi 2009).

Talent enhancement through training, development and performance appraisal

In this discussion of how managers approach talent management, we have talked about the importance of recruitment and selection as the 'buy' option in human capital. These in-flow activities, however, are inevitably complemented with some use of the 'make' option: developing the people who are already in place. Key activities include employee training and development

(T&D) and types of performance appraisal, in which managers attempt to make better use of the potential of the employees they have hired.

A simple, but crucial, distinction we must observe here is between training and learning, which are not equivalent terms. Training is something that managers provide, or provide access to, with a range of intentions. Much, to be sure, is aimed at enhancing the skills needed for performance but some is oriented at ensuring compliance with standard operating procedures or management policies and some is a form of reward aimed at improving employee retention (Felstead et al. 2010). Learning is something we do ourselves, often without realising it. As Poell (2014: 23) explains, the process of workplace learning 'is always there in all workplaces at all times'. Individuals who apply themselves to work inevitably learn how to do things through on-the-job experience (e.g. Marsick and Watkins 1990, Billett 2006). A critical predictor of our rate and quality of learning is the nature of the work we are asked to do and the extent to which we are given assignments that stretch our abilities. If we are offered little responsibility, or have few opportunities to make decisions, our scope to learn is that much reduced (e.g. Gallie et al. 2012). Workplaces, and particular jobs within them, vary in the extent to which they offer 'expansive learning environments' in which we can exercise discretion and grow our capabilities (Felstead et al. 2009: 27). This is a key factor in how employees think about whether the organisation is meeting their needs, as we shall explain when we look at their interests.

On-the-job training is a way of facilitating, or channelling, the natural human propensity to learn. Managers often expose new workers to the skills of experienced performers through 'buddy' systems or what was sometimes called the 'SBN' system – 'sit by Nellie' (with the sub-text: 'and do what she does').[3] Alternatively, the direct line manager may play the crucial role of the initial job trainer (e.g. Purcell and Hutchinson 2007). There is little doubt that on-the-job training is widespread because employers have an obvious incentive to help new employees familiarise themselves with their job as quickly as possible, which will lead to a faster pay-back on the expense of hiring them.

For new recruits, then, training is often organised on a 'deficit model', where the concern is with enabling them to meet their immediate job demands. The extent to which this is complemented by more costly forms of investment in human capital is another matter altogether. Major training investments do occur when firms are implementing new technology and no one has much experience with it or when major production or operating systems are being reformed. This typically occurs, for example, when firms implement lean

---

[3] For a reference to the role of 'Nellie' in employee training, see Crichton (1968: 33–4).

production systems, which require training in methods of identifying and eliminating waste in work processes and materials (e.g. De Menezes, Wood and Gelade 2010, Sterling and Boxall 2013). Such systems can impose new demands on workers in terms of teamwork and on supervisors in terms of facilitating worker involvement.

Apart from when a new business or production model requires a substantial proportion of the workforce to be upgraded in terms of skill levels, investments in training and development tend to be segmented in firms, as argued by researchers studying workforce differentiation (e.g. Lepak and Snell 1999). Managers, professionals and the more highly educated tend to be the higher priorities (e.g. Felstead et al. 2010). Large firms often invest in some level of management training, recognising that the skills associated with managing others are not the same as those associated with being a good operator or specialist. This form of training is typically off-the-job, in management short courses or educational programmes, but it can be complemented by mentoring and coaching from higher-level managers and/or HR specialists. In large firms, management development programmes may be linked to a process of succession planning to ensure that the organisation can replace key managers as they are promoted, relocated, retired or dismissed. A key role for a senior HR specialist may be focused on the development planning and succession processes on which renewal of the management cadre depends.

Apart from such investments in management development, firms are likely to target their discretionary training budget at the high potentials and high performers in the workforce (Collings and Mellahi 2009). In the larger firms, methods used may include a mix of formal training, further education, internal mentoring, external coaching, more demanding job assignments, taskforce participation and transfers across functions. In multinational firms, expatriate secondments and appointments are part of this mix. This, however, is a controversial process because some are included and others are not. How well are these decisions made?

Performance appraisal: enhancing alignment or entrenching the problems?

This brings us to the role of performance appraisal (PA) systems in identifying, developing, rewarding and retaining the organisation's talent. Such systems, which are growing, involve formal methods of planning and evaluating employee performance, including interviewing of employees to discuss work goals and outcomes (typically, annually, although there may be various informal meetings across a year). The percentage of British workplaces in which all non-managerial employees have formal appraisals rose from 38 per cent in 2004 to 63 per cent in 2011 (van Wanrooy et al. 2013: 98). PA systems frequently require the line manager to make a recommendation about pay and provide a basis for making decisions about promotion and succession. It is typical for them to include some form of planning for employee development, although some organisations separate these activities in case the 'developmental' discussion is impeded by the 'evaluative' discussion going on around the individual's performance.

PA systems, then, are among the most complex kinds of HR practice. A lot can go wrong with them, which can undermine employee trust and commitment rather than enhancing these underlying variables. Good intentions in the PA area have often been associated with disappointing outcomes (e.g. Marshall and Wood 2000, Latham, Sulsky and MacDonald 2007). As well as huge variability in how (or even whether) managers conduct formal interviews, research has long confirmed the existence of 'rater bias', stemming from use of invalid performance criteria and lack of representative data on performance (amongst other things). As a result, some industrial psychologists now routinely distinguish between 'objective' and 'rated' performance in organisations (Hunter et al. 2000). The implication of this distinction is that good performers may be under-recognised while poor performers may be over-recognised.

PA systems make some major demands on managerial time and skills. Line managers are expected to prepare for meetings, conduct them and record the outcomes, often in a climate of work pressure, and then there are the questions around skill. Can they set appropriate goals or performance standards? Can they do so consultatively? Can they then accurately discern performance differences and give performance feedback that is fair? Can they have the aptly named 'difficult conversation'? Can they identify the factors that contribute to an individual's performance and recommend good ways of developing their careers? Can they see how to have the kind of conversation that will retain high performers? Just listing this string of questions suggests we have a tall order here, which makes a high demand on the people-management skills of managers. These are often called the 'cognitive problems' of PA systems and management training can be useful in dealing with them, especially if it involves practice, with feedback, at better techniques (Latham and Latham 2000). The need to develop managerial skills in these difficult tasks is now widely recognised as important in implementing a PA system.

However, it is also very clear that the performance of managers in PA systems is not simply about the 'can do' factor, their knowledge and skills. It is also concerned with managerial motivations and politics (Murphy and Cleveland 1991, Huber and Fuller 1998). As Longenecker, Sims and Gioia (1987: 190) put it, 'few (performance) ratings are determined without some political consideration'. In any organisation where people 'rub shoulders' daily, a common syndrome is conflict avoidance, leading to inflated appraisals (Longenecker, Sims and Gioia 1987). Managers who must continue to work with the people they appraise tend to avoid actions that involve conflict escalation. They are therefore often prepared to give soft appraisals that 'don't rock the boat'. This can mean that poorer performers drift up the rating scale and gravitate to higher pay levels, making them less likely to leave (a 'honey trap'). On top of this, when higher-level managers do not support lower-level managers who wish to challenge poor performance, there is very little chance of building an organisational culture in which it is appropriately managed. Addressing poor performance is a risky personal strategy in such an organisation: better to leave the problems alone and pass them on to the next manager.

Soft appraisal ratings are probably the most common political syndrome in PA systems, but, at the other extreme of the political spectrum, there are the managers who are motivated to 'do down' the talented individuals or 'rising stars' who threaten them. Some managers, as Kets De Vries and Miller (1984) argue, have dysfunctional personality syndromes including 'power-holic' problems and infantile jealousies of more productive people. Politically shrewd managers may use the PA system to exact their revenge on political rivals or to hobble an individual's chances of advancement.

Admitting the possibility of political problems implies that senior managers must improve accountability mechanisms around PA systems – for example, requiring lower-level managers to summarise and justify all proposed evaluations in advance of interviewing any employees (Marshall and Wood 2000). This means the higher-level manager can form a sense of how rational the proposed ratings are, based on their knowledge of the people involved and the unit's results. If they are all being rated highly, but the team, as a whole, is doing poorly, something is probably wrong. Similarly, if some people are being rated harshly when other evidence suggests they are high achievers, who also happen to speak their mind, something is probably wrong. Senior managers can also improve systems by spending more time clarifying their purposes and how key linkages to rewards and development will actually be achieved in practice (Marshall and Wood 2000), including through ongoing training and coaching of managers. All of this is hard work and senior managerial commitment to doing it sets the context for effectiveness in performance appraisal.

In terms of talent management, then, performance appraisal systems are something of a mixed blessing. When used skilfully and positively, they can help to create better alignment between organisational and individual interests. Organisations that want to retain talented people benefit more fully from them when they offer a setting for individuals to discuss how they see their personal development and the issues they have with where their career is heading. When used badly, or incompetently, they can demotivate good performers and entrench problems with the poor ones.

This brings us to the end of this section looking at the management perspective on talent management. Managers in all firms are engaged in an ongoing process of constructing and renewing a workforce. Even organisations that appear to hold the upper hand in labour markets face issues of human capital that can severely affect their performance. On the quantity side, there are major risks associated with under-staffing and over-staffing an organisation that can affect both short-run profitability and the capacity to remain financially viable. On the quality side, managers must deal with the fact that human abilities and performances are extremely variable. They need to build a workforce in which there is an appropriate mix of current and potential performances for their organisation. Firms in which there are talent blockages, talent ghettos or chronic, unaddressed performance issues underperform as a result of these problems.

Job quality and organisational attractiveness

We are now at the point where we need to turn the tables and think about talent management from the employee's perspective. Employees have a major interest in investing in their own human resources or human capital, as we explained in Chapter 1. This includes investments in education and in a range of human experiences, inside and outside workplaces and across a lifetime. If managers wish to foster alignment between individuals and organisations, they need a theory of what employees are seeking: what needs are workers trying to meet and what do they consider a good bargain for their talents? Like the employer, the employee is motivated to enter an employment relationship when the anticipated benefits outweigh the costs. For an employee, this typically means that the rewards such as the wage level, the intrinsic enjoyment and the social standing of the job exceed the mental, physical and emotional effort that the work implies and are worthwhile in the light of alternative job offers. In other words, there must be a relatively balanced relationship or sufficient levels of reciprocity in the relationship if employment is to be stable (e.g. March and Simon 1958, Boxall 2013). The extent to which employment relationships are mutually beneficial is, of course, very variable. One form of balance occurs when both parties are making high levels of investment in the relationship, but moderate and low levels of investment can also be stable if they are mutual. Whatever the context, the problem arises with those relationships in which one party contributes significantly more than the other. If the reasons for this imbalance are not addressed, that party's commitment is undermined and the relationship may be heading for a break-up. It is particularly damaging for a firm if it continually loses talented people from roles that are critical to the organisation's success (Collings and Mellahi 2009).

In analysing how employees respond to a job and an organisation, it is standard to distinguish between intrinsic and extrinsic drivers of motivation. Intrinsic sources are associated with the work itself and with the workload experienced. Extrinsic factors cover the material and social rewards that holding the job confers, such as the level of pay, the status accorded to the role and the degree of employment security.

The intrinsic quality of work

In terms of intrinsic factors, then, what makes a job desirable and an organisation attractive?

Vocational interests, skill utilisation and personal growth

We must begin with the fundamental point that people differ in the kinds of work they find attractive or a meaningful use of their time. Some people will only consider work for which they have a consuming passion or a sense of calling, even if this means a low level of material well-being. More generally, people differ in their vocational interests, which are 'relatively stable individual differences that influence behaviour through preferences for certain work activities and work environments' (van Iddekinge et al. 2011: 1168). Holland (1973) identified six vocational types: some people approximate the 'realistic' type, who gravitate to practical work, or the 'conventional' type, who seek an ordered environment, while others are much more drawn to 'artistic', 'social', 'investigative' or 'enterprising' kinds of work. These underlying preferences tend to attract people into certain kinds of occupation or help to retain them in those jobs that turn out to be a good fit with their values and personality. The work of nursing, for example, appeals more strongly to 'social' types, who are interested in caring for others. This means that nurses typically respond more positively to emotionally demanding work, such as the care of patients with complex illnesses, when other personality types find it demotivating or debilitating (Bakker and Sanz-Vergel 2013).

Whatever their vocational preferences, people generally prefer jobs that deploy the skills they have developed and that sit within an organisational context that offers them opportunities to grow. A series of studies of

Australian workers in the 1970s and 1980s demonstrated the importance of 'skill utilisation' as a driver of job satisfaction (O'Brien 1982, 1983). This line of research was also explored in Britain by Michael Rose (1994) who defined three categories of worker. The first are the 'underutilised' whose skills are greater than those needed in the job. University students doing low-skilled jobs while studying often fall into this category but so too does anyone working in a job which does not make sufficient use of their talents. The second group are the 'matched', whose skills approximate those needed in the job, while the third category are the 'underqualified', whose skills are less than those needed. Rose's (1994) analysis of some 4,000 workers shows that people whose skills are underutilised are the least satisfied, while those whose talents are well matched are generally satisfied with their work, and those who are underqualified are the most satisfied (Rose 1994: 258).

The underqualified (who may therefore be marginal performers or chronic underachievers) can pose a serious risk to employers but the key implication of such studies is that if management wants the employment relationship to last beyond the short term, it is important to get a good match between the individual's skills and the demands of their job. In general, people who feel their skills are underutilised have a greater propensity to look for another job (Allen and van der Velden 2001). Studies of skill utilisation also imply that most people can be happy in their work, irrespective of how educated they are or how many talents they have. The key factor for the individual is finding a job that uses the talents *they do* have. Hairdressers, for example, who have good opportunities for personal expression, come out very highly in British studies of job satisfaction while solicitors, who have much higher academic qualifications, are among the least satisfied.[4] It may be that the actual experience of legal work is much less glamorous than people imagine in law schools, which is why many of those who acquire law degrees eventually consider other avenues for expressing their talents.[5]

We need to understand the issue for employees in a dynamic way, however. People's knowledge and skills grow over time and lead to a demand for new challenges. In time, a job that once matched our talents becomes boring. Unless the organisation can find a more stimulating job for us, one that uses our expanded capabilities, we are likely to seek 'greener pastures'. Studies in adult life-cycle theory suggest that there will be several times over a person's life when they will seek major developmental challenges (Levinson 1978,

---

[4] http://www.bath.ac.uk/news/2007/8/6/jobsatisfaction.html, accessed 20/1/15.
[5] See, for example, http://legalcareers.about.com/od/practicetips/a/lawyermyths.htm, accessed 20/1/15.

Levinson and Levinson 1996). According to life-cycle theorists, the adult life consists of alternating periods of stability (structure-building) and transition (structure-changing). In each stable period, the emphasis is on pursuing one's goals and values within a given structure of choices. In the transitional periods, one 'questions and reappraises the existing structure, to explore various possibilities for change in self and world, and to move towards commitment to the crucial choices that form the basis for a new life structure in the ensuing stable period' (Levinson 1978: 49). At the transitional points, some people 'externalise' their inner turmoil more than others: changing their job, their address, their spouse, perhaps even their country of domicile. Personal change can be particularly profound when an individual experiences what is popularly known as a 'mid-life crisis'. What an individual once found meaningful may now be much less so and may even be repudiated.

While the pattern of stability alternating with change across the life cycle is likely to be similar for both sexes (Levinson and Levinson 1996), there is greater variety in women's patterns (e.g. Gilligan 1982) and there is variety in the way people manage the caregiving responsibilities in their lives (van Engen, Vinkenburg and Dikkers 2012). Women who become mothers, and have no paid employment after their first child is born, have a life pattern that is very different from the typical male. On the other hand, women who have no substantial caregiving roles, either with children or in eldercare, may have very similar career orientations to the traditional 'male breadwinner'. Paid employment is a central life interest, if not the most important thing. A third pattern includes those women, and increasing numbers of men, who try to balance family and employment (Buxton 1998), either on the basis of part- or full-time employment.

Where paid employment makes up a significant element of the life, we can expect both men and women to seek some regular growth opportunity. At earlier stages of the career, this may be about gaining a serious promotion, or a chance to switch across functional tracks, which opens up more challenging work and/or higher rates of pay, positioning the individual for the next step. Labour turnover rates are generally much higher among the under-thirties than other age groups as people seek these kinds of improvement in their prospects (Burgess and Rees 1998, Boxall et al. 2003). At later stages of the career, when individuals have made their major moves and consider they have enough responsibility, it may simply be about learning how to use a new information tool or about honing one's core skills or extending one's network.

This analysis puts an interesting spin on the issue of change in the workplace. We are frequently told that employees are resistant to change, and there is no doubt that individuals react against threats to their interests. However, research on job satisfaction and life-cycle theory suggests that people leave firms because their employer cannot offer them *enough* stimulating change (Boxall et al. 2003). Firms face risks to their human capital if they fail to foster developmental opportunities for those individuals seeking personal growth. Rose (2000, 2003) talks of the rise of 'expressivism' in the workforce, something that Bryson (2004: 22) calls the 'aspirational agenda' of today's workers. The challenge of retaining outstanding performers over the long run, then, is one of providing a setting in which they can reach their developmental goals without leaving the organisation. Talent management is more problematic for those employers who are not in touch with this because they are not offering individuals a regular opportunity to talk about their personal development. As discussed above, a useful function of a performance appraisal system can be providing a setting to have this kind of conversation.

In sum, when the firm does not offer a good match with an employee's capabilities and their rate of learning, we can expect them to look outside for other avenues for personal growth. Losing talented people this way has consequences for the quality of human capital in the firm. How to align these sets of needs is an issue we now take further in thinking about other intrinsic factors.

Work demands and resources

Research in Anglophone and European contexts also underlines the fact that most people prefer jobs in which they can exercise some influence over *how* they do the work (e.g. Bauer 2004, Gallie 2013). Not only is the 'what' of work important but our motivation in a job, and our opportunity to make an impact in it, is connected to the level of discretion we can exercise as we go about it. Several theoretical traditions recognise the scope for control as central to the quality of working life, enabling employees 'to make use of their individual creativity in work and to develop their abilities over time' (Gallie 2007: 212). One prominent example can be found in sociological theories of the labour process, which see the drive of workers to control their working lives as a fundamental dynamic in employment relationships (e.g. Thompson and Harley 2007, McBride 2008). Another example, in the psychological literature, is the theory of self-determination developed by Deci and Ryan (2000), which argues that human beings have inherent needs for autonomy (along with needs for competence and relatedness). A third example is associated with 'job characteristics theory' (Hackman and Oldham 1980), which builds on studies of job enrichment to argue that autonomy at work fosters the individual's sense of responsibility for outcomes. Along with other characteristics, such as skill variety and good levels of feedback, greater control leads to better motivation and higher satisfaction, although not all workers are considered to be interested in personal growth at work.

The importance of control for employee well-being is also central to the theory of work-related stress. Paid employment requires people to expend energy to meet the demands of the job. Some level of stress, or performance pressure, is to be expected. When people have the energy they need, and can recover through their rest breaks, at work and at home, this is usually a healthy situation, which we take for granted. Job strain, however, entails feelings of exhaustion and depression due to the pressure of work. In a highly cited model, Karasek (1979) placed jobs into four categories based on the relationship between job demands and the employee's level of control. 'High-strain jobs' combine high work demands with low levels of employee control, while 'passive jobs' are low in both pressure and employee control, and 'low-strain' jobs combine low pressure with high levels of employee control. The argument is that the fourth type, 'active jobs', which are demanding but offer plenty of scope for employees to apply their skills and decide their responses, are the best for learning and personal development. In a landmark analysis of Swedish and US workers, Karasek (1979: 303) concluded that 'the working individual with few opportunities to make job decisions in the face of output pressure is most subject to job strain'. The influential Whitehall II study of 10,308 civil servants found that those reporting low levels of control at work had more than twice the risk of heart disease (Bosma et al. 1997, 1998) as well as increased risk of psychiatric disorder (Stansfield et al. 1999). Originally known as the 'demand-control' model, this theory has been extended to include support, becoming the 'demand-control-support' (DCS) model (Karasek and Theorell 1990). This extension of the theory implies that higher levels of employer and/or peer support may soften the effects of stressful work environments on individuals. In other words, a high level of pressure is more tolerable when colleagues help us to cope under these demands.

The range of resources that can help individuals to cope with job demands is now more fully recognised in the job demands-resources (JDR) framework (Demerouti et al. 2001, Bakker, van Veldhoven and Xanthopoulou 2010), which has progressively built on the DCS model. The JDR framework sees participation in work as generating two processes. The 'motivational process' is stimulated by job resources, such as 'performance feedback, job control and support from colleagues', and from personal resources, which are 'aspects of the self that are associated with resiliency' (Schaufeli 2014: 26). People working in an environment with the kind of resources they seek are more 'engaged', which has become a key term when talking about employee motivation. As Schaufeli (2014: 26) puts it, 'resources foster engagement in terms of vigor (energy), dedication (persistence) and absorption (focus)'. Job demands, on the other hand, generate a 'health impairment process', which is dangerous when demands are excessive or when work pressure is unrelenting. 'When recovery is inadequate or insufficient, employees may gradually exhaust their energy backup and might eventually burn out' (Schaufeli 2014: 27). Refinements within this tradition now make the distinction between hindrance and challenge demands (LePine, LePine and Jackson 2004, Schaufeli 2014). The idea is that job demands vary in their impact: a good challenge is positive for us, drawing out our abilities and helping us to grow, while hindrances frustrate our efforts. The latter may, for example, include obstacles that management could have anticipated but has failed to deal with, such as insufficient access to information. What, however, is challenging and what is a hindrance may well vary across people, jobs, organisations and time-frames (Parker 2014).

As this discussion of the JDR model indicates, social support is often an important resource in the workplace. Jobs typically involve some level of interaction with other human beings, even if they don't involve a highly interdependent form of teamwork. It is now increasingly recognised that most employees benefit from the social dimension of work, which can be a major source of satisfaction (e.g. Parker 2014). Human needs for relatedness can be met, at least partially, by the opportunities to meet and make friends with other people at work (Deci and Ryan 2000). The impact of social interaction on our well-being may vary over the course of our lives. An interesting study on this question has been conducted by Sanders et al. (2011), using longitudinal data from the Netherlands Working Conditions Study. They examine the work ability and motivation of lower educated workers over 45 years of age, using an augmented version of Hackman and Oldham's (1980) job characteristics model. What they show is that the path to retaining more of these workers in the workforce lies not so much in enhancing their autonomy but in improving the quality of their social interactions: in the support that supervisors give them, in the support that they give each other and in the opportunities they have to interact positively with customers. Workers of this kind may consider that they have enough responsibility and value more highly the ways in which going to work enables them to meet other people and participate more fully in their community.

The intrinsic quality of work, then, depends not simply on one factor but on the way that demands and resources come together in a particular situation to create the overall impact on employee well-being. The JDR framework is a useful tool for analysing the intrinsic quality of work whenever there are concerns that a job lacks a good balance in terms of the demands on the individual and the resources they have available to them. This is a useful way of thinking about how to create long-term sustainability in working conditions, ensuring that people can enjoy their work and have a good level of work–life balance (Halbesleben, Harvey and Bolino 2009, Robertson and Cooper 2011). If managers are worried about high levels of burnout, poor safety performance or dysfunctional levels of employee absence and turnover, analysis through the JDR framework can pay dividends in identifying the contributing factors.

An interesting complication on the employee side, however, concerns those who are willingly overworking, who are so absorbed in their work that they are indifferent to its impacts on their personal life (Boxall 2013, Schaufeli 2014). 'Workaholism' of this kind is potentially a killer for the individual as well as a problem for colleagues and family members, who must somehow cope with an individual whose life is out of balance. Such individuals may have come to the point where their work *is* their well-being. Work is very important to us all but for most people this is going too far. The general conclusion must be that individual well-being depends on achieving healthy balances between demands and resources at work and between work and the rest of life.

The extrinsic quality of work

This brings us to extrinsic rewards and to the whole question of the relationship between intrinsic and extrinsic factors. Which of these sets of factors looms larger as employees weigh up job offers or think about whether to stay in an organisation? Research regularly confirms that both matter. For example, Table 5.1 lists the results from a survey of 7,000 British workers, showing the factors they rated as priorities in searching for a job (Rose 2003). The nature of the work itself is clearly very important to whether someone is motivated to do a job. This is chosen first by 27 per cent of people and adding the two columns in Table 5.1 shows that some 45 per cent of people give it as either their first or their second priority, a finding backed up by other major surveys of worker opinion (e.g. Clark 2005). However, Table 5.1 shows that intrinsic factors are not all that matters. People value job security and pay, which are rated either first or second priority by 43 and 48 per cent in this survey. This is hardly surprising. The vast majority of people need to earn money to live, which is sometimes called the 'provisioning motive' for work (Rose 2000, 2003). A primary reason for changing jobs is therefore to get higher levels of income. This is a critical factor among the low paid and among those who, for whatever reason, feel they are currently underpaid relative to their value (Griffeth, Hom and Gaertner 2000).

Extrinsic motivators should not therefore be underestimated, including what some people would now regard as old fashioned: the desire for job

Table 5.1 Job facet priorities of British workers

Job facet priorities	Chosen first (%)	Chosen second (%)
The actual work	27	18
Job security	25	18
Pay	22	26
Using initiative	10	13
Good relations with manager	8	13

Source: Based on Rose (2003).

security. But this desire is far from old fashioned. Concerns about personal insecurity were heightened by the Global Financial Crisis of 2008–9 and the sovereign debt crises that followed it (van Wanrooy et al. 2013: 36–7). Economic crisis and uncertainty have made feelings of insecurity pervasive and have made gaining, and retaining, a permanent job more important to people (e.g. Kalleberg 2011). Guy Standing (2011) talks about the rise of a new class, the 'precariat', people whose lives are dominated by insecure, irregular forms of work, which make it difficult for them to join the materially successful strata of society. Employment security is essential for taking on life's larger financial commitments, such as home ownership and child support.

The implication is this: intrinsic interest may draw a person to a job, but they are unlikely to remain with an employer if they feel seriously under-recognised in their rewards or seriously disadvantaged in their employment conditions. We must understand that intrinsic and extrinsic factors are tied together in jobs, affecting the quality or fairness of the 'effort-reward balance' as perceived by employees (e.g. Baldamus 1961, Siegrist 1996). It is therefore important to spend some time thinking about the role of rewards in aligning employee and organisational interests.

Reward strategy: issues of fairness and alignment

Most reward theory revolves around the problem of how to establish and maintain equity or fairness in the pay system, although much of the argument can be applied to other types of reward, such as rates of internal progression through promotion. There are three objectives that have traditionally been advocated in this regard (e.g. Bowey 1989, Milkovich, Newman and Gerhart 2013). The first of these is 'external equity' or 'external relativity', which is the goal of ensuring that the reward system supports the recruitment and retention of suitably qualified people in the labour market. If such people accept the firm's employment offers, and do not leave because of dissatisfaction with their rewards and recognition, the firm is achieving a fundamental level of alignment with employee interests on this criterion.

Firms that fail on this primary criterion have little chance of creating sustainable advantages because of instability in their workforce and may be fatally weakened by the problem. Concern with this fundamental goal is what generates interest in salary surveys and wage-trend data. Remuneration consultancies will typically advocate that employers pay at or near the market median. Lagging behind the market too much is obviously dangerous but how far an employer needs to go to 'meet the market' is a moot point. As Guthrie (2007: 357) explains, there are 'diminishing returns to increases in market pay position'. Firms that systematically pay near the top of the market ('upper and top quartile payers') definitely attract job candidates and do have a better chance of retaining people. However, they also run the risk of creating 'honey traps' where people can't afford to leave. This will apply just as much, if not more, to the poor performers in the workforce and aligning too much with their interests is hardly a good business outcome.

The second goal advanced by reward theorists is associated with 'internal equity'. There is a job hierarchy of some kind in every organisation and employees typically judge the fairness of the distinctions in levels of pay and associated status. The idea is that the reward system should be perceived by employees as fair in terms of rewarding with higher pay and status those jobs that involve greater demands. Job evaluation systems, such as the well-known Hay system,[6] were historically developed to foster a sense of internal equity (Rock 1984). A job evaluation or 'job-sizing' process typically looks at three (and occasionally four) dimensions of job difficulty:

1. *skill* (the extent of education and prior experience needed to do the job);
2. *effort* (the extent of cognitive complexity involved in the job);
3. *responsibility* (in classical job evaluation, this boils down to the extent of control over people and money); and
4. *working conditions* (relevant only in physically dangerous jobs and often not used at all in executive job evaluation).

Measuring, weighting and summing these factors in some appropriate way leads to a set of pay brackets into which jobs of different difficulty can be placed after a formal job analysis (for a good explanation, see Armstrong and Baron 1995 or Kilgour 2008). This then constructs a hierarchy of positions in

---

[6] http://www.haygroup.com/en/our-services/evaluate/, accessed 20/1/15.

terms of status and reward. Job evaluation systems constitute a huge part of the work carried out by remuneration consultancies. It is unusual to see them used in small firms, which rely much more on their sense of the 'going rate' or low-cost advice on a suitable pay offer. However, they are often found in large, bureaucratic firms with a plethora of managerial and specialist roles and in those public sector bureaucracies, such as the policy ministries, the police and the armed forces, where there is a difficulty in making comparisons to an external labour market.

Job evaluation can become very important in responding to questions about gender neutrality in pay. When men and women largely fall into different occupational groups in an organisation, there can be an issue around whether there is 'comparable worth' or 'equal pay for work of equal value' (e.g. Bowey 1989, Chicha 2009). A systematic approach to job evaluation can help an employer respond to this concern but the courts can look closely at whether the specific system is gender-biased. In an interesting case, Birmingham City Council, one of the largest local authorities in the UK, came seriously unstuck when it was ruled that some 5,000, mainly women, workers had been underpaid for at least ten years.[7] The council had been paying bonuses to workers in some male-dominated jobs, such as garbage collectors, but not to workers in female-dominated jobs, such as school cooks, now deemed of 'equal value'. One estimate put the cost of correcting these anomalies at £600 million.

Skilful handling of issues of internal equity in a reward system helps to reassure employees that rational standards are applied to the way their pay is compiled. However, it should be apparent at this point that the goals of external and internal equity can come into serious conflict. The external labour market is hardly ever under the control of an individual organisation, and strongly held views of an internal job hierarchy, or of fairness in relative pay, can easily be disturbed by movements in the external labour market. The need to offer remuneration packages that will retain top performers has been used by banking executives as part of their argument for extraordinary levels of pay among the banking elite. The chief executive of Barclay's went so far as to talk of a 'death spiral' for the organisation after hundreds of staff left its American investment bank.[8] Although HR practices in the banking sector are highly controversial, as we shall discuss further below, there is an important issue here, which is of general significance. It is about the fact that a firm's reward system has to operate in a labour market, in which some occupational

---

[7] http://news.bbc.co.uk/2/hi/uk_news/england/west_midlands/8647072.stm, accessed 20/1/15.
[8] See http://www.telegraph.co.uk/finance/newsbysector/banksandfinance/10676908/Barclays-We-paid-bonuses-to-avoid-death-spiral.html, accessed 20/1/15.

groups rise and others fall and in which people can leave, including migrating to other countries. This is why job evaluation experts argue that firms need to periodically relate their internal job distinctions to the external labour market (e.g. Armstrong and Baron 1995, Kilgour 2008). It is important, then, to take care that the goal of internal equity works within the fundamental priority for the business of recruiting and retaining talented employees effectively.

The third goal typically espoused by reward experts in the Anglophone world is that of 'performance equity'. As noted earlier, within any given job, some people will perform at a much higher level than others, and this variation grows as jobs become more complex. Some form of variable or performance-related pay (PRP), and a career path that recognises their growth in productivity, is therefore important to higher-performing employees, who may leave if they feel they are poorly recognised for the quality of their contribution (Trevor, Gerhart and Boudreau 1997). Some form of PRP is also common when management wants to incentivise certain kinds of behaviour and is not constrained by rules negotiated in collective bargaining. Instead of having a single 'rate-for-the-job', many organisations now have a salary range. PRP can take the form of 'merit pay' where an increase based on performance is permanently added into the pay packet, typically following an annual process of performance appraisal. Higher-performing employees are thus advanced up the salary range for their role. It can also take the form of some kind of bonus (not permanently added into the pay packet), on an individual, team or company-wide basis. These forms of PRP are not mutually exclusive. Some firms have layers of PRP, especially for their senior executives.

What kind of effects can such systems achieve? An interesting analysis in this regard is contained in a study of individual bonuses conducted by Lazear (1999), who gained access to the records of the Safelite company, a firm that installs automobile window glass, and which changed in 1994 from time-based to piece-based pay (with a minimum hourly wage guarantee). Full data was available on worker output before and after the change in the pay system. The data revealed that overall productivity increased by 44 per cent after the change to performance-related pay. Lazear was able to show that the firm benefited through high-potential workers increasing their output (an 'incentive effect'). But he was also able to show a 'sorting effect': the rate of turnover of higher performers dropped and more workers of high potential were attracted to the firm. At the same time, lower performers tended to leave in search of more secure payment regimes elsewhere. By the end of 1995, Safelite's workforce was on average much more productive than it had been when associated with time-based wages alone. The alignment of interests had become much better from a management perspective.

The study is particularly valuable because Lazear (1999) notes some of the critical contingencies where individual bonuses will work well: the work is individualised, it is observable and cooperation in teams (for which group bonuses may be more appropriate) is not important in this company's business. Based on this and other studies (O'Neill 1995, Campbell, Campbell and Chia 1998), we summarise the factors that favour individual PRP and those that favour team-based PRP in Box 5.1.

Box 5.1   Supporting conditions for performance-related pay

Good conditions for individual performance-related pay:

1. Individuals have high job control
2. There is high performance variation among individuals due to individual abilities or efforts, not primarily due to their context
3. Management can make fair individual performance attributions and will reward for them
4. High-performing individuals expect the firm to reward them, by pay and/or promotion, for their individual productivity (or will leave or reduce effort)

Good conditions for team-based performance-related pay:

1. There is a high level of interdependence among team members
2. There are only minor performance differences among team members (i.e. there is little 'social loafing' or 'free riding' in the team)
3. Management can, and will, work with the team to create a fair system of team goals (with good 'line-of-sight' from team efforts to them)
4. Management can, and will, work with the team to create good team development and ongoing support (many people will need greater training and coaching to become better team workers)
5. Performance rewards are not overly diluted by large numbers of recipients
6. High-performing team members see performance rewards as fairer at the team level than at the individual level

---

Most pay researchers validate the importance of these conditions and argue that various contingent factors will affect choices of pay systems over time (e.g. Kessler 1998, Guthrie 2007). Wood's (1996) study of pay systems in a sample of British manufacturing firms pursuing 'high-commitment management' is instructive. Many 'best-practice' models of HRM would advise such firms to adopt a serious element of variable remuneration but Wood finds that UK manufacturers pursuing higher employee commitment are circumspect about bonuses. If using any form of PRP, they are more likely to add merit pay permanently into the salary, so it is not 'at risk' from year to year. When one reflects on Wood's findings there is an intuitive logic to them. Employers may well avoid individual bonus systems if they discourage the kind of flexible attitude the firm seeks (Wood 1996: 65, 72). If wanting higher production quality, it can be safer to use the supervision process to brief employees on a regular basis and to change their focus when necessary. The advantage of time-based pay systems (either an hourly wage or an annual salary) is that they are actually more flexible in terms of managing priorities as they change. The company is not locked into a specific set of targets linked to pay and can more readily shift its goals without undermining confidence in the pay system.

It is, in fact, far from essential to manage employee behaviour through variable pay. Time-based payment in the context of instructions and feedback from a supervisor ('direct supervision') is actually a much more common method of managing employee behaviour. The major risk in PRP systems is that they will create 'perverse incentives': for example, when goals linked to pay channel the employee's actions too narrowly or towards a misguided target (Kessler and Purcell 1992). The worst fears about PRP schemes materialised in the Global Financial Crisis of 2008–9. In the banking sector, it was common practice for mortgage brokers, retail bank staff and investment bankers to receive a bonus based on selling mortgages and refinancing them through mortgage securities. This went along swimmingly for several years as property markets boomed. Unfortunately, these performance bonuses were based on short-term targets and faulty assumptions about property prices (Stiglitz 2010). Many loans were sold to people at high risk of not repaying them ('sub-prime loans') and then repackaged via investment banks to investors around the world who were ill-informed about the true risks. Tragedy struck when the property bubble burst, to the disillusionment of those who thought that property inflation would go on forever. Tragedy turned to farce when bankers profited not only from the bonus-generating financial instruments that helped to fuel the boom, but also from the government bailouts afterwards, while bank shareholders lost capital and tens of millions of people were laid off around the world (Stiglitz 2010). Excessive levels of bonus pay linked to short-term sales of risky, poorly understood financial products not only tripped up financial institutions but contributed to a wide-ranging economic disaster.

If we ever needed an example of the power of ill-conceived approaches to HRM to do more harm than good to society, this was it. The saga of the

Global Financial Crisis is a grim reminder of the way in which dysfunctional HR practices can undermine the social legitimacy of a management strategy and bring about responses from politicians and regulators. In an attack on the perversities of the bonus culture, the British Labour government instituted a 'bank payroll tax' on bonuses of more than £25,000 paid to employees between 9 December 2009 and 5 April 2010.[9] In the USA, the outrage was, if anything, greater. The Obama administration appointed a 'Pay Czar' to regulate the remuneration of top executives in US companies bailed out by public money in the crisis.[10] By early 2014, the European Parliament had developed a proposal to limit bonuses in banking to no more than the equivalent of one year's salary.[11]

The huge level of public interest in bankers' pay has continued unabated and may have prompted some re-thinking, with bankers making promises to better link their remuneration to long-term measures of a bank's performance. The sad facts of the Global Financial Crisis underline the point that the question of how to align employer–employee interests through reward strategy needs very careful handling, including healthy processes of consultation that help to identify equity concerns and perverse incentives (Bowey and Thorpe 1986, Purcell 1999). This used to mean consultation with workforce groups, such as unions and works councils, and this is still very advisable. However, the recent anger over banking pay, and over executive pay generally, has led to growing legal requirements to obtain shareholders' approval of executive pay plans, as in the UK's 'say on pay' laws, introduced in 2013.[12]

How do we sum up such a controversial area? As a general rule, it is still important that pay systems, and rewards generally, are designed to recruit and retain the kind of people the firm needs ('external equity'). This requires competitive, but not necessarily excessive, levels of pay and implies some way of fostering 'performance equity' in order to retain high achievers, including ensuring that people are promoted through the job hierarchy at a rate consistent with their growth in value to the firm. Serving 'internal equity' is important, too, because this plays an important role in building faith in rational or fair treatment throughout the firm. Care needs to be exercised, however, that overly rigid notions of internal equity do not undermine the firm's ability to recruit and retain. And there is a need for great care whenever

---

[9] http://www.guardian.co.uk/business/2009/dec/09/bank-bonus-super-tax, accessed 20/1/15.
[10] http://www.reuters.com/article/idUSN2220981520100322, accessed 20/1/15.
[11] For a review of the history, debate and responses around bank bonuses, see http://www.theguardian.com/business/2013/feb/28/bonuses-the-essential-guide, accessed 20/1/15.
[12] See, for example, http://www.irmagazine.com/articles/proxy-voting-annual-meetings/19788/uk-investors-get-binding-say-pay-votes/, accessed 20/1/15.

the goal of performance equity is expressed in schemes that incentivise particular kinds of behaviour. Such schemes work best when certain conditions are met to minimise perverse incentives. If major perversities are possible, as is the case with many bonus systems, other forms of performance management are more desirable or bonuses need to be much more carefully linked to the firm's long-run success.

Conclusions

The challenges of 'talent management' are absolutely central to HRM in all types of organisation. Organisations depend on the human capital developed by individuals, and managers in all firms are engaged in an ongoing process of constructing and renewing a workforce. There are major risks associated with under-staffing or talent shortages that can affect the firm's profitability, its reputation and its chances of remaining viable. The more successful firms in the labour market are able to offer an interesting 'employment value proposition', something that requires careful thought in firms or industries with attractiveness problems. Similarly, over-staffing or talent surpluses generate financial risks, and it is typical for managers to develop some forms of staffing flexibility to reduce the impact of these problems on performance. In addition to these difficult issues of workforce size or quantity, there are challenging questions of quality stemming from the fact that human performances are variable in any kind of workforce, no matter how well resourced the organisation is. Organisations in which there are talent blockages, talent ghettos or chronic, unaddressed problems of human performance perform less effectively as a result of these issues.

The firms that address these challenges more effectively are those in which managers are more attuned to questions of mutuality or reciprocity in employment relationships. They are more aware of the importance of interest alignment in employment relationships and more proactive in their responses to it. This involves an understanding of the intrinsic and extrinsic factors that attract individuals to jobs and to organisations. Whether a job is working well for an individual depends on whether they see it as a meaningful use of their abilities: something that appeals to their vocational interests and that enables them to utilise their skills at work. Furthermore, there is a dynamic element to this. Research points to the rise of 'expressivism' in the workforce, to the drive of many employees to find greater avenues for personal fulfilment as they develop over their working life. Where managers are concerned about improving the long-term retention of critical employees, then, attention should be given to ways of opening up scope for their personal growth. Firms that cannot provide growth opportunities are likely to lose many of their more talented workers, and the more powerful forms of 'human capital advantage' will be beyond them. In addition, the intrinsic quality of any job can be assessed by analysing the particular blend of job demands and resources that an individual, or an occupational group, is experiencing at work. This can help to identify imbalances that undermine motivation, such as insufficient control over the job or insufficient support from the line manager or colleagues. Most people, apart from workaholics, are seeking a good work–life balance to enable them to engage not only in healthy forms of work but also in caregiving or other interests in life.

In terms of extrinsic rewards, people are generally looking for a fair match between what they invest in their job and their outcomes. Those who feel underpaid relative to their contribution, or who are experiencing a high degree of insecurity, are likely to search for better alternatives. For the employer, it is important to ensure that the firm's reward strategy enables it to recruit and retain the individuals it needs ('external equity'), as well as maintains confidence in the fairness of the reward structure ('internal equity') without undermining the capacity to make good job offers as the labour market changes. As a general rule, within the Anglo-American context, employees will expect to be recognised for their productivity and the way they have grown in their work ('performance equity'). Ensuring that they are, however, takes some very careful management because reward systems always carry the potential to create 'honey traps' and perverse incentives, which are conditions in which the alignment between organisational and employee interests is poor.

6

Management power, employee voice and social legitimacy

We are concerned with underpinning principles of HRM in this part of the book and the fundamental question in this chapter is how much influence do, and should, employees have over decisions that affect them at work. What forms of employee voice prevail in organisations and why? And how should management develop HR strategy in this area? Answering the latter question is not simply a matter of management considering the economic value of different voice options because this aspect of HRM is deeply embedded in notions of social legitimacy. The voice dimension of HRM raises the question of what sort of limits should be placed on managerial power in a democratic society. The answer does not lie solely within management's control. Employees are deeply affected by how managers exercise their power and typically react to managerial approaches that threaten their interests while many governments around the world attempt to regulate managerial power in the wider interests of society. Furthermore, supranational bodies like the International Labour Organization (ILO) and the European Union (EU) have major policy agendas in the area of employee voice: the former is committed to an international baseline of employee rights, including rights to freely associate in trade unions and to negotiate with employers through collective bargaining, while the latter is fostering higher levels of employee information and consultation. Thus, the chapter must begin by discussing the contested, essentially political, nature of employee voice. It then enters into a review of contemporary trends in voice, including the growth of voluntary forms of employee involvement and the decline of trade unions in the private sector. We then review evidence on the impacts of employee voice systems, examining the way they affect the socio-political and economic outcomes of HRM.

With the backdrop of research on the impacts of employee voice, the chapter concludes with a framework enabling managers to reflect on the 'should question': what should be their underpinning styles in employee relations as they respond to the demand for voice in their organisation?

The contested nature and changing contours of employee voice

'Employee voice' is a term designed to cover all types of opportunities for employees to have a say and exert influence over the decisions that affect their interests. It covers a very diverse terrain. One way to describe the types of employee voice is to distinguish between those that are direct and those that are indirect.

Direct channels for voice can operate at individual, team and workforce levels. At the individual level, direct voice starts at recruitment when individuals have a say in their terms of employment and continues in the workplace when they exercise control over how they do their jobs, including how to choose among different methods of working and the pace at which they work. Such forms of employee control tend to be higher where individuals are more highly skilled and must make non-programmed decisions based on their accumulated knowledge (e.g. Zoghi and Mohr 2011). They are also central to management reforms of work organisation that foster higher levels of employee involvement in decision-making because low-skill, low-discretion models of working have ceased to be competitive in a particular market (Lawler 1986, Appelbaum et al. 2000). Firms adopting such systems take steps to create greater scope for employee discretion and have an incentive to recruit more carefully, to train workers more comprehensively and to pay them better. As we will explain further in Chapter 8, such 'high-involvement work systems' are seen as a way of improving the utilisation of employee skills, tapping into the latent potential of the workforce, and thus improving the company's problem-solving and adaptability. Employee voice in how to work a machine more efficiently, in how to reduce the incidence of faults or cut down waste or in how to better meet a customer's needs is central to such types of work organisation.

Employee voice may also include some say over the locations and hours of work. For example, it is now more common for employees working on a personal computer to spend at least some of their time working from home, thus cutting commuting costs, or at hours of the day that suit their caring responsibilities. These forms of accommodation to personal needs often evolve informally in the relationship between the individual and their supervisor, and they tend to grow as employees become more experienced and are trusted as someone who will not abuse the greater level of control they are granted (Green 2008).

Direct voice can also occur at higher levels, in work teams and at workforce level. Team briefing, problem-solving groups and self-managing teams are all examples of groups of workers exercising more say in decisions about the work itself and the conditions that impact on it. Giving greater control to teams of workers was at the heart of the interest in 'socio-technical work systems' (STS) that developed in Europe in the 1950s. STS models of work organisation encourage the growth of 'responsible autonomy' (Trist and Bamforth 1951, Winterton 1994) through 'minimal critical specification' of how work should be done (Cherns 1976). This kind of voice is often supported by training in interpersonal skills. At the workforce level, direct voice sits within management communication systems, which may include open meetings, notice boards, newsletters, e-mails, the firm's intranet, engagement or employee attitude surveys and social media, such as Facebook and Twitter. It is now common for workforce meetings to be held on a regular basis where senior managers address employees about future plans or about production and workforce issues (Adam, Purcell and Hall 2014: 31). These are sometimes referred to by the American term, 'Town Hall' meetings. A key question here, of course, as in team-briefing sessions, is whether employees are given the opportunity to ask questions and make comments. Managers did so in just under half of British workplaces with five or more employees in 2011 (van Wanrooy et al. 2013: 65).

These types of direct voice can be contrasted with those that rely on some kind of indirect or representative system. In this second type of voice, managers inform, consult and/or negotiate with representatives elected by employees or appointed by trade unions. Senior managers are critical to this process, including HR specialists who may manage it on behalf of the management team. The classic types of indirect voice include collective bargaining through trade unions, which leads to 'joint regulation' of employment conditions, and thus imposes some legal restrictions on management power (e.g. Flanders 1970). They also include consultation with workers through joint consultative committees (JCCs) or works councils. In Europe, many countries have laws giving works councils rights to information, consultation and some decision-making in employee relations.[1] Indirect voice is typically more formal and

---

[1] For an overview of the rights of works councils in Germany, for example, see http://www.worker-participation.eu/National-Industrial-Relations/Countries/Germany/Workplace-Representation, accessed 20/1/15.

	Voluntary	Legally enforceable
Direct	- Individual say over how, when or where to do the job - Team briefing - Self-directed teams - 'Town Hall' meetings - Engagement surveys - Social media	- Individual rights to agree their terms of employment - Individual rights to consultation during work restructuring
Indirect	- Management-instigated consultative forums	- Recognition of trade unions - Legally mandated consultation through works councils or consultative committees

Figure 6.1 Contrasts in, and examples of, employee voice

less regular, and it takes place in meeting rooms away from the point of production or delivery of service.

As this discussion implies, a second type of contrast in employee voice is whether it is voluntary or legally enforceable, as depicted in Figure 6.1. The activities of trade unions and the operation of works councils, for example, are underpinned by societal regulation. Many countries have employment statutes that uphold the requirements of the ILO, which sees union recognition and collective bargaining as fundamental worker rights, although the extent of the regulation, and the quality of its enforcement, vary enormously. In the EU, supranational regulation is more powerful than in most other parts of the world: for example, considerable attention has been given to the development of collective consultation on business changes. This includes consultation when large-scale redundancies are proposed, when mergers or acquisitions take place and when decisions are likely to lead to substantial changes in work organisation or contractual relations.

Senior managers often, but not invariably, find the management of legal rights to information, consultation and negotiation less appealing than voluntary forms of employee voice, which they can shape around the needs of the business. Such rights involve a sharing of power or, at the least, a requirement to discuss business proposals before a final decision is made. Consultation does not mean having to reach an agreement, as is the case with collective bargaining with trade unions, but it does imply entering into a meaningful dialogue with employee representatives, even if the final decision is for management to take. This makes the management process more time-consuming and makes senior managers more widely accountable, not simply to their shareholders but to the workforce and to the society in which they are operating. It is thus not possible to look at questions of employee voice solely through an economic lens. Rather, issues of social legitimacy are involved, and these can clash with managerial power, as we explained in Chapter 1. Few nation states leave this area to employers to resolve themselves, unfettered by legislation. The issue for the state to determine is how much restriction should be placed on the 'right to manage'. If modern democracies are based upon political citizenship, how far should there also be a concept of industrial or employment citizenship? If the exercise of arbitrary power by those in authority in government is constrained by laws giving rights to citizens, and enforced by the judiciary, how far should equivalent rights be applied in the world of paid employment and how far can they be enforced in workplaces?

Ultimately, the justification for employee voice is as an end in itself in a society committed to democratic values and in a world order, or international trading environment, in which the ILO and various governments have an interest in baseline labour standards (Hughes 2002, Haworth and Hughes 2003). As such, it is always contentious and subject to reinterpretation as different generations of power-holders in enterprises and the wider world of politics debate the ethics of employment relations and reform the law to reflect their values. Social democratic governments, which often have historical links to the trade union movement, typically see it as their role to nurture the opportunities for worker representation. Conservative governments tend to opt for a position which believes it is up to managements to evolve their own voice arrangements voluntarily with workers. Sometimes they will seek to roll back trade union rights, although doing so can backfire at the ballot box because the majority of electors in any society are workers.

It has often been noted that the fashion for employee voice tends to come in waves or what Ramsay (1977) called 'cycles of control', a point also noted by Fox (1974) in his influential analysis of management styles in industrial relations. The pressure to adopt more participative styles of management is greatest during periods of strong economic growth, when people have good job opportunities, and management raises wages, improves working conditions and enhances channels for worker voice in order to recruit, motivate and retain. If trade unions are well organised in such upswings, managers will tend to introduce various forms of voice that share greater control with workers in order to hold the enterprise together. This need to accommodate labour power tends to recede during economic downturns when jobs are scarce and the voice of organised labour is more muted. We think it useful to recognise that a 'demand for voice' is always present among employees in organisations

(Boxall, Freeman and Haynes 2007), but it is evident that the degree of pressure that workers can bring to bear in their employment relationships tends to vary across different economic and political contexts.

What are the trends in employee voice?

What, then, are the major trends in employee voice? The most commonly noted shift in voice practices is the declining significance of employee representation through trade unionism, something that is most apparent in Anglophone, liberal-market economies as opposed to more coordinated economies, such as the Nordic countries, with stronger traditions of representative voice, although even here union membership is falling. For example, it fell in Sweden from 81 per cent in 1999 to 67 per cent in 2012.[2] In a comparative study of the Anglo-American world, Boxall, Freeman and Haynes (2007: 207) note that 'outside the public sector, unions are no longer the "default" option for worker voice in any (Anglophone) country'. In the UK, only around 10 per cent of workplaces with five or more employees in the private sector now recognise a trade union for collective bargaining compared with 90 per cent of public sector establishments (van Wanrooy et al. 2013: 59). While a substantial minority of workers feels vulnerable and seeks much better access to union representation, it is fair to say that most private sector workers in the Anglo-American world are now relatively indifferent to what unions offer, preferring direct over union forms of voice (Boxall, Freeman and Haynes 2007: 211–15). Direct dealing with management over training and career issues and a philosophy of self-reliance in the labour market have grown.

A difficult management problem, then, is how far to support a recognised union when its membership is falling. In the UK, one option managers take is to create dual channels of voice: they instigate a collective consultation body for all employees while preserving collective bargaining on pay and conditions with the union. An alternative is to persuade the union to join a hybrid consultative forum and work alongside non-union representatives, although some union leaders object to this (Hall and Purcell 2012). Such dual and hybrid channels of voice have become more common over the last 20 years than union-only voice regimes (Willman, Bryson and Gomez 2007: 1321). It seems that British unionised employers have developed a model of employee voice that widens the engagement with employees, both in the sense of opening voice opportunities up to a greater range of employees and in the sense

---

[2] According to OECD statistics: http://stats.oecd.org/Index.aspx?DataSetCode=UN_DEN, accessed 20/1/15.

of expanding what is discussed. Dual voice systems may be enabling them to handle distributive or conflictual issues through the union channel while handling integrative or cooperative issues more effectively through the more broadly based consultative channel. This may explain why productivity outcomes are better in dual voice systems than in union-only regimes (Charlwood and Terry 2007, Purcell and Georgiadis 2007).

More dramatically, management may decide to de-recognise the union, but this step is rarely taken. An option that does not undermine the union's legitimacy is to seek a new form of working relationship based on 'partnership'. This is where discussion focuses on possible mutual gains and exploration of a much wider range of topics, including business strategies that affect the workforce. The notion of 'partnership' is now widely accepted among industrial relations practitioners in Britain and Ireland (e.g. Haynes and Allen 2000, Martínez Lucio and Stuart 2004, Samuel and Bacon 2010). As a rhetoric, it is very powerful, implying a markedly new role for trade unions, both with employers and with union members. In its idealised form, it is

> a qualitatively different form of indirect participation or employee representation.... and offers each of the parties significant gains: employers are able to secure a greater degree of job flexibility and stronger commitment of employees and union representatives to organisational goals; trade unions are offered a more cooperative form of involvement in enterprise-level employment regulation; and employees are promised greater employment security and the opportunity to participate in new forms of consultation (Tailby and Winchester 2000: 365).

One of the reasons for a shift to a partnership style of industrial relations is that the traditional union roles of job protection through restrictive work rules and gaining above-average pay rises through collective bargaining have been eroded by intense international competition (Brown 2009). Higher labour costs, unless these can be passed on to the customer, make it more attractive to move work overseas or to invest in labour-saving technologies and work methods that increase productivity. In effect, with the collapse of unions' traditional roles in many, but not all industries, they are left with a difficult choice of either being marginalised and continuing to lose members, or seeking new forms of relationship based on cooperation and joint problem-solving (Evans, Harvey and Turnbull 2012). This presupposes that management is willing to accept a joint philosophy and work to make it meaningful. It is management's response that is critical here because it is extremely difficult for unions to insist on a high level of cooperation or a climate of partnership (Boxall and Haynes 1997).

As union density in the private sector has fallen, trade unionism in the Anglo-American world has become increasingly dominated by the public sector unions. The public sector is characterised by tensions over wage levels and work pressures and an ongoing clash between professional work cultures, on the one hand, and managerial ideologies and bureaucracy, on the other (Bach and Kessler 2012). Budget constraints have been applied while client demands, as in public education and health, have risen, fuelling employee discontent. This discontent has been readily organised by public sector unions which have the advantage of operating on much larger worksites and in much larger organisations than is true, on average, in the private sector.

Has the realm of employee voice receded with the decline of trade unionism? Has management decided that voice can be dispensed with as an area of HR practice? The answer is clearly 'no'. As Willman, Bryson and Gomez (2007: 1321) put it, the decline of trade unionism does not mean that employers have lost 'their appetite' for employee voice. The key change is in the *how* of employee voice: direct, voluntary types of employee voice (the upper-left box in Figure 6.1) have grown since the 1980s. In the UK, the most recent analysis of the Workplace Employment Relations Survey (WERS 2011) shows that 80 per cent of workplaces with five or more employees hold workforce meetings and two-thirds have team briefings (van Wanrooy et al. 2013: 64). Looking at workplaces with 20 or more employees, 95 per cent have one or other, or both, of these types of communication system. Half regularly use e-mail to communicate with employees and 38 per cent have an employee survey, a form of employee voice that grew in popularity through the 2000s (van Wanrooy et al. 2013: 65). Social media, including discussion among staff through such networks as Facebook, Twitter and Yammer, is also gaining in penetration, something that may offer a fundamentally new style of employee voice because it can quickly connect physically remote managers, as well as other employees, with what people are saying about management initiatives (CIPD 2014). Its potential cuts both ways: it can be used to organise protest but it also offers management a way of responding to employee concerns. The pattern of increasing use of these direct forms of employee involvement is repeated both in other Anglophone countries (Boxall, Freeman and Haynes 2007) and in continental Europe (Poutsma, Ligthart and Veersma 2006).

The more formalised expressions of employee voice are, of course, more common in large enterprises (e.g. van Wanrooy et al. 2013: 66). Does this mean that small firms are some kind of realm where workers have very little influence because managers go about their work with a high degree of autocracy? The empirical data does not generally suggest this. There is autocratic behaviour in some small firms, but worker satisfaction with their influence on the job and with the quality of communication is typically higher in them (Forth, Bewley and Bryson 2006, Macky and Boxall 2007). In small firms, there is likely to be much more face-to-face contact between management and workers, something that fades rapidly when the workplace gets above 40 to 50 employees. Even in financially vulnerable firms operating in highly competitive markets, critical workers, such as chefs in small restaurants, have some bargaining power. This means that the employer often takes their voice into account and makes concessions to accommodate their interests (Edwards and Ram 2006).

To be sure, less critical workers are less likely to get management consideration but the problem with larger firms is that they tend to be more impersonal and more bureaucratic. The social and power distance between top decision-makers and the workforce is much greater and individual voices are more muted. Formal schemes for employee voice can therefore be imagined as antidotes to these tendencies, but it must be doubted how successful they are unless managers at various levels give them support and bring them to life. A key variant in formal voice is always in the extent to which it is 'embedded': applied extensively across the workforce of a large organisation and regularly practised (Cox, Zagelmeyer and Marchington 2006).

What, then, do we know about trends in indirect or representative schemes, such as works councils and consultative committees? In most of continental Europe, the legal requirement for works councils ensures that they are widespread. In the UK, these are unusual in small firms, but 63 per cent of workplaces with 100–199 workers have JCCs, either at the workplace itself or through access to one at a higher corporate level (Adam, Purcell and Hall 2014: 14). This figure rises to 74 per cent in workplaces with between 200 and 999 workers and 80 per cent in workplaces with 1,000 or more employees. In 2008, the Information and Consultation of Employees Regulations came fully into force in the UK following the enactment of this legislation in the EU. There is some evidence that this may have stimulated a growth in JCCs at the workplace, especially where there are between 150 and 249 employees (Adam, Purcell and Hall 2014: 18), but overall in workplaces with five or more employees there has been no growth in JCCs. The proportion of employees in workplaces with a JCC was 38 per cent in 2004 and 37 per cent in 2011 (van Wanrooy et al. 2013: 62). The regulations are generally regarded as weak, or 'half-hearted', and enforcement is difficult so the predicted rapid growth in consultation through JCCs did not happen (Hall and Purcell 2012: 88–113).

There is another trend hidden by these summary figures relating to JCCs operating at a level above the workplace in multi-plant or multi-site organisations. Here there has been a marked decline in JCCs, falling from half in 2004 to just over a third in 2011 (Adam, Purcell and Hall 2014: 18). What this means is that it is increasingly unlikely that senior managers in large, highly dispersed companies will meet employee representatives to discuss strategy and hold a dialogue on the plans and prospects of the company. This decline was most marked in the biggest companies with 10,000 or more employees where the fall was from 68 per cent in 2004 to 44 per cent in 2011 (ibid.). In this context, it is not surprising that surveys consistently show that there is a low level of trust of senior managers (Purcell 2014a). They are increasingly 'out of the loop', not wishing to get involved with what are deemed to be workplace employment relations matters, although social media may help them to get a feel for what people are thinking (CIPD 2014). We pick up the implications of this in Chapter 10.

What these statistics cannot tell is what is actually meant by consultation or voice in practice. This is particularly important in the handling of change. In the UK, some 80 per cent of workplace managers currently agree or strongly agree that they would not introduce changes 'without first discussing the implications with employees', an increase from 72 per cent in 2004 (van Wanrooy et al. 2013: 56). Managers, it seems, are in tune with the need to discuss changes with the workforce. Much of this type of consultation is face-to-face via workforce meetings and team briefing, but it is interesting to note that those managers who first discuss changes with employees are also much more likely to have a JCC (Adam, Purcell and Hall 2014: 37). Direct and indirect forms of voice often go together. The authors of the WERS analysis find some interesting twists to the managers' views on consultation in change. Regression analysis, which controls for factors that can influence attitudes like sector and workplace size, shows that 'female managers were seven percentage points more likely than male managers to agree that changes would only be introduced after discussing the implications with employees' (van Wanrooy et al. 2013: 56). Agreement was also more common among longer-serving managers and was 8 per cent more likely in organisations with a formal strategic plan in which job satisfaction was considered.

It is well known that if management wish to render formal consultation in JCCs an empty process they can easily do so with the agenda of JCCs being restricted to 'tea and toilets'. Meaningful consultation, which the UK's Involvement and Participation Association calls 'option-based consultation', requires employee representatives to have a right to express their views on issues before final decisions are taken.[3] To be effective, they need a lot of information from within and outside the company, time to draw up proposals, an opportunity to present them and time for the proposals to be treated seriously

---

[3] http://www.ipa-involve.com/information-consultation/option-based-consultation/, accessed 20/1/15.

by management. Managers who had a JCC in their workplace were asked, in WERS 2011, how they approached consultation (van Wanrooy et al. 2013: 62–3). They were asked if they discussed issues at the meeting, meaning before options for change had been formulated, or took a range of options for review at the meeting. The third option was just to consider one preferred option, meaning that management had already decided what action to take. The first two approaches meet the requirement for option-based consultation. Some 80 per cent of managers said this was their approach, while 20 per cent said that they only discussed their preferred option, meaning that consultation was very restricted. When asked the same question, 8 per cent of the employee representatives on JCCs said that managers took this restricted approach in 2004 but 7 years later this had jumped to 28 per cent, a higher proportion than managers reported. A large number of both managers and employees reported that their JCC was very influential when it engaged in option-based consultation (Adam, Purcell and Hall 2014: 37). In contrast, managers using restrictive, single-option consultation were much more likely to consider their JCC had little or no influence at all. It would seem that some managers are scaling back on their support for consultation, while many others have no JCCs or any involvement with trade unions. The preference is for direct communication with employees. The 2009 European Company Survey found that across the whole of the EU, despite extensive legal provisions for collective consultation, 60 per cent agreed that 'we would prefer to consult directly with our employees'. In the UK, this rose to 72 per cent (Purcell and Hall 2012: 4).

A common format for consultative committees is a meeting two to four times a year, lasting from two hours to a whole day. Such meetings can be quite challenging for managers, even though they usually meet in a spirit of cooperation, not conflict (van Wanrooy et al. 2013: 62). This is because 'the root of employee voice lies in influence being shared among individuals who are hierarchically unequal. In essence, it relates to employees' ability to influence the outcome of organisational decisions by having the opportunity to advance their ideas and have them considered' (Farndale et al. 2011: 114). This fits with the legal definition of consultation being 'a right for employees to be informed of planned measures in advance and to have an opportunity to express an opinion prior to implementation' (Budd and Zagelmeyer 2010: 492). This does not happen that often, at least in the Anglo-American world, and many managers dislike having to do it. Hall and Purcell (2012) studied 26 consultative committees over a two-year period. Two of the JCCs collapsed after a short period. It has often been observed that JCCs come and go and may have a short life if meaningful consultation fails to take root. A minority of their case study companies had developed healthy systems of 'active consultation'. This is where senior managers are prepared to discuss strategic issues and decisions; there is a wide agenda put forward by both parties; senior managers attend the meetings; there is a close relationship with direct involvement via team briefings and workplace communications; the employee representatives are well organised and given appropriate facilities; and, above all, there is mutual trust. Things go much better when both management and employee representatives support the consultative process. In one company studied, Mobile Phone, although the JCC was introduced to keep unions out, as often happens, over the five years of operation it had developed into a highly effective body with senior managers taking issues for debate and claiming that the quality of change introduced, including some difficult decisions to cope with a volatile industry, had improved significantly (Hall and Purcell 2012: 139–41). The experience of active consultation can lead managers to change their views and give greater support.

The other type of consultative committee was found in organisations that did not discuss policy or decisions about change with the employee representatives but rather saw the role as exclusively a matter of communication. These 'communicators' made up the largest proportion of Hall and Purcell's (2012) case study companies. One conclusion to draw from this UK experience is that the law may be a catalyst encouraging the adoption of good practice, but it is never sufficient.

The picture in the Anglo-American world, then, is that management's preference is to foster direct and voluntary forms of employee voice, such as workforce meetings and team briefing. In the larger organisations, more formal methods of direct voice, such as employee surveys are important, as are indirect forms of employee voice, such as JCCs. These are typically used to enhance the quality of communication and cooperation with the workforce and have a greater universality about them by covering all employees. They can operate either alongside or instead of trade unions. Where unions are strong, collective bargaining retains its role but it is much more prevalent in the public than in the private sector. And, across all these types of practice, the quality of employee voice is extremely variable.

What are the impacts of employee voice systems?

What, then, are the impacts of employee voice systems? Who benefits and how? In thinking about this question, we must take care to consider the full range of goals in HRM, as described in Chapter 1. Voice practices impact on both the economic and the socio-political goals of management, and it pays to start with the latter in this case. When societies have laws requiring certain forms of employee voice, such as union recognition, the primary justification for employee voice is that society requires it, not that it will make the firm more profitable. In terms of outcomes, willing compliance with the law on employee rights will make the firm a more legitimate member of the society in which it operates. This will typically enhance its reputation beyond the circle of its shareholders or, at the least, help to shield it from public criticism. This is particularly true of larger organisations, which are more visible in society and which have workforces that are more easily organised by trade unions. Firms whose managers comply with the law of employment are taking an important step towards demonstrating that they are responsible corporate citizens. At the transnational level, those who make it clear that they are working positively with the international regulation of worker rights enhance their global citizenship. This message also transmits within the organisation, and it can enhance the 'social order' in the workplace, the sense that those in authority are handling their power in a responsible fashion and that there are certain norms of behaviour that we all recognise. An open acknowledgement of the value of listening and responding to employee interests can help to stabilise management power inside the workplace, showing that management is not insecure and recognises the legitimate interests of its workforce. In the oft-quoted words of the industrial relations theorist Allan Flanders (1970: 172), management 'can only regain control by sharing it'.

But voice practices cover a large terrain, much greater than the minimum legal requirements, and there is huge variety in the level of sincerity and perseverance that managers bring to them. This makes a big difference in how much employees benefit. There is plenty of evidence, for example, that voice arrangements can be no more than 'bolt-ons' that become an additional burden on managers who fail to provide the necessary support to make them effective (Marchington 1989, 1995, Danford et al. 2009). This is particularly clear in the chequered history of problem-solving groups like quality circles (Collard and Dale 1989, Hill 1991). Here, developing and encouraging employee voice in problem-solving can be a fashionable fad, or worse, a sop, with little expected or experienced from its introduction. Not surprisingly, voice systems that are disconnected from organisational decision-making, and are irritants to line managers, have a short life. However, when linked to more sincere and sustained changes in management style, they can have very positive impacts on employees. We know that employees who perceive that they have greater authority in decision-making, and who hold more positive perceptions of the quality of two-way communication with their manager, report higher levels of job satisfaction (e.g. Boxall and Macky 2014).

Millward, Bryson and Forth (2000: 130) show how positive employee attitudes are strongly associated with the existence of arrangements for individual involvement. One link is with perceptions of fairness or justice, one of the bedrocks of social legitimacy. It has often been observed that people will rate a management action as fair as long as they have had a voice in it 'even if they knew that what they said had little or no influence on the decisions made ... voice has a value beyond its ability to shape decision-making processes and outcomes' (Tyler and Blader 2003: 351). Employees form perceptions about the justice of major changes, such as who is selected for redundancy or who is chosen to receive an important promotion ('distributive justice'); how fair the processes are for making these decisions ('procedural justice'); and how individuals feel they are personally treated ('interactional justice') (e.g. Folger and Cropanzano 1998, Saunders and Thornhill 2003). Employees who have positive experiences of these forms of justice are much more likely to believe that the organisation's management supports them. 'Perceived organisational support' (POS) is strongly linked to employee voice and is an important predictor of employee engagement (Saks 2006).

The crucial variable for employees is *how*, and *to what extent*, line managers support and activate their involvement as an ongoing process. Research that asks if a practice exists, or even what proportion of the workforce is covered by a practice, is not particularly helpful because structure does not equate with process (Purcell 1999). In the area of voice arrangements, the supporting organisational climate, especially the level of trust, is crucial in providing the seedbed for effective participation to germinate (Ichniowski, Shaw and Prennushi 1997). Purcell and Georgiadis (2007) show that well-embedded, direct and indirect voice systems are strongly associated with higher levels of organisational commitment, job satisfaction and the amount of discretion workers have in their job. This makes a lot of sense since direct and indirect involvement can play different roles. While a consultative committee can provide employee participation with senior management on strategic issues, individual involvement with the line manager can have a more immediate influence on everyday working life (Delbridge and Whitfield 2001).

It is more difficult to find hard evidence on the economic outcomes of voice systems, those that enhance profit performance in the short run or improve an organisation's long-run agility. We do, however, have some important clues. Kessler and Purcell (1996) in a study of joint working parties, where managers and employee representatives jointly deal with workplace problems, found that trust between them increased markedly. This was especially the case where employee representatives, and the employees themselves, were actively involved in all stages of a change process, overseen by a joint working party. Where this happened well, over half of the managers considered that their organisation had benefited a lot from this form of involvement. The 2010 European Company Survey found that firms where managers and employee representatives made 'sincere efforts to solve common problems' had higher than average productivity and experienced increases in it. These firms had, unsurprisingly, a good work climate (Purcell and Hall 2012: 3). Research by Sako (1998), on the impact of employee voice in the European car components industry, is particularly interesting. She showed how the combination of individual involvement and collective consultation had the strongest effect in this industry. Thus, rather than these two forms of voice being alternatives, it was the combination of the two that enhanced performance. The outcomes of combined types of voice arrangements were also clear in a large-scale European survey of participation in the mid-1990s. The greater the types of voice used, the more likely it was that managers reported benefits: from declining absenteeism through to increased output (Sisson 2000). This is confirmed by analysis of the link between employee engagement and economic outcomes (Rayton, Dodge and D'Analeze 2012).

These findings are repeated when the question of worker needs or problems is assessed. Here researchers ask what needs employees have and whether they are resolved. Bryson and Freeman (2007) show that a combination of collective consultation and open-door policies, where employees can raise issues with managers, reduces the number of problems reported by British employees. The combination of open-door policies, meetings with the workforce, problem-solving groups and collective consultation seems particularly effective. Interestingly, these authors find that the mere existence of an HR department has no effect in reducing worker needs or problems. It is those HR departments that foster effective systems of employee voice that add greater value.

Surveys of employee perceptions of management responsiveness are similarly revealing. In these, the focus is on the extent to which managers seek the views of employees, respond to suggestions, share information and treat employees fairly. Both Purcell and Georgiades (2007) and Bryson, Charlwood and Forth (2006) find that the experience of individual involvement is closely associated with positive worker evaluations of management responsiveness. Bryson, Charlwood and Forth (2006: 448–9) go on to relate responsiveness to productivity, showing that firms reporting much higher labour productivity than their competitors are more likely to have employees who say that their managers are responsive to their voice. WERS 2011 asked employees about their satisfaction with the level of involvement in decision-making (van Wanrooy et al. 2013: 74). Of those who reported that were satisfied with their involvement in decision-making, 87 per cent said they were proud to work for their organisation, which is one of the classic tests of organisational commitment. In contrast, of those who were dissatisfied with their involvement, only 38 per cent expressed pride in their organisation.[4] If management is worried about losing key people, these differences in commitment are not trivial.

One of the major justifications for the development of voice regimes is that they can contribute to the successful management of change. The facilitation of change is sometimes strategically more important than a fixation with current financial outcomes (Purcell 1999). In Chapter 1, we referred to the achievement of organisational flexibility as one of the key goals of employers. Employee involvement is often critical in the pursuit of flexibility or responsiveness to change. We see this at various levels in the organisational hierarchy. Giangreco and Peccei (2005: 1825) looked at middle managers and their responsiveness to change, reminding us that managers are employees too. They concluded that 'the more deeply involved … middle managers were in the various aspects of the development and implementation of the change programme [in the Italian firm they studied], the more positive they were about the change and the lower the level of resistance to change that they exhibited'.

Overall, employee voice has a number of critical impacts, and we affirm here one of the key themes of this book: HR strategy serves multiple 'bottom lines'. Employee voice institutions are important for reasons of social legitimacy, both inside the organisation and in wider society. They help to ensure that companies respect employment laws and important social norms, and they help to enhance the legitimacy of management within the organisation. This, ultimately, is their justification. But well-implemented voice practices can also have economic value, both in the short run through reducing problems in a workplace and, in the long run, through helping to build trust and facilitate the management of change. A climate in which trust levels are high may, in fact, help to lay a basis for more advanced forms of cooperation and higher levels of innovation, which can lead to competitive advantage.

These are important arguments but we must also note that voice, like much else in HRM, is unlikely to be evenly distributed in or across organisations (Kaufman and Miller 2011). The more central individuals are to an organisation's mission, the more they are likely to be listened to by senior managers. When managers make higher investments in an individual through greater

---

[4] The 2011 *Workplace Employment Relations Survey* First Findings, p. 19, https://www. gov.uk/government/uploads/system/uploads/attachment_data/file/336651/bis-14-1008-WERS-first-findings-report-fourth-edition-july-2014.pdf, accessed 20/1/15.

pay and career development, they are more likely to want to take account of that individual's views so as not to waste their investment. Similarly, when they have decided to compete through higher employee involvement in decision-making, voice practices become important in reaping the benefit of the recruitment, pay and training investments that this will involve. Managers making a much lower investment in a group of workers, or operating in a market where skills are easily replaced or outsourced, are not likely to be easily persuaded that there is a 'business case' for employee voice, especially in its more time-consuming and politically challenging forms. In these contexts, voice practices are likely to remain fairly basic and reflect the beliefs of particular managers as they come and go.

Management style in employee relations

As our review of trends in employee voice indicates, union influence has receded in the Anglophone world, and management now has a greater impact on the shape of voice regimes inside organisations, choosing what type of involvement to pursue with individuals and how to respond to societal regulations on collective consultation and negotiation. How do, and should, managers think these issues through? What sort of management style does the company want with its employees? Management style can be defined as 'a distinctive set of guiding principles, written or otherwise, which set parameters to, and signposts for, management action regarding the way employees are treated and how particular events are handled' (Purcell and Ahlstrand 1994: 177).

It is top management who make the critical choices on what sort of relationships they want with employees through trade unions and/or employee representatives in joint consultation. That is, strategic choices in higher-level voice arrangements, while to a greater or lesser extent constrained by legislation, employee expectations and societal beliefs on legitimacy, need to be taken by senior management. Do they wish to avoid, live with or embrace forms of partnership with employee representatives? Relationships with unions and non-union or hybrid collective bodies range along a continuum from avoidance to high levels of cooperation (Boxall and Haynes 1997). Some, often American firms, seek to avoid all forms of collective representation. Others have to come to terms with a union because it has gained recognition and has a significant membership in the firm, and their responses to it are visible in wider society. Yet others may reluctantly accept the collective consultation imposed by law but choose to do so with a minimal level of interaction: a 'hands-off' approach.

Another group is more positive, seeking collaborative relationships with employee representatives, providing strategic information, discussing major proposals for workforce change and valuing employee opinion.

The bargaining stance that will be taken in collective negotiations or the atmosphere that will be fostered in joint consultation does heavily reflect what senior managers, particularly the board and the top team, want to achieve. Further down the hierarchy, however, management style is less amenable to central control. It cannot be assumed that what top management seeks, or seeks to avoid, will necessarily be enacted by middle and front-line managers. Such managers need to get things done with people who are generally in close proximity, and it is up to them to set the tone in the 'leader-member exchange' (Uhl-Bien, Graen, and Scandura 2000). In crude terms, their behaviour can range from a 'command-and-control' style to one favouring high levels of employee commitment. It is here that the extent of individual involvement comes into play. We have noted that this is more likely to be extensive where workers are highly skilled and where managers see their cooperation as critical to the achievement of more demanding operating objectives, such as higher goals for quality, innovation and responsiveness to customers. Here, higher levels of involvement are more likely to be found and managers are likely to work hard to retain their best workers. In contrast, where labour is easily recruited, where investment in terms of training and development is low or where work is repetitive or easily outsourced, a command-and-control style of managing individual workers may come to predominate, including violations of employee rights (e.g. Theodore et al. 2012).

Figure 6.2 shows the main options. Choices in such countries as the Netherlands or Sweden, with long traditions of collective worker representation, may well be different from those taken by the same type of firm in the USA or the UK. While Figure 6.2 stylistically describes six distinctive management styles, in practice each of the axes is a continuum, and all styles are the outcome of the complex interplay of tensions and choices between conflicting demands.

Organisations operating with an avoidance strategy, seeking to prevent trade unionism and trivialise voice systems, do so either by forceful opposition (Box 1) or by competition in the sense of preferring to provide competitive conditions of employment and extensive use of direct voice arrangements (Box 2). The former, described by Guest (1995) as 'black hole' firms, have neither high-commitment policies in their relationship with their employees nor any positive industrial relations policies of working with trade unions. These firms will tend to utilise low-skill employees and minimise investment in people, as seen in low pay, little training and little job discretion. Box 2 firms, like management consultancy organisations or software houses, place

Relationship with employees	Avoidance	Adversarial	Cooperative
Commitment-Involvement	Individual-based, high-commitment management Extensive direct voice systems Box 2	Emphasis on high-commitment management and direct voice Hands-off relationship with representatives Low trust of external unions Box 4	High-commitment management Partnership with unions and/or non-union representatives Extensive direct and indirect voice systems High trust Box 6
Command-Control	Low trust No voice Box 1	Low trust Restricted voice Conflict Box 3	Emasculated representatives No real voice 'Sweetheart unionism' Box 5

Relationship with trade unions and elected works councils/JCCs

Figure 6.2   Voice systems and management style

emphasis on human capital and knowledge management, seeking to get the best out of their core employees and emphasising policies that encourage high performance and retention of the best. They avoid any form of collective representation but emphasise individual involvement through e-mail, intranet, social media, employee surveys and management meetings.

Boxes 3 and 4 include companies caught in adversarial, hands-off relationships with trade unions. Traditional patterns of conflict, and autocratic control systems, are found in Box 3. These still exist in some manufacturing companies (especially in developing countries), in parts of the public sector and in parts of the service economy like routine, short-transaction call centres. While formal methods of consultation may exist at corporate and workplace levels, they are generally seen to be ineffective, being marked by distrust and posturing and come to be relegated as 'communication only' bodies.

Box 4 organisations are usually in transition. While formal relationships with trade unions or works councils are marked with distrust and a failure by each party to communicate effectively with the other, direct forms of voice are used, often to bypass and undermine the unions while work organisation places emphasis on high levels of individual involvement. It is here that non-union collective consultation bodies may be created as a union substitution device in the hope that union membership will fade away.

Box 5 is where work organisation is traditionally 'command and control' and where relationships with unions or works councils exist more for show than for substance. They do not function as robust participation channels, but employee leaders enjoy personal favours and benefits from management. This is sometimes called 'sweetheart unionism' and can occur where the union representatives are more concerned with their own pay and careers than with fighting for their members' interests. While examples are rare, they are sometimes found where company unions or staff associations exist, in part to keep out external unions. In Box 6 firms, in contrast, there are strong voice arrangements, combining both direct and indirect arrangements. It is likely that a variety of schemes operates in tandem, embedded in a bundle of HR practices that encourage high involvement and employee well-being. These forms of involvement are supported by structures involving union and/or non-union representatives.

A key question that a framework like this raises is how management can shift its style. Management styles, like the organisational culture of which they are a part, evolve over time but, once established, become difficult to change. It is hard to eradicate embedded assumptions and values held by key groups (e.g. Martin 1992, Batt 2004). These assumptions and mental maps set the parameters for 'how we do things here'. Studies in supermarkets by Rosenthal, Hill and Peccei (1997) and Ogbonna and Harris (1998), for example, show the difficulties that planned cultural change programmes can run into. The assumption that senior management has the power to easily change perceptions of the managerial culture is severely challenged in such studies. Where the prevailing climate is one of low trust, managers will need to build up a track record of fair, trustworthy and consistent leadership. This will take time, determination and a lot of goodwill in the face of cynicism and suspicion. Turnover, or removal, of key managers who are advocates of a more trusting climate can set things back very quickly. As Chapter 4 explained, achieving a high-trust culture is not an easy feat and is something that may help to underpin competitive advantage.

Conclusions

A critical choice at the heart of HR strategy in any firm concerns the extent to which employees are offered a voice in job, workplace and company-level decisions. The climate for employee voice is influenced both by senior management's values and by how line managers behave in their work teams. Voice practices may include direct forms of individual or group involvement or indirect consultation and negotiation through employee representatives or some combination of both. The more central employees are to competitive success, and the more heavily firms are investing in them, the more likely methods to encourage their voice will be developed. On the other hand, where employees are less critical to competitive success, which may hinge more on financial and outsourcing strategies, voice activities may be minimal.

However, a key principle we have emphasised in this chapter is that it is important not to imagine that choices in voice arrangements are solely about the economic performance of firms. The interests of employees, and the values of the society of which they are part, make a critical impact. Much of the activity we observe in employee voice exists because such practices play an ethically important role in democratic societies *irrespective* of economic outcomes. They are there for reasons of social legitimacy, both inside the organisation and in terms of its wider relations in society. To be really effective, however, societal regulation of employee voice needs to have a catalytic effect on beliefs, especially on managers who are required to share power and to be accountable to their subordinates, as in representative voice systems. The politics surrounding social legitimacy in employee voice varies from one generation to another and from one society to another. The move to market individualism or neo-liberalism in the last two decades of the previous century, especially in Anglo-American societies, has challenged traditional notions of legitimacy, especially in regard to the role of trade unions. On the other hand, in Europe, the EU has increasingly emphasised the rights of employees, including the right to a voice in the affairs of the company for which they work.

The development of voice systems giving employees access to, and involvement in, management decisions is dependent, then, on strategic choices at organisational, national and supranational levels. Historically, many employers have opposed new regulation constraining their prerogatives, yet adapted to it as a political expedient (Hall and Purcell 2012: 6–20). Taken in isolation, and grudgingly accommodated, voice systems may have little impact, or can become a focus for negative adversarial relationships between management and labour, or can destroy employee engagement and commitment. Seen as an important ingredient in high-involvement models of work organisation, or in its own right, employee voice can positively influence the way people are managed and impact on their sense of commitment. There is evidence in various countries of a growth in voice practices, partly stimulated by managerial awareness that higher levels of employee engagement are necessary for higher levels of quality, innovation and customer satisfaction. Management is not giving up on employee voice but is expressing a strong preference for direct and voluntary forms of it.

In terms of HRM, a lot is at stake here, which is why this domain merits its own chapter. Questions of employee voice are ethical choices confronting organisational leaders in the way they, personally, engage in communication and dialogue with their staff and encourage their managers to do the same. This has profound implications for every other aspect of HR policy. There are many ways in which voice practices can be approached, as we have reviewed, but let us finish by emphasising the principle that underpins them all. Trust is the critical underlying variable, and it is this, or rather the lack of it, which limits the effectiveness of systems of worker voice. This principle is relevant in any size of organisation: it is not so much the particular voice practices that matter but the level of managerial sincerity and degree of responsiveness that comes through them, which then pays a dividend in terms of the level of trust in the organisation. If there is an owner-manager or CEO with a strong belief in valuing employees, who walks this talk, healthy trust levels are easier to achieve in a small organisation. Higher trust levels are much harder to achieve in larger, more layered organisations in which there is greater managerial turnover, greater variability in management attitudes and greater potential for slippage between management intentions and management actions. For such organisations seeking to compete through a high level of employee skill and commitment, evidence points to the way in which well-integrated, highly embedded channels of employee voice (using both direct and indirect practices) can bring positive outcomes for the organisation and its members. To achieve this, senior executives need to be clear on the fundamental management style that should be adopted in their firm and need to build a high level of integrity into the management process across time. Conflicts between organisational and employee interests are bound to occur, but organisations recover more effectively from them when managers are perceived as handling them with respect for employee voice and strongly held views about organisational justice.

7

Workforce performance and the 'black box' of HRM

This is the last chapter in our part on the general principles underpinning strategic HRM. We have talked about the importance of contingency and configurational theory in understanding HR strategy, which varies significantly across the societal, industry and organisational contexts of the firm. We have explored the way in which relating HR strategy to an organisation's specific needs may help managers to develop competitive advantages, especially through the build-up of socially complex forms of learning and cooperation that are hard for other firms to imitate. We have emphasised the role that human capital plays in creating a viable organisation: it is vital that managers employ people with the sort of talents that will enable their organisation to survive. All this has to be done cost effectively, but if managers want to enhance employee commitment to their firm, they need to think hard about the other side of employment relationship: what will attract, develop and retain talented people? We have also underlined the principle that organisations are embedded in societies and have a political side to them. The social legitimacy of a firm's approach to HRM matters for its performance, at least to those managers who wish their firm to act as a responsible corporate citizen. For those who take this view, respect for employee rights is an end in itself, and there is value in accepting some constraints on management power to enhance employee voice.

In this chapter, we are concerned with how HRM contributes to what is actually achieved by an organisation's workforce. We are thinking here about such business outcomes as the levels of productivity and quality that characterise a workplace and the level of profit that is generated in a business unit. These operating and financial outcomes are requirements for organisational survival and matter for the personal careers of managerial leaders. The literature for several years has underlined the difficulties in identifying, and improving, the complex relationships that transmit HR activities into such outcomes. These are the opaque and troublesome links inside the 'black box' of HRM (Wright and Gardner 2004, Purcell and Kinnie 2007). The chapter reviews important theory on the mediating links between HRM and performance, drawing on both quantitative and qualitative research. Much of this is grounded in the AMO framework, which is a fundamental building block in understanding human performance at the individual level. The chapter then takes its analysis to the collective level, examining the nature of HRM as a social process in organisations and identifying critical relationships among the actors. We look here at the intentions and actions of senior managers, the central role of first-line managers in shaping HRM, and the importance of employee perceptions, responses and strategies. Managing this web of relationships is a tall order, especially in the larger organisations in which problems with broken promises, managerial politics and misperceptions of motives are that much greater.

The AMO model of performance

As shown in Figure 7.1, the AMO model is now the established starting point in attempts to explain how HRM affects performance. Stemming from a variety of sources, such as the pioneering work of Vroom (1964), it argues that performance depends on the individual's ability, their motivation and their opportunity to perform (Blumberg and Pringle 1982, Guest 1997, Appelbaum et al. 2000). The implication is that the role of any HRM process is to put in place the policies and practices that will enhance employee ability, motivation and opportunity to perform, each of which add value to performance in a particular context (Boselie, Dietz and Boon 2005, Jiang et al. 2012). This is true in any kind of job, whether we are talking of simple performances, such as those involved in preparing hamburgers, or very complex ones, such as those involved in brain surgery. In mathematical notation:

$$P = f(A,M,O)$$

In other words, individuals perform when they have:

- the ability (A) to perform (they *can do* the job because they possess the necessary knowledge, skills and aptitudes);
- the motivation (M) to perform (they *will do* the job because they want to do it or feel that they must do it); and
- the opportunity (O) to perform (their work structure and its environment provide the necessary support and avenues for expression).

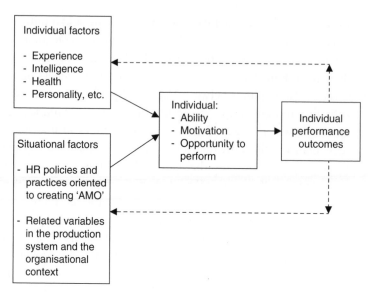

Figure 7.1 The AMO model of individual performance

Factors shaping individual performance

The mathematical shorthand we use here, $P = f(A,M,O)$, is simply a way of indicating that no one knows the precise relationships among ability, motivation and opportunity. There is no exact formula here, but we do know that all three factors are involved in generating an employee performance, and we also know that two broad sets of factors exert an influence over these variables. These contributing factors are associated with the individual and with the situation (Barrick, Mount and Li 2013).

The first set of contributing factors relates to what individuals bring to their work. As explained in Chapter 5, individuals have differing levels of human capital. For example, those who have accumulated a long-term understanding of what is involved in a job will typically outperform a novice who may be highly motivated but is much less efficient (Frese and Zapf 1993). Experience, as they say, is 'a great teacher', which is a major reason why we need feedback loops in Figure 7.1: the better a person performs in a job, the greater will be their confidence and know-how and, typically, the greater the learning by their managers about how well the productive system is working. On top of this, research demonstrates the impact of intelligence or 'general cognitive ability' on our performance (Hunter and Hunter 1984, Judge et al. 1999, Hunter et al. 2000). Except in cases of very deprived or traumatised backgrounds, more intelligent people typically secure a better education and gravitate towards more intellectually challenging work (Baumeister and Bacharach 2000). The process of tackling mentally challenging work then develops their abilities further, increasing their value to employers in knowledge-intensive roles. On the other hand, physical fitness makes a big difference to whether individuals will have the stamina for physically demanding work (Campion 1983). A long day pruning grapevines or labouring on a construction site will convince many intellectuals that they would rather do something else for a living. An individual's health, of course, includes not only their physical fitness but also their mental health. Those who are burnt out from emotional overload do not generally perform well (Maslach and Jackson 1984). Personality also comes into play in various ways, exerting a major influence over the kinds of work that individuals find meaningful and over the extent to which they will persevere in them (Van Iddekinge et al. 2011, Barrick, Mount and Li 2013).

The second set of contributing factors is associated with the situation in which individuals find themselves. This includes the model of HRM in the work unit or relevant to their occupational group, such as the policies and practices that managers use to hire and train people to a level where they have sufficient ability to perform in a job. HRM also includes motivational practices, such as those associated with personal supervision and with the organisation's pay system, that are designed to ensure that workers are willing to apply their abilities in the organisation's interests. In addition, HRM includes policies and practices that influence the opportunity to perform. This includes the way in which the job is designed and the avenues that are offered for employee voice. Where individuals are offered greater freedom over how to do a job, and when their opinions are taken more seriously, their scope to influence outcomes is that much greater.

But HR policies and practices are only one part of the situational context. The work of all individuals is in some sense embedded in a wider set of factors that shape how the organisation produces its goods or services. Managers are engaged in a process of constructing and renewing production systems to meet the needs of their customers, either external or internal to the organisation. This includes, for example, making decisions about the technologies to adopt and obtaining funding to purchase working materials. In the health sector, for example, the absence of sufficient funding to equip an operating theatre will simply rule out certain kinds of medical procedure. Many medical performances are heavily dependent on advanced equipment and the availability of drugs. The same point applies to making hamburgers:

without the funding to purchase cooking equipment, food materials and an energy supply, there is no hamburger. As a general rule, it is easier to perform when a firm is financially successful and can invest more fully in developing its productive resources.

This broader context around the individual and their job is not, however, simply technical. It is also deeply social (e.g. Cherns 1976, Morgeson and Humphrey 2006). Individual performance is enhanced when the social context of the firm is supportive: when managers and colleagues are helpful, sharing their know-how and offering assistance when difficulties arise. Some people are highly independent in their working environment, as teachers are in their own classroom, but many other types of human performance are team based, as they are in hospital surgery, or depend on chains of cooperation inside the firm and/or with external suppliers or customers. Some kinds of social relationship are always present, particularly the relationship with the direct line manager, with whom performance expectations are negotiated over time, and there are nearly always some colleagues or co-workers whose opinions and level of support can make a difference. It is commonplace in research on HRM to talk about both 'task performance' and broader concepts of performance such as 'organisational citizenship behaviour' (Organ 1988), which includes a range of cooperative and caring behaviours that can be very valuable to collegial relations, teamwork and client service in a firm (e.g. Kuvaas and Dysik 2009).

How have HRM academics gone about testing the links from these sets of variables to performance outcomes and vice versa? Theoretical development has been led by studies of mediating processes, using statistical techniques that allow us to map out the links across independent, intervening, control and outcome variables. An important meta-analysis (an analysis of the relevant quantitative studies) by Jiang et al. (2012) has now confirmed these mediating links, showing that HR practices designed to enhance employee ability, motivation or opportunity transmit their impact on financial outcomes through improving the human capital and motivation of employees and thereby improving operational outcomes and reducing employee turnover. The authors note that other mediators, unmeasured in their study, such as the quality of social capital in a firm, may also be one of the pathways through which HRM affects organisational performance.

This meta-analysis confirms the key argument made in Chapter 5, that human capital is indispensable to organisations. There is no performance unless managers can attract sufficient people with the kind of skills needed to do the job. In effect, all performances depend on the organisation's strategies for talent management. Given this essential premise, HRM academics have been interested in studying the employee attitudinal variables in the 'black box'. It is usual to consider a range of relevant employee attitudes under the heading of the 'M' or motivational variable in the AMO framework. Measures of employee engagement are now commonplace in assessing employee motivation (e.g. Soane et al. 2013) and researchers often consider the interrelationships among attitudinal variables such as job satisfaction, trust and employee commitment. For example, in a study of 404 workers in New Zealand, Macky and Boxall (2007) found that higher levels of job satisfaction are associated with higher levels of trust in management and higher levels of affective commitment to the organisation, which is a measure of longer-term motivation.

In terms of thinking about the relevant research on employee motivation, we have already canvassed much of the relevant theory in Chapter 5 where we focused on the factors that attract people towards a job and an organisation. These factors, and the relevant theoretical principles, have a degree of overlap with what will predict performance inside the organisation. It is important to note, however, that employee well-being and employee performance are not equivalent outcomes because individuals and organisations have a mix of common and competing interests. What makes for a good job in the eyes of a worker is not entirely the same as what makes for a good performance in the context of a production system and as perceived by management.

Some theories have proved more popular than others in the stream of research on employee motivation. For example, a large group of researchers has deployed the notion of 'social exchange' to explain why employees choose to perform and with what degree of energy and dedication (e.g. Shore et al. 2004, Guest 2007, Hom et al. 2009). Drawing on classical sources such as Gouldner (1960) and Blau (1964), the principle of reciprocity is central to these accounts of employee motivation. The idea is that employees reciprocate the treatment they receive at work, so that they perform well for an organisation when it performs well for them. If, for example, managers invest more heavily in an individual's training and development, this is argued to call forth a greater response in terms of work effort and dedication. Measures of employee perceptions of 'perceived organisational support' (POS) (Eisenberger et al. 1986) are now widely used in studies of the motivational mediators inside the 'black box' (e.g. Gould-Williams 2007, Takeuchi et al. 2007). This then brings in notions of equity, fairness or justice. Individual perceptions of fairness in the employment relationship are closely related to whether an employee sees their organisation as supportive of them and of their colleagues (e.g. Zhang and Agarwal 2009). The general conclusion is that employees who rate their organisation more highly in terms of POS and organisational justice will try to respond with better performances.

Conversely, where employees become dissatisfied with the support offered by management, they are more likely to withdraw some of their 'discretionary effort' or to quit when another job comes along. The results of these studies are usually consistent with social exchange and justice theories, although it would help if more researchers referred to the employment relationship as an *economic* and social exchange because a sense of fairness in the economic returns from work is a clearly a key factor in this process.

Other studies of critical motivators of employee behaviour have argued that social exchange and justice theories need to be complemented with, or tested against, theories that assess the intrinsic dimensions of work (e.g. Kuvaas and Dysik 2009). A very important pathway to higher performance passes through the intrinsic characteristics of work (e.g. Hackman and Oldham 1980, Barrick, Mount and Li 2013), as discussed in Chapter 5. Snape and Redman (2010), for example, compare the role of perceived organisational support as a mediator with that of work practices that enhance the degree of employee influence and discretion. In a study of 114 workplaces in northeast England, they find that employees' self-reported work behaviours are enhanced by greater job influence but not by a greater perception of organisational support, which challenges the general line of research on POS.

This kind of study underlines the way in which the motivation to perform is deeply affected by how an individual's work is organised and reminds us that we need to consider all three AMO variables and how they interact. One line of analysis is to look at the way in which changes in the design of work influence the 'O' variable and have consequent implications for the 'A' and 'M' variables (Appelbaum et al. 2000, Sterling and Boxall 2013). Where work reorganisation creates greater opportunities for workers to control how they do the job (the 'O' factor), this can utilise more of their skills (the 'A' factor) and can be more intrinsically motivating (the 'M' factor). Work-design research shows how more empowering forms of work design can improve employee skills and foster higher levels of individual development (e.g. Morrison et al. 2005, Felstead et al. 2010). In Chapter 5, we noted the way in which employee well-being can be enhanced through this process and here we wish to underline the way in which greater scope for employee discretion can contribute to better performance. Whether senior management will see it as worthwhile to make the sort of investments and political changes that are needed to increase employee involvement in decision-making is, however, another matter.

Much more literature could be cited but the underpinning principle ought now to be clear. To bring about desired performances, management must engage in a process of influencing the variables of employee ability, motivation and opportunity to perform. This, however, is not simply a principle that applies at the individual level. It has important parallels at the level of work teams and at the level of the entire workforce in a business unit or organisation (Takeuchi et al. 2007, Jiang, Takeuchi and Lepak 2013). These higher levels are critical in the theory of strategic HRM, in which we must try to understand how HRM generates collective outcomes through a workforce with the kind of capabilities, attitudes and behaviours the organisation needs. We turn now to consider the key principles that are involved in this complex process.

Analysing the management process in HRM

To understand the 'black box' of HRM, we must recognise that it is a *social* process played out in an organisation. It involves a range of actors with a variety of roles who interact in complex ways. This approach is underlined by Ferris et al. (1998: 239) who advocate a 'social context theory of HRM', recognising the role of 'culture, climate, politics, and social interaction processes' in the way that people function in organisations. As Morgan (1997: 129) put it in a classic analysis, 'organizations are mini-societies that have their own distinctive patterns of culture and subculture'. They have major issues with 'relational coordination', with creating relationships among individuals and groups that enable interdependent activities to be performed (Gitell, Seidner and Wimbush 2010). Some organisations, like the US military and the UK's National Health Service, employ millions of people and exhibit the complexity of a small country. Analysis in strategic HRM must address the social nature of organisational life if it is to be useful in explaining the performance outcomes of workforces and in suggesting ways to improve them.

In analysing the roles that different actors play in an organisation's HRM process, the logical place to begin is with senior management, who have accountability for setting overall goals and exercise a key influence over workplace culture. What do senior managers in an organisation want to achieve in HRM and how clear and consensual are they about their intentions? This then leads directly to another crucial group because senior managers are reliant on those below them to get things done. What do line managers actually implement in HRM and to what extent is this consistent with what senior managers envisage? As we explained in Chapter 6, line managers form their own agendas and may operate in terms of a preferred personal style in managing the members of their team. There is then the critical issue of what the majority of the workforce perceives and how they respond. What signals are they actually receiving from senior managers, HR specialists and their direct line manager? How do they process and interpret these signals?

Like line managers, employees form and enact their own agendas, much of this driven by their personality disposition (Barrick, Mount and Li 2013). As labour process analysts recognise, employees can form strategies that challenge management goals and that express their own interests and identities (e.g. Thompson and Harley 2007, McBride 2008). At the extreme, forms of employee protest, such as strikes, endemic absenteeism and wilful sabotage, can interrupt or seriously diminish performance. Our discussion will now explore these issues more fully.

Managerial intentions and actions in HRM

What do senior managers want to achieve from a workforce and how do they envisage doing so? In other words, what is their 'theory of HRM' (Boxall, Ang and Bartram 2011)? In-depth case studies using qualitative and quantitative methods are often used to discern this. For example, in a study of a British supermarket chain, Peccei and Rosenthal (2001) used interviews and documentary evidence to study management intentions. This showed that senior managers were leading a shift in business strategy towards competing less on price and more on service quality: 'they judged that quality of customer service would join, and perhaps supersede price, as a major competitive issue within mass market food retailing' (ibid.: 835). This, in turn, implied a more empowering model of HRM in which managers would need to be good exemplars of customer service and in which employees would have greater degrees of freedom to respond to customer problems. In this case, major resources were allocated to making these changes, and Peccei and Rosenthal (2001) were able to use quantitative analysis to identify positive impacts on the customer-oriented behaviours of employees. This is a case where a major change in HR strategy was clearly distinctive, seems to have been approached with a high level of consensus in management, and in which managers followed through with a high level of consistency. Bowen and Ostroff (2004) consider these the kind of attributes that characterise a 'strong' HRM system, one that transmits itself through the 'black box' in a recognisable and highly effective way.

The problem of 'internal fit'

A key concern of theorists in strategic HRM, however, is that the various HR practices of a firm may lack much reinforcing power. This concern is encapsulated in the idea of 'internal fit', which was first developed by Baird and Meshoulam (1988), and is otherwise called 'horizontal fit'. To what extent are HR practices 'bundled' or clustered in mutually supportive ways (MacDuffie 1995)? In general terms, bundling is a search for coherence or 'powerful combinations' among HR practices (Becker et al. 1997). The corollary is that managers should avoid 'deadly combinations' (Becker et al. 1997): practices that work in directly opposite directions, such as strong training for teamwork but appraisal which only rewards highly individualistic behaviour. Coherence in HRM implies designing policies that pull in the same direction. In any large organisation, as in Peccei and Rosenthal's (2001) supermarket chain, there is an important role for senior managers in identifying the mix of policies that they want and how they want them enacted in the particular production system or in the organisation more generally.

The notion of consistency, which overlaps with coherence, is also used in discussions of internal fit. One of the more useful summaries is provided by Baron and Kreps (1999: 39) who define three types of consistency in HRM. The first type is 'complementary' fit or what they call 'single employee consistency': for example, ensuring that where firms use expensive selection approaches they also invest in training and promotion policies that aim to reduce labour turnover, thus increasing the chances of reaping rewards from their investment in individuals. In effect, this is about coherence in HR policy design and entails the search for 'powerful' rather than 'deadly combinations'. The second type of fit Baron and Kreps (1999) argue for is consistency across employees doing the same kind of work ('among employee consistency' but better known in everyday usage as 'standardisation' of employment conditions). There are often strong normative or ethical pressures for standardisation in HR policies in firms: one of the main ways employers argue they are treating people equitably is by treating them all the same when it comes to employment conditions (e.g. standard working times and leave policies for people in the same occupational category or more generally). The third kind of consistency is what Baron and Kreps call 'temporal consistency': consistency of employee treatment across a reasonable period of time. 'In general, how employee A is treated today should not differ radically from how she was treated yesterday' (Baron and Kreps 1999: 39). Again, and assuming employee A has not done something radically different in the last 24 hours, this principle makes good sense: employees like to be able to predict an employer's behaviour and can be seriously demotivated by violation of their 'psychological contract' (Rousseau 1995).

As far as it goes, the theory of internal fit seems very reasonable. Critical reflection suggests, however, that it is somewhat oversimplified as a way of understanding how the HRM process evolves in the social life of organisations. While rightly emphasising the value of various forms of coherence and consistency, which help to create stability and build trust, the notion of 'internal fit' tends to be discussed in a way that overlooks the paradoxical elements that emerge as managers try to organise work and manage people. The problem stems from the fact that there are multiple goals in HRM and these bring about a range of strategic tensions (e.g. Evans and Genadry 1999).

As an illustration, consider work by Pil and MacDuffie (1996) on automobile manufacturing. At the time they wrote, Pil and MacDuffie (1996) observed a general increase in the use of high-involvement practices in this industry around the world. These are practices that foster higher skill and solicit greater commitment to, and creativity in, problem-solving. However, at the same time, firms were pursuing downsizing, often of major proportions. The same picture is described by Bacon and Blyton (2001) in the international iron and steel industry: new work systems designed to increase employee involvement in decision-making were introduced at the same time as firms introduced more contingent employment contracts (fixed-term contracts and sub-contracting of jobs) and as they continued to carry out redundancy programmes. As anyone with experience of downsizing and sub-contracting processes knows, these sorts of actions typically raise suspicions, reduce trust in management and undermine employee commitment to the firm (Zatzick and Iverson 2006). This climate of insecurity, however, did not prevent management in these firms from seeking higher involvement from the remaining workforce. Here, then, is a critical tension: between needing more skilful, more creative work while not being able to hold traditional staffing levels and offer traditional levels of employment security. Management, in fact, often needs a blend of 'forcing' and 'fostering' behaviour as it wrestles with the problem of renewing an organisation that has lost competitiveness (Walton, Cutcher-Gershenfeld and McKersie 1994). Processes designed to foster greater employee involvement can operate alongside processes of work intensification (e.g. Eurofound 2012). Furthermore, the former may be more openly discussed or signalled through new forms of teamwork and training investments, while the latter may be less transparent, gradually emerging as the budgets of line managers are whittled away over time.

We must be careful, then, with the concept of 'internal fit'. It rightly underlines the value that managers may gain by seeking coherence among the HR policies aimed at a particular group of employees and through consistency in their application. Where, for example, management aims to introduce a new style of working, such as one that implies higher levels of skill and creativity, striving for reinforcement across the HR policies needed, and their consistent application, will most likely add significant value. However, striving for 'internal fit' in this sense does not rule out the possibility that management will simultaneously adopt strategies that intensify work or generate higher insecurity, with mixed impacts on employee well-being. Managers, as we have noted, are involved in constructing and renewing production systems, and such systems often involve wrestling with a range of tensions associated with limited resources and with changes in the firm's environment.

Rhetoric versus reality

In general terms, the potential for a gap between employee expectations and experience is always present in HRM. Legge (2005) makes the point by talking about the difference between management rhetorics and realities. Grant (1999) explores the difficulties that can arise by taking the concept of psychological contracting to the collective level of analysis to define four types of psychological contract between management and a workforce:

- the 'congruent contract' (where management's 'rhetoric' in HRM appeals to employees and 'coincides with their perceptions of reality'). Previous experiences 'tally with the content of the rhetoric'.
- the 'mismatched contract' (where 'the rhetoric fails because it has no appeal to the employee and does not match the perceived reality'). This can happen, for example, when past experience tells employees management cannot deliver on its rhetoric.
- the 'partial contract' (where 'parts of the rhetoric appeal to the employees and parts do not'). 'For example, the employee may feel that rhetoric promising personal development reflects reality, while at the same time they may feel that rhetoric linking personal development to increased levels of pay does not.'
- the 'trial contract' (where 'rhetoric is given a chance to prove itself and become reality'). This can happen where employees are prepared 'to "buy in" to the rhetoric on a "wait-and-see basis" ' (Grant 1999: 331).

In discussing this typology, Grant (1999) examines a case in the UK consumer electronics sector ('Renco') where data was obtained through two periods of data gathering on employee attitudes, some 18 months apart. Renco, a Japanese-owned company, opened a greenfield site at which Japanese practices of worker participation in decision-making and a cooperative approach to industrial relations were promised. Workers were keen to give this approach a chance (a 'trial' psychological contract). After 18 months, however, management practice had diverged significantly from the initial rhetoric. Japanese-style consultative practices were allowed to decay. Employees did not experience consistent opportunities for involvement. The trial contract passed away as employees revised their effort (e.g. lowering the quality of work) in a quid-pro-quo for a disappointing management performance.

The psychological contract shifted back to a 'mismatched' one. The case illustrates the danger of raising expectations which are then subsequently dashed because management does not care about follow-through or because the internal politics within management derail top management's espoused values. Cynicism is bred in this kind of environment, and any future change engineered by management will have serious credibility issues.

Case study research of this nature frequently underlines the importance of bringing senior management's espoused values – or cultural signals – closer into alignment with the collective actions of both senior managers and the various layers of line and specialist managers that report to them. Large organisations in which there are high levels of inconsistency in management values and, thus, in the HRM process, do not have strongly positive workplace cultures (Gordon and DiTomaso 1992, Ferris et al. 1998). Stronger cultures are more readily built in small, owner-managed organisations where trust levels tend to be higher (Macky and Boxall 2007). Because those who own the firm directly manage employees, there is much less chance for miscommunication to occur and for debilitating internal politics to take root. Where small business owners retain control for long periods of time, they are in a position to bring a high degree of consistency into the way the firm is managed. This does not mean to say that all do or that small business owners will give employees everything they want – far from it, because they usually lack the resources to do so – but they are in a better position to follow through on the promises that they do make. Such consistency is much harder to achieve when organisations are large and subject to frequent changes in ownership or in senior management leadership. Violation of the psychological contracts of employees is naturally greater when there are multiple agents involved in the management process (Guest 1998).

The crucial role of line managers

The possibility for gaps between rhetoric and reality underlines the need not only for senior managers in large organisations to figure carefully what they want to achieve and then follow through on their pledges – achieving greater consensus in their attitudes and greater consistency in their own behaviour – but also indicates how dependent they are on lower-level line managers to achieve the results they seek.

While this includes both staff specialists, such as HR specialists and line managers, the latter are particularly important if desired changes are going to occur in HRM. Line managers are not simple conduits or pipelines. Line manager action or inaction is often responsible for the difference between espoused HR policies and their enactment. Many HR policies can only be converted to practice by line managers. This is particularly true in the case of complex practices, such as performance appraisal, which are very sensitive to how they are implemented, as we explained in Chapter 5.

This does not mean that line managers are necessarily trying to be perverse. They can be trying to make the organisation function more effectively but find themselves struggling with a wider system that is not supportive or that scapegoats them for the problems that emerge (Fenton-O'Creevy 1998). If the firm's executives are financiers rather than people with deep industry experience, the role of line managers in making things work on a daily level becomes even more important. Loyal supervisors and middle managers may be all that stands between viability and operational collapse. Thus, at times, line managers help to keep the ship afloat. At other times, they may be letting a policy die because it works against their political interests (e.g. Batt 2004). This can happen if senior managers or HR specialists have introduced a policy without consultation with those who must implement it. The relationships between senior, HR and line managers are important and often contested (e.g. Hope-Hailey et al. 1997, McGovern et al. 1997, Cooke 2006). Involvement of line managers in HR policy development is critical if policies are to be workable and if their commitment is to be won when radical changes are desired.

The crucial role of the line manager in shaping the actual character of HRM is now widely recognised and the quality of the relationships between line managers and their team members is receiving greater attention in the analysis of HRM (Purcell and Hutchinson 2007, Purcell et al. 2009). Uhl-Bien, Graen and Scandura (2000: 138) adopt the term 'leader-member exchange' (LMX) to describe the quality of interpersonal relationships that line managers develop with their workers. Research on managers and their subordinates, they suggest, 'shows that more effectively developed relationships are beneficial for individual and work unit functioning and have many positive outcomes related to firm performance' (ibid.: 143). There is no doubt that ties within a work team can be much stronger than those with remote senior executives. It is much easier to trust someone you know, especially if you share their values and find them to be a person of competence and integrity (Macky and Boxall 2007). Becker et al. (1996) find a stronger relationship between commitment to supervisors and performance than that found between commitment to the organisation and performance. As Liden, Bauer and Erdogan (2004) comment, the 'immediate supervisor plays a critical role as a key agent of the organization through which members form their perceptions of the organization'.

Thus, research on the links between HRM and performance needs to take account of the mediating role of line managers since the HR practices that employees perceive and experience will be heavily influenced by the quality of their relationship with their direct manager. The quality of this relationship is, in turn, heavily shaped by the extent to which senior leaders and HR specialists in the firm invest in the selection, coaching, appraisal and reward of middle and first-line managers (FLMs). This is strongly illustrated in Purcell and Hutchinson's (2007) case study of the Trafford Park store of the Selfridge's retail chain. Data from a staff survey showed weaknesses in terms of how FLMs or team leaders carried out official HR practices, such as performance appraisal, and in their personal supervisory style, such as whether they listened to employee views. As a result, senior managers decided to make a greater investment in the recruitment, development, support and reward of team leaders in the store, and the value of this showed up in better employee attitudes and outcomes, as measured in a subsequent employee survey and in reduced levels of employee turnover. Purcell and Hutchinson (2007: 17) concluded that:

> The example of Selfridges has clear implications for practitioners who wish to improve organisational performance as far as possible via people management. In particular, paying particular attention to FLMs as an occupational group with numerous responsibilities and often competing priorities is necessary. This can include building involvement and problem solving activities to allow access to decision-makers and provide means for mutual support, better selection with greater emphasis given to leadership behaviours as well as technical skills and knowledge, access to further development, coaching and guidance and career management.

The ways in which first-line managers perform, then, depends on the extent to which they experience a supportive relationship with their manager and benefit from the sort of training, coaching and voice practices that help them with the challenges involved in managing people. Their behaviour can also be influenced by performance appraisal and pay systems that incorporate recognition of their critical role in how people are managed or make it more stressful by focusing only on such targets as production or sales volumes. A key implication is that HR-function strategy in large firms needs to pay close attention to how to develop and support line managers in their role as the front-line managers of people in the organisation. How HR departments can add value as 'business partners' in this sense has become an important focus of the literature on the roles of HR specialists (e.g. Beer 1997, Ulrich 1998, Caldwell 2008).

Variation in employee perceptions, responses and strategies

Employees, then, are going to be influenced not simply by top management values and formal policies but by the reality of what they experience on a daily basis. Some formal HR policies (such as their base rate of pay and the details of their pension) can be directly transmitted from policy to practice without slippage but much else is filtered through line managers, positively or negatively. In addition, employees gain experience of the quality of material and financial resourcing in their organisation. High-sounding policies for employee rewards and development that are not met with good resources are unlikely to be very convincing after a while. What may be pressing down more heavily on employees is the level of work pressure, which is driving them towards certain production targets, something which has increased in Britain over the last few years (van Wanrooy et al. 2013: 102–4).

All of this means that employees are receiving signals on various levels in a large organisation, with the potential for conflict among them. Not only this, but there is a question around whether they hear the same thing in relation to any one signal. In a sophisticated study of employees in a supermarket chain, Nishii, Lepak and Schneider (2008) show that employees can make quite different 'attributions' about management's purposes in implementing what seem to be the same HR practices. One employee can perceive a performance-related pay scheme as fostering service quality and their well-being while another perceives it as an attempt to control costs and intensify their work. Different attributions then connect to different levels of satisfaction and commitment: predictably, those who interpret management's motives more positively are happier. Such variability in the attributions that employees make about managerial motives reinforces the importance of studying employee experiences of, and responses to, HR practices, rather than relying solely on management reports of a company's HR practices (Geare, Edgar and Deng 2006, Nishii, Lepak and Schneider 2008). Any one individual manager who is asked to respond to a survey about an organisation's HR practices can only reliably report their own perception of what the HR practices are supposed to be and their own experience of them in practice. They cannot authentically describe whether *other* individuals, including the vast bulk of employees, perceive the firm to have these HR practices in reality and how they affect their interests.

For each employee, then, there is a 'psychological climate' in the workplace: their own, individual sense of what is happening in their employment relationship and how it affects their well-being, which will then affect their individual attitudes and behaviour (James and James 1989). When employees, however, form a relatively common perception of management's intentions and actions, we can also talk meaningfully of a 'social' or 'organisational' climate in the workplace (James et al. 2008), which then becomes a collective mediator, or intervening variable, in the links between HRM and organisational performance. A good test of any HR strategy, as Lepak et al. (2006) emphasise, is whether managers have succeeded in creating the kind of productive climate they intend. Management's intentions can be quite diverse: some management teams seek to create a climate for service, others a climate for innovation, while yet others may be seeking to build a climate of occupational safety and so on. Some productive climates may contain a range of themes.

In stronger climates, with high levels of distinctiveness, coherence and consistency, there is 'a shared perception of what the organisation is like in terms of practices, policies, procedures, routines and rewards – what is important and what behaviours are expected and rewarded' (Bowen and Ostroff 2004: 205). When management is seeking high levels of commitment, this shared perception needs to be as positive as possible with management deemed trustworthy. This does not rule out the need for difficult decisions at times, such as an unavoidable period of downsizing. These, as we have noted, are to be expected. Workers, however, are likely to adjust to these events more quickly when the overall pattern of management style is deemed ethical (Zatzick and Iverson 2006). Hall and Purcell (2012: 141–4) describe the case of an American-owned manufacturer which reduced headcount in its UK plant by two-thirds and shifted much of its production to Turkey and Poland. Through extensive consultation and negotiation with unionised and non-unionised staff on the fine details of a complex change process, a package of measures was agreed to save the UK plant and to manage redundancies. In their survey of staff before and after the event, Hall and Purcell found that employees' approval of management, and their commitment to the firm, had considerably improved.

The role of shared perceptions in HRM is demonstrated in McKay, Avery and Morris's (2009) study of the 'diversity climate' in 654 stores in a large US-based retail organisation. They define a work context as 'pro-diversity when, consensually, employees feel they have an equal opportunity to succeed on the job and are made to feel like integral members of the organization' (ibid.: 771). This means, for example, that both men and women and people of different ethnicity feel treated fairly and respected for their views. What McKay, Avery and Morris (2009) find is that the link between diversity climate and organisational performance is greater in those stores where both employees and their managers perceive there to be a pro-diversity climate. Performance is lowest in the stores where both report a less hospitable approach to diversity.

The higher-performing stores, then, have a high level of positive consensus about the climate for diversity: this, clearly, is a 'strong' climate in Bowen and Ostroff's (2004) terms. The point, then, is that organisations will vary in the extent to which individual psychological perceptions are shared across the group. Where they are, they can have strongly positive implications when management's motives are welcomed and management is trusted. However, it must be said, strongly shared negative perceptions of managerial motives and behaviour can do major damage, creating a legacy of low trust, as studies such as Grant's (1999) demonstrate.

Before leaving this discussion of employee perceptions and responses in HRM, it is important to recognise the role that the strategies of workers can play in shaping performance, both positively and negatively. The need to do so is underlined by labour process theorists, who are critical of mainstream HRM theory, which they see as overlooking inherent conflicts of interest in capitalism and underplaying worker activism (e.g. Thompson and Harley 2007). Drawing heavily on, but also adapting, the critique of managerial strategy developed by Braverman (1974), labour process theory (LPT) focuses on the ways in which managers try to control employee behaviour and the ways in which workers resist those aspects of control that threaten their interests (e.g. Burawoy 1979, Littler 1982, Hyman 1987). Although some LPT researchers use quantitative analysis (e.g. Harley, Sargent and Allen 2010), the major research method employed is the qualitative case study.

An interesting example is the study by McBride (2008) of worker strategies in the shipbuilding and maintenance industry in northeast England. What her work shows is that workers in these shipyards have developed strong occupational and union cultures. They are active in the development of work practices rather than passive recipients of management initiatives, showing high levels of engagement in union-management negotiations and in inter-union politics. In these shipyards, workers help to shape what work quality means and how they will achieve it, bringing their pride to the job, including a commitment to producing good work on time in each contract won by their employer. This is an example of a sector in which a traditional model of industrial relations has survived but the point that McBride (2008) makes is actually more general. It is the need for us to avoid casting workers as acquiescent by depicting HRM as something that is done to them rather than something that is forged with, or by, them. Whether on an individual and/or collective basis, it is much more desirable in an analysis of HRM to see workers as independent agents who bring their own agendas and enact their own strategies in the workplace, a point that is also made in the organisational behaviour literature through the concept of 'job crafting' (Wrzesniewski and Dutton 2001).

The extent to which this will imply conflict with management strategies is clearly variable but the point about the need to recognise worker activism is important. There are various ways in which workers may seek to renegotiate the nature of their jobs or the terms of their employment, both as individuals and as groups. The case cited by McBride (2008) is one of a strongly collective response from a workforce but individual strategies are often being played out, in addition to, or instead of, such collective actions. Professionals, for example, such as lawyers in a firm with a culture of long working hours, may seek to negotiate more family friendly terms or, if this fails, may resign as a form of individual resistance and move to a smaller practice where they have greater control over the length of their working time. Where highly talented individuals are lost this way, and are not easily replaced, there will be reputational damage and implications for the performance of the firm they leave behind.

An expanded model of the 'black box'

We are now in a position to look at an expanded model of the mediating links that influence the effectiveness of HR strategy. Following the work of Wright and Nishii (2013) and Purcell and Kinnie (2007), this model (Figure 7.2) tracks intentions, actions, perceptions and responses, and it aims to take the analysis to the collective level we have talked about. HRM involves attempts to build the abilities, motivations and performance opportunities of entire workforces.

At the far left of Figure 7.2 is a box containing the intended elements in HRM – such things as top management's espoused values and employee relations style and the organisation's HR policies. Alongside these intentions for how the firm will conduct its HRM are other relevant aspects of the organisational context, including policies that set marketing goals, decisions about technologies and techniques that structure operations and strategies for finance. What we are emphasising here is that the experience of work is not simply about policies and practices that are explicitly related to HRM. Much that is done in marketing, finance and operations shapes the production system and affects what people experience at work, including the degree of work pressure they experience, and the possibilities they have to express themselves.

The next box in Figure 7.2 is the one where we represent management actions. There are three aspects here. First, senior managers not only form intentions but they also take direct actions, such as deciding actual budget levels and deciding what they will say in an important team briefing when financial results are disappointing. There are also direct actions by HR specialists in those parts of HRM, such as collective negotiations, which depend

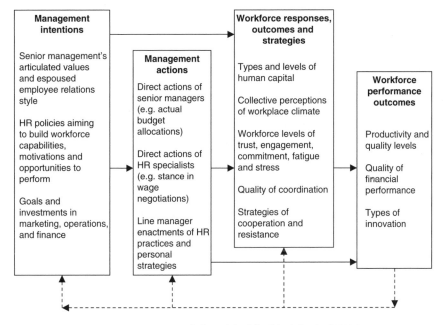

Figure 7.2 An expanded model of the 'black box' of HRM

on their expertise. How senior managers and HR specialists actually behave in carrying out the organisation's espoused voice practices is a key issue, as Chapter 6 explained. Then, very importantly, there is the behaviour of line managers as they enact HR policies – to the extent that they need to and want to – and also express their own beliefs and personalities in the way they do things. Line managers are responsible for converting much of HR policy into actual HR practice, given the resources they are allowed to work with and their judgement about what will work or what serves their interests. What we are emphasising here is that HR practice is rarely a 'straight line'. It is more useful to think of HR practice as a 'curve' or a range of actual managerial behaviour around a notional policy line.

The next box in the figure represents the perceptual, motivational and behavioural responses of employees, including outcomes that matter to them and the strategies that they form. This is a complex set of variables with a number of interrelationships that we have simplified into one box. In a careful study, these variables would each be measured in an appropriate way. One key variable is the extent to which the HRM process has developed the pool of knowledge and skill in the workforce or the way it has affected the quantity and quality of human capital available to the firm. Other variables include individual and collective perceptions of the nature of the productive climate (e.g. to what extent do employees perceive that there is a good climate for providing service in a hotel or restaurant?) Motivational and behavioural variables include levels of engagement and commitment, the level of trust between management and labour, levels of fatigue and stress and levels of coordination and cooperation among work colleagues. To handle conflicts of interest, employees may form strategies around where they will resist management control or negotiate more acceptable work norms. As we have been at pains to emphasise, these perceptual, motivational and behavioural variables are key mediators which then feed into operating and financial performance, along with other factors in the way the organisation is resourced and managed. The figure is completed with feedback loops. This helps to make the point that more successful organisations are likely to build better human and social capital over time: success often breeds success. Similarly, workers who experience positive outcomes are more likely to remain with the firm and contribute their enhanced capabilities to future performances.

Figure 7.2 provides a general template that can help managers identify weak links in the HRM–performance chain in their firm. This is particularly important in larger organisations, which are more prone to internal contradictions, confusions and power struggles, all of which can contribute to a loss of value from the funds invested in HRM. For those managers who want to enhance the quality of their HR strategies, then, a process of surfacing the 'theory of HRM' is very useful. As shown by in-depth case studies (e.g. Peccei and Rosenthal 2001, Boxall, Ang and Bartram 2011), it is necessary to begin with identification of senior management's goals for managing people and identification of the major ways in which they see these being achieved. This is a qualitative process requiring a good series of interviews and the analysis of company documents. This can then lead into a set of propositions or hypotheses, connecting independent variables in HRM to mediators, controls and outcomes, which can be tested through surveys and quantitative data analysis. With e-mail and intranet systems, surveys like this can be put online, inviting employees to respond on their attitudes and experiences and then measuring the outcomes of performance through responses from their managers or through indicators of operating and/or financial outcomes. Ideally, the best kind of data source or informant is chosen for each step in the measurement process and data are collected longitudinally so that we can assess relationships over time and build up a picture of causality (e.g. Purcell and Hutchinson 2007, Cascio and Boudreau 2010).

The growth of surveys for measuring employee attitudes or engagement, noted in Chapter 6, is a sign that many business leaders want to see some performance metrics for HRM (Cascio and Boudreau 2010). However, our perception is that many of these surveys are not surfacing the particular theory of HRM being pursued by the organisation in its specific context and assessing its fitness for purpose. For this, more customised forms of research, rather than general indicators of engagement, are needed.

Conclusions

The literature in strategic HRM has for several years underlined the difficulties in identifying, and improving, the complex relationships that transmit HR activities into workforce outcomes. There are fragile links between what is intended, what is enacted and what is perceived in HRM that lead on to employee attitudes and behaviours and thence to productive outcomes. In a nutshell, this is the 'black box' problem.

The AMO model has become the established starting point in attempts to explain how HRM affects performance. Developed at the individual level of analysis, it argues that performance is a function of ability, motivation and the opportunity to perform in a particular context, implying that the role of any HRM process is to put in place the policies and practices that enhance these variables. HRM academics have been particularly interested in testing the human capital and attitudinal linkages in the HRM–performance relationship. They have placed emphasis on 'social exchange theory', with its ideas of reciprocity, perceived organisational support and organisational justice. In addition, HRM researchers have studied the intrinsic motivational value of job characteristics with work-design researchers helping to emphasise the way in which work organisation not only affects employee motivation and the opportunity to perform but also influences skill utilisation and the extent to which the firm will tap into employee potential.

To understand the 'black box', we must recognise that HRM is a social process in organisations, involving a range of actors who play a variety of roles. What senior managers want to achieve with a workforce, and how they envisage doing so, is the logical place to start in an analysis of the black box. This is their 'theory of HRM', and a good role for HR research projects in organisations is to help them surface it and test its assumptions. The extent to which senior managers form a distinctive and consensual view of HRM and carry it through consistently is very variable. The extent to which it achieves the ends they desire, and in the way they desire, is very variable. The concept of 'internal fit' places a premium on achieving high levels of coherence and consistency in HRM. Clearly, coherence and consistency offer value to management but the social reality of organisations is rather more complex than the concept implies. For example, changing economic fortunes lead to trade-offs between organisational and employee interests. A management team that respects employee voice in these conflictual situations, ensuring that there is a strong level of substantive, procedural and interpersonal justice, will negotiate these difficulties more effectively, thus building a reputation for integrity and doing less damage to the culture of the firm.

Tensions between management rhetoric and reality are emphasised by critical theorists of HRM, who highlight the damage to employee attitudes that can stem from major gaps between management intentions and actions. The potential for these gaps also underlines the way in which senior managers are dependent on lower-level line managers to achieve results with the workforce. Research on the links between HRM and performance has increasingly recognised the crucial role of line managers and their impact on the well-being of their team members. The quality of this relationship is heavily shaped by the extent to which senior leaders and HR specialists in the firm invest in their development and support. Managing line managers more effectively helps to equip, and motivate them, to manage the workforce more effectively.

In any kind of large organisation, employees are receiving signals on various levels, with the potential for conflict among them and the potential for shifting philosophies, leaders and resources to destabilise trust. On top of this, individuals can make quite different attributions about management's purposes in implementing what actually seem to be the same HR practices. Individual employees form their own perception of the 'psychological climate' in their organisation, but we can talk meaningfully of a social or organisational climate when they form a relatively common perception of management's intentions and actions. This, of course, can be positive or negative, with the more positive climates, in conjunction with good levels of human capital, leading to better levels of engagement and cooperation. In thinking about the critical role of employee responses in any kind of workplace, it is important, however, to avoid casting employees as acquiescent or passive conduits of management strategy. As labour process theorists remind us, workers are independent agents who may assert their own identities and pursue their own interests in the workplace, helping to shape what performance means and how the organisation will achieve it.

part 3

Specific contexts

8

HR strategy in manufacturing

As we explained in Chapter 3, firms need to respond to their environments or they fail. The 'law of context' has serious implications for HRM, as it does for other parts of a business. We dedicate four chapters in this part of the book to understanding important types of context and to analysing the HR strategies that characterise them. We begin with manufacturing, which covers the activities of firms engaged in making physical goods or products, ranging from such staples of human consumption as groceries and clothing through to advanced devices such as computers, smartphones and jet engines. Largely because of the labour-saving impacts of mechanisation, the manufacturing sector now accounts for a much smaller proportion of employment in advanced societies (typically, 10 to 20 per cent), but 'it generates 70 per cent of exports in major manufacturing economies – both advanced and emerging – and up to 90 per cent of business R&D spending' (McKinsey 2012: 3). Manufacturing is at the forefront of technological development in the global economy, and has major spillover effects, creating jobs in a range of services associated with designing, financing, insuring, transporting, warehousing and selling goods. It draws supplies from mining industries and provides the processed materials for the whole of the construction sector. Its impact is felt across society. The recruitment of people into factories, and the associated growth of cities, has had a profound impact on human living conditions. It continues to do so. In China, for example, around a quarter of a billion people have migrated from farming into factory work over the last 30 years, arguably the largest human migration ever.[1]

---

[1] http://en.wikipedia.org/wiki/Migration_in_China, accessed 27/1/15.

We start, then, with a review of the nature and development of manufac-turing, including the rise of the factory system and the techniques of mass production. This historical backdrop is important for understanding how models of HRM have evolved in manufacturing and how they continue to influence the way we think about the management of work and people. We then examine the competitive challenges to mass production that arose in the latter part of the twentieth century and that led to the development of high-involvement models of HRM, which aim to make better use of the skills and potential of the workforce. This leads into an analysis of how globalisation is currently transforming manufacturing. Manufacturing is being redistrib-uted around the world, and both companies and governments have a large stake in its impacts. Outsourcing and offshoring have become very impor-tant approaches to HR strategy. This leads, finally, into a discussion of 'lean production', which has become the dominant philosophy in manufacturing management, and which poses important challenges for HRM. Those who are employed in services should not skip this chapter simply because it is about manufacturing. The history, models and philosophies discussed in this chapter have direct relevance for the next one on services, as we shall see.

Manufacturing and its impacts on models of HRM

'Manufacturing' is an English word with its origin in the Latin words to do with making ('facere') an article by hand ('manus'). The capacity to make physical products, including tools, is an ancient characteristic of the human species, as anthropologists explain (e.g. Tattersall 2012). Various sites of early human habitation contain piles of flints left behind as our early ancestors made cutting tools.[2] Manufacturing is now a diverse set of activities, incor-porating a range of types of production and models of HRM.

Craft and batch production

When humans make articles by hand or with a few, well-chosen tools, we talk of 'craft production' to describe the close fashioning of an object to a par-ticular set of needs: for example, in a hand-made dress or a homemade piece of furniture. For most of recorded human history, people have worked on

---

[2] In the oldest find so far in the UK, flint tools dating to 800,000 years ago were uncovered at Happisburgh in 2010, http://en.wikipedia.org/wiki/Happisburgh, accessed 27/1/15.

the land in the seasonal tasks of food production, such as ploughing, sowing and reaping, and in the farming of animals. Much hand-based production occurred in this context as families sought to be as self-sufficient as possible or sought to supplement their income in such activities as cloth production on hand-made looms.

More specialised forms of craft production occurred among the smaller proportion of the human population located in market towns and cities. In medieval times, craft workers – such as carpenters, masons, shoe-makers, glass-blowers and lock-smiths – organised themselves into guilds, which were regulated by the public authorities in exchange for being able to control admission to the trade (i.e. 'restrictive entry') and its methods of work (e.g. Pirenne 1937: 176–88). People learned their trade through the apprentice-ship system in which new workers were trained on the job by a master of the craft. At the end of this process, individuals could expect higher wages and could potentially move into self-employment. The artisan or craft worker exercised a high level of control over which techniques to use and how to use them, allowing significant room for the expression of the individual's skills and personality (Blauner 1964). Wherever this kind of worker control over production methods continues to exist, we talk of a 'craft model' of HRM.

In craft production, the volume of output ('scale') is typically low and there can be significant variation in the characteristics of each product made. Craft manufacturing remains prevalent among small firms that cater to market niches of various kinds in all societies. Larger runs in the making of more standardised goods, such as bread-making in a bakery, are known as 'batch production'. Here, the manufacturer is responding to a more uniform type of demand with a product that has more of a formula about it and through a production process that has a greater degree of repetition. Larger, more expensive equipment is typically applied to the process, as for example in the baking industry, and the production workforce may have a lower, or more general, level of skill than is characteristic of the classical craft worker.

The factory system and the rise of mass production

The great expansion of manufacturing came with the advent of the Industrial Revolution, in which an explosion of scientific research and inventive activity led to the application of greater machinery to production. In the UK, the home of modern manufacturing, this movement started in the eighteenth and continued throughout the nineteenth century.[3] Other large economies,

---

[3] http://en.wikipedia.org/wiki/Industrial_Revolution, accessed 27/1/15.

like Germany, the USA, Japan and France, joined in the process, gaining major momentum over the course of the nineteenth and twentieth centuries.

At the time when Adam Smith was writing his famous text in 1776, *The Wealth of Nations*, with its analysis of the efficiency gains to be achieved by the detailed division of labour, factory owners in the emerging British industry of cotton manufacture were taking advantage of new mechanised processes to create radically new forms of work organisation. New forms of power applied to newly invented machinery made it profitable to concentrate workers, including large numbers of children, at the point of production (Deane 1969, Jones 1994). The technological revolution in power sources, such as the steam engine, and more efficient machinery, such as the 'spinning jenny', led to a large-scale migration of families from villages into factory towns and cities.

Under the factory system, operators became 'machine minders' working at the pace set by the machines owned by the capitalists and the factory's time clock, not by themselves. They were paid a wage, often linked to output and, working very long hours, undertook a single task or a small number of linked tasks requiring physical stamina and some dexterity but few intellectual skills. Each task took no more than a few seconds or minutes and then had to be repeated again and again. This process of 'job simplification' reduced the amount of training needed and made workers more replaceable. Using the AMO model we discussed in Chapter 7, the opportunity of workers to perform was channelled into a narrow set of tasks. As Adam Smith (1776) understood, workers who specialised at a simple set of activities learnt to do them quickly and their rate of production rose. However, in the interests of greater efficiency, their scope to explore their human potential was heavily restricted and much of the work was boring. The language of the time, of 'the master and his hands', gives the game away. Factory workers were like appendages to the machinery, needed much more for their physical attributes than for their mental abilities (Watson 1986).

Factories were designed by engineers to function as large sets of cogs and wheels rationally linked together. This metaphor of organisations as rationally co-ordinated, interlocking parts is still prevalent today and brings with it a denial of human emotional and social life (see Morgan (1997) for a wonderful analysis of the ways of thinking about or imagining organisation). As work was 'de-skilled' through breaking it down into the simplest tasks, and as workers no longer owned their own means of production, being reliant, as 'wage slaves', on factory owners and their management agents, much about the process was dehumanising. In a wider sense, this was no more than a reflection of social structures and beliefs in society at the time on the brutish nature of the emerging working class. However, questions were increasingly being asked by British novelists like Charles Dickens and Elizabeth Gaskell, and by a growing group of social reformers, about the consequences of rapid industrialisation and urbanisation.[4]

The mental models of the early factory owners about the way work should be organised became the standard or 'default' model for the design of work in industrialised societies. In what Cordery and Parker (2007) call the 'mechanistic' model of work design, managers did the thinking and directing while workers were required to obey instructions and mind the machines. As this implies, factories depended on two work systems operating under different principles: one for workers involving low discretion, low scope and low skill and one for managers involving much higher levels of discretion, responsibility and skill (Fox 1974). Subsequent developments, whether that pioneered by Henry Ford, or turned into a new science of management by Frederick Winslow Taylor, continued to rest on these premises.

The key figures we have just mentioned – Henry Ford I and F.W. Taylor – were both Americans. While Britain may have industrialised first, the USA rapidly caught up in the nineteenth century and it was American engineers and business leaders who escalated the rate of innovation in manufacturing. A stream of advances in machinery, in materials, in plant layout and in methods of management created much higher rates of throughput or 'economies of speed' (Chandler 1977: 281). This included the application of more rigorous work measurement processes and the ruthless division of responsibility between management and labour (Braverman 1974, Meyer 1981, Warner 1998). Formal processes, such as 'time-and-motion study', were used to investigate the informal methods workers had developed on the job, quantifying how long it took them to carry out their tasks and how they moved within the work space, interacting with materials, tools and machines. Work practices were then redesigned by a management-appointed 'work study' expert to make human activities more efficient and to create a basis for identifying normal output and for linking pay incentives ('bonus systems') to higher levels of output. Under Taylor's (1911) concept of 'Scientific Management', the efficiency gains inherent in task specialisation were heightened and incentivised.

It is wrong to suggest that the Taylorist practice of 'de-skilling' work permeated all manufacturing industries or all manufacturing jobs (Burawoy 1979, Littler 1982). At one extreme, craft production remained important in small-scale industries while at the other extreme, in highly mechanised industries in which continuous-flow production was possible, workers with a strong

---

[4] For two of the classic sources, see Dickens' novel, *Hard Times*, and Gaskell's novel, *North and South*.

capacity for problem-solving were needed to oversee complex processes and maintain production (Blauner 1964). However, much in-between became subject to the process of work simplification in which core operating jobs were reduced to a simple set of tasks that were constantly repeated. In the expanding automobile industry, Henry Ford's contribution came in linking these highly specialised jobs to the *moving* assembly line (Lacey 1986). This minimised the need for operating workers to move around the floor to pick up tools or parts: instead, they remained at their work station and the work came directly to them, creating the basis for 'speed-up'. The Ford Motor Company smashed production records and used these gains to deliver major reductions in the price of cars and thus expand the market, fostering a process in which car ownership eventually spread beyond the upper and middle classes to factory workers themselves. Although these principles had their precursors, the innovations of Taylor and Ford, more than anything, epitomised the American system of mass production or what has widely become known as 'Fordism'.

The development of the industrial model of HRM

Work systems matter enormously to workers. The organisation of work deeply affects the extent to which individuals can express their abilities, and poorly designed work has major impacts on an individual's physical and mental health (e.g. Karasek and Theorell 1990, Parker 2003). Workers did not necessarily take these new production methods lying down, nor did they meekly accept working conditions where wages were low, work pressures were high and working conditions were unsafe. Early factory legislation, bitterly opposed by the owners, outlawed the employment of the youngest children and limited some of the worst excesses of dangerous working conditions. This forced the factory system to adapt and it did so despite the warnings of dire consequences of economic collapse from capitalist leaders. New efficiencies were found, often by replacing people with advances in technology.

From the nineteenth century onwards, governments, disturbed by threats to social order, began to enact labour legislation supportive of worker rights. This responded to, and was accompanied by, the growth of trade unions. From such beginnings in the nineteenth century, unions grew more strongly in the first part of the twentieth century: at the end of the First World War, throughout the Great Depression of the 1930s and during the Second World War (e.g. Clegg 1994, Hannan 1995, Kaufman 2004).

Inside the factory, managers responded with steps to shore up the stability of the factory system. Wherever workplaces were big (and large factories in steel-making, ship-building, textiles and automotive assembly could employ several thousand workers on one site), unions tended to be strong, and senior managers moved to appoint labour relations' specialists to their staff. These specialists worked on mechanisms to channel industrial conflict. This meant working with unions through a process of collective bargaining to jointly regulate the terms and conditions of work and employment (Flanders 1970), as explained in Chapter 6. It led to the adoption of such bureaucratic control systems as job evaluation, discussed in Chapter 5 as a way of bringing greater order into payment methods by developing a hierarchy of jobs and pay grades. Through such methods, the role of the industrial relations managers was to keep the peace with the unions and help to ensure the continuity of production, which led directly to profitablity. However, while the accommodations to organised labour that came through this process significantly improved levels of wages and benefits, they rarely challenged the structure of the work itself. In the Anglophone world, what unions with strong shopfloor power did achieve was improvements in pay, employment security, staffing levels and work norms. They helped to build what economists call the 'internal labour market' (ILM) (Doeringer and Piore 1971, Jacoby 1984).

This is a strange term because the whole idea of an ILM is to minimise market influences. ILMs are administrative regimes, not markets. They are a system of bureaucratic rules for defining jobs, allocating workers to them, enhancing employment security and determining pay. In the most developed systems, recruitment at the bottom levels of the job ladder leads into a structure which offers promotion from within and a set of valuable benefits in pay escalation, training, pensions and security. Unions played a major role in fostering such systems. They often negotiated seniority rules to protect workers with longer tenure and they helped to create the manufacturing wage premium. Manufacturing is a sector in which firms typically pay wages above the national average (UKCES 2012: 48–9). However, unions rarely challenged the division of labour (between managers and workers and between different types of worker) on which the Fordist production regime rested. In many cases, they magnified it through inter-union 'demarcation' disputes in which boundaries between different types of labour (and, thus, union memberships) were contested and policed.

In Chapter 1, we talked about the way in which the field of HRM encompasses a range of options or systems for managing work and people. In effect, what the Industrial Revolution gave birth to was a new kind of HR system: the 'industrial model' of HRM (Osterman 1987, Jacoby 2004), characterised by jobs that are low in discretion, responsibility and scope ('Taylorised' jobs) and with workers subservient to a hierarchy of management authority. These are the fundamental features of the industrial model although it has been modified by the responses of trade unions and governments, which have reinforced and expanded its bureaucratic rules.

The industrial model was developed to foster the efficiency advantages of high degrees of specialisation and economies of scale in mass production. However, reformers within management and, more importantly, pressure from trade unions and governments helped to ensure that wages and employment conditions were improved (e.g. Jacoby 2004). While many firms continued to adopt a style of limiting union influence or keeping the unions at 'arms-length', as discussed in Chapter 6, the overall result was greater workplace stability and higher levels of social legitimacy. The industrial model was enormously influential. Its core features of specialised jobs embedded in strong 'internal labour markets' spread into large service firms and the public sector and across the world.

The salaried model of HRM: necessary corollary of industrial expansion

It was never possible, however, to run the whole of the HRM process in an expanding manufacturing firm on an industrial model of HRM. The necessary corollary of such a model is the 'salaried model' of HRM (Osterman 1987, Pinfield and Berner 1994). This model of HRM was developed to manage the managers and specialists who were essential to manufacturing firms requiring high levels of capital, energy and coordination (Chandler 1977). In the USA, companies expanded on the back of a growing market and the success of the new techniques of mass production and distribution, creating a demand for a range of specialists in engineering, management accounting, personnel, purchasing, marketing and so on (Chandler 1977). Other industrialising countries also developed their hierarchies of professional managers with engineering and business schools springing up around the world to educate them.[5]

Under the salaried system, the individual is paid an annual salary rather than a wage calculated on the actual hours worked. This in itself conveys more trust and suggests that more flexibility is desired of people in the way they carry out their roles. Managers and specialists employed in this way enjoy higher levels of responsibility, pay and security than other employees (Fox 1974). Jobs are more open to interpretation, as is necessary when people are working on complex and open-ended problems, such as how to design a more stylish motor vehicle or how to set up a new distribution system. Career development within the firm is more strongly fostered so that 'institutional

---

[5] The French were the first to establish business schools but the US schools, such as Wharton and Harvard, became the exemplars within the Anglophone world: http://en.wikipedia.org/wiki/Business_school, accessed 27/1/15.

memory' can be preserved and highly productive people retained. While such bureaucratic practices as job descriptions, job evaluation and performance appraisal are prevalent in large organisations, there is often scope to recognise the particular strengths of individuals through performance-related pay, as explained in Chapter 7. At the highest levels of management, reward levels, including bonuses and share options, have now become extremely attractive and, in some societies, highly controversial because of their largesse. Like the industrial model, the salaried model spread from manufacturing to other large-scale organisations, such as those that developed in major service firms and government departments as economies grew.

Competitive challenges to mass production

Throughout the process of industrial expansion, management was not entirely insensitive to worker reactions to mechanistic work systems and university researchers were well aware of the human problems associated with industrialisation. In the middle decades of the twentieth century, the 'Human Relations Movement' showed interest in how work and supervisory practices affected employee motivation and in how the impacts of industrialisation could be ameliorated (see Watson (1986) for an excellent analysis). From the 1950s, the theory of 'socio-technical work systems' encouraged the development of 'autonomous or semi-autonomous work groups' in order to enhance the capacity for workers to make their own decisions and use more of their skills (e.g. Trist and Bamforth 1951, Winterton 1994). Then, in the 1960s, industrial psychologists laid increasing emphasis on ways of enhancing employee discretion through 'job enrichment' (Herzberg 1968, Hackman and Oldham 1980), as noted in Chapter 5. Job enrichment, involving increases in workers' responsibility and authority, was argued to improve satisfaction and employee commitment, reducing problematic levels of employee turnover. Most of these ideas, however, made little substantive impact in factories. There were celebrated experiments with work redesign, such as Volvo's development of semi-autonomous teamwork at its Uddevalla plant (Berggren 1992), but these were often marginal and short-lived (MacDuffie 1995).

It was not until the 1970s that management thinking about the organisation of factory work really started to be challenged. While the sort of ideas we have just noted had been talked about in management education for some time, the impetus for sustained changes to work systems had much more of its origin in serious competitive challenges that started to shake management confidence. In the 1970s, Japanese manufacturing firms began to show that they had mastered a new form of production which delivered better quality products at lower prices, seen most graphically in the Toyota Production System (Ohno 1988, Oliver and Wilkinson 1988). Japanese factories had adopted ways of manufacturing that reduced wasteful stock levels and involved workers (and not simply managers) in enhancing production quality. Ironically, they had taken American quality gurus, such as Deming (1982), much more seriously than had managers in the West and had used post-war reconstruction to build a manufacturing model which directly challenged Western manufacturers (Oliver and Wilkinson 1988). Japanese methods of 'lean production' (Womack, Jones and Roos 1990) and 'total quality management' (e.g. Wilkinson and Willmott 1995) began to take their toll, surprising Western manufacturers by the way in which Japanese firms could simultaneously enhance quality and reduce costs. The British motorcycle industry, flat-footed by Japanese production of a range of more reliable, cheaper and more stylish bikes, was one of the early casualties.[6] In the USA, smaller, more fuel-efficient Japanese cars began to gain market share and challenge the hegemony of such household institutions as Ford and General Motors.

What was painfully realised in the light of Japanese manufacturing success was that work systems for operating workers could no longer be ignored by senior managers. Unchanged, the old forms of work organisation could become a source of competitive *dis*advantage. On the other hand, transformed to focus more on quality and on more flexible types of working, new forms of work organisation had the potential to contribute to competitive advantage in a way unimaginable in the 1960s.

The development of high-involvement models of HRM

The threat to Western manufacturing associated with Japanese production systems generated enormous interest in the 1970s and 1980s and forced a rethinking of work organisation in key industries (e.g. Piore and Sabel 1984, Appelbaum and Batt 1994). Out of this re-thinking, a reformed version of the industrial model of HRM emerged, one which placed greater emphasis on tapping into the skills and underlying potential of production workers (i.e. 'working smarter' rather than 'working harder'). In various Western firms, manufacturers have made attempts to reform their low-discretion work systems towards a 'high-involvement' model of work organisation (Lawler 1986). Such a model was seen as necessary to improve quality, and the capacity to respond more flexibly to markets, including through higher

---

[6] For an excellent analysis of the rise and decline of the British motorcycle industry, see Ian Chadwick's website: http://www.ianchadwick.com/motorcycles/britbikes/index.html, accessed 27/1/15.

levels of innovation in products and manufacturing processes. Some use the high-involvement term synonymously with 'high-performance work systems' (HPWSs), which we discussed in Chapter 3 in our examination of best-practice models of HRM. While the HPWS terminology has become very prevalent, we think that talking of a high-involvement model of HRM, or a high-involvement work system (HIWS), is more useful because it is a more descriptive term, signalling a shift away from the low-involvement characteristics of traditional factory work.

In terms of their role in production reforms, high-involvement work systems encompass a range of practices that attempt to reverse the Taylorist process of centralising decision-making and problem-solving in the hands of managers and technical specialists. One way to foster greater involvement is to redesign jobs so that production workers have greater scope to make their own decisions about how to do the tasks in the job, using more of their skills and their learning capacities. This is the process of 'job enrichment'. Another way is to give this kind of power to a team of workers who then have greater control over their part of the production process, as in autonomous or semi-autonomous work groups (also known as self-managing or self-directed teams). Such changes often necessitate improvements in management communication, so employees have better information to work with and greater opportunities to have their say about issues in production, safety and work quality. They frequently involve greater investment in training and development, to foster skills in problem-solving and human relationships, and in pay incentives so that workers are better rewarded for the improvements they make in operating outcomes. As Appelbaum et al. (2000) explain, greater employee involvement in decision-making benefits from a reinforcing set of changes in the abilities, motivations and opportunities of workers to contribute to performance. The 'AMO' characteristics of HIWSs are a significant step up from those associated with the traditional factory system.

Lawler (1986) developed a useful way of describing these changes in work and employment practices. In his 'PIRK' model, high-involvement work processes improve employee perceptions of workplace power (P), information (I), rewards (R) and knowledge (K). In other words, high-involvement work processes empower workers to make decisions that affect their work, improve the information they have available and their opportunities to express their voice, link their rewards to their contributions and improve their access to training and development. This should then improve the utilisation of workers' skills and their intrinsic motivation while also having direct benefits for employee outcomes (Vandenberg, Richardson and Eastman 1999, Boxall, Hutchison and Wassenaar 2015). The linkages and impacts envisaged

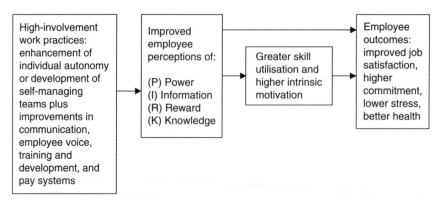

Figure 8.1 High-involvement work systems: envisaged linkages and impacts

in HIWSs are shown in Figure 8.1. The diagram makes this seem very straightforward, but that would be an unwise conclusion. As we explained in Chapter 7, real implementations of change are variable, depending on a complex set of motives and links inside the 'black box' of HRM. Whether the positive effects envisaged in Figure 8.1 can be achieved in a workplace reform, such as a move to lean production, is very much a moot point, as we shall see.

Greater employee involvement in decision-making is not, of course, likely to be the only way in which management responds to competitive pressure. Management moves to reform production systems have often started with investments in advanced manufacturing technologies, such as robots, computer-aided design (CAD), computer numerical control (CNC) machine tools and electronic data interchange (EDI) systems (Boyer et al. 1997, Challis, Samson and Lawson 2005). The combination of company investments in new manufacturing and information technologies *and* in the related work practices and employee skills is often argued to bring the greatest productivity benefits (Brynjolfsson and Hitt 2000, Black and Lynch 2001). When these new technologies are implemented, work redesign that enables production operators to solve technical problems as they occur reduces reliance on the need to call in specialist technicians and thereby enhances productivity (Wall et al. 1990, Wall, Jackson and Davids 1992). The more that machine operators are empowered, and trained, to address machinery problems, the quicker the response to these problems and the lower the amount of machine downtime. With highly automated technology, higher levels of error-free machine operation translate directly into higher output (Blauner 1964). There is also an 'anticipatory' benefit when operators learn more about the reasons why faults occur in the first place and find ways to reduce their incidence (Wall et al. 1990, Wall, Jackson and Davids 1992).

As underlined in Chapter 3, we must bear in mind that the specific work practices used to bring about greater employee involvement can be expected to vary across contexts. In some situations, HIWSs will involve reforms to create greater teamworking, either online (during production) or offline (away from the production process) or some mix of the two (e.g. Pil and MacDuffie 1996). But there are contexts in which teamworking can be counterproductive. It is more likely to be effective when people are working in a highly interdependent production process, where they must interact at a high level to improve how things are done (e.g. Sprigg, Jackson and Parker 2000, Langfred 2005). In situations where workers are largely independent of each other, imposing teamworking can actually reduce both performance and job satisfaction, and individually based job enrichment is a more sensible approach. Whatever the specific practices adopted, the key point we wish to make here is that an involvement-oriented model of HRM is now part of the HR strategies of a range of manufacturers. It is not a panacea, however, for manufacturing survival or something that finds favour across all societies. The extent to which high-involvement models are adopted, and how they are implemented, largely depends on whether their benefits outweigh their costs, and this is something that has to be considered in the light of the increased globalisation of manufacturing since the 1980s, a subject to which we now turn.

Globalisation and HR strategies in manufacturing

'Globalisation' of production was strong in the nineteenth century under the 'Pax Victoriana', when Britain ruled the waves (Krugman 1997), and under the continuing impetus of industrial innovations, including the growth from the 1820s of steam shipping (Solar 2006). International trade, however, suffered major setbacks in the first half of the twentieth century as a result of the two world wars and the Great Depression. Globalisation is not a new phenomenon but is something that has reasserted itself since the Second World War through a process of reduction in trade barriers between countries and regions (e.g. Gereffi and Frederick 2010). This has been a fraught, imperfect process but other factors, such as the liberalisation of financial markets, the collapse, or reshaping, of Communism as an alternative economic system, the growth of improved modes of transport (better air travel and containerised shipping), and higher speed and more comprehensive communications through the internet, have all played their part in opening up the world to higher levels of trade in goods, services and ideas.

Outsourcing and offshoring as models of HRM

Globalisation has made a major impact in those manufacturing industries where technology has been less successful in automating production and, thus, where production remains labour-intensive (Bernard, Jensen and Schott 2006). This is the case, for example, in clothing, footwear, consumer electronics and toy manufacture, in which China and other low-cost producers have become so dominant. In these sorts of industries, as Table 8.1 indicates, operations in high-wage countries are extremely vulnerable to differences in labour costs. In these terms, the least competitive countries are the high-cost northern European countries such as Sweden, Germany and the Netherlands. Australia also currently has a high level of labour cost. In the next tier are Canada, the USA, Japan and the UK, with New Zealand and Korea tracking

Table 8.1 Hourly compensation costs in US dollars for production workers in manufacturing, 2012: selected countries

Country	US$/hour, 2012
Sweden	49.80
Australia	47.68
Germany	45.79
Netherlands	39.62
Canada	36.59
USA	35.67
Japan	35.34
UK	31.23
New Zealand	24.77
Korea	20.72
Slovakia	11.30
Taiwan	9.46
Poland	8.25
Mexico	6.36
Philippines	2.10

Note: Hourly compensation includes direct pay plus employer social insurance expenditures and other labour taxes.
Source: Selected from U.S. Department of Labor, Bureau of Labor Statistics, http://www.bls.gov/fls/ichccindustry.htm, accessed 27/1/15.

somewhat below this group. However, hourly compensation costs in eastern Europe and in Asia and South America are markedly lower. In Slovakia, they are around one third of US levels, while those in Mexico and the Philippines are around 18 and 6 per cent of US levels, respectively.

Such large differences in labour costs place intense pressure on manufacturing operations in the developed world. A fundamental response in these circumstances is to consider which parts of the business can be outsourced to more efficient suppliers. Outsourcing can be either domestic or international. It is a strategy for buying inputs or services from another firm rather than employing one's own staff, except for the core people who manage the outsourcing process. In effect, outsourcing is a model of HRM, one in which firms try to gain access to the fruits of human labour in a way that is more cost-effective than employing their own staff. When this process is international, we talk of 'offshoring'. Offshoring can be through establishing one's own plant in a foreign location or through sub-contracting the work to other firms.

Offshoring production to countries in which labour costs are markedly lower, and where labour regulations are less demanding, has become one of the preferred HR strategies of manufacturing companies (Cooke 2001, 2007b). In labour-intensive industries, a strategy of trying to save a plant in a high-wage country through a high-involvement work system may not work because the difference in the unit costs of production with plants in low-wage countries is just too great. Multinational clothing or apparel manufacturers, for example, have chosen to sub-contract their production to a range of suppliers in newly industrialising countries where workers have the capabilities they need (principally, good skills in sewing) and where companies can meet their standards for quality and delivery times, but where labour costs are much lower than in their home countries. China has been the major beneficiary of this process along with other developing nations such as Vietnam, Indonesia and Bangladesh (Gereffi and Frederick 2010). Offshoring is the strategy that clothing multinationals use to achieve cost-effectiveness, while building a network of suppliers across countries and regions enhances their flexibility, helping them to manage the risks that can come from over-reliance on a single source or from political instability and natural disasters in a country or region.

As we explained in Chapter 1, however, these economic goals are not the only motives driving HR strategy: firms are embedded in societies and can be the focus for protest and consumer boycotts. An issue that the leaders of multinational firms cannot easily avoid concerns the social legitimacy of their foreign operations. We illustrated this in the case of the global supply chain in the fashion industry, in which the ethics of employment practices and of workplace safety are regularly put under the spotlight. The social legitimacy of multinational companies can be compromised if their suppliers are engaging people on crude forms of the industrial model of HRM or in life-threatening conditions. This risk particularly affects the larger firms that are household names. Such firms are increasingly taking steps to audit the employment practices and working conditions of their suppliers and are publicly disclosing the results in corporate responsibility reports.[7]

Cost is therefore a very large consideration driving outsourcing in labour-intensive industries but decisions in outsourcing cannot simply be reduced to the cost factor. Jensen and Pedersen (2011: 357) demonstrate this in a study of a large sample of Danish firms, explaining that globalisation and technological advances have enabled firms 'to disaggregate their activities into progressively smaller segments'. Which pieces they offshore where, however, depends on the fit between the characteristics of the activity and the attributes of the location. Besides cost levels, Jensen and Pedersen identify three other sets of factors in the decision: the availability of the types of human capital required, the attractiveness of the business environment, and the 'interaction distance between onshore and offshore locations' (ibid.: 356), which includes language and cultural issues. While their Danish firms found central and eastern Europe (CEE) attractive for manufacturing operations because of its proximity and low costs, the USA was more attractive for R&D and for advanced manufacturing activities. Asian countries also showed some importance in terms of a location for R&D activities, which is consistent with the strategies of several Asian nations to move up the value chain. It is also consistent with the fact that developing economies are creating their own mass markets of consumers: 'some 1.8 billion people are expected to join the global consuming class by 2025' (McKinsey 2012: 9).

This Danish study underlines the complexity of manufacturing and the way that different aspects of it are being redistributed around the world. In their review of global manufacturing, McKinsey (2012: 13) argues that 'companies must look beyond the simple math of labor-cost arbitrage to consider total factor performance across the full range of factor inputs and other forces that determine what it costs to buy and sell products – including labor, transportation, leadership talent, materials and components, energy, capital, regulation and trade policy'. A case in point is the range of factors that encouraged BMW to move engine production from Brazil back to its

---

[7] See, for example, the steps being taken by the large British retailer, Primark, including its participation in the Ethical Trade Initiative, and links to external reviews: http://www.primark.com/en/our-ethics/our-performance/annual-performance, accessed 27/1/15.

Birmingham plant in the UK in 2006, despite labour costs in Brazil being two-thirds of British costs.[8] The move worked synergistically with the production of the highly successful Mini at the company's Oxford plant. BMW Oxford, the old Cowley works of Morris Motors and British Leyland, was notorious for poor industrial relations in the 1960s and 1970s. It is now a classic case of a successful HIWS. This probably contributed to the decision along with the fact that labour costs only contributed 15–20 per cent to total costs and, by getting major suppliers within one hour of Oxford, the relocation significantly reduced transportation costs. It also increased flexibility for customers in the important British market by enabling them to change their choice of engine up to a week before the car is made.

Advanced manufacturing and the development of workforce capabilities

While access to suppliers in countries with a reputation for low labour costs and reliable performance is critical to producers of labour-intensive goods, the BMW case shows that this is not necessarily the formula for success in advanced manufacturing. Advanced manufacturing is both capital- and knowledge-intensive with high levels of investment in R&D (UKCES 2012). Advanced manufacturing firms are at the forefront of applied scientific research, including the development of nanomaterials in semiconductors and electronics, the creation of light-weight composite materials in aircraft manufacturing and automobiles and the fusing of engineering with biological science in food production, health products and medical equipment (McKinsey 2012). Such firms offer a blend of high-value products and services and are experimenting with new business models for growing their profitability (e.g. Teece 2011, Roos 2012). At this end of modern manufacturing, locating a plant in a cluster of firms with close connections to research-intensive universities and scientific laboratories, as well as in societies with access to world-class pools of scientists, engineers and managers, can be critical for success.

However, access to the human talent needed in advanced manufacturing cannot be taken for granted, even in the world's leading economies. It is interesting to note the ways in which the German manufacturers that have located in the affluent American market are collaborating with US community colleges to create a stream of employees with German-style apprenticeship skills in 'mechatronics', which combines mechanical and electrical engineering with computing and software skills (Aring 2014). German manufacturers,

---

[8] http://www.theguardian.com/business/2006/sep/14/politics.motoring, accessed 27/1/15.

such as VW, BMW and Siemens, are taking it on themselves to address a major weakness in the US talent pipeline, at least as far as their own operations are concerned. These, of course, are very large firms. Smaller manufacturers cannot be expected to have the financial or managerial resources to emulate them (UKCES 2012: 24–5). Most firms actually need the support of industry bodies and the higher education sector to have any chance of accessing the skills they need to be competitive in advanced manufacturing. To address this issue, in recent years, British governments have taken steps to increase the proportion of graduates in the 'STEM' subjects (science, technology, engineering and mathematics) (UKCES 2012: 37). Whether the UK has a sufficient supply of well-qualified scientists and engineers is an ongoing concern in advanced manufacturing.[9] There are general lessons here about the ways in which HRM is affected by societal attitudes to manufacturing and the educational institutions that develop, or fail to develop, the skills on which it depends (Winterton 2007).

Manufacturing firms, then, need leaders who think not only about the management of their costs but also about the development of the capabilities of their workforces. Cost dynamics are always in play, as the continued importance of outsourcing demonstrates, but HR strategy in manufacturing is increasingly about talent-management strategies. To secure a future in manufacturing, firms and their industry associations need to work collaboratively with governments to ensure that educational institutions and immigration policies generate the quantity and quality of people needed in the talent pipeline. This is particularly critical for enabling SMEs to compete on the world stage. Some societies are much better prepared than others for the talent shortages that are growing in manufacturing (McKinsey 2012: 76–7). Thinking about HR strategy solely at the level of the firm is very problematic in this sector.

Lean production and HRM

As we have seen, issues of labour cost, human talent, organisational flexibility and social legitimacy are all implicated in the HR strategies of manufacturing, with varying degrees of emphasis in different industries and countries. But another concern is also vital: how manufacturers make use of the talents of the people they have attracted to create the productive

---

[9] http://www.managementtoday.co.uk/news/1228358/dyson-hoover-3000-new-engineers/, accessed 7/11/14.

outputs desired by their customers. HRM plays a major role in the implementation and improvement of production systems. A production system is a set of choices around the technologies and know-how to use, the way the work is organised and the way people are employed in the particular operation. As discussed above, the Japanese development of lean manufacturing, exemplified in the Toyota Production System (Ohno 1988), directly challenged the production models of Western manufacturers in the 1970s (Womack, Jones and Roos 1990). Lean manufacturing is a philosophy or set of ideas relating to production. It combines high utilisation of manufacturing capacity with low inventory, eliminating the wasteful 'just-in-case' buffers of traditional approaches to mass production. It incorporates the Japanese emphasis on 'total quality management', a process that places great emphasis on enhancing the quality of the product as perceived by the customer (e.g. Hill 1991, Wilkinson and Willmott 1995). As de Treville and Antonakis (2006: 101) explain it:

> The Toyota Production System was born out of scarcity in post-World War II Japan. The buffers required to maintain high capacity-utilization given line imbalances, quality problems, alienated workers with narrow skills, and other sources of variability were too costly for Toyota. The solution was to operate with minimum inventory buffers while attempting to maintain a high capacity-utilization.

Lean producers focus on how customers perceive the value of the product and develop a production system that responds to a defined customer order in a highly efficient flow (i.e. production is 'pulled' by the customer rather than 'pushed' by the manufacturer).[10] In this process, waste is reduced through just-in-time (JIT) inventory, careful problem-solving to achieve continuous improvement ('kaizen') and close liaison with suppliers to enhance quality throughout the supply chain (e.g. Niepce and Molleman 1998, Shah and Ward 2003). This is not a radical break with the techniques of mass production, which was also concerned with how to reduce waste, such as poor coordination between material supplies and manufacturing processes (Chandler 1977: 273), but it takes waste reduction to a new level.

Lean production, then, calls for the application of skills that are not required, or that are less important, in traditional types of mass production, including technical skills in the diagnosis of waste and quality problems, and skills in working with others in teams (Sterling and Boxall 2013). Womack, Jones and Roos (1990), leading advocates of the lean philosophy, argue that operators should be able to stop the assembly line if they notice

---

[10] For an excellent introduction, see http://www.lean.org/WhatsLean/, accessed 30/10/14.

defects, and they also instigate problem-solving techniques to ensure they are not repeated. A successful transition to lean ways of working hinges on whether workers will learn and apply the relevant skills. To perform well in a lean context, they need better resources, such as real-time information on operating performance, and a style of supervision that is supportive of their skill development and involvement in decision-making. These changes imply that management needs to make investments in HRM that exceed those historically required by Fordism. Using a data set that spans a 24-year period, de Menezes, Wood and Gelade (2010) demonstrate that those British firms that first learnt to integrate the operational and HR practices implied by lean manufacturing outperformed later adopters. HRM is deeply embedded in the configuration of practices on which lean production depends (Shah and Ward 2003).

The adoption of lean techniques in manufacturing is now extensive (Delbridge 2007). It shows no sign of abating because there is still a major need to achieve efficiency gains in manufacturing, including in the drive for more efficient and more sustainable uses of raw material and energy inputs (McKinsey 2012: 122–4). There is considerable debate, however, around the impacts of lean production on worker well-being. Does it really represent a rupture from Fordism, in which workers experienced limited control and high levels of pressure, or does it represent a heightening of it (e.g. Vidal 2007, Hughes 2008)? Does it really have the characteristics, and benefits, of the high-involvement work systems we described above or is it more about work intensification? The fundamental issue can be summed up as follows: while lean production involves workers in problem-solving groups, it is a highly interdependent system of production that works by reducing work buffers and that leads to greater standardisation of work processes than was true historically in mass production (Oliver and Wilkinson 1988). This process reduces the opportunity for individual workers to vary their working methods and creates the risk of greater work intensity (e.g. Danford et al. 2004, Lorenz and Valeyre 2005).

What, then, are the consequences for employee well-being? This question continues to be the subject of research in employment relations. On the one hand, some research points to largely negative outcomes. This can occur if a lean implementation brings about a reduction in the skills and autonomy of operating workers (e.g. Parker 2003), which is hardly what lean advocates envisage. On the other hand, a lean implementation may enhance opportunities for involvement where these have, in fact, been more restricted historically. Based on his analysis of the Toyota production system in the NUMMI plant, Adler (1993) argues that worker involvement in developing operating standards can create genuine possibilities for influence and learning.[11] This view is developed into a series of propositions by the operations management theorists, de Treville and Antonakis (2006), who accept that lean production reduces the discretion of workers to vary their working methods but see it as fostering their involvement in the design of the production system in which they are embedded. They argue, however, that 'excessive leanness' can reduce the time that both workers and managers need to foster involvement in decision-making. This situation can then challenge its sustainability as a production system.

In recent research, Cullinane et al. (2013) apply the job demands-resources (JD-R) framework, discussed in Chapter 5, to the question in a study of 200 employees from a pharmaceutical manufacturer in Ireland. The JD-R framework contains the fundamental insight that all work involves resources that can engage or motivate us, while containing demands in terms of work pressure and performance targets that will deplete our energy, and may threaten our health through debilitating forms of exhaustion. As explained in Chapter 5, the JD-R framework sees such factors as a good level of employee control, helpful feedback from the supervisor, support from colleagues and the availability of relevant training as 'resources' that can help an individual to engage at work (Demerouti et al. 2001, Bakker, Van Veldhoven and Xanthopoulou 2010). Assessing job demands and resources in a lean implementation, Cullinane et al. (2013: 15) conclude that 'managers should focus their efforts on the provision of resources which complement the increased work pace, responsibility and dependency on others, allowing them to be perceived as challenges rather than hindrances'. Research by Sterling and Boxall (2013) illustrates the point. In their case study of the implementation of lean manufacturing in a consumer-goods manufacturer, there was a general improvement in quality, and workers reported much greater role clarity, but it was evident that some work teams were much more engaged in problem-solving and decision-making than others. The latter groups had the lowest levels of literacy and were working in those parts of the plant with higher levels of production pressure. The resources they needed to become more engaged included literacy programmes to enable workers to participate more confidently and greater support to their supervisors to cope with production pressure.

The debate around the impacts of lean philosophies on worker well-being, and how HR strategy should respond to them, will continue for some time.

---

[11] The plant lasted from 1984 to 2010 when it was closed in the light of differences about future plans and severe difficulties facing both parties in the Global Financial Crisis: http://en.wikipedia.org/wiki/NUMMI, accessed 31/10/14.

It is a critical issue in manufacturing because excessive levels of stress, as well as limited possibilities for involvement and development, affect the attractiveness of manufacturing firms and the sustainability of working lives in the sector. What we need to bear in mind is that while we talk of lean manufacturing as a particular style of manufacturing, individual implementations of it are variable, as with so many management philosophies (Koukoulaki 2014). Some aspects are more relevant in certain industries than others, some managers emphasise some aspects more than others, some anticipate the difficulties better than others and so on. The JD-R approach, utilised by Cullinance et al. (2013), offers a methodology for HR directors in manufacturing to assess the particular combination of resources and demands in their specific context and make responses accordingly. A case-by-case evaluation of the kind of demands the workforce is facing, including those confronting its frontline managers, can guide the development of the kind of resources needed to address them. This should then make lean production more sustainable.

Conclusions

There is no society on earth that doesn't have some level of manufacturing, even if only craft and batch forms of production. Manufacturing activity comes naturally to human beings and the organisation of work in it has created lasting legacies in our economies and on our well-being. Mechanisation in the Industrial Revolution created the basis for mass production – or 'Fordism'– and gave birth to the industrial model of HRM in which the jobs of production workers were characterised by low levels of discretion, responsibility and scope ('Taylorised' jobs). Trade unions and governments challenged, and reformed, the early excesses of this pattern, expanding its bureaucratic rules and the protections of workers through 'internal labour markets' and progressive legislation. The necessary corollary of the industrial model is the 'salaried model' of HRM, which was developed to manage the managers and specialists who were also essential to factory operation. The Fordist regime remained in place for a long period of time, and its practices influenced work systems well beyond manufacturing. It was destabilised in the 1970s when Japanese firms showed they had mastered a new form of 'lean production', which delivered better quality products with less waste at lower prices. Part of the response has been the development of 'high-involvement work systems', which aim to make better use of workers' skills and potential, often in association with more advanced forms of technology. These systems are reforms of the industrial model but the extent to which they are adopted, and how they are implemented, depends heavily on whether their benefits outweigh their costs.

Economic globalisation, including the massive development of production capacity and consumer markets in China, is redistributing manufacturing around the world. Globalisation has made a major impact on those industries where production remains labour-intensive. Here, cost levels are critical to profitability and offshoring to the developing world has been extensive, although the larger firms, particularly, have to be sensitive to the risk of being associated with exploitative or unsafe employment practices. Decisions about manufacturing locations are now finely grained and involve systemic choices around a range of business factors. In advanced forms of modern manufacturing, locating a plant in a cluster of high-technology firms with close connections to research organisations, and in societies with access to world-class skills, can be crucial to long-run competitiveness. Talent management, including ensuring access to a complex pipeline of scientific, vocational and managerial abilities, is critical in this. Some individual firms, such as the elite German firms operating in the American market, are more proactive in taking on the talent challenges posed by advanced manufacturing, but all are ultimately affected by the strategic HR choices that governments make.

Costs, capabilities and questions of flexibility and legitimacy are all involved in the HR strategies of manufacturers. Strategic HR choices also arise in the adoption and implementation of production systems, such as lean production, which continues to evolve as managers seek more efficient and more sustainable uses of resources. There is an important question, however, around the impacts of lean production on worker well-being and, simultaneously, on its business outcomes. Is it really an example of a high-involvement model of HRM or is it more accurately understood as a process of work intensification? The picture is mixed because each implementation is in some way different. As Cullinane et al. (2013) demonstrate in their study of an Irish manufacturing plant, the job demands-resources (JD-R) framework offers a way of assessing the particular combination of resources and demands in a lean implementation, which can help to shape responses that will enhance the outcomes in a specific context. This is an area in which HR directors can, and should, be making their mark.

9

HR strategy in services

In the previous chapter, we noted the enormous impact of manufacturing, which has lifted economic standards, radically altered human living conditions and left its mark on our thinking about how to manage people in organisations. In the second of our chapters on the critical contexts of HRM, we turn to an analysis of HR strategy in services. The industrial, salaried, high-involvement and outsourcing models of HRM, discussed in the previous chapter, all have their counterparts in services, and the philosophies of lean production are increasingly influencing the behaviour of service organisations (e.g. Bamber et al. 2014). But we must now consider services in their own right. This, as Chapter 8 explained, is absolutely essential: services, after all, account for 80 to 90 per cent of employment in advanced economies. We begin by looking at what is distinctive when a service is offered to a customer rather than a physical good produced. Both are designed to meet a human need or want but there are key differences that affect the character of HRM. We then analyse the nature of HR strategy in three broad categories of private sector services: standardised and simple services, differentiated services and knowledge-intensive services. HRM varies very significantly across these broad domains and across industries and strategic groups within them. The chapter then turns to an analysis of HR strategy in the public sector before reaching its conclusions.

What's different about services?

Services are conventionally understood as valuable experiences or human interactions rather than physical goods (Segal-Horn 2003: 478). While there is major overlap between the two sectors because service firms often provide goods (e.g. meals in a restaurant) and manufacturers often provide services (e.g. after-sales support for operating a computer), the service sector does differ from manufacturing in a number of important ways. First, service firms are typically much more labour-intensive than manufacturers (Frenkel 2000). For example, an Irish study estimates labour costs at 54 per cent of operating costs in convenience stores and 46 to 49 per cent in department stores[1] while labour costs in US law firms have been estimated at an average of 78 per cent of total costs.[2] Labour costs thus have a major impact on pricing in a way that is generally not true in capital-intensive, large-scale manufacturing. Wherever they have serious competition, the leaders of service firms are naturally focused on monitoring and managing the cost of the people they employ. If competitors can offer the same service with less costly labour, or if a major business downturn comes along, the managers of service firms tend to think fairly quickly about how to adjust their staffing budgets. A case in point concerns Aviva, Britain's largest insurer, which owns Norwich Union and RAC, among others. On 14 September 2006, the company announced a cut of 4,000 jobs, made possible by more sales being handled over the internet and a merging of back-office functions. When union leaders protested, Norwich Union's chief executive commented that the company was 'always looking for ways of working smarter with fewer people'.[3]

Second, services differ from manufacturing in terms of the balance between tangibility and intangibility in the offering to the customer (e.g. Bowen and Ford 2002, Lovelock, Patterson and Wirtz 2010). In a rental-car company, for example, the tangible parts of the service include the cars available for hire and the branch sites owned by the company while the intangibles concern the human-provided customer services, such as the level of staff efficiency and friendliness, the quality of car cleaning and the possibility of home delivery of the car. Services generally have a higher level of intangibles than manufacturing and thus a greater range of quality levels or 'heterogeneity', to which customer satisfaction can be very sensitive (e.g. Segal-Horn 2003, Batt 2007). Service workers typically have a much higher level of contact with customers than is true among manufacturing workers: 'the service product is, at least in part, the attitude the employee displays as he or she delivers the service experience' (Bowen and Ford 2002: 460). While large service firms often try to standardise the service encounter (as, for example, in fast-food chains and

---

[1] http://www.forfas.ie/media/forfas081222_retail_running_costs.pdf, accessed 27/1/15.
[2] http://www.altmanweil.com/dir_docs/resource/64272ef8-56f0-4b9a-b519-95351ee0310a_document.pdf, accessed 27/1/15.
[3] http://www.theguardian.com/business/2006/sep/15/1, accessed 5/11/14.

in cinema complexes), services are inevitably affected by the skills, personalities and moods of those who provide them (e.g. Aryee et al. 2012).

Third, services are typically produced and consumed as and when customers demand them ('simultaneous production and consumption') while manufactured goods can generally be stored, sometimes for very long periods of time (e.g. Segal-Horn 2003, Lovelock, Patterson and Wirtz 2010). 'Service organizations must find ways to balance capacity with demand without the benefit of the manufacturer's physical inventory buffer or risk losing customers who refuse to wait for service' (Bowen and Ford 2002: 455). Services are often seasonal with peaks of demand, such as the 'Christmas rush' in retailing and the peak in air travel, resort accommodation and hospitality during the summer months or when major events are occurring, such as the Olympics. As a result, service firms often develop flexible staffing systems, scaling up their staffing through temporary or casual workers to cope with spikes in demand and maintaining a smaller core of permanent workers who retain the company's know-how and provide training to the short-term staff (e.g. Siebert and Zubanov 2009). The implication of this is that managers try to avoid over-staffing a service business when customers are not there because this cuts directly into company profits. This motivation has undoubtedly been behind the controversial growth of zero-hours contracts in the UK where workers are not given any guaranteed hours and are paid only when the work arrives and they are called in to perform it.[4] The attraction of such contracts to managers in the retail and hospitality industries is obvious.

Fourth, customers are involved in 'co-producing' a range of services (e.g. Bowen and Ford 2002, Lovelock, Patterson and Wirtz 2010). Customers increasingly play a large role in less-skilled services, such as putting petrol into a vehicle, booking travel or entertainment and conducting banking transactions online or at an automated teller machine. Co-production or self-service helps to reduce labour costs and keep prices down. It is, however, limited in quality-sensitive and knowledge-intensive services, such as legal work, dentistry and healthcare. Conducting one's own child-custody case is rarely done or one's own root-canal treatment or heart surgery! As these illustrations suggest, we must treat the service sector as a diverse set of industries trying to meet a range of human needs and wants. We need some way of organising this diversity in order to analyse the nature of HR strategy in services.

---

[4] http://www.theguardian.com/news/datablog/2014/apr/30/new-data-on-zero-hours-contracts-adds-to-a-worrying-picture, accessed 25/11/14.

HR strategy in private sector services

We will turn our attention, first of all, to private sector services. To understand HR strategy, we are adapting a framework developed by Boxall (2003) to define three broad types of service, describe the business dynamics associated with them and the skills required in them (Table 9.1). This then enables us to identify the major models of HRM that are used in these service categories and analyse the way in which they affect organisational, employee and societal outcomes.

Standardised and simple services

Standardised and simple services cover all those service activities where human beings have fairly straightforward and regular needs. This includes

Table 9.1   Business dynamics and HR strategies in services

Service category	Business dynamics	Skills involved in the service	Typical approaches to HR strategy
Type One: Standardised and simple services	Cost-based competition except to the extent limited by unions and state regulation; outsourcing and substitution of labour for technology and self-service	Key managers and specialists have critical knowledge but front-line workers use generic know-how and basic skills	Dualistic models: an elite model for the core managers and specialists but 'scripted' HRM for front-line workers; informal models of HRM in small firms
Type Two: Differentiated services	A mix of cost and quality-based competition; profit opportunities for firms that identify and serve higher value-added segments	Key managers and specialists have critical knowledge but a higher level of skill is now needed in the front-line workforce	A continuation of dualistic models of HRM but greater use of high-involvement models of HRM for front-line workers
Type Three: Knowledge-intensive services	Competition is based on advanced expertise and high quality; premium prices, with elite firms clustering in the highest bracket	High knowledge intensity except where some parts of jobs or some services become routinised or outsourced	Much higher levels of investment in HRM per capita: professional and expert models of HRM with high levels of skill, pay and discretion

Source: Based on Boxall (2003).

such industries as service stations, public transport, fast-food outlets, super-markets, cleaning and security services and child- and elder-care services provided in the home. Customers often have choice in where to buy these sorts of services, or who to buy them from, and tend to be price sensitive.

Because this is the less-skilled end of services, customers will often engage in self-service or co-produce the service, thus helping to reduce its cost. This may include printing their own rail ticket, carrying their food to a table at a fast-food outlet, weighing their own fruit and vegetables in the supermarket and 'swiping' their purchases through the bar-code reader at a check-out. Large firms offering low-priced services to mass markets are continually looking for ways to take out costs. The more these firms engage customers in co-production, and the more they automate services and off-shore 'back-office' functions to lower-cost countries, the lower their unit-costs will be (Farrell 2005). De-skilling of work can be central to reducing costs. In the Australian retail sector, for example, large supermarkets have 'used various strategies to reduce the overall cost, and reliance, on skilled labour' (Price 2011: 95). In the baking department, bread is often par-baked at a central facility and then only requires re-heating in the stores, reducing the level of skill required. As a result, the supermarkets can employ bakery assistants rather than qualified bakers, 'thereby saving over $2 per hour in labour costs' (Price 2011: 97). In retail, as in many basic services, wage levels for front-line staff are among the lowest in the modern economy (Oster-man 2001). Most adults in society could do this kind of work if they wished to because it relies on simple skills in operating basic types of equipment or in offering some level of personal attention and care. Such work rarely commands a wage premium.

As this discussion indicates, business strategies in basic services are often focused on reducing the costs of producing the service. This implies a dual-istic approach to HR strategy. Mass-service firms concentrate their critical skills in a small cadre of managers and specialists. Senior managers at the Head Office, supported by specialists in marketing, supply-chain, finance and HRM, and a network of store-based and regional managers, make up the corporate elite (e.g. Bozkurt and Grugulis 2011). As in the salaried model of HRM developed to enable manufacturers to expand, mass-service firms need a well-trained, well-remunerated and loyal team of managerial and special-ist employees. It is this core group that develops strategy and, to the extent possible, finds ways of differentiating the service offering. The front-line workforce, however, makes up the vast majority of labour costs and here an equivalent of the Taylorist practice of de-skilling is often adopted (Bozkurt and Grugulis 2011). We call this 'scripted HRM'.

The scripted model of HRM

Scripted HRM is an attempt to standardise how front-line service workers deal with customers. Training in the chain stores, the supermarkets and the cinema complexes often includes scripting in an attempt to ensure that customers are processed in a standard way (e.g. Boxall, Ang and Bartram 2011). In other words, front-line workers are required to follow a particular set of steps in how they greet and sell services to a customer standing in a queue, much like an assembly line. In the cinemas, for example, this can include a set of questions about which food and beverages the customer would like, potentially adding significant value to the sale ('upselling'). These kinds of scripted interactions naturally diminish the scope for workers to use their discretion and can be connected to monitoring systems. Retailers often use surveillance via closed-circuit TV and video cameras and may use 'mystery shoppers', who secretly score sales assistants on their willingness to smile and be helpful (e.g. Guy 2003). Similarly, in the high-volume, in-bound call centre industry, managers often rationalise work practices by measuring such variables as call-length against prescribed time, the calls waiting to be answered, the abandoned-call rate and the time taken to 'wrap up'.[5] There will frequently be recording of calls and remote monitoring where managers listen in to ensure that scripts are used properly (e.g. Frenkel et al. 1998, Batt 2000, 2002). In these ways, managers use the scripted model of HRM to drive efficiency improvements and reduce heterogeneity in the service encounter. They seek to process large volumes of customers as rapidly and as consistently as possible, which enhances profitability and reduces customer frustration with waiting times for standard services.

It is not surprising that such situations have often been seen as the service sector equivalent of the factory system and that questions have been raised over their impacts on employee well-being (e.g. Korczynski 2001, Bozkurt and Grugulis 2011). The scripted model of HRM mirrors the industrial model of HRM, and an equivalent of the manufacturing 'speed-up' can occur, increasing stress levels and leading to high levels of employee turnover (Deery, Iverson and Walsh 2002, Cordery and Parker 2007). Furthermore, attempts to specify the kind of attitudes and facial expressions that employees should display, including smiling and showing interest ('emotional labour' (Hochschild 1986)), can be stressful, especially when customers are rude or abusive (Korczynski 2001, Bowen and Ford 2002). The picture in terms of employee well-being is not entirely negative, however. Scripting of interactions can bring

---

[5] http://en.wikipedia.org/wiki/Call_centre#cite_note-13, accessed 27/1/15.

a welcome order into the chaos of high-demand services and the taping of calls can actually protect employees from ill-founded customer complaints or management criticism (Rosenthal 2004). And, as with any model of HRM, individual line managers can do things to make life more tolerable and to help their team cope with the stresses they face (Frenkel et al. 1998, Purcell and Hutchinson 2007). In their study of an Irish call centre, which was heavily dependent on standardised policies and scripts imposed by its principal client, Harney and Jordan (2008) show how team leaders nonetheless found ways of building morale through personally treating their employees well. This meant that the call-centre representatives had much higher levels of loyalty to their supervisor than to the organisation of which they were a part.

Family firms and the informal model of HRM

The scripted model of HRM is not, of course, uniformly applied across firms operating in less-skilled services. Alongside the mass-service providers are many smaller organisations in which owner-managers try to make a living by 'keeping out of the way of the big boys' and offering more localised and customised services. This includes many small shops, regional trucking or taxi services, cleaning and gardening businesses, and a host of local bars, restaurants and caterers. The vast majority of these firms are family-owned with family members providing capital and the core human resources the firm needs. Retaining wealth, employment opportunities and leadership succession in the family can be more important than making the highest rate of return (Colli, Fernández Pérez and Rose 2003, Marchington et al. 2003). Profits grow in a bubbly economy but downturns in the discretionary income of their customers during a recession, or costly failures in service, can easily wipe them out.

The leaders of these firms use a much more informal model of HRM. They rarely use the bureaucratic practices that the big companies adopt for their large workforces, relying instead on their personal networks to hire workers and on their personal control of service operations (e.g. Marchington, Carroll and Boxall 2003). The outcomes for workers are typically mixed. At one extreme, some owner-managers are dictatorial and some pay below the minimum wage (Osterman 2001, Green et al. 2013). Where they exploit poorly informed workers, such as young workers or new migrants, by denying them their employment rights, and resist opportunities for individuals to have their say or join a trade union, researchers often talk of a 'bleak house' model of HRM (e.g. Sisson 1993). This kind of disregard for social legitimacy in HRM tends to be more possible in small firms because they are much less visible to regulators and the public eye than the large firm 'trading on the High Street'. On the other hand, while the prospects for internal promotion are limited in small firms, which tends to generate higher levels of turnover among more ambitious people, work is more open to individual discretion (e.g. Ortega 2009), making it more possible for individuals to adapt their working methods or express their personalities. In terms of employment practices, small firms can also provide a more trusting and flexible working environment when the owner fosters a climate of 'give-and-take' over working conditions (Edwards and Ram 2006). In this context, the owner is an approachable person, someone who may make adjustments for things like an employee's needs for after-school care of children.

Overall, then, in standardised and simple services, HR strategy is heavily affected by the dynamics of cost-based competition. In the large-scale operations, this drives a process of reducing unit costs through installing greater technology, fostering self-service, de-skilling work and outsourcing at least some of the activities behind the scenes. This turns on a dualistic approach to HR strategy, in which an inner core of managers and specialists are responsible for strategic direction and manage a much larger pool of front-line workers. The latter group works in a more scripted way and under less attractive and more insecure conditions. Predictably, this tends to foster higher levels of absenteeism and employee turnover (e.g. Green et al. 2013). At times, the level of dissatisfaction with the quality of work leads to such a low level of employee engagement and commitment that service quality suffers and firms acquire a bad reputation for it, which damages their market share and profitability (Batt 2007). However, as long as it is not difficult to replace people who leave, the approach to HRM tends to be stable enough to support business models in low-skilled services. The small firms in the sector are somewhat different and feel discernibly different to work in: they face the same cost pressures but rely much more on the personal control of the owner and an informal approach to HRM. This can be oppressive, and contains firms that disregard the employment laws, but it can also work effectively when owners accommodate the personalities and personal needs of the workers on whose skills they are dependent (Marchington et al. 2003, Edwards and Ram 2006). When labour markets provide plenty of low-skilled workers, this approach to HRM can also be stable but the risks of poor service are always present and such service failures can quickly sink the small firm.

Differentiated services

When we talk of differentiated services, we are referring to those markets where customers will pay a premium for a higher quality of service (Boxall 2003, Batt 2005, 2007). This is commonplace in hospitality and travel services, for example. The world's largest hotel chains often operate at multiple levels of the accommodation market, offering budget hotels for the cost-conscious traveller and luxury hotels for wealthier ones.[6] The long-haul, international airlines are also great differentiators, offering customers first-class, business class and economy options. We are also thinking here of service markets in which firms are competing to sell people riskier and more expensive items such as houses, new cars, fine art and personal loans or where firms are engaged in critical forms of business-to-business sales, such as major computer installations, high-tech medical equipment and personalised advertising campaigns. These sorts of higher-value activities depend on employees who have a higher level of product knowledge and who have skills in discerning differences in the needs of customers and nurturing their trust over longer periods of time.[7] For example, sales representatives in the pharmaceutical sector typically have greater education and training, which they need to intelligently discuss drug options with doctors and develop a personalised selling strategy for people who face many demands on their time.[8]

At this point, however, it is vital to reinforce a key point of difference between manufacturing and services. As we saw in the previous chapter, lean manufacturers in such spheres as automobiles and motorbikes have shown that it is possible to create improvements in quality and reductions in price at the same time. This process has now unfolded in many capital-intensive manufacturing industries (e.g. consumer electronics) where customers have become used to buying better models as they are released at lower prices. There are many service industries, however, where improvements in quality will *only* come at a higher price because of the strong relationship between higher levels of service and the higher costs of service provision. The airlines make this very visible in the prices charged for different classes of seat. It is also extremely apparent in the hospitality industries where the larger part of the service is geographically fixed. For example, someone wanting to stay in a good hotel in Paris will likely make the booking through the internet, which reduces costs, but the bulk of the service provision will take place with staff working in Paris and being paid Parisian wages. While companies in differentiated services continue to apply new technologies and offshoring wherever they can to reduce costs, higher-quality service in the geographically fixed components of services translates into higher costs and prices.

---

[6] See, for example, the branding of Sofitel and Novotel in the Accor hotel chain: http://www.accor.com/en/brands.html, accessed 27/1/15.

[7] See, for example, http://www.mckinsey.com/insights/marketing_sales/the_basics_of_business-to-business_sales_success, accessed 27/1/15.

[8] For an excellent explanation of the work of a pharmaceutical rep, see http://www.jobshadow.com/interview-with-a-phizer-pharmaceutical-rep/, accessed 27/1/15.

The high-involvement model in service work

Moving 'up-market' has implications for the package of tangibles and intangibles in the service offer, and thus for HRM. A study by Haynes and Fryer (2000) of a five-star hotel in New Zealand illustrates the point. Like all luxury hotels, a desirable location, special amenities and the quality of guest rooms drive one aspect of the hotel's strategy. Luxury hotel owners create the kind of opulent facilities, including larger, better-furnished bedrooms, swimming pools, bars and restaurants, that position them in the four-or five-star segment of the market. However, the rate of room occupancy and revenue per customer, and thus the hotel's profitability, is also affected by the way front-line staff deal with customers in the context of these surroundings (the intangibles in the service offer). This includes the way in which guests are greeted, and their preferences discovered and catered for, leading to higher levels of customer loyalty. It includes the ways in which staff respond when there has been a service failure. The demand of their clientele for a higher quality of service then justifies a greater investment in the HRM model for front-line workers: in more careful employee selection and more comprehensive training, in regular reviews of employee performance and in staff committees and suggestion systems through which management learns about quality problems and about employee motivators.

When firms aim for higher value-added segments in services, then, investments in creating the kind of high-involvement work systems we talked about in the manufacturing chapter are more likely to be justified (Batt 2000). This often implies a greater degree of investment in employee training, as in those airlines that seek to offer a better quality of cabin service (Heracleous and Wirtz 2009). A greater degree of empowerment may be encouraged among front-line employees, enabling them to tailor the service offering to individual needs and respond with some discretion when service failures occur ('service recovery'). This is typical among business-to-business sales representatives who have a high level of control over how they deal with customers in their territory or set of accounts. And, in these sorts of cases, remuneration strategy is also important: rather than relying on controls over their behaviour (i.e. scripting), such sales representatives are typically managed by output controls: an important percentage of their pay is directly linked to their sales performance.[9]

A greater degree of empowerment is also likely in those standardised services where firms are trying to move away from competing solely on costs.

---

[9] See, for example, the interview with a medical equipment sales rep at http://www.jobshadow.com/an-interview-with-a-medical-device-salesman/, accessed 27/1/15.

In Peccei and Rosenthal's (2001: 835) study of a supermarket, which was seeking to compete on quality of service and not simply on price, management relaxed the scripting and empowered front-line workers to 'give exchanges or credit for unsatisfactory products', take the customer's word on disputed prices and remove stock of poor quality from the floor. These may seem like small changes but they can actually be significant in the context of large-scale retail operations, making better use of employee skills, enhancing employee commitment and thus improving the quality of service and customer loyalty. Research on the 'employee-customer-profit chain' at the American retailer, Sears, is interesting in this regard. Sears uses the idea that the company will become a 'compelling place to invest' if it is a 'compelling place to shop' and a 'compelling place to work' (Rucci, Kirn and Quinn 1998). Data gathered from surveys within the company suggest that 'a 5 point improvement in employee attitudes' leads to 'a 1.3 point improvement in customer satisfaction' and 'a 0.5 per cent improvement in revenue growth' (ibid.: 91).

Much about the character of HR strategy in differentiated services is similar to the pattern we see in standardised services. Dual tracks for the elite and for the majority of the workforce are still apparent. What may shift, however, is the degree to which the front-line workforce is empowered, incentivised and enabled to offer more expert, more customised and more responsive service. In these conditions, managers often develop models of HRM that have parallels to the high-involvement work systems developed to make better use of employee skills in manufacturing. This typically implies a higher level of investment in HRM, which managers seek to recoup in higher prices or greater revenue.

Knowledge-intensive services

By knowledge-intensive services, we mean the classical professions, such as those that control services in law, accounting and medicine, along with newer forms of knowledge-intensive service, such as specialised forms of software development and expert work in financial services. Like scientists and professional engineers working in advanced manufacturing, workers in knowledge-intensive services are very much what we might call 'human capitalists'. Knowledge is their stock-in-trade: both knowing about a difficult subject and knowing how to meet a client's needs (Swart 2007). Individuals are motivated to seek ever more interesting or challenging work that enables them to explore their potential. While many such individuals work as independent contractors, others are employed in firms. They compete by attracting clients who will come back for more because of their respect for the quality of the expertise being provided to them and the relationship of trust that has been established. Very successful individuals and firms become something like a monopoly: they develop the kind of specialist know-how and quality of relationship that makes them the first choice of their clients. Pricing is never irrelevant, with the elite individuals and firms charging fees in the highest brackets and the less-well-known ones charging somewhat less, but all of them are building in a high level of remuneration (Boxall 2003).

Professional and expert models of HRM

We refer to the 'professional model' of HRM to describe the management of people in the classical professions and we refer to the 'expert model' of HRM to describe how other types of knowledge worker are managed. Both groups typically have advanced tertiary education with professionals requiring an approved qualification that meets the standards of their professional body.[10] Professionals are socialised through their higher education and specialist training into ways of working that have been developed by the professions themselves, much as the medieval crafts, discussed in Chapter 8, developed their own methods and controlled their own training. Service to the client is critical and the professional code of ethics is important. The profession disciplines its own members when they act unethically: for example, when the Bar Standards Board disciplines a barrister for some form of misconduct with a client.[11]

Professionals typically organise themselves into partnerships in which the shareholding partners form the supreme decision-making group (Boxall and Steeneveld 1999). This is an elite form of employee ownership and junior professionals are often highly motivated to rise through the ranks and 'make partner'. Working as an HR specialist in this context involves a need for sensitivity to professional forms of governance, including collegial, though not necessarily straightforward, decision-making and to the autonomy that individual partners can preserve for themselves. Building up their own set of clients, each partner can act like an independent agent, albeit contributing to, and drawing resources from, the larger partnership of which they are a member. This form of ownership is less common in other forms of knowledge-intensive work, such as advanced IT services, where large corporations have grown up on the worldwide expansion of computing and communication technologies.[12]

---

[10] In the case of the General Medical Council, see http://www.gmc-uk.org/, accessed 27/1/15.

[11] https://www.barstandardsboard.org.uk/, accessed 27/1/15.

[12] Apple, Microsoft, Google, and Facebook are examples.

In knowledge-intensive services, there is a conjunction of high qualifications, high discretion and high pay: or, at the least, everyone starts out with high qualifications and can reach high levels of discretion and pay if they learn fast, work hard and impress their superiors. This implies that the level of investment per capita in HRM will be high and clients have to pay high prices if they want the service in question. To be sure, there is some scope to economise on costs when some advanced services become 'routinised'. This happens where professional or consultancy firms roll out standardised solutions to the more common business problems they deal with and use more junior employees to deliver them (Doorewaard and Meihuizen 2000). There is also a growth now of 'knowledge-processing offshoring' where aspects of such services as insurance underwriting and legal and financial research are conducted in low-wage countries, most notably in India.[13] However, the more complex or esoteric the knowledge, requiring a high level of adaptation to each client's needs, the higher the control exercised by the knowledge worker, the higher the cost of employing them and the higher the price that will be charged.

A high-involvement approach to HRM is therefore commonplace in knowledge-intensive services in order to use the professional or expert's judgement in how to solve a problem or meet a client need. The world of HRM in these firms is well endowed and the HR specialists in the elite firms are charged with recruiting the brightest graduates from the best universities or proactively finding new employees who have the right kind of experience but are currently employed elsewhere. Talent management looms large with HR strategists in these firms needing to think hard about the mix of intrinsic and extrinsic motivators that will attract and retain expert workers. Knowledge workers can be expected to have greater employment opportunities than less skilled workers and to be more mobile, creating angst about the impact of their departure on the competitive capabilities of firms (e.g. Horwitz, Heng and Quazi 2003). They often have links to wider networks and communities of practice in which knowledge-sharing is fostered (e.g. Swart 2007).

When it comes to their preferred style of working, however, many prefer to work as independently as possible and may need support to develop skills in teamwork when this is important to build social capital and innovation in an organisation (Lee-Kelley, Blackman and Hurst 2007). It is important to provide them with an environment that fosters personal growth, one in which

---

[13] http://www.theguardian.com/business/2006/nov/06/india.internationalnews, accessed 27/1/15; http://www.smh.com.au/business/sourcing-cheaper-staff-the-new-growth-industry-20120127-1qlou.html, accessed 27/1/15.

they have the kind of work that stimulates them and in which their achievements are well recognised (Horwitz, Heng and Quazi 2003, Lee-Kelley, Blackman and Hurst 2007). Personal attention from senior executives who take an interest in the firm's stars is important along with access to start-of-the-art technology in high-tech industries (Horwitz , Heng and Quazi 2003). However, firms that boast in their 'employer branding' of their ability to offer interesting work and continuous career development need to deliver on this promise if they are to retain the more effective professionals and experts. A reasonable level of retention in a productive environment is critical if firms are to gain sufficient value from the high level of investment in knowledge workers, providing, of course, that their skills have not atrophied or been made obsolete by newer developments.

A mismatch between what an employer claims and what is delivered is clearly a major risk in professional and expert models of HRM. Another major issue is associated with the problem of work-life balance among successful knowledge workers. British professionals, for example, are increasingly experiencing heavy demands on their time (Green 2006, Gallie and Zhou 2013). The best individuals come under pressure to take on more work or, in many cases, willingly immerse themselves in work that fascinates and fulfils them. This drive for learning and mastery further extends their human capital but can, in time, undermine their health (e.g. through high blood pressure, heart attack or stroke) and alienate them from their family and friends who 'hardly ever see them'. Helping such individuals to achieve a better balance in their lives and helping the professions, such as law, to enable their highly skilled workers to balance work with care-giving remains a key challenge and a question of ongoing interest in the debate around gender equity in society.[14]

We have come, then, to the end of our tour of HR strategy in private sector services. What should be readily apparent is the extent to which HRM varies across this huge sweep of the economy. The kind of skills needed in a human-service activity, and the nature of the competition that plays out in particular service industries, makes a profound impact on the character of HRM. The folly of thinking about HRM as a set of 'best practices' across these contexts should now be very obvious. What we need to be able to do is identify the models of HRM that characterise different service contexts, understand how they have arisen in these circumstances, and assess their impacts on firms, workers and society, including shifts in outcomes as change occurs. We have,

---

[14] See, for example, http://www.theguardian.com/law/2011/jul/01/law-firms-work-life-balance, accessed 27/1/15; http://www.forbes.com/sites/deborahljacobs/2014/08/05/at-law-firms-mommy-track-still-holds-women-back/, accessed 27/1/15.

in fact, understated the degree of variety that exists in HR strategy in services by talking only about three broad categories. Closer research finds finer variations in these patterns. We turn our attention now to the public sector, an enormous site of employment in most economies and one of the most contentious fields in contemporary HRM.

HR strategy in public sector services

The state, whether at national or local level, has always had to provide some services to citizens. In the nineteenth century, these began with free schools, the 'work house' for chronically impoverished families, a police force and the armed services. At the least, these services needed to be administered and financed, leading to the creation of a cadre of civil servants. The major expansion in the role of the state as the provider of services, with the corollary of tax and national insurance, came after the economic depression of the interwar years and reconstruction following the Second World War. The Welfare State in Britain came in response to the Beveridge Report of 1942, concerned to tackle the 'giant evils of squalor, ignorance, want, idleness and disease' with government the lead reformer.[15] This reform process created the National Health Service (NHS), national insurance for unemployment, family allowances and pensions. The failing railway network was nationalised, along with other key industries, while the road infrastructure, the postal service and communication networks were expanded to meet the needs of the modern economy.

The public sector became huge. In the UK in 2013, it employed 5.7 million workers, amounting to 18.8 per cent of the total workforce.[16] This is even after cuts in employment in the period since 2010. Of this 5.7 million, a third work in education, 31 per cent in health and social work and just below a quarter in public administration and defence. Around two-thirds of employees are women, compared to 40 per cent in the private sector, and one-third work part-time, compared to a quarter of private sector employees (Bach and Kessler 2012). Over time, education and the NHS have come to dominate the public sector. The management of the public sector has been subject to attempts by governments over many decades to gain control of this enormous expenditure, ensure value for the taxpayer's money and create greater responsiveness to user needs. For 30 or more years in OECD countries, the search for cost-effectiveness has been a constant theme among policy makers

---

[15] http://en.wikipedia.org/wiki/Beveridge_Report, accessed 27/1/15.
[16] http://www.ons.gov.uk/ons/taxonomy/index.html?nscl=Public+Sector+Employment, accessed 27/1/15.

(Hebdon and Kirkpatrick 2005, Eliassen and Sitter 2008). The heart of the challenge has been the management of the workforce since labour costs as a proportion of total costs often exceed two-thirds.

The evolution of the New Public Management

Public sector management, as it evolved in the mid-twentieth century, placed emphasis on central control and standardisation through bureaucracies, emphasising public accountability and public values. The provision of services in health, education and the justice system was dominated by professionals. The notion of the 'customer' was alien and 'market values' anathema. The key term for the reform programme that took root in many countries, including Australia, New Zealand and the UK in the 1980s, and which continues (Greener 2013), was the New Public Management (NPM). It encouraged the implanting of private sector–style initiatives into the public services, a focus on competition among service providers, stronger managerial authority and enhanced forms of centralised performance management (Bach and Kessler 2012: 8). The state 'became less about the direct provision of services and more concerned with establishing a policy and budgetary framework ... the regulation and licensing of providers, and the collection and dissemination of performance information' (ibid.: 44).

While different British governments have approached the management of the public services in marginally different ways, strongly influenced by the state of the economy at the time, the fundamentals of NPM have remained unaltered. These have been summarised by McLaughlin, Osborne and Ferlie (2002: 9) as seven doctrines:

- Hands-on and entrepreneurial management
- Standards and measures of performance
- Output controls
- Disaggregation and decentralisation of public services
- Competition in provision
- Private sector styles of management
- Discipline and parsimony in resource allocation.

There have been three phases in the adoption of NPM, in England and Wales at least (Scotland has been less enthusiastic about NPM, a factor of some influence in the independence referendum of 2014). At first, in the 1980s, and much of the 1990s, the emphasis was placed on empowering the management cadre while seeking to reduce the dominance of public sector professions and championing private sector management techniques by developing markets to rebalance customer–producer relations (Hebdon and Kirkpatrick 2005). Market forces were used to discipline the workforce: for example, by decentralising pay determination and introducing performance-related pay. Additionally, the programme of privatisation was begun through selling off the public utilities, such as energy and water supply, and then by encouraging private investment and control in parts of the health service, the prison system and in local authorities, which were required to engage in 'compulsory competitive tendering'. This was most vividly seen in the real-location of 'bin men' (and women) to the private sector in many towns. There was a clear divide between purchasers and providers of public services.

By the time the UK Labour government came to power in 1997, it was evident that this basic NPM agenda was not producing the expected results. The reform agenda was uneven in its application and was neither understood nor accepted by public sector employees. This tended to undermine staff morale, labour turnover increased and, as a result, service quality declined. It proved much harder than anticipated to decentralise collective bargaining and weaken unions at the national level (Bach and Kessler 2012: 157). Neither for the first time, nor for the last, government found that importing (assumed) private sector models of performance management into the public sector was a challenge. The inability to manage the workforce was the Achilles' heel of NPM.

The second phase of NPM, in the decade 1998–2008, redefined the problem but continued with many of the solutions. There was a crisis of 'fiscal legitimacy' with much of the public disillusioned with the quality of public sector provision and questioning the huge funding requirements. Emphasis was placed on service to the user, for example in 'The Patient's Charter' developed in the UK's health system. At the same time, the Labour administration recognised that, in a global economy, modern public services, especially in education and health, were essential to national competitiveness (Bach and Kessler 2012: 157). The state found that it was required to support the country's education, health, welfare and transport infrastructure to a much greater extent. The solution was to continue to rely on markets and contracts and, where possible, the commodification of public services with the expansion of low-skilled, unqualified work in social care, health and education. At the same time, emphasis was given to the active encouragement of a diverse set of providers to deliver services from private, voluntary or not-for-profit organisations alongside, or competing with, existing public sector providers. One typical example is the privatisation of home-care services for the elderly in Japan in 2006 (Broadbent 2014). The intention of NPM was to give service users more choice, open up more public services to competition and grant more freedom to local management by allowing for semi-autonomous provider units once quality standards, set centrally, had been met. Schools and hospitals were able, in theory, to determine their own models of HRM. One outcome was to search for employment patterns outside traditional grade structures, and at reduced cost. This led to a growth in outsourcing and the use of temporary contracts, as well as an expansion in unqualified staff as 'assistants' in schools and hospitals (Kessler, Heron and Dopson 2012).

This rapid expansion in the number and types of providers of public services led to the adoption of coordinating bodies building on the latest theory in management strategy in large multidivisional companies, that of networking or the N-form Corporation (see Chapter 10). 'Public network management is about managing networks of different providers, many of whom may not be public providers, into coherent services' (Greener 2013: 41). The implications for employment strategies were that government 'became acutely aware that public service quality based on NPM consumerist sentiments relied on the commitment and capability of the workforce; the ability to recruit and retain and motivate staff as well as providing the necessary skills and capabilities' (Bach and Kessler 2012: 160–1). This was expensive and pressure for achieving 'value for money' led to imposed targets, regular and sometimes intrusive monitoring, further emphasis placed on performance-related pay and appraisals, new forms and times of working, an emphasis on team performance and multi-agency working with closer involvement of users in service design and provision.

The third phase of 'austerity NPM' is currently being adopted in many countries in response to the recession triggered by the Global Financial Crisis in 2008. Public sector employment has been a prime target of government responses to the crisis (Bach and Bordogna 2013). Common responses have been structural reorganisation, pay freezes and job losses (especially among managerial and administrative staff (ibid.: 286)[17]; further contracting out to the private sector; increased use of temporary staff; and re-centralisation and unilateralism in pay and conditions decisions. Job losses in the UK are expected to be just under 1 million between 2009 and 2017, around 1 in 6 (Tailby 2012). This has broad implications 'for what people can expect to experience in terms of pay, conditions of work, management practice and workplace cultures' (ibid.: 457). Within the health system, further radical reorganisation took place following legislation in 2012, bitterly opposed by all professional groups and trade unions.[18] This established new commissioning groups at the local level required to seek tenders from private and

---

[17] In 2010, the UK government's White Paper setting out the restructuring of the NHS predicted that 30,000 management jobs would be lost in the cost-saving exercise (Department of Health, *Equity and Excellence: Liberating the NHS.* Cm 7881).

[18] The Health and Social Care Act 2012.

public providers. While much has been made of the opportunities such commissioning provides for voluntary organisations and social enterprises, in practice it is large companies that gain most of the contracts, especially in social care and specialist health provision. The same is occurring in prisons and among probation staff. Private-equity funds are very active in health and social care and 'are likely to expand their presence as part of the shift towards more diverse, market-orientated funding of public services' (Bach 2011: 9).

This is very challenging for trade unions and professional associations originally structured to service centralised collective bargaining for very large numbers of employees. The decentralisation of bargaining in the civil service in England and Wales meant that instead of a handful of national agreements there are now around 150. Yet the government Treasury department closely controls the bargaining parameters by enforcing a 'remit' on management negotiators (Bach and Kessler 2012: 66). Increased use has also been made of pay review bodies where a panel of experts takes evidence from government, employers and trade unions and makes pay awards. What seems like a non-conflictual way of determining pay has proved to be controversial.[19] While the second iteration of NPM in the 1990s gave substantial pay awards, often linked to re-grading, in the 'austerity NPM' of 2010–2017, pay in the public sector in many countries has either been frozen or significantly constrained below the level of inflation (Bach and Bordogna 2013). Low-paid jobs are increasingly moved to the private sector (Hebdon and Kirkpatrick 2005), and are more often part-time, with many undertaken by women on temporary or zero-hours contracts. Private sector employment in areas previously provided by the state is most evident in 'nursery nurses' and assistants, growing from less than 40,000 in 1994–5 to over 100,000 in 2010–11, and in social care, up from just over 200,000 in 1994–5 to over half a million in 2010–11 (Cribb, Disney and Sibieta 2014: 26–7).

It is hard for unions to recruit and service members in this fragmented public-service provision. The main public sector union in the UK, Unison, reports that while it used to be normal for a union branch to deal with one public sector employer, by 2009 45 per cent of Unison branches dealt with 10 employers and 17 per cent had to deal with more than 50 (Waddington and Kerr 2009).

Public sector organisations, including 'approved' semi-autonomous hospitals and schools, are subject to oversight, targets and performance measures

---

[19] In 2014, the Doctors and Nurses pay review body awarded a pay rise of 1 per cent. The government refused to accept this and only paid this amount to staff that were not on an incremental pay scheme. A national strike took place for 4 hours on 13 October 2014, the first such strike for 32 years.

from the centre via quasi-independent bodies such as the Health Commissioning Board, and Monitor, which is concerned with financial and organisational viability.[20] Crucially, Monitor sets the prices or tariffs that British purchasers and providers of healthcare have to follow. This places emphasis on local management and staff to achieve efficiencies and cost saving since price competition is ruled out. The expectation is that there will be mergers among providers, cross-service partnerships involving public and private providers, new forms of work organisation merging professional practice, the growing use of shared-service models across organisations, especially in HR services, and pressure on staffing. This is particularly intense in local government. One of the largest city councils, Birmingham, expects to have lost two-thirds of its jobs in the period 2010–2017, down from 20,000 to 7,000.[21]

NPM: implications for HRM

Historically, HRM in the public sector was regulated through a process of centralised collective bargaining with the relevant unions. Within this structure, the public sector was seen as a 'model employer', setting an example in social legitimacy for the private sector (e.g. Greener 2013). There was little scope for local management to vary the national formula or challenge the high levels of autonomy enjoyed by professionals like doctors, nurses and teachers on the ground. Under NPM, 'HRM is regarded as one of the key ways that an organisation can achieve a competitive edge over its rivals and to make the most of those working within it' (ibid.: 197). One aspect of this is the determination of performance standards, measurement to ensure compliance and intervention when performance is not up to scratch. Another policy goal is proactive recruitment of key individuals, if necessary from abroad; training and development with an emphasis on new ways of working; and ensuring that skills and professional knowledge are kept up to date. Central to performance management is individual appraisal, increasingly linked to performance-related pay. This is a huge agenda and, in the complex and conflicted context of the public sector, extremely challenging.

Professional HRM in the public sector: a model under siege

Within health and education, a high proportion of employees are professionals. Half of the employees in the NHS are professionally qualified and 44 per cent have been educated up to degree level, compared to 24 per cent

---

[20] https://www.gov.uk/government/organisations/monitor, accessed 27/1/15.
[21] http://www.bbc.co.uk/news/uk-england-birmingham-29226844, accessed 27/1/15.

in the private sector (Bach and Kessler 2012: 101). Professionals have long been accused of 'producer capture' by enforcing inflexible and self-serving work practices (Bach and Kessler 2012), protected by the professional associations that determine entry standards and rules of conduct. This is less so after 30 years of NPM but the management of professionals continues to exercise, and frustrate, governments (Hebdon and Kirkpatrick 2005). The attempt to bring them under the control of public sector managers through the techniques of performance management and performance-related pay has not been easy. 'The central paradox of dealing with professionals in public management is that professionals often don't regard their primary responsibilities to be to the organisation that employs them but to their clients and to their professional grouping' (Greener 2013: 124). Hutchinson and Purcell (2011), in their study of ward managers (senior nurses), asked respondents to rank the groups they identified with. First was the patient, second their team, third their profession and last their employer, the hospital.

With public sector professionals, the use of performance measures and rules-based standards may, in fact, be counter-productive (Hood 2006). Fisher and Ferlie (2013) trace how rules-based standards erode ethics-based engagement. A rules-based system can have a perverse effect, undermining professionals' and clients' confidence in each other, while producing a 'tick box' culture that protects managers and officials from criticism. The tension is between the drive for transparency and accountability, and the desire of professionals to deliver a high-quality treatment without some bureaucrat looking over their shoulder. Professionals have high-discretion jobs and expect to be provided with the tools to undertake the work in accordance with professional standards and their judgement of the needs of the patient, student or client. When this principle is continually challenged in the public sector, the outcome is 'intractable conflict'.

Devolution has shifted responsibility for management, and especially HRM, to the local level but within the context of centrally determined performance targets. Typical performance measures include the proportion of 16-year-olds gaining a minimum number and standard of exam passes, or waiting times for operations in hospitals. Performance rankings are published and widely reported, and resource decisions are made in the light of these measures. The outcomes for failing to meet the targets are not trivial. They can involve a decision to put the school or hospital into 'special measures' with a new top-management team imposed.

Such controls can have perverse consequences with evidence of 'gaming' to meet standards: for example, delaying the arrival of ambulances to ensure that waiting-time targets are met in Accident and Emergency departments, or schools giving preference to able students to ensure the required pass rate is achieved. Perversely, 'one of the consequences of the imposition of managerial practices, of which centrally prescribed performance management systems are perhaps the most visible example, ends up taking away discretion from public managers and reducing their autonomy and ability to manage their organisation' (Greener 2013: 202). It becomes harder to manage despite the theoretical freedoms that devolution gives to local management. In part, this is because of the problem of multiple stakeholders. A study of an Australian Blood Service organisation (Fletcher et al. 2003) identified 11 stakeholder categories, with all the diversity that this implies in targets for, and perceptions of, quality.

It is the need to recognise multiple stakeholders, and attempts by central authorities to impose performance targets in close detail, in the context of professional workers with low levels of affinity to their employer, which make the challenges faced by public sector managers very different from those pertaining to the private sector. An added dimension is that public sector organisations rarely fail in the same way as they do in the private sector. Private sector firms that fail close down and cease to exist. In the public sector, the need for health, education and welfare remains. A new organisation has to take over from the failed provider, often employing the same staff in the same premises. If units cannot fail in a private sector sense, change management is harder, especially when change initiatives from the centre are endemic, leading to 'change fatigue'. Furthermore, the acceptance of performance-management initiatives, and cooperation with them, is much harder to obtain when the fundamental purposes appear to be more punitive than developmental, dubbed 'targets and terror' (Bevan and Hood 2006). Managers find that they have much less room to develop policy initiatives to suit their local circumstances.

In the decade since 2004, the need to promote the canons of performance management has led, at the local level, to action to improve the take-up of appraisals, encourage teamwork and promote training. This is particularly the case in the health sector where off-the-job training was provided to at least 80 per cent of experienced staff in 70 per cent of workplaces in 2011, compared with only 46 per cent of workplaces in 2004 (van Wanrooy et al. 2013, figure 6.4, p. 111). The proportion of non-managerial employees being appraised also rose from around half in 2004 to 87 per cent in 2011. A quarter of the appraisals in 2011 were linked to pay, compared to 11 per cent in 2004 (ibid.: figure 5.3, p. 99).

There are mixed outcomes, however, often dependent on how well the policy is implemented. Van Wanrooy et al. (2012: 194) observe that when appraisals are linked to pay and target setting, 'they are as much about monitoring as anything else. This type of appraisal may have contributed, along with pay freezes, reorganisations and increased job insecurity to lower levels of well-being and job satisfaction in the public than the private sector'. According to the NHS staff survey, 32 per cent of staff had a well-structured appraisal 'which helped them improve how they did their job, involved setting objectives for their work, and left them feeling valued by their hospital Trust' (West et al. 2011: 7). These staff had substantially higher engagement and commitment to their employer. In contrast, the 39 per cent of staff who had a poor quality appraisal had engagement levels *lower* than staff who did not receive an appraisal at all.

The strategy of using appraisals to enforce patient-care values was vividly illustrated in the UK in the Francis Report (2013) on a failing NHS Trust hospital with exceptionally high levels of patient mortality.[22] Francis observed that 'appraisal systems are a key tool to monitor and enforce standards and to reinforce a caring culture' (2013: 78). He recommended that as part of 'the mandatory annual performance appraisal, each clinician and nurse should be required to demonstrate their ongoing commitment, compassion and caring using feedback evidence from patients and their families, colleagues and co-workers' (ibid.). This would be very bureaucratic and would take appraisals and their importance to a new level.

Individualised pay and appraisals can actually be at odds with another HR priority: to break down the barriers between professions and encourage cross-professional collaboration. This is often attempted by promoting teamwork. The NHS staff survey showed that where there is a well-structured team environment with clear objectives, interdependent working, regular reviews of team performance and discussions on improvements, engagement and commitment are higher (Purcell 2014b: 250). Good team-working fosters mutual respect and information sharing among co-workers and directly connects to outcomes such as the length of patient stay, satisfaction and post-operative mobility (Gitell 2009). The strategic challenge in the health sector especially, but also in schools, is to balance the inevitable tensions between rewarding individuals in appraisals and pay and the need for team-working, and between meeting imposed targets and gaining consensus over change initiatives. This cannot be achieved by training alone.

---

[22] The key failings in the Mid Staffordshire NHS Trust Hospital ('the worst crisis a district general hospital has ever known') were that senior management focussed on financial performance to meet targets set nationally while ignoring patient care and allowing a climate of bullying to develop. The report showed how all of the bodies concerned with performance management and measurement at the national level had failed to identify and act on the growing crisis of care.

Kessler (2015) summarises the research on associations between HR policies, especially training, teamwork and appraisal, and positive outcomes. For example, West et al. (2006) show the connection between such policies and mortality after emergency surgery and in hip operations. In Canadian nursing homes, Rondeau and Wagner (2001) show the linkage between HR policies of communication, training, team-working and compensation, and patient satisfaction and hard outcome measures such as operating costs. Similarly, 'the application of lean production techniques to emergency departments highlighted how changes to data monitoring, staff training and communication with process improvements introduced through bottom-up staff involvement reduced the length of patient stay and the incidence of adverse events, and increased patient satisfaction' (Kessler 2015: 12). The data came from 18 studies in the USA, Australia and Canada (Holden 2011). However, the problem of introducing such techniques taken from private sector manufacturing remain formidable. In the UK, Radnor, Holweg and Waring (2012) warn how limited the scope is to improve work organisation within the context of the tight commissioner-provider contractural relations. Kessler (2015: 12) concludes that lean techniques have often been viewed by hospital staff with scepticism and resistance when they are seen to be a managerial initiative to reduce cost, rather than a professionally driven process to improve service quality.

In the public sector, then, the challenges facing HRM are still those associated with the New Public Management, but in a heightened form. The issue remains how to meet performance standards, but with reduced budgets, and in the context of an aging population, which creates more complex, long-term needs in health and social care. The management of conflict is critical in the public sector and especially so when further budget cuts are imposed that require a reconfiguration of service delivery with remaining staff undertaking new roles or working with increased loads and responsibility. This is particularly pertinent in the management of professionals with high-discretion jobs, 'keen to protect their jurisdiction' (Currie, Koteyko and Nerlich 2009: 308). While the cuts can be imposed unilaterally, the subsequent reorganisation requires, at the minimum, a level of staff compliance and involvement to maintain service quality, as discovered in the first phase of NPM. New forms of partnership with private sector providers will continue to be developed, often involving staff moving from the public to the private or voluntary sector.

At the same time, while the days when public sector organisations were 'model employers' have long gone, there remains an expectation that, with a high proportion of women workers, and ethnic and sexual-orientation minorities, the public sector will deliver HR policies at the forefront of social legitimacy in employment. The trend, however, looks to be in the opposite direction: HRM in the public sector suffers from too much restructuring and divisiveness to qualify as a progressive model in contemporary society. Ongoing restructuring and attacks on professional discretion generate low trust and high levels of conflict and characterise a model of HRM that is fractured and struggling, with impacts on the desirability of careers in the public sector. Given the level of complexity and politics in the public sector, the question of how to create greater stability in its employment relations is extremely challenging. It is a problem with impacts on much more than the direct parties involved because public sector services are critical to a competitive economy and a cohesive society.

Conclusions

HRM in the service sector owes much to ideas and practices developed in manufacturing during the process of industrialisation but also has its own character, deriving from the labour-intensive nature of services, the greater level of intangibility in the service encounter, the conjunction between production and consumption and the growth of self service. Labour costs in services have a much greater impact on pricing than is true in capital-intensive, large-scale manufacturing. In terms of analysing patterns of HR strategy and their outcomes, it helps to group the service sector into three broad categories: standardised and simple services, differentiated services and knowledge-intensive services. These are gross categories, which cover an enormous variety of industries and strategic groups within them. However, this simple framework helps us to make some contrasts between services in which competition is heavily driven by cost dynamics and those in which complex, specialist knowledge plays the leading role. Large service firms offering standardised services depend heavily on a dualistic HR strategy: nurturing an inner core of managers and key specialists while employing the front-line workforce on less attractive, less secure conditions. A scripted model of HRM is popular where managers are trying to make the service business a more efficient processor of customers, very much like a factory operation. As this implies, the impacts on employee well-being of this approach to HRM are very variable. Smaller firms, which are often family owned, use more informal models of HRM. These are less bureaucratic, which can have its advantages, but career development is typically limited.

As service firms move up-market, they seek to differentiate through higher levels of quality or customisation and aim to recoup their greater investments in tangibles and intangibles through higher prices or greater revenue. They retain their dualistic models of HRM but tend to adjust their HR strategy to open up greater scope for employee skill and discretion. This process reaches its high-water mark in knowledge-intensive services where firms are competing through the quality of human capital that their employees possess and the social capital they can create through team-based innovation. Here, in professional and expert models of HRM, the highest levels of employee skill, autonomy, pay and development are to be found but firms face significant challenges in attracting and retaining knowledge workers and appropriating good value from their contributions. In this 'hothouse environment', work pressures are high and work-life balance is often fragile.

Conflicts of interest are apparent in all forms of service work, nowhere more so than in the public sector, which has changed enormously over the last 30 years as governments have tried to incorporate private sector models of performance management and create much higher levels of competition (the 'new public management'). Here, the professional model of HRM is under siege and the outcomes for government, for the workforce and for the public are very variable. The unknown now is whether, and when, governments will announce yet another set of structural changes. In the British health sector, for example, there were 15 such reorganisations in the 25 years to 2010 (Walshe 2010). Restructuring is often expensive, reducing productivity in the short to medium term, and often less than effective in improving services (Andrews and Boyne 2012). HRM in the public sector is being asked to work within the constraints that these reorganisations impose and respond to the pressure for efficiency gains. In a very general sense, the management objectives remain much the same as in the private sector but they are more difficult to achieve in huge, politically charged organisations open to public scrutiny and in which a key portion of the workforce can be expected to have goals at odds with their rationale. In situations when there is a plethora of stakeholders, the balancing of priorities poses major difficulties for management at all levels of the system. In our view, the model of HRM in the public sector is in poor shape. How to re-establish it with higher levels of employee trust and engagement is one of the most difficult problems in contemporary HRM. If politicians could create a longer-term basis for cooperation with public sector workers, on whose skills and goodwill the quality and efficiency of public service is dependent, there would be a greater chance of improving outcomes in the sector.

10

HR strategy in multidivisional firms

Most studies of HRM start from the assumption that the firm is an independent entity engaged in a single or predominant kind of activity. In the previous two chapters, we looked at HR strategy in manufacturing and service organisations in this way. All modelling of the real world needs to reduce the complexity of organisational life through a process of variable reduction, enabling us to make some sense of what is going on and extrapolate trends. Sensible though this is, it often reduces complexity too far. We aim in this chapter to understand the effect on HR strategy of being a multidivisional enterprise, one in which multiple business units report to a corporate office. These firms are among the most complex and politicised contexts in which HRM takes place and they are critically important for economic and social well-being in advanced economies. Multidivisional firms are large, diverse and widespread. It is common in developed economies for many workplaces to be part of larger organisations where top management is geographically remote, either domestically or internationally. For example, in the UK, in 2011, around half of all workplaces with at least five employees were branches of multi-site organisations (van Wanrooy et al. 2013: 52).

The goal of this chapter is to assess the implications for HRM of multi-business firms, including the ways in which they grow and decline. What is distinctive about multidivisional firms and what are the implications for HR strategy? We first examine the structural arrangements of multidivisional firms, paying particular attention to philosophies of corporate control. This leads into a discussion of the rise of private-equity investment. Over recent times, private-equity firms have increasingly taken control of long-established multidivisional firms and removed them from stock market listing into private ownership, searching for ways to generate greater financial returns from these complex organisations. This is a matter of considerable controversy with conflicting evidence on the outcomes for companies, workers and societies. We need to examine this phenomenon closely. This is followed by our analysis of the different models of HR strategy in multidivisional firms, in which we distinguish between bonus-driven and development-oriented models of HRM. We also discuss the impacts of mergers, acquisitions and divestments, which are regular challenges for HRM in multidivisional firms. These strategies, however, need careful handling. Besides affecting employee well-being, they can easily destroy corporate value when the HR issues are poorly managed.

Structure and control in multidivisional firms

To get to grips with the ways in which HRM is a strategic issue in the management of large, diverse firms, we need to begin with an understanding of the ways in which they are structured and controlled. To what extent do multidivisional firms centralise or decentralise their decision making and with what implications? Do they try to integrate the different businesses they own or treat them as separate entities? How do they seek to make their portfolio of businesses successful? The crucial question is how does the centre add value, how does it develop what has been called 'parenting advantage' (Goold, Campbell and Alexander 1994)?

Most firms start as a single business. As this 'legacy business' (Feldman 2014) matures, and as the market it serves changes, a number of critical choices must be faced. Will the firm's competitive position in its current markets be sustainable once new entrants arrive, is there sufficient capital available from revenue to fund future investment needs, is the market maturing such that growth potential and margins are likely to be eroded? Another type of question is whether there are opportunities to use distinctive technologies or know-how to enter other markets. What is certain is that doing nothing is rarely viable and, for many business leaders, rather boring too. One route to growth is to branch away from the traditional market: in other words, to diversify. This could be to do the same thing in a new market, as the British retailer, Tesco, did by expanding into central and eastern Europe and the Far East, especially China, and into the USA with the acquisition of Fresh & Easy. By 2010, two-thirds of its floor space was outside the UK.[1] But this is risky and many a firm comes to grief in seeking to 'export' its business

---

[1] http://www.theguardian.com/business/2010/jun/08/tesco-terry-leahy-profile, accessed 28/1/15.

recipe to another country and culture. Tesco found this out the hard way in its US expansion in 2007. It never made a profit and in 2013 it pulled out at a cost of around £150 million.[2] Another route is by vertical integration, seeking both to protect the supply chain and to enter new markets where there is growth potential. It may also be that another firm possesses knowledge of a technology or market that the single-business firm lacks or, indeed, its leaders may feel the lack of general management expertise. Whatever the reason, the critical choice that follows is how far to pursue diversification and how best to manage a diversified business.

To begin with, the traditional firm adopts a functional or unified form ('U-form') in which specialists in marketing, operations, finance and HRM each coordinate their own areas, linked to the board of directors through the chief executive (CEO) and, usually, a separate chairman (Chandler 1962). The board will most likely contain non-executive directors drawn from 'the great and the good' in the business world to provide oversight, advice and access to networks. As firms diversify, this structure is placed under severe strain. Policy and operating decisions become increasingly difficult when managers have responsibility for multiple sites and markets, which each require some unique adaptation to their particular situation.

In a famous study of the evolution of American corporations, Alfred Chandler (1962) explained how companies such as Du Pont and General Motors developed multidivisional structures to deal with this problem. This involved the creation of a series of subsidiary business units, each of which was organised around a particular product or geographical area and reported to an elite group of executives in the corporate office. This is the 'M-form' or multidivisional company in which corporate strategy is driven from the centre and 'structure follows strategy' (ibid.: 14). We depict what this means in Figure 10.1. Decisions about the long-term direction of the multidivisional firm and the scope of its activities ('first-order' decisions) set the context for decisions on the structural arrangement of the corporation. The latter are 'second-order' decisions, including the organisation of subsidiaries and their relationships with the centre and with each other. Functional strategies in business units are then tackled as a 'third-order' activity or 'downstream' process, deeply influenced by the first- and second-order decisions.

Thus, the distinctive feature of the M-form organisation is a clear separation of business-unit managers from the executives in the corporate office. Profits are returned to the corporate office and regular reports are required

---

[2] http://www.bbc.com/news/business-24040346, accessed 28/1/15.

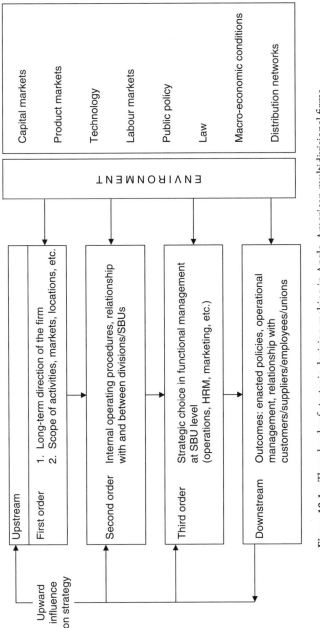

Figure 10.1 Three levels of strategic decision making in Anglo-American multidivisional firms
Source: Purcell (1989).

on performance, such as rate-of-return on sales (ROS) or rate-of-return on investment (ROI). In effect, the M-form company is composed of a number of U-form profit centres or, to use the preferred term, 'strategic business units' (SBUs). Between SBUs, which face distinctively defined markets, and the corporate office, divisional structures may exist to coordinate whole sectors (e.g. a consumer foods division) or geographic areas (e.g. Europe). In the rational minds of industrial economists, M-form companies have five advantages over other forms of corporate control. Williamson (1970: 120–1) argues that these are:

1. The responsibility for operating decisions is assigned to (essentially self-contained) operating divisions.
2. The elite staff attached to the general office (i.e. the corporate headquarters) performs both advisory and auditing functions. Both activities have the effect of securing greater control over operating division behavior.
3. The general office is principally concerned with strategic decisions involving planning, appraisal and control, including the allocation of resources among the (competing) operating divisions.
4. The separation of the general office from operations provides general office executives with the psychological commitment to be concerned with the overall performance of the organization rather than becoming absorbed in the affairs of the functional parts.
5. The resulting structure displays both rationality and synergy: the whole is greater (more effective, more efficient) than the sum of the parts.

The M-form structure grew first in the US private sector and then spread throughout the Anglo-American world and beyond: for example, into China.[3] In a copy-cat way, the new public management (NPM), which we discussed in Chapter 9, was built on the philosophy of separating strategic planning and monitoring from operational delivery, adopted with new reporting requirements and a vigorous pursuit of greater efficiency. The typical evolution of the M-form structure is that firms move from being single businesses through a process of diversification and divisionalisation into a collection of related businesses, each serving a different market, but with some overlap in terms of a core process, raw material or business logic, allowing for some cross-fertilisation of ideas and sharing of resources. The next step, or an alternative approach altogether, is diversification into essentially unrelated businesses, usually called a 'conglomerate' (Williamson 1981).[4] In conglomerates, there may be few links across businesses apart from the fact that they report to

---

[3] http://en.wikipedia.org/wiki/Multi-divisional_form, accessed 28/1/15.
[4] For a good definition, see http://www.investopedia.com/terms/c/conglomerate.asp, accessed 5/2/15.

the same head office. The conglomerate spreads the risk of failure in any one firm or industry but the challenge facing the corporate leadership is to how to make such a diverse collection of businesses successful.

In multidivisional firms, individual business units are often judged according to two criteria: the attractiveness of the market served, and the share of the market controlled by the business (Hedley 1977). Market attractiveness relates to whether the market is growing, has reached maturity, or is declining. The share of the market is the extent to which the SBU or division is a leading or dominant player in the market. A common problem for the M-form company, however, is that it is likely that the market served by the legacy business is mature, with limited prospects for growth, or that it is even declining as taste and fashions change. United Biscuits, one of the M-form companies studied in the UK by Purcell and Ahlstrand (1994), dominated the market for sweet biscuits, such as the ubiquitous 'digestive biscuit', but the market was flat and showing signs of secular decline. In the framework developed by the Boston Consulting Group (BCG), companies with a high share of a mature market are called 'cash cows' since they are capable, with lower unit costs, of producing high rates of return on capital expenditure, and their needs for capital investment are low (Hedley 1977). Their profits are returned to the centre and can then be invested in other businesses in the group and in takeovers. In the case of United Biscuits, such profits enabled diversification into frozen foods and snacks, as well as the acquisition of Keebler, the largest cookie and snacks manufacturer in the USA.[5] Reallocated profits can help to foster 'stars', which have a high share of a growing market (ibid.: 10–11). Stars generate high profitability but their investment needs are high in order to fuel further innovation and expansion. Some other investment goes into 'question-mark' businesses, which have high growth but low share, representing something of a long-run gamble. A particularly bad pattern is the 'dog', which has low growth and low share (ibid.: 11). Questions marks that do not grow into stars and dogs that cannot be rescued are candidates for divestment because they consume resources that could be used better elsewhere in the portfolio.

Thus, the role of the executive leadership of the multidivisional firm is to evaluate the performance and potential of the different businesses in their portfolio, drawing funds from where they are not needed and allocating them to areas where there are promising prospects. Having the spare cash to invest in emerging markets can give the multidivisional firm a very threatening financial advantage over small firms ('deep pockets'). However, the firm's leaders face a complex set of questions around which businesses to acquire, which to invest

---

[5] http://en.wikipedia.org/wiki/Keebler_Company, accessed 3/2/15.

in (and at what level) and which to divest (and when). As the BCG framework argues, it is clearly unwise to treat all businesses in the portfolio in the same way but how to manage the mix effectively to maximise the overall value of the firm is a complex, multidimensional problem carrying a high level of risk.

The implications of private equity for the multidivisional company

The growth of private-equity firms has challenged the model of the multidivisional firm we have just described. As firms, they are typically constituted as limited partnerships rather than companies. The standard formula involved is for the 'general partner', the private-equity firm, to create a fund seeking investors as 'limited partners', typically made up of public-pension funds, insurance companies, sovereign-wealth funds, wealthy individuals and so on (e.g. Wright et al. 2009). The funds raised are used to take over existing businesses and are managed by the general partner, not by the investors.

In the broader sense, private equity is part of a trend over recent decades towards the 'financialisation' of capitalism: a process in which the finance sector has greatly expanded in influence and in which business people, including bankers, investment professionals and wealthy executives, have increasingly been pursuing the profits to be made from the sourcing and structuring of financial investments ('financial leverage') and the trading of currencies and financial securities (e.g. Dore 2008, Thompson 2011). The move into private-equity ownership often leads to an increase in 'leverage via more debt which, in the British case, involves shifting a typical [share quoted] public company structure of 70 per cent equity and 30 per cent debt to a typical private equity structure of 30 per cent equity and 70 per cent debt' (Froud and Williams 2007: 410). This debt risk is held by the acquired company, not by the general partner. Interest payments to the general partner are deducted before corporation taxation is paid, adding to the attraction of the debt. In addition, the general partner often charges 2 per cent administration fees on the funds committed to the portfolio firms and receives 20 per cent of all investment profits once a hurdle rate of return has been achieved. This is known as the '2 and 20' model (Appelbaum, Batt and Clark 2013: 502). This is taken as capital gains, not income, and incurs a lower rate of tax. The motive, clearly, is to find ways of using these funds to make significantly greater returns for investors, albeit with a higher level of risk. The success of the fund depends heavily on the quality of the decisions made by private equity leaders, and their investment staff, and those who are appointed by them to run the businesses in a portfolio.

Why has this come about? What was wrong with the companies listed on the stock exchange, including the firms with deep pockets? The major criticism of the publicly owned corporation, as multidivisional companies usually are, is most clearly stated by the financial economist, Jensen (1989). He argues that managers in public corporations often sit on large surpluses of cash or waste them in unwise forms of expansion, which enhance their remuneration but can have the opposite effect on shareholders. They get away with this because shareholders are passive and have few ways of influencing managers apart from selling their shares. Jensen (1989: 72) asks: 'who can argue with a new model of enterprise [the private-equity firm] that aligns the interests of owners and managers, improves efficiency and productivity and unlocks hundreds of billions of dollars of shareholder value?' The answer, he says, is that many people do argue the point, accusing private-equity firms, which have pioneered a new form of financial capitalism, of 'asset stripping and profiting from reselling assets within short periods of time … instigating restructuring within firms that negatively impacts employment … and using leverage and off-shore holding companies to reduce tax charges' (Wright et al. 2009: 354). Thompson (2003) describes an era of 'disconnected capitalism', one in which the pursuit of greater value for shareholders means that managers, while wanting greater employee performance, are less and less committed to employment security and employee development. The evidence is not, however, clear cut and we need to look carefully at the theory, practice and outcomes of this form of investor behaviour and its implications for HRM.

The basic theory that Jensen (1989) draws on is known as 'agency theory' (Jensen and Meckling 1976), which we noted in Chapter 1 in discussing questions of managerial power. Agency theory deals with the principal/agent problem in organisations. It asks: how can 'principals' (i.e. the shareholders who own the firm) ensure that their agents (i.e. the managers they employ) act in their interests? This problem, it is said, is especially acute in multidivisional companies where 'investment funds may not be allocated to divisions to use on the basis of rates of returns but as a result of internal power dynamics' (Wright et al. 2009: 355–6). It will be recalled that the profits of 'cash cows' are returned to the corporate office where they are used as executives see fit. 'According to agency theory, managers – especially those in mature firms in low growth industries – should return free cash flow to investors and shareholders via share buy-backs and dividends and use debt to finance new investments, subjecting these decisions to a market test' (Appelbaum, Batt and Clark 2013: 501). It is no surprise that what is termed 'free cash flow' is most likely to be found 'in mature, cash rich firms with few growth options' (Wright et al. 2009: 356). These types of businesses have been a favourite target of private-equity firms. When taking over all or part of a multidivisional company, the private-equity firm can often pay in excess of 40 per cent of the stock market valuation of the business (Goergen, O'Sullivan and Wood 2011: 264) in expectation of significant gains from asset sales (often property that is rented back to the business) and efficiency savings (Froud and Williams 2007: 414).

The fund will have an exit strategy to dispose of the acquired firm within a few years (Wright et al. 2009: 355). The experience of United Biscuits, which we referred to above, is typical. It was bought by a consortium of private-equity investors in May 2000 who rationalised the company to focus on the sweet-biscuit market. It was sold again as part of financial re-engineering in October 2006 for £1.6 billion to another private-equity group with further rationalisation following. Then, in November 2014, it was bought by the Turkish food group, Yildiz for £2 billion, returning it to the food sector.[6] By then, United Biscuits employed 7,100 people worldwide, of whom 4,600 were in the UK. This compares to over 25,000 employees in the UK in 1984. Passing through the hands of private-equity ownership can have dramatic consequences.

The main source of investment return will come on exit, largely because of efficiencies achieved and assets sold (Wright et al. 2009). The principal/agent problem is reduced because senior managers are given much greater responsibility to manage and are heavily incentivised through stock options and performance-related pay. 'A buyout creates entrepreneurial incentives and discretionary power for the new management team' (Wright et al. 2009: 356).

The private-equity industry grew significantly in the peak years of 2006–2007, before the Global Financial Crisis.[7] The Global Financial Crisis affected the industry significantly but latest figures show that it has bounced back, accounting for 21.9 per cent of global M&A activity in 2014.[8] There is some evidence that it is the USA's and the UK's 'liberal economies' that are more attractive for private-equity investment because 'attitudes towards entrepreneurial risk and the willingness of management to undertake a buyout (are) noticeably more positive … than in most other European countries and Japan' (Wright et al. 2009: 568). This may be so, but the influence of private equity is spreading. 'US buy-out houses were part of all deals exceeding €3 billion in Europe and more than a quarter of all European deals of more than €400 million since 2003; meanwhile, 45 per cent of UK private equity funds were invested overseas in 2004' (Froud and Williams 2007: 416).

---

[6] http://www.theguardian.com/business/2014/nov/03/united-biscuits-jaffa-cakes-mcvities-yildiz-two-billion-deal, accessed 28/1/15.
[7] http://en.wikipedia.org/wiki/Private_equity, accessed 28/1/15.
[8] http://fortune.com/2015/01/05/2014-was-a-huge-year-for-ma-and-private-equity/, accessed 28/1/15.

Types of buyouts and their consequences

Not all types of buyout, however, are created equal. In assessing the consequences of private-equity ownership, it is useful to distinguish three different types.[9] Insider-driven deals involve an existing management team, say in a division or an SBU, seeking finance from a private-equity firm to mount a 'management buy-out' (MBO). Where an investment leads to the replacement of the existing management team with a new Board of Directors, it is called a 'management buy-in' (MBI). The use of private-equity houses, or other institutional forms, to create a fund that purchases a portfolio of businesses is called an 'institutional buy-out' (IBO). 'IBOs are private equity acquisitions undertaken by specialist investors or investment banks, typically involving a change of management. The IBO management team does not own significant equity once the acquisition is completed' (Goergen, O'Sullivan and Wood 2014: 147).

Some people suggest that the effects of MBOs may be less threatening in terms of the HR consequences. A number of studies have shown that while employment drops immediately after the buy-out, the firm often shows significantly higher employment growth rates 4 or 5 years later than found in their non-MBO counterparts (Goergen, O'Sullivan and Wood 2011: 263). Bacon, Wright and Demina (2004) show an increase in the importance attached to HRM in MBOs, which include increased employment, greater employee involvement, increased training and greater flexibility. In a major study of European MBOs, Bacon et al. (2010: 1361) find that 'under private equity ownership, more firms report consultation committees, managers regard their consultative committees as more influential on managerial decisions, and more managers report discussing firm performance and future plans'. In an associated study, Bacon et al. (2008) find that management buy-outs in the UK and the Netherlands have led to a greater use of high-commitment HR practices. 'The subset of private equity-backed buy-outs was less likely to report introducing new high commitment management practices but did not necessarily reduce them' (ibid.: 1425). These studies suggest that it would be unwise to apply a blanket form of criticism to private equity. It could well be the case that the milking of a good business by corporate executives in a multidivisional firm gets redressed by private-equity managers who start to reinvest in the business for the long term (Bacon et al. 2008).

In contrast, Wood and Wright (2009: 371) suggest that the effects on employment are 'particularly adverse' in MBIs and IBOs. One reason for this is that 'new buyers may have a greater interest in rapid value realization' (ibid.: 371),

---

[9] http://www.investopedia.com/terms/m/mbo.asp, http://www.investopedia.com/terms/i/institutional-buyout.asp, accessed 29/1/15.

rather than long-run competitiveness. The new, external management team is 'less likely to be loyal to the existing workforce, especially if employees had opposed the takeover transaction' (Goergen, O'Sullivan and Wood 2011: 264). This is where MBOs may gain an advantage: by having 'more detailed knowledge about the nature of human assets which may be essential for long-term organizational competitiveness' (Wood and Wright 2009: 371). A second reason why the employment effects of MBIs are likely to be worse is that 'MBIs are typically more likely to have been underperforming and require restructuring to restore viability' (ibid.: 371). This may be the case, but is hard to prove.

Those researchers who question the impacts of private-equity investment for workers and societies tend to use selected case studies which have been in the media for the 'horror stories' they tell (for four of the most tragic and well-known cases, see Appelbaum, Batt and Clark 2013). It is not possible to advance from these specific instances to the general experience of MBIs and IBOs. There are, as suggested above, 'good news' cases as well: for example, Westcott's (2009) study of Myer Retail Stores in Australia where a new management team with extensive experience in retail was appointed after an MBI. After the initial fall in employment, achieved by natural wastage rather than redundancy, staff numbers grew again. The union was not derecognised but a new, tougher contract negotiated emphasising flexibility in rostering, rather than cutting benefits. The central Melbourne site (which is huge) was sold and redeveloped and is leased back to the store, as is typical in private-equity transactions in the retail sector. 'After less than 18 months of ownership the company had increased sales, increased sales margins and, with the sale of the retail site, reduced net debt' (ibid.: 540).

The best evidence on the effect of IBOs, especially on employment matters, comes from surveys by Goergen, O'Sullivan and Wood (2011, 2014) over a number of years, enabling a considered view to be taken beyond the first year. Their 2011 paper concludes by stating that 'the main finding ... is that employment in acquired firms reduces significantly in the year after the completion of the IBO transaction, compared with non-acquired firms [and] further analysis fails to find any parallel or subsequent increase in productivity or profitability' (Goergen, O'Sullivan and Wood 2011: 273). They explain this by asserting that 'restructuring may result in a loss of ... accumulated capabilities; hence any gains through discipline and more effective divisions of labour will be offset' (ibid.: 273). The 2014 study uses the same data set but provides further analysis. The target firms, taken over by the IBO, had lower wages pre-acquisition than the control group of non-acquired companies (implying lower productivity) but this lower wage profile continued after the IBO. 'This would suggest that incoming managers neglect the human dimension, other than in terms of controlling costs … The lack of attention to enhancing productivity might suggest that the priorities of incoming managers lie elsewhere, such as financial engineering, and that HR issues may be of only secondary concern to enhancing returns through non-HR interventions, such as the liquidation of assets or the servicing of the debt' (Goergen, O'Sullivan and Wood 2014: 155). One of the difficulties with coming to a definitive conclusion is that private-equity firms are privately owned and not subject to the same level of reporting requirements faced by publically quoted companies. And, as everywhere in studies of strategy, there is a wide variety of practice, including different approaches in different industries.

Overall, we ought to be cautious about making sweeping generalisations about the impact of private equity on HR strategy and on employee well-being. There is some evidence that private-equity managers may try to put a neglected business, with good long-term potential, back onto a more sustainable basis before selling it to a 'natural owner'. On the other hand, the limited duration of private-equity partnerships, the high use of debt to fund businesses and the incentives to maximise the exit value of the investment within a few years are fundamental characteristics of this type of ownership. New managers appointed by a private-equity firm are in a strong position to make radical changes, through laying people off and renegotiating the conditions of those who remain, in pursuit of a better balance sheet and a bigger bonus. This is never without risk: downsizers and restructurers who are not deeply familiar with a business can damage its core capabilities and alienate its best staff and suppliers when they vigorously pursue ways of taking out costs (Appelbaum, Batt and Clark 2013). Long-run investment may be more likely when an MBO is involved because of the knowledge that existing managers have about the sources of value in the business. However, even here, it would be unwise to over-generalise. All managers are operating under the disciplines of the capital markets, which have undermined their capacities to sustain long-term commitments to employees (Thompson 2003).

Challenges for HR strategy in the multidivisional company

Given what we know about the strategies and structures of multidivisional firms, what models characterise the corporate approach to HRM in them? These firms are large and nearly always have HR specialists, but what would it pay an HR director to understand about a multidivisional firm before accepting employment in it? As the previous section makes clear, the restructuring and downsizing associated with acquisitions, mergers and divestments are certainly going to figure prominently. HR specialists inevitably play a critical role in dealing with the human consequences of restructuring, as graphically depicted in the book and film, 'Up in the Air'.[10] Before we get to this critical problem, however, we need to consider the impact of the corporate leadership of multidivisional firms on the fundamental philosophy underpinning HRM.

Corporate HRM: bonus-driven or development-oriented?

The previous chapters have talked about models of HRM that apply within business units or workplaces within them, such as a scripted model of HRM in a retail chain. Here we need to analyse the types of HRM that apply at the level of the multidivisional firm. In our view, there are two fundamental approaches to corporate HRM. One occurs in multidivisional firms that emphasise financial targets and controls, keeping the business units at arm's length from the centre and often from each other. This leads to what we call a 'bonus-driven model' of HRM. The other occurs where a multidivisional firm aims to build synergies, emphasising collaboration and knowledge sharing across the group, as in the 'N-form' or networked company (Hedlund 1994). This leads to what we call a 'development-oriented model' of HRM. Rather than stark categories, these two models can be thought of as two ends of a continuum with individual firms located somewhere along it. All multidivisional companies have ways of incentivising and developing people but the labels are useful because they indicate where the balance of emphasis falls in corporate HRM.

In the bonus-driven model of HRM, corporate executives focus on the setting and monitoring of monetary targets for SBUs. They are heavily concerned with forces in the capital markets that seek higher rates of return from multidivisional firms and that can quickly lead to the break-up of long-established corporations (Thompson 2003, 2011). Budgets are negotiated or imposed annually, planning horizons are short and performance targets are monitored frequently: 'these companies are willing to act speedily to exit from the businesses that are not performing or do not fit ... and are quicker to replace managers, fiercer in applying pressure through the monitoring process and more effective in recognising and acclaiming good performance' (Goold and Campbell 1987: 126, 132).

As Goold and Campbell (1987) note, this approach can be liberating for SBU managers and the use of high-value performance-related pay, where stock options and bonuses can easily constitute one third or one half of an executive's

---

[10] http://en.wikipedia.org/wiki/Up_in_the_Air_%282009_film%29, accessed 29/1/15.

remuneration, and sometimes more, can be a strong incentive. The rise of private-equity ownership has most probably heightened the process of financial control and incentivisation in multidivisional firms. However, the decentralisation of operating decisions, in the context of centralised control over budgets, can have important implications for people. It means that there are rarely corporate requirements for particular HR policies, such as a defined level of investment in training and development. It is up to local management to adopt the training and career-development investments they want to, and can pay for from their budgets. The problem is that management by short-run financial targets tends to render long-run development more difficult to achieve (McGovern et al. 1997). In responding to their financial targets and their performance incentives, SBU managers will often look for ways to reduce 'HR overheads', including through outsourcing. In addition, strong decentralisation and separation of businesses to expose profit responsibility renders it difficult to emphasise or build on relationships between business units. Each is treated as an atomised unit. On top of this, in some multidivisional firms, managers beyond head office simply have contracts of employment with the operating company, not with the corporation. This means that they are not considered as a corporate resource and management development across the group can suffer.

The evidence suggests that the decentralisation of responsibility for HRM is growing in multidivisional firms. Data from the UK in 2011 show that the average number of HR issues where decisions are made in the workplace in multi-site firms, without consultation with higher level management, increased from 5.6 in 2004 to 6.4, with the private sector being more decentralised than the public sector (van Wanrooy et al. 2012, table 4.2, p. 53). There are, however, some important exceptions: few corporations, for example, give carte blanche to SBUs on questions of trade union recognition, and pay, pensions and holiday entitlement are controlled by higher managers in three quarters or more of multi-site organisations (ibid.: 52). These areas can become a threat to managerial power and the overall economic performance of the firm. The leaders in the corporate office may have strong views on such matters, with US-owned corporations being notorious for favouring union avoidance wherever they can while finance departments keep a close eye on the parameters of reward policies.

The predominance of organising the management of SBUs through the use of financial controls is a particular feature of Anglo-American corporations. It is explained in large measure by the dominance of short-term capital markets emphasising shareholder returns (Thompson 2003, Sisson and Purcell 2010). It is not, however, a model of capitalist management that enjoys universal support. Jacoby's (2005) analysis of US and Japanese corporations shows how, despite facing common competitive pressures unleashed by globalisation, Japanese firms still retain a more stakeholder-oriented perspective, which gives employees a greater role in corporate strategy and governance. This applies, too, in much of continental Europe: for example, in the Netherlands (Paauwe and Boselie 2007). HR departments in these countries are typically more influential than in their US or British counterparts.

There are, then, alternative philosophies of corporate control that place more emphasis on 'synergy', sharing and deepening the firm's special know-how across the group. This leads to a more 'development-oriented model' of corporate HRM. Where M-form companies organise around related businesses, there are likely to be knowledge or technological links between divisions. For example, this may be through vertical integration along the supply chain, requiring integrated production and distribution. Alternatively, synergy may be pursued through a process of building and spreading product or process innovations, as is often the case in aeronautical manufacturing. Inter-business relationships may be designed to achieve 'scope' economies through the exploitation of a common-root technology, as we explained in our discussion of core competences in Chapter 4. Here, organisational practices which focus on knowledge creation and sharing are crucial (Volberda 1998), meaning that managers will be encouraged to communicate more frequently and assist one another without simply thinking of their own sectional interest. They are likely to be moved across divisions to gain greater insight and build their personal networks.

The critical point of this search for synergies is that corporate management cannot easily achieve both the financial economies of separation and those of synergy. Choices have to be made, structural models have to shift and HRM needs to come into some kind of alignment. The networked organisation entails a different managerial style (Hedlund 1994). 'The N-form works best with the Eastern appreciation of the tacit, the embedded and the ambiguous, rather than the explicit, tightly specified knowledge systems of the West' (Whittington and Mayer 2000: 81). An apt metaphor is between the masculinity of the M-form and the femininity of the N-form. An example of what this might mean comes from the transformation of General Electric (GE) from a financially controlled corporation to a more synergistic one under the leadership of Jack Welch (who retired in 2001):

> By 1990, Jack Welch had formulated his notions of coordination and integration within his view of the 'boundaryless company'. A key element of this concept was a blurring of internal divisions so that people could work together across functions and business boundaries. Welch aimed at 'integrated diversity' – the ability to transfer the best ideas, most developed knowledge, and most valuable people freely and easily between businesses (Grant 1998: 415).

This kind of highly networked approach to knowledge draws on high levels of sharing and trust and, underpinning this, high levels of commitment to employees and favoured suppliers. This means it requires higher levels of investment in the workforce and, inevitably, in larger teams of HR specialists to support this. The development-oriented model of corporate HRM is one in which HR departments are more generously staffed, giving them time to pay attention to employee development and be concerned with the transmission of innovative practices, and the tacit skills that underpin them, across the group. This does not mean that executives are going to be poorly paid, or that the labour markets for advanced forms of 'talent' are going to be ignored, but it does indicate where the balance of emphasis is going to fall in corporate HRM.

All of this begs the question of which way multidivisional firms are heading. What is the big picture? In the light of continuing pressures from capital markets, we think it is likely that most Anglo-American firms are leaning more towards the bonus-driven end of the continuum rather than the development-oriented end. Since the Global Financial Crisis, they have been heavily concerned with cost levels and profit outcomes, and they are continuing to adopt outsourcing of non-core operations when they consider it delivers better performance. This implies a more restricted or 'focused' investment in the workforce, rather than high-commitment policies across the board, as Thompson (2003, 2011) argues. If the multidivisional firm is to be astutely led, an elite core of managers and specialists does need to be nurtured but there are likely to be fewer HR specialists in the corporate head office, employee and supplier contracts are more contingent, and there is a more restricted investment in employee development throughout the group.

The HR implications of divestments, mergers and acquisitions

As we have noted above, restructuring and downsizing are regular occurrences in the multidivisional sector, aided and abetted by the growth of private-equity ownership. In the USA in 2012, while the number of divestments was down to the lowest level in 6 years, Deloitte reports that the average deal grew from US$129 million to US$149 million in size.[11] In their survey, 93 per cent of the executives polled, all with experience of divestitures, said that managing employee morale was very or somewhat challenging. A study by Feldman (2014) of legacy divestitures, where the original part of the business is sold off, shows some of the problems associated with doing this.

---

[11]http://deloitte.wsj.com/cfo/files/2013/01/us_fas_ma_Divestiture-Survey-Report-2013_printable_012313.pdf, accessed 28/1/15.

She found that 'the stock market responds favourably to announcements of legacy divestitures, especially when they remove business units that operate in declining industries or when they are accompanied by corporate name changes that reflect the extent to which the firm is shifting away from its past. By contrast, in the 4 years after the divestitures, the operating performance of firms that divest their legacy business is lower than that of firms which retain their legacy units' (Feldman 2014: 815). After a while, the stock market performance slips too.

The position is worse when the divestiture is made by a newly appointed CEO, who is 'significantly more likely to undertake legacy divestitures ... and the most operationally costly legacy divestitures are undertaken in firms managed by the CEOs with the shortest tenures in their organizations' (ibid.: 829). The reasons for this take us back to the notion of core competences and the integration of related business activities. Feldman (2014) shows that the legacy business is the one most likely, after many years, to be the hub of these competences, 'part of the organization's taken-for-granted reality, which is an accretion of decisions made over time and events in corporate history' (Leonard-Barton 1992: 114). The newly appointed CEO is likely to have little appreciation of these competences and the nature of the linkages between businesses, and employees, in the group. They may be more impressed by the short-term hike in stock market performance, which will affect their bonuses.

Worldwide, the volume of mergers and acquisitions peaked in 2007 at US$4,191 billion and then scaled back significantly in the Global Financial Crisis.[12] However, it had risen again significantly by 2014. When new owners arrive, of course, there are already HRM models in place and some modes of behaviour are deeply embedded. The problem of integration or embedding practice from elsewhere is likely to be especially difficult. It is regularly argued in the literature on mergers and acquisitions (Buono and Bowditch 1989) that half or more are failures in the sense of either an inability to provide shareholder value greater than the sum of the previous two companies or an inability to maintain market dominance.[13] Such reorganisations often fail to achieve the promised cost reductions or build the anticipated synergies. Difficulties in achieving organisational fit, especially the meshing of cultures or management styles, are often identified (Buono, Bowditch and Lewis 1985, Datta and Grant 1990). This can be exacerbated in multinational firms, which are the subject of

---

[12] http://www.statista.com/statistics/267369/volume-of-mergers-and-acquisitions-worldwide/, accessed 29/1/15.
[13] http://www.bmmagazine.co.uk/columns/opinion/many-mergers-fail, *Business Matters* 29 November 2013, accessed 28/1/15.

the next chapter. 'Cross-border M&As frequently fail to deliver the synergistic or other benefits strived for, lead to human resource and cultural problems, result in power plays, and often produce problematic consequences for various internal and external stakeholders' (Soderberg and Vaara 2003: 11).

Most often, the failure of M&As occurs not at the negotiation or purchase stages, although this can be important if a firm pays excessively for a purchase, but at the implementation stage when the two firms come together. KPMG (1999) distinguishes between 'hard keys' to successful mergers, which need to happen at the start of the process, such as synergy evaluation, integration project planning and due diligence, and 'soft keys'. These soft keys include classical HR issues such as the selection of the management team, the resolution of cultural issues and communication inside the two companies, which needs to be compatible with communication externally to shareholders and the business press. Thus, 'human factors' loom large in M&As, and become especially acute during the post-acquisition implementation phase, and beyond that in what is sometimes called the stabilisation period (Hubbard and Purcell 2001). Reviewing research on the performance of M&As, Schmidt (2002: 8) finds that the top seven difficulties all 'directly or indirectly relate to the management of people'. Mergers and acquisitions, especially in the post-merger rationalisation stage, involve highly political processes.

The problem is particularly acute in hostile takeovers where the target company resists the blandishments of the acquirer but the shareholders eventually accept the deal against the advice of their board of directors. Most inside directors resign following a hostile takeover. White-collar staff are vulnerable, especially when headquarters are consolidated (Conyon et al. 2001: 430). It is also the more tenured, long-serving staff who tend to leave, taking with them their tacit skills and insider knowledge (Gokhale, Groshen and Neumark 1995). The consequences of hostile takeovers are troubling. In the UK, while all takeovers, whether hostile or friendly, show a 'decrease in labour demand, averaging about 7.5 per cent', 'hostile transactions are associated with immediate substantial falls in output and employment which are not present after friendly transactions' (Conyon et al. 2001: 438). The authors conjecture that this occurs because of a 'high level of post-merger divestment of divisions and subsidiaries' (ibid.: 438). Schleifer and Summers (1988) argue that hostile takeovers provide an opportunity for the new owners and their incoming management team to override explicit and implicit labour contracts in what amounts to a 'breach of trust' (see also Appelbaum, Batt and Clark 2013). This has efficiency implications, as we saw with IBOs, by reducing employee commitment and the willingness to learn new ways of working. The level of employee cooperation falls.

Impacts of M&A activity on employee attitudes and organisational justice

It is hardly surprising to find that employees suffer from uncertainty in mergers and acquisitions (Buono and Bowditch 1989) and that this is linked to perceived violations of their psychological contracts with the employer, especially the new employer. Such violations can lead to a withdrawal of support for the organisation and a reduction in discretionary behaviour and motivation (Robinson 1996). In an acquisition, this psychological process can occur on a large scale, covering groups of employees, and leading to damaging consequences for the acquirer through the withdrawal of trust and commitment. In practice, the political environment of an acquisition severely reduces the opportunities to participate. People often feel powerless. They may ask their direct managers what is happening but it is rare for them to know any more than they do. Trade unions may be informed one or two days before the public announcement but are generally unable, at that time, to raise issues of concern about the acquisition's consequences, unless provided with the legal right to do so, as in the EU under the Transfer of Undertakings (Protection of Employees) (TUPE) regulations.[14]

Beyond this, there can be a profound sense of loss – a form of bereavement (Cartwright and Cooper 1992) – when a long-established company is swallowed up and effectively dies. Mergers and acquisitions frequently lead to a round (or rounds) of job cuts. They can also lead to a substantial increase in voluntary labour turnover, to reductions in effort and cooperation and to resistance to integration moves, which thus take longer and cost more in terms of performance dips than anticipated. Maguire and Phillips' (2008) analysis of the merger in 1998 between Citicorp and Travelers Group is a case in point. Citicorp, whose core business unit was 'Citibank', had grown organically since its founding in 1812. By contrast, Travelers, a diversified financial services company involved in a range of activities including lending, brokerage and insurance, had grown rapidly through acquisitions. Their merger resulted in the massive Citigroup, which naturally lacked a commonly understood or shared culture. Maguire and Phillips (2008) argue that immediately following the merger, institutional trust suffered because of ambiguity surrounding the identity of the newly merged organisation. This was compounded when 'Citibankers' came to the view that, in effect, it was not a merger of equals but a takeover by Travelers' executives whose style of organisation and management became dominant. As a result, Citibankers, who had closely identified with 'their' company, experienced low institutional trust

---

[14] http://en.wikipedia.org/wiki/Transfer_of_Undertakings_%28Protection_of_ Employment%29_Regulations_2006, accessed 29/1/15.

with Citigroup because they could not identify with it. Many left the organisation, which was seen by HR staff as a serious drain of human capital (ibid.: 393).

Low levels of organisational trust are linked to perceptions that organisational justice has broken down. Organisational justice, discussed in Chapter 6, is about the way people evaluate the fairness of a decision (Folger and Cropanzano 1998). There are various elements of justice in an organisational context. Distributive justice concerns the fairness of the outcome, procedural justice is about fairness in the way in which the decision is taken and interactional justice focuses on the extent to which individuals feel treated with respect. Some argue there is a fourth dimension to justice, being 'informational justice': 'accounts and explanations provided by organisational authorities about [key decisions] and why certain outcomes [are] distributed in a certain way' (Fuchs and Edwards 2012: 41–2). In mergers and acquisitions, this can be especially difficult since two firms are involved and executives can feel constrained by commercial confidentiality from explaining the merger and its outcomes before the final announcement.

Senior managers can often take the view that the only HR issue of immediate concern in an acquisition announcement is to deal with job security and job loss. This is the question that is always asked by the press. In Hubbard's (1999) acquisition research, there was quite commonly an early announcement that it was to be 'business as usual' and that both companies would be stronger by coming together. This was rarely the case and, at times, announcements to employees of 'business as usual' were at odds with statements to the business press on the need to reduce costs and increase margins. Of course, employees read these and note the incompatibility of the internal with the external statement.

The employee response to an acquisition announcement, especially those in the 'target' firm to be acquired, is much more multi-faceted than a single concern with job security. Hubbard (1999) calls this 'dual expectations theory'. This covers both the individual's perception of their immediate future (what will happen to *me*, do I have a job?) and their concern with their team and the wider social network (what will happen to *us*?). Thus, for the individual, the issue is 'what sort of job will I have, what type of future, how do I know what is expected of me in terms of performance and will I fit into the new organisational culture?' These concerns of individuals often coalesce into wider group or collective worries about the style of the new management. This 'cultural behaviour' means learning about, and internalising as a group, 'the shared patterns of beliefs, assumptions and expectations held by organisational members, and the group characteristic way of perceiving the organisation's environment and its norms, roles and values as they exist outside the individual' (Schwartz and Davis 1981: 33). This is especially difficult in multinationals where there are differences in language and behavioural expectations across societies.

Clearly, then, a major challenge for a management team that wants to manage mergers and acquisitions more effectively is how to plan for the impacts on employee attitudes, including perceptions of organisational justice. Helping senior managers plan for, and implement, these disruptive strategies is an important aspect of the work of HR specialists in these firms.

The challenges of organisational integration

A strategic factor in M&As is the degree of organisational integration required for the combined firms and the underlying reasons for it. The greater the degree of organisational integration, the greater the HR issues that will come to the fore since sites are likely to close, rationalisation occurs in departmental amalgamations (a single sales team, a single finance office, etc.), and there will be 'winners' and 'losers' in the organisational musical chairs that follow (Hubbard and Purcell 2001: 21).

The most frequent way acquisitions are intended to create value, for the shareholder at least, is by 'resource sharing' (Haspeslagh and Jemison 1991). Primarily, although often dressed up in terms of synergistic value creation, this means a focus on cost reduction, while at times increasing the scope of business activities. Resource sharing is seen, for example, in branch closures where there is overlap in a town or city, operational rationalisation in the home country or overseas, and contact-centre amalgamations, often linked to offshoring of certain activities. Significant savings can occur within management from specialist departments coming together and from property sales. And we shouldn't think that these rationalisations are just a problem for the acquired company. In the manufacturing sector, 'post acquisition job losses are more likely to occur in larger factories owned by the acquiring firm' (Goergen, O'Sullivan and Wood 2011: 261). The 'forced' mergers of banks in 2008–9 as part of governments' rescue activities also provided plenty of examples of this.

The problem is how this can be done quickly, leaving behind a committed, integrated, innovative workforce able to maximise customer service. Performance often dips in a major change programme and in M&As this can be exacerbated because of the loss of institutional trust. In an integration programme, there is often a need to change old ways of thinking (competence destruction) prior to new learning (Pil and MacDuffie 1996). This takes time and can lead to a loss of performance at first. Where the 'competency destruction' is linked to large-scale redundancies, for those that remain, the requirement to learn new operating procedures and deal with new bosses, can be especially difficult. It is often observed that employees who stay in a firm after a major redundancy programme suffer from 'survivor syndrome' where guilt, a sense of loss and the intensification of work, lead to a collapse of commitment (Baruch and Hind 2000). The loss of productivity or profitability, while anticipated, is both deeper and lasts longer than hoped for, and this often greatly exceeds that told to shareholders in the prospectus. It is easy to see how shareholder value is lost, let alone employee value. Cultural integration is especially hard but even IT integration is difficult and requires planning, project teams and high levels of involvement at operational level between employees from the two companies, learning to work together.

Conclusions

Multidivisional organisations are those in which a corporate office of senior executives presides over an array of strategic business units. They face the challenge of managing vertically, in their relationships with subsidiaries, and the challenge of managing horizontally, in the way in which the parts of the business collaborate or compete with each other. These are not simple matters. Value is not added simply by owning the assets in a multidivisional company and can, in fact, be squandered. Corporate executives are under pressure to secure a financial return from the whole corporation that is greater than the sum of its parts. The challenge is to achieve a 'parenting advantage'. The rise of new forms of investment, led by private-equity partnerships, has made multidivisional firms more vulnerable to takeover, and size is no defence. The multidivisional company is now more likely to question itself and divest businesses that no longer fit.

We have seen how the logic, in economic terms, of the multidivisional firm has tended to favour the separation of the firm into discrete accounting units, allowing the centre to 'manage by the numbers' in pursuit of financial outcomes. This is a very prevalent philosophy among large Anglo-American firms, spawning a bonus-driven model of HRM in which executives have high levels of performance-related pay. It is a corporate philosophy dominated by strong financial controls over the performance of subsidiary units but limited loyalties to their work sites and workforces, one which has probably been heightened by the growth of private-equity takeovers. An enhanced ability to switch investments, terminate contracts and offload assets does bring a certain kind of organisational flexibility but it also runs risks. It may overemphasise short-run profits at the expense of longer-run investment in management development and skill formation across business units, and it can sap employee cooperation. Too little may be invested in professional HR support to the organisation's line managers. At the very least, senior leaders at corporate headquarters need to ensure that a diverse company of this type can develop and renew its elite group of managerial leaders and technical experts.

An alternative philosophy focuses more on synergistic economies. This includes multidivisional firms that aim to develop core competences stretching across business units, and including favoured suppliers, which can be used to foster innovation in products or processes. When synergies are fostered, the way people, especially managers and expert workers, are managed plays a crucial role in building competitive advantage. Since knowledge sharing is critical, a more liberal, more trusting exchange of it is encouraged through practices that facilitate horizontal networking and organisational integration. The corporation then needs to invest more extensively in the development of its employees and in the HR specialists who, in turn, support them. Higher levels of corporate commitment to the workforce are needed to protect this level of investment. This is the development-oriented model of HRM. Quite how many large organisations tend towards this more synergistic and developmental philosophy is hard to say. In the Anglo-American world, capital market pressures and levels of economic uncertainty are more favourable to firms emphasising the bonus-driven model of HRM.

Many multidivisional firms pursue growth through mergers and acquisitions, while divesting parts of the firm to improve profitability. These are complex, risky and uncertain actions in the business world. All too often, they are badly handled and end up destroying shareholder value despite promises to make greater profits through enhancing efficiency or building synergy. Business leaders are well advised to give very careful attention to the management of these changes, including the deeply human and cultural dimensions of implementation. Poorly focused cost-cutting can trim lean muscle rather than fat, weakening or fatally sapping the competitive strength of a business. Questions of distributive, procedural, interactional and informational justice come strongly into play. A disgruntled reaction from employees and/or suppliers can damage both the firm's core capabilities and its wider reputation as a corporate citizen. Modern capitalism is constantly throwing up opportunities to restructure large or mature firms, selling off under-valued assets or laying a basis for a more profitable future, as the rise of private equity indicates. In so doing, however, corporate executives face major decisions about people and the productive capabilities they have evolved that have fateful consequences for all concerned.

11

HR strategy in multinational firms

This chapter is the last one in Part 3 that analyses the way HR strategy varies across different contexts. Here we examine HRM in multinational firms. Multinational companies (MNCs) are typically multidivisional firms, meaning that the analysis in the previous chapter remains highly relevant, but here we add in the complexities associated with managing across societies and cultures. Multinationals include the world's largest, most recognisable, most powerful and most controversial organisations. What should we understand about their strategies and the ways they organise the network of their activities? What are the leaders of these firms trying to achieve in HRM, and what challenges do they face in doing so? How do their approaches to HRM affect the individuals they employ and the societies in which they operate? We look first at the growth of the MNC phenomenon and then consider wider questions of strategy and structure in multinational firms, including the influence of multinationals on global value chains. This leads into our analysis of HR strategy in MNCs. Here we focus on questions of local adaptation and social legitimacy in multinational operations and then examine how the models of corporate HRM we discussed in the previous chapter – bonus-driven HRM and development-oriented HRM – play out in multinational firms.

The growth of multinational firms

Sometimes referred to as transnational companies (TNCs), multinational corporations have long been a feature of world trade. The English and Dutch East India companies, for example, were chartered in 1600 and 1602, respectively, and given a mandate to exploit trading opportunities with countries in Asia.[1] An MNC is defined as 'any company that has an organizational presence in two or more countries' (Morgan 2005: 555), a definition which encompasses both large and small multinationals. The term 'organizational presence' is important since the stretch and influence of MNCs is not restricted simply to the assets they own and manage. It often includes joint venturing or sub-contracting where the MNC works with business partners or with suppliers rather than through its own subsidiary companies. This wider set of relationships beyond the strict boundaries of the MNC is referred to as the global value chain, or GVC for short (Gereffi 1995). This is an important term, which we will be using in this chapter, on the understanding that we do not use the word 'chain' in a vertical or linear sense: global value chains are better understood as multi-party networks of relationships (Lakhani, Kuruvilla and Avgar 2013). Recent years have seen an increasing vertical *dis*integration of the GVCs in which multidivisional companies are embedded (ibid.: 457), as they move away from the need to make everything along the supply chain to buying from third parties. This classic 'make or buy' choice has profound consequences for the strategy and structure of MNCs, as well as its suppliers.

One of the clearest ways to look at the growth of MNCs is by comparing foreign direct investment (FDI) over a number of years. This is only a partial measure since it excludes sub-contractors, but it does reveal the trends. Léonard et al. (2014: 173) cite the database of the United Nations Conference on Trade and Development (UNCTAD), showing that outward flows of FDI grew 30-fold from US$51,590 million in 1980 to US$1,451,365 million in 2010 (i.e. US$1.45 trillion). Developing economies now attract more investment than either Europe or the USA.[2] This points to a seismic shift away from the historic dominance of the latter, also evidenced in the fact that investments abroad by developing and transitional economies grew from around 12 per cent of all FDI at the beginning of the 2000s to 39 per cent in 2013. MNCs are to be found everywhere in the world. UNCTAD (2007) estimated that there were 37,000 MNCs in the world in the early 1990s, but this had grown to 77,000 by 2006, with more than 770,000 foreign affiliates. These affiliates generated an estimated US$4.5 trillion in value added, employed 62 million workers and exported goods and services valued at US$4 trillion. By 2013, employment in foreign affiliates was 72 million (UNCTAD 2013: 23).

---

[1] http://en.wikipedia.org/wiki/East_India_Company,http://en.wikipedia.org/wiki/Dutch_East_India_Company, accessed 22/1/15.
[2] http://unctad.org/en/publicationslibrary/wir2014_en.pdf, accessed 4/2/15.

We can see the impacts in a country like the UK where foreign ownership more than doubled between 1980 and 1998 (Millward, Bryson and Forth 2000: 32) and has continued to grow since. While few small firms are foreign owned, 28 per cent of businesses with 250 or more employees were foreign owned in 2011.[3] These contributed 40 per cent of the value added by UK companies, showing that, on average, the foreign-owned ones are more efficient that their indigenous counterparts. Just over half of these firms were owned by MNCs based in Europe with a further third being from the Americas. Much of this development has been through company mergers and acquisitions. The UK has one of the most open economies when it comes to such transactions. This is often a matter of some controversy, as, for example, in the takeover of the iconic British company Cadbury by the US multinational Kraft in 2010.[4]

Among the OECD (advanced industrialised) countries, around one in five employees works for an MNC and a further one in five is employed in companies supplying MNCs (Marginson and Meardi 2010: 207). This says something about the extent of multinational influence. In the 1980s, the ownership and leadership of MNCs was heavily based in the richest countries, in 'the Triad' of the USA, western Europe and Japan (Ohmae 1985). In 2005, all but four of the top 50 multinationals were headquartered in the Triad (Croucher and Cotton 2009: 16). However, MNCs are now developing strongly in the BRICs (Brazil, India, Russia and China). In recent years, a growing number of MNCs from other regions have bought UK firms, such as the Indian conglomerate, Tata Group, which acquired Jaguar Land Rover in 2008.[5] The expansion of Chinese MNCs is becoming one of the biggest business stories of the twenty-first century (Cooke 2014).

Multinational strategies, structures and value chains

What are the consequences of this growth in multinational firms? To understand this, we must look more closely at their strategies and structures and their influence in global value chains.

---

[3] http://www.ons.gov.uk/ons/rel/abs/annual-business-survey/foreign-ownership/sty-abs-who-owns-businesses-in-the-uk.html, accessed 15/1/15.
[4] http://en.wikipedia.org/wiki/Cadbury, accessed 22/1/15.
[5] http://www.jaguarlandrover.com/gl/en/about-us/our-history/, accessed 15/1/15.

Multinational strategies and structures

Dunning and Lundan (2008: 68–74) argue that the strategies of multinationals can usefully be understood in terms of four sets of motives underpinning international business activities. The first group is associated with multinationals that are 'natural resource seekers'. For example, this includes companies in oil and gas production, in mining and in agricultural products, which are pursuing resources they lack in their home country or which they can obtain more cheaply elsewhere. Much of the internationalisation of British firms in the nineteenth century was motivated by a desire to extract the natural resources of countries like Australia, South Africa and India in order to fuel the increasing demands of industrialisation in Britain and beyond. Dunning and Lundan also include among resource-seekers firms that are 'seeking plentiful supplies of cheap and well-motivated unskilled or semi-skilled labour' (2008: 68). This, as we noted in Chapters 1 and 8, has been a prime reason for offshoring strategies in manufacturing. We have discussed the decision by the electrical appliance manufacturer Dyson to relocate production to Malaysia while keeping R&D in the UK. This started as a joint venture with the Singapore-based firm, the Meiban group.[6] Then, in 2007, a partnership was formed with a Malaysian electronics manufacturer, VS Industry Bhd (VSI), to take a major role in the Dyson supply chain, from materials and production to distribution. Around 4,000 employees at VSI are now devoted to Dyson-sourced work. This is a joint-venture route to MNC expansion, which is now often seen as preferable to operating a wholly owned subsidiary. As Chapter 9 explained, offshoring is also prevalent in certain kinds of services, which can be obtained more cost-effectively in foreign countries.

Dunning and Lundan's (2008) second category includes the 'market seekers'. Going international is a logical step for any firm that has saturated its home market and run out of ways to grow profitably. Firms often begin by exporting from their home countries but then find that it would be more feasible or more desirable to establish their own subsidiaries in a foreign country to deal with political impediments, to better understand and respond to the foreign market and to deal more effectively with competitors. For example, the world's largest market, the USA, drew Japanese automobile manufacturers in the decades following the Second World War as they sought to reach the American consumer and challenge the dominance of the US auto manufacturers, both in the USA and on the global stage. Now China, the world's second largest economy, is an enormous magnet. Both the USA and China

---

[6] http://en.wikipedia.org/wiki/Dyson_%28company%29, accessed 5/2/15.

are complex and dynamic markets, presenting not only great opportunities for firms but also many risks for the ill-prepared and the poorly connected.

'Efficiency seekers' are firms trying to 'rationalise the structure of established resource-based or market-seeking investments' (Dunning and Lundan 2008: 72), making the point that an ongoing aspect of multinational activity is about restructuring existing operations to enhance profitability. 'Strategic asset seekers' are multinational firms 'acquiring the assets of foreign corporations' (ibid.: 72), aiming to 'augment the acquiring firm's global portfolio of physical assets and human competences' (ibid.: 73). An example is the purchase in 2005 of IBM's PC business by the Chinese firm Lenovo, and another is the acquisition of Jaguar Land Rover, referred to above. These two sets of activities bring into play all the issues associated with divestments, mergers and acquisitions, which we discussed in the previous chapter, and which are more complex for multinational firms because of differences in regulations, cultures and political responses.

Standing back from this detail, it is possible to suggest that the strategies of multinationals are typically developed to address two major business questions: how to obtain better access to resources, including more cost-effective production capabilities than they have in their home country, and how to take advantage of greater market opportunities than they have at home. Clearly, many firms are simultaneously, and continuously, addressing both questions. But we should not imagine that these strategic activities are simply based on economic rationality. The world of the multinational is a highly politicised one, influenced by the policies and powers of governments and supranational bodies as well as trade unions and 'people power'. Large multinationals are exposed to political forces and wield their own. For example, the 'geographical scope of a multinational's operations (may give) it a powerful position in its dealings with nationality based institutions … able to negotiate tax breaks and aid packages with governments' (Edwards and Rees 2006: 56). In addition, through internationalising, a multinational firm may put political pressure on its home-base workforces to accept changes in employment practices, a form of *reverse* diffusion where the MNC learns from overseas experience and imports it back into its home country. Multinationals are politically complex entities, both externally and internally.

As this suggests, governments are very interested in multinational firms. They often try to influence the investment decisions of MNCs, seeking the benefits in resource development, in technology transfer, in employment opportunities and in revenues that can come from their presence, and trying to avoid or minimise the adverse effects of resource depletion, tax avoidance and social exploitation. In this competition, some countries have a kind of 'regime advantage', which attracts foreign investment. The UK and Ireland are good examples of what this means in terms of competition for plant locations in Europe. Government ministers in the UK often point to the UK's relatively 'flexible labour market' as attractive to MNC investment. What this euphemism really means is that, compared with continental Europe, it is easier to make workers redundant in the UK: there are fewer employment rights given to workers, especially temporary and agency workers. MNCs in the UK use agency workers more than domestic firms and have done so consistently over many years (Edwards and Walsh 2009: 298). In effect, the costs of exiting the business in the UK are significantly lower than, say, in France or Germany, a matter of bitter complaint among trade union leaders. Much the same applies in Ireland where FDI has been crucial in expanding the economy. Over the last 20 years, and helped by very low corporate tax rates (another dimension of regime competition), this enabled Ireland to become 'the Celtic tiger'. The withdrawal of major firms in the global recession of 2008–9 has been a body-blow to the economy. Dell, for example, came to Ireland in 1990 and became the country's biggest exporter with revenues amounting to 5 per cent of GDP. In January 2009, it announced that much of its Irish-based production would move to Poland with the loss of around half its jobs in Ireland.[7]

As is often observed, MNCs that seek greater efficiencies in their international locations can be 'foot-loose and fancy free'. Multinational firms, after all, are international companies whose managers seek to serve their shareholders. They often have strong roots in a particular country (French MNCs retain a lot about them that is French, for example), but their interests are not necessarily the same as those of nation states or of particular communities where they may have operated for many years. They do not necessarily aim to retain plants or service centres in a particular country 'come hell or high water'.

Not surprisingly, multinationals typically create some kind of division-alised structure. They are, in effect, more complex variations of the multi-divisional companies we discussed in Chapter 10, exhibiting a layering or meshing of structures to cope with transnational diversity (Edwards, Marginson and Ferner 2013: 569). One thing should be overwhelmingly obvious about MNCs as organisations: they face challenging issues of coordination. They often begin with an international division to coordinate their foreign activities (Evans, Pucik and Barsoux 2002: 16–21, Dunning and Lundan 2008: 241–9). This, however, can be very inadequate for multi-product firms, which may set up an international division within each major product grouping or a matrix structure 'involving both product and geographical reporting

---

[7] http://www.finfacts.ie/irishfinancenews/article_1025198.shtml, accessed 16/1/15.

lines' (Evans, Pucik and Barsoux 2002: 17). Within these broad umbrellas, it is often necessary to manage coordination through a structure of regional offices. For example, a logical grouping is to establish a European division to deal with the legal and institutional frameworks of the European Union, a North American division to adapt to its more individualistic institutions and a North-East Asian division to nurture the tacit and group relationships for which the region is famous. These are still very gross categories. As corporate expatriates know, there are many variations across countries within these broad categories, not to mention the Middle East, Africa, Southern and South-East Asia, Oceania and South America. Experimentation and restructuring is certainly going to occur as multinational leaders react 'to changing markets and ... search for a workable structure' (Drahokoupil 2014: 202).

Multinational subsidiaries and value chains

Within whatever kind of international structure they establish, multinationals go on to create subsidiaries in various countries. Historically, setting up subsidiaries was necessary to get in behind the protectionist barriers, such as import duties, quotas and procurement policies, set in place by national governments to foster their own industry and induce multinationals to play a role in it (Dunning and Lundan 2008: 159–60, 181–2). This gave the managers of multinational subsidiaries quite a degree of power in their relations with the headquarters of their firms because they made it possible for the firm to adapt to, and take advantage of, their local environments (Murray et al. 2014). The global environment, however, has moved on. There is now less protectionism; growing forms of regional integration, such as the European Union; a highly connected, communication-obsessed world dominated by the internet; major improvements in transportation; and a world in which finance is highly mobile, often with disturbing results. All these changes raise the question of what has been happening to multinational investments in their subsidiaries and supply chains.

The activities of multinationals are increasingly being analysed within the literature on global value chains or networks. The researchers working within this body of theory are interested in how multinationals create value, including where they locate particular types of activity, who benefits from the way they do so, who might be exploited by more powerful actors in the process and how to influence or regulate them to achieve better outcomes for the societies in which they operate (e.g. Riisgaard and Hammer 2011, Léonard et al. 2014). A value chain is not simply about an individual firm but about the web of relationships in which it is embedded. Drawing on the influential work of Gereffi, Humphrey and Sturgeon (2005), Lakhani et al. (2013) examine the implications of different types of value chain for local suppliers and employment systems. They suggest that four criteria may be used to analyse these choices: the lead firm's (i.e. the MNC's) influence on supplier employment relations; the type of skills and knowledge of employees required in the supplier firm; the stability of employment in the supplier firm; and the national institutional influences on employment relations. Using these criteria, they describe five types of relationship between an MNC and its suppliers and argue that we should see a diverse range of impacts (ibid.: 452–6):

- *Market value-chain configurations.* Here, the contract is for the supply of standard products requiring only low levels of skill, with tasks easily codified. The asymmetric power of the MNC over the supplier means that it is easy to exit from the contract and move to a new supplier. Low task complexity is associated with low employment stability and high levels of labour turnover. Workers are easy to replace, and casual employment is frequently used. National systems of employment relations apply to the supplier but not to the MNC. An example given is that of fruit growers in South Africa.
- *Modular value-chain configurations* are where suppliers make products or services to the lead firm's specifications, known as 'turnkey' operations. Suppliers will try to use generic machinery to supply a number of customers to minimise their dependence on one MNC. In the American electronics industry, the contract manufacturers receive highly formalised specifications for the product manufacture from the lead firm, but they are 'responsible for purchasing required component parts, re-design-for-manufacturability, circuit-board layout, testing, final product assembly, final packaging and after-sales service' (ibid.: 453). The supplier retains full control over their employment system. There will be moderate levels of employee skills and some stability, with national employment systems applying to the supplier.
- *Relational value-chain configurations* exist where the tasks performed by the supplier are complex and not easily codified, but suppliers are highly competent and 'provide lead firms with an incentive to outsource to gain access to complementary competencies. The need to exchange tacit knowledge results in high explicit coordination' and a high degree of mutual dependence fostering high levels of trust (ibid.: 454). The employment systems are jointly influenced by the lead firms and their suppliers. It is likely that employees will be highly skilled. The lead firm will take a close interest in training and ensuring employees understand the market needs for the product. Examples of this relational configuration can be found in the

global automotive industry where sub-contractors sometimes take a role in co-designing complex parts. This also applies to software design and R&D in life sciences.

- *Captive value-chain configurations* exist where suppliers are dependent on the lead firm, which provides 'detailed instructions' and engages in 'high levels of monitoring and control' (ibid.: 455). The aim, in part, is to lock in the suppliers they have invested in. 'Examples of captive value chain configurations can be found in food industries such as chicken where lead firms ("integrators") exert significant control over suppliers (independent farmers, referred to as "growers") who are responsible for raising chickens and are dependent on integrators for market access and key inputs' (ibid.: 455). Another example is offshoring of dedicated call centres to India. 'Readily available call-centre technologies routinize work practices while electronic monitoring systems allow lead firms to monitor progress and standards' (ibid.: 458). In this pattern, the lead firm attempts to dictate certain aspects of the employment systems of the supplier firm. Training programmes are often designed by the lead firm: for example, to ensure that call-centre workers speak with an American accent and use American names. However, the lead firm is also taking advantage of the low labour costs and minimal regulations of these offshore sites.

- *Hierarchical value-chain configurations* relate to vertically integrated subsidiaries. 'Tasks are highly complex and uncodifiable, and because highly competent suppliers cannot be found outside the firm, these tasks are kept in-house' (ibid.: 456). Information technology companies, for example, may retain research and development activities in their own subsidiaries because the protection of their intellectual property rights is important. Innovations in one subsidiary can then be spread to other units in other regions. This use of integrated subsidiaries can also be found in the reorganisation of professional service providers: for example, in the creation of HR shared-service centres covering the whole of a company, helping it to keep track of managers and professional staff around the globe (Smale 2008: 137).

The argument is that these configurations can change and develop, either with the supplier becoming more embedded within the MNC by developing their own expertise, or by being downgraded by the lead firm and losing their contract. In essence, the choice for the MNC is between being 'hands on', characterised by long-term contracts and regular engagement between the centre and the subsidiary, or 'hands off', relying on product specifications, explicit standards and monitoring (Riisgaard and Hammer 2011: 172).

The implication of these analyses of global value chains is that there is now greater volatility in MNCs, in part as a result of the Global Financial Crisis but also because of trends in the changing nature of the relationships with subsidiaries and suppliers. To summarise a complex field, the general move is to use suppliers from outside the MNC and have fewer subsidiaries, but the pattern can vary from one firm to another and from one industry to another.

Financialisation and multinational behaviour

If the picture is not complicated enough already, we must add in the impact of the financialisation process discussed in relation to multidivisional companies in Chapter 10. Morgan (2014: 192), talking of the 'global financial value chain', argues that the impact of financialisation is greater on MNCs because 'unlike firms located in a single state, they have the capability of being able to shift around their resources between different national jurisdictions in ways which enable them to maximise financial benefit' (ibid.: 185). Thus, 'MNCs' strategies for outsourcing, relocation and the formation of global value chains are dependent on the ability to raise and shift capital across national borders as well as a relative freedom to repatriate profits or leave them offshore' (ibid.: 185).

Morgan (2014) points to several features of this financialisation process. One is the reorganisation of boundaries in order to reduce costs, increase efficiencies, improve flexibility and respond to short-term market changes to maximise short-term shareholder value. Another is heavy borrowing from the London and New York financial markets 'to set up new plants overseas, to acquire facilities in other countries through mergers and takeovers, to set up flows of cash across national boundaries to purchase commodities and services from sub-contractors and to transfer earnings from one country to another' (ibid.: 186). In the past, these sorts of acquisition activities were funded from retained profits or rights issues, raising investment funds from shareholders. This came to be regarded less favourably by the share market. The preference became the issuing of bonds and the use of sophisticated financial instruments, such as credit default swaps and risk-hedging derivatives managed by financial advisers and international banks for heavy fees.

Another feature has been the use of transfer pricing between subsidiaries and the MNC. Here, 'the central allocation of overheads and other costs to subsidiaries can make their actual profitability seem very unclear' (Morgan 2014: 192). A key issue is the question of allocating intellectual property rights (IPR). 'MNCs have increasingly taken to allocating IPR to specific subsidiaries, usually in environments where there is a tax advantage due to high allowances and low taxes on anything than can be associated with innovation and the development of IPR' (ibid.: 193). The use of tax minimisation strategies by MNCs has become controversial: for example, the way they can utilise the very low tax rates and generous allowances of Luxembourg.[8] In the case of Amazon, a recent '23-page provisional decision paper from the competition commission in Brussels said Amazon EU Sarl, the group's Luxembourg trading hub' with 'sales of €13.6 billion (£10.3 billion) in 2013, had been paying inflated royalty fees to another Amazon entity', Amazon Europe Holding Technologies SCS (AEHT), thus reducing its reported profits and tax liabilities.[9] In effect, the argument is that many MNCs have excellent opportunities to 'make money out of money' and, indeed, it is often the case that they generate more profit from financial dealings than from production and service.

In summary, the strategies of multinational firms have their roots in two fundamental drives: the desire to obtain greater or cheaper resources than those available at home and the desire to penetrate new markets in the search for greater profitability. This sounds simple but the world is a complex place in which to pursue these goals. As multinationals grow, their structures become more complicated, adapting to the needs of different regions and countries, and their activities become increasingly politicised. The world's largest multinationals are highly adaptive organisations but also highly influential ones, flexing their economic muscles through the deployment and withdrawal of their subsidiaries, through their actions in the wider value chains in which they are embedded and through the financialisation of their international activities.

What's different about HR strategy in the multinational firm?

To become an MNC, then, is to face a whole new layer of economic, social and political complexity, both in terms of opportunities and risks. What does this mean for HR strategy in MNCs? We begin with the fundamental point that all multinationals adapt their HR strategies to the local contexts in which they operate, and we analyse the way in which their HR strategies are subject to scrutiny in terms of social legitimacy. We then extend the analysis from the previous chapter of bonus-driven and development-oriented models of HRM to the multinational context.

---

[8] http://www.theguardian.com/business/2014/nov/05/-sp-luxembourg-tax-files-tax-avoidance-industrial-scale, accessed 16/1/15.
[9] http://www.theguardian.com/technology/2015/jan/16/amazon-eu-sarl-paid-too-little-tax-says-brussels, accessed 6/2/15.

Local adaptation in multinational HRM

A key issue in the literature on HRM in MNCs has been the tension between global integration and local adaptation or decentralisation (e.g. Evans, Pucik and Barsoux 2002, Dowling, Festing and Eagle 2013). This is an increasingly complex debate involving analysis of large, multi-country data sets (e.g. Brewster, Wood and Brookes 2008, Edwards, P. et al. 2013). Clearly, as underlined above, multinationals face a very challenging task in coordinating their operations across countries, one which is made more difficult as they traverse more countries and which is disturbed whenever mergers and acquisitions are used to restructure a global firm. But to what extent does this critical problem of coordination imply conformity in HRM?

We take the view that coordinating operations (i.e. managing flows of supplies and intermediate outputs to meet targets for delivery of a product or service to a customer) and standardising HRM (e.g. each subsidiary having the same policy on remuneration levels and components) are not the same thing. To coordinate work demands and deliveries among subsidiaries and suppliers is one thing; to tell them all to manage their employees in the same way is quite another. The obvious fact is that any multinational establishing a foreign operation is going to need to gain permission from local officials, address local laws and set up agreements or contracts with local people. This means that it is not a question of *whether* multinational firms adapt to local circumstances but of understanding the ways in which they do actually adapt. As Evans, Pucik and Barsoux (2002: 160) put it:

> Sensitivity to local conditions has important advantages associated with better market acceptance. By providing a local face, behaving like domestic firms, and adjusting products to local tastes, the foreign entrant is likely to have wider customer appeal or to compete more effectively in local labor markets. Local responsiveness helps to overcome the 'liability of foreignness'.

An inescapable feature of HRM is that it is a domain of management in which the need for societal adaptation is very strong, as Chapter 3 explained. In MNCs, the problem is magnified whenever there are language differences and, underneath them, different cultural values and expectations. This is illustrated in a fascinating study of Japanese retail firms opening stores in China, in which Gamble (2010) shows how a high level of customer service, which flourished in Japan, was nurtured in China. Like most Japanese MNCs, the firms placed a heavy reliance on expatriates to manage the Chinese operations. One way of improving customer-service standards in China involved recruiting staff with no work experience 'because you need them to do as they are told', as one manager put it (ibid.: 718). On the other hand, cultural expectations about the promotion of women, which is rare in Japan but common in China, led the firms to adopt the local practice, partly because many talented people would otherwise leave. Some of the firms used seniority-based pay as in Japan, while others did not because this is not necessarily helpful in the Chinese labour market in which good performers expect higher pay more quickly. Labour retention is a big issue in Chinese cities whereas in Japan loyalty and long service to the corporation remain cultural norms. One small illustration of cultural differences is that in Japan employees' bags are checked when they leave the store. This was done at first in China but stopped after a week as expatriate managers felt constrained from exercising harsh discipline outside their home country (ibid.: 721) – a wise decision.

The general point is this: multinationals need to subscribe to some sensitive local adaptation of HR practices if they wish to succeed in a foreign environment. The level of adaptation is less extensive when there are strong cultural similarities and a common language, but the need for adaptation is always present. Even if they were inclined to, how far MNCs can impose a standard set of HR policies in all operating units is limited. There is no doubt that some multinationals want to ensure that certain key policies are widely adopted or not adopted. This is most often the case with US multinationals, which show a higher propensity to try to control HR policies than multinationals from any other country (Ferner et al. 2013). Part of this is the well-known desire of US managers to avoid union recognition and collective bargaining, something that governments and workforces in other countries either insist on or concede in order to secure the investment. Britain is an example of the former while Ireland, from the mid-1980s, became an example of the latter (Geary 2007: 101).

Despite the fact that the USA is a dominant influence in world business, the actual level of success of American managers with a more controlling approach to HR policy is mixed (Ferner et al. 2013), and a more common approach among multinationals is to let key policies in HRM 'take the form of frameworks or "global footprints", which lay down the main principles and parameters, but leave detailed implementation to the individual businesses and countries in the light of local regulation, conventions and practice' (Marginson and Meardi 2010: 217). The framework principles are supposed to be taken seriously, but it makes much more sense if practices can be adapted to local conditions. As Gamble (2010) emphasises, subsidiary managers, including expatriates, soon come to appreciate the need to respond to local labour markets and attitudes, which can vary both within and between countries. In a study of Finnish-owned subsidiaries in China, Smale (2008: 149) noted that the larger the Chinese subsidiary, the greater was the desire of headquarters to ensure integration with the MNC in Finland. However, full integration was never possible and the monitoring of it was beyond the capacity of the MNC's HR information system (HRIS) given the extensive differences in language and cultural meanings. The gap was filled by 'people-based integration' in the way that expatriate managers from Finland worked alongside local Chinese management. This led, very naturally, to local adaptations rather than centralised conformity. The local HR manager, always Chinese, 'assumed several "bridge-type" roles', linking 'the expatriate supervisor and voice of MNC headquarters' with 'line managers and shop-floor employees, and intra- and inter-MNC HR contacts' (ibid.: 144).

As implied by our discussion in Chapter 10, any MNC in which executives aspire to greater integration of their favoured HR practices will find it harder to achieve where growth comes through acquisitions of companies in other countries with established patterns of employment relations. In a study of international mergers, including the period of post-merger rationalisation, Rees and Edwards (2009) show how political and institutional factors in host countries slowed or significantly modified the integration process. In one company, SnackCo, the plan involved a move to a standardised individual incentive plan, but 'in many European countries, HR managers argued that they needed works council approval. The reaction from corporate and European HQ was pragmatic, reluctantly accepting that many pre-existing practices should be left in place' (ibid.: 32). Similar resistance was experienced in EuroFuel through a combination of labour law and collective bargaining. 'Two years after the merger' ... it was 'admitted that there was little hope of meaningful integration across all sites and that a "patchwork quilt" of different sets and conditions would persist indefinitely' (ibid.: 32). The authors conclude that 'the rationalisation process in the post-merger period is not simply determined by market and institutional factors but is also an intensely political process in which the interests of many actors are challenged, leading them to respond with whatever resources they have at their disposal to influence outcomes' (ibid.: 36).

We should not really imagine that the leaders of MNCs are somehow desperate to export the specific HR practices used in their home country and terribly disappointed if they can't. They do often bring HR managers together from around the world to discuss global HR policies and challenges in HRM and, no doubt, to hear presentations on 'best practice' in different parts of the group (see e.g. Edwards, Marginson and Ferner 2013: 569). However, we need to step back from an obsession with what is happening in HR practice and set HRM within the context of the business motives and production networks of multinational firms. What matters most to the directors of multinationals is their ability to obtain the resources they seek and to compete effectively in the markets they target.

Without necessarily specifying particular kinds of HR practice, what this does imply is that benchmarking – comparisons of production or service performance – are very popular in the multinational world (Farndale and Paauwe 2007). Analysis of comparative statistics on business performance is commonplace in multinational firms and typically leads to corporate pressure on local managers to improve plants or sites that are seen to be under-performing. The use of sub-contractors, rather than wholly owned subsidiaries, makes it easier to use 'coercive comparisons' (Mueller and Purcell 1992) and wield the deterrent of contract termination if performance improvement or cost reduction fails. Greer and Hauptmeier (forthcoming) show how Ford, General Motors and VW have used benchmarking to compare labour costs across their European plants where they make automobile components or assemble final vehicles. If a plant is characterised by much higher costs than its sister plants (e.g. as a result of taking much longer to assemble a car or doing so with significantly higher employment costs), the clear implication is that management will shift production to other plants within the group or outsource it to cheaper providers. This has led to a process of 'whipsawing' in which unions have agreed to major concessions to retain production volumes and unionised jobs in their plant or country. The threat of plant closure is greatest when there is excess capacity in an industry, and a company has multiple sites producing standardised outputs.

As this example illustrates, multinationals, like multidivisional firms generally, require their different businesses, work sites and suppliers to meet performance benchmarks. The business priority is typically to achieve certain performance outcomes rather than to export or import HR practices *for their own sake*. Managers whose plants/sites have a low-productivity performance will often get help through the transfer of technologies or know-how developed elsewhere or their subsidiaries will be sold off. As Cooke (2007b: 501) explains, multinationals tend to emphasise the transfer of 'technological capabilities over HR capabilities'. This means that change in under-performing sites is most likely to be led by operations managers, who may, for example, push for the adoption of lean production systems or, alternatively, for outsourcing and reconfiguration of the supply chain. They tend to be the innovators in workplace change with HR specialists following their lead (Guest and Bryson 2009, Wood and Bryson 2009). There are, thus, important 'downstream' impacts on the management of people, but these, as Chapter 3 explained, will involve a large measure of adaptation to the local social and political context. For example, ArcelorMittal, the world's largest steel manufacturer, has a European Works Council and holds regular meetings between senior management and union leaders to discuss issues of mutual interest, such as health and safety and environmental concerns, both highly important in steel production.[10] Employee relations specialists from Europe and North America meet regularly in London to share knowledge, coordinate initiatives and ensure that collective bargaining remains at the plant or local company level.

Being a downstream activity does not, however, mean that the work of local HR specialists is unimportant or that it is totally circumscribed. Local HR professionals are important for their knowledge of national and regional cultures, labour markets and regulation, which is vital for effective integration of the MNC into the local economies and societies. In any large multinational company, HR departments are critical for dealing with regional bodies such as European Works Councils and for negotiating with trade unions seeking to establish standards of employee treatment. These are areas that depend on specialist HR expertise and on trust-building with counterparts in the public bureaucracy, in works councils and in trade unions.

The social legitimacy of multinational HR practices

There is, however, a serious problem when MNCs are seen to be exploiting local conditions in a way that offends international standards for human rights or humane conditions of work. Sensitive adaptation to national laws and culture is one thing: exploitation of vulnerable workers in developing nations, or exploitation of a particular country's lax levels of legal enforcement, is quite another. As we explained in Chapters 1 and 6, social legitimacy is an important goal in HRM for all firms whose managers want their firm to be recognised as a responsible corporate citizen. The spotlight often falls most sharply on multinational behaviour. There can be consumer boycotts of multinational firms reported to exploit labour in low-skill operations, like clothing manufacturing in Bangladesh or toy-making in China.[11]

To counter this criticism, many MNCs now subscribe to codes of conduct. Some of these are issued at a world level, like the OECD Guidelines on Multinational Enterprises or the UN Global Compact (Seifert 2008). Yet others are voluntary codes issued on a sectoral level. Within Europe, the regulation of MNCs has been taken much further through the creation of European

---

[10] http://corporate.arcelormittal.com/news-and-media/press-releases/2007/apr/19-04-2007?lang=english, accessed 20/1/15.

[11] http://www.ethicalconsumer.org/home.aspx, accessed 22/1/15.

Works Councils. Trade unions also have a strong interest in MNCs and more than 60 International Framework Agreements (IFAs) have been signed between the predominantly continental European MNCs and international trade-union federations (Croucher and Cotton 2009: 58–60). The influence of these agreements in Europe has so far been weak with the creation of a dialogue but with little sign of collective bargaining or active coordination of terms and conditions of employment. This is left to workplace activities, and it is extremely difficult to organise concerted union action across national boundaries if this is premised on strike action.

In developing countries, there is some evidence that IFAs have been more effective. For example, in banana growing, distribution and marketing, the five MNCs that dominate the market have been forced by a multinational labour coordinating body, COLSIBA, of 42 unions and 45,000 workers, to sign an IFA enforcing ILO standards on freedom of association and collective bargaining (Riisgaard and Hammer 2011). However, even with this, there is evidence of production being relocated to non-union areas and outsourcing to labour contractors, making meaningful implementation difficult. A newer form of labour standards' enforcement has emerged in collaboration between ethical trading consumer interest groups and COLSIBA, promoting 'private social standards' (PSSs), which gains agreements from producers. Another example comes from the cut-flower producers in Kenya where a PSS has been important in gaining recognition of an international code of conduct, especially by major European retail MNCs that buy directly and not via the wholesale market (ibid.: 180–3).

The clothing industry disaster at Rana Plaza in Bangladesh in 2013, where over 1,000 workers died, has led to an unprecedented coordination attempt by major companies, such as H&M (even though it had no contracts with firms in Rana Plaza). There is now an 'Accord on Fire and Building Safety in Bangladesh' signed by over 190 brands, clothing firms and importers from around the world and a North American 'Alliance for Bangladesh Worker Safety'.[12] These bodies are concerned to raise standards, engage in auditing and enhance the voice of workers on safety. Some clothing brands have refused to join these efforts but the requirements of social legitimacy will influence them, too.[13] HRM in MNCs is not immune from social requirements and employment ethics even if the relationship is with sub-contractors producing low-cost items with low-skill labour in a less visible part of a complex

---

[12] http://bangladeshaccord.org/about/, http://www.bangladeshworkersafety.org/about/about-the-alliance, accessed 22/1/15.
[13] http://www.theguardian.com/world/2014/apr/19/rana-plaza-bangladesh-one-year-on, accessed 20/1/15.

value chain. It has proved impossible for them to 'wash their hands' or deny responsibility in a world of global communication, 24-hour news coverage and social media, as Nike discovered with allegations of child labour and sweatshops among its sub-contractors.[14]

Although they are powerful and influential, large multinational firms, then, are still vulnerable in the domain of social legitimacy. This responsibility is more important for their HR strategies than it is for many smaller or solely domestic firms that can 'fly under the radar', and it is something that can consume a high level of time and energy in research, negotiation and compliance activities, if it is to be done credibly. The old adage comes to mind: 'with great power comes great responsibility'.[15]

Bonus-driven and development-oriented models of HRM in multinational firms

As mentioned above, multinational firms are also typically multidivisional firms. In Chapter 10, we described the ways in which corporate approaches to HRM vary along a continuum from bonus-driven to development-oriented models. We see the same tension in multinational firms with an added realm of complexity associated with operating across borders. While financialisation undoubtedly creates greater opportunities for executive bonuses, the development of a cadre of internationally competent staff, particularly managers and advanced specialists, is a critical challenge for any multinational (Evans, Pucik and Barsoux 2002, chapter 8). Even if the bonus culture is strong (as it is in the international banks, for example), long-standing multinationals have usually developed a more extensive framework for employee development than have firms based only in one country (Mabey 2008).

Employee development in MNCs includes the selection and management of individuals to serve abroad as expatriates, the development and career management of indigenous managers from host countries, and the provision of training and development programmes to new managers (e.g. Dowling, Festing and Eagle 2013). As firms increasingly organise themselves across national boundaries, their talent-management activities must adjust to a variety of labour markets and must take into account the extent to which individuals show an ability and willingness to be deployed in different countries, including those in which there are language and cultural challenges. This is a more demanding agenda than that faced by firms operating in only

---

[14] http://en.wikipedia.org/wiki/Nike,_Inc, accessed 20/1/15.
[15] Attributed first of all to the French sage, Voltaire.

one country and it places greater demands on HR specialists (e.g. Cooke 2014). At least some HR specialists are allocated to transnational issues: they may develop competency-based frameworks for employee and management development, pursue global talent-sourcing strategies, support the use of performance management processes and help develop corporate 'employer brands' (Evans, Pucik and Barsoux 2002, Sparrow et al. 2004). Hird, Marsh and Sparrow (2009: 25) give an example of Vodafone. The company has a European HR director and there is an HR director in each of the nine European operating companies. There are specialists in reward and organisational development in 'centres of expertise' with business-partner HR staff at the operating companies. The HR director explains that 'on an annual basis we get the operating company HR directors together with the centres of expertise to discuss and debate internal and external factors which will drive the people agenda for the coming year. During the session, we jointly prioritise and plan the initiative list for the year. It is a very powerful way of creating mutual buy-in and a shared agenda' (Hird, Marsh and Sparrow 2009: 25).

Although the models applied show cultural variations, among the world's largest multinationals, management development is a critical priority (Evans, Pucik and Barsoux 2002: 372–6, Mabey 2008). As Cooke (2014: 13) demonstrates in a series of case studies, the need to develop 'managerial talent capable of managing international operations' is something that is exercising the leadership of Chinese multinationals as they expand around the globe. A company long admired for its approach to management development is Unilever, the Anglo-Dutch MNC with a range of well-known food and cleaning brands (Goold, Campbell and Alexander 1994, Jones 2005).[16] Although it is heavily decentralised, there is a strong culture of coordination and linkages between businesses, fostered by the fact that executives in the company have always needed to operate in both the Dutch and Anglophone worlds and their spheres of influence. This is achieved by building elaborate networks and lateral relationships between managers in different businesses and retaining tight control over career management and promotion decisions. All managers worldwide are considered a corporate resource. The process starts with recruitment. 'The greatest challenge of recruiting is to find the best and the brightest who will fit into the company.... For international careers in our current operating company, we look for people who can work in teams and understand the value of cooperation and consensus' (Floris Maljers, then joint chairman of Unilever, quoted in Goold, Campbell and Alexander 1994: 154). After graduate trainees

---

[16] Unilever is highly rated in Hay Group's study of the best companies for leadership development, http://www.haygroup.com/bestcompaniesforleadership/, accessed 22/1/15.

are recruited each year, career movement for the best takes on a triple spiral: between functions, between divisions and between countries. As Jones (2005: 229) explains:

> The higher up the hierarchy a manager progressed, the more important it was that he or she had a sense of identity as a Unilever manager, rather than a company one. To have worked in more than one company, probably in more than one product group, and in more than one country, was regarded as essential for career advancement. Unilever's stress on international experience and mobility contrasted with most US-based multinationals, where employment outside the United States for any length of time was routinely regarded as the death knell of a successful career, although total mobility within the United States was often expected.

Looking at Unilever's 'parenting advantage' in the way the centre adds value, strategy analysts conclude that 'Unilever's system for managing (people) creates a direct linkage benefit by providing the businesses with a larger pool of suitable management talent to draw on. It is also a mechanism that promotes other linkages. By fostering a common culture, promoting networks and exposing managers to a broad range of experiences, the Unilever system speeds up the circulation of product knowledge and best practice' (Goold, Campbell and Alexander 1994: 155). In effect, Unilever has developed a global HR strategy for recruiting and developing its managers.[17] Providing firms such as Unilever can provide a high level of employment security, their programmes for employee development, and their diverse array of working environments, make them very attractive and highly admired places to work. The same is true of the elite group of pharmaceutical multinationals, which have contributed to extraordinary scientific discoveries and innovations in healthcare.[18] MNCs are frequently under scrutiny for their employment practices in the developing world but the other side of the coin is that they are world leaders in knowledge and career development for their management and specialist cadres. Countries in which a strong concentration of development-oriented multinationals is headquartered are likely to be at a societal advantage in terms of management and scientific capability.

This example of Unilever shows how some MNCs build social capital through organisational processes that foster networks and generate trust across boundaries. Lengnick-Hall and Lengnick-Hall (2005: 477) define

---

[17] For a helpful description, see http://www.humancapitalreview.org/content/default.asp?Article_ID=1282, accessed 22/1/15.
[18] See, for example, http://www.pfizer.com/research/rd_partnering/centers_for_therapeutic_innovation, accessed 12/2/15.

social capital in an international context as 'the intangible resource of structural connections, interpersonal interactions and cognitive understanding that enables a firm to (a) capitalize on diversity and (b) reconcile differences'. Social capital helps MNCs to manage the tension between pressures for integration on a global scale and pressures for local adaptation: to cope with the challenges that arise from diverse national value systems, economic systems and workplace conditions (Sparrow and Braun 2007). MNCs can be expected to vary in the extent to which they wish to build this kind of social capital, with the bonus-driven ones less concerned about it, but a significant presence in transnational operations typically makes a firm more development-oriented, at least for its management cadres and 'high-potentials'.

Conclusions

The growth of multinational companies, which have an organisational presence in two or more countries, has been a dominant feature of the global economy over the last 40 years. In terms of their significance, a telling statistic is that one in five people in Europe are directly employed in a multinational while another one in five works in a firm supplying multinationals. The Global Financial Crisis made a slight dent in the growth rates but the advance of MNCs was never in doubt. Among the factors facilitating this growth have been the increasing liberalisation of world trade, the development of global financial markets, the impact of more sophisticated information technology and the emergence of global brands. MNCs are looking out upon a world that offers them great opportunities, but one which still imposes great challenges in coordination. The integration–decentralisation dilemma faced by all multisite companies is made more complex in MNCs, which need to coordinate product or service delivery across countries, made all the more difficult by different languages, belief systems and regulations. Governments also look out upon the world of multinationals and think about their interests: can they tame the beast, gaining the benefits of new technologies and standards of living, or will they be tamed by its appetite for resources and rewards? There is clear evidence of 'regime competition' to persuade an MNC to invest in a given region or country. This can include incentives or tax breaks. In some countries, it may involve finding means by which the corporation is exempt from social legislation on trade unions or collective bargaining.

Researchers looking at MNCs are increasingly studying their influence in global value chains or the network of relationships in which they are embedded. This suggests a range of models of value creation rather than one dominant model. Standardised production of global products allows for sub-contracting, often in low-cost countries, either as commodities or as 'turn-key' operations where the sub-contractor works with a number of MNCs in the same industry. A requirement for an institutional presence in a local market – for example, in insurance – predicates the need for a local provider, either as a subsidiary or as a joint venture. The need for bespoke production, or R&D, will mean that the MNC pays close attention to the subsidiary and control of intellectual property is likely to be critical.

What, then, is different about HR strategies in multinational firms? Despite regime competition, we have argued that they are inevitably adaptive in HR strategy. To be sure, there may be 'global footprints' or principles that set out an important framework of ideas, and a demanding set of performance benchmarks, but the actual process of HRM is one of those 'sticky', contextually sensitive parts of management. The value of some adaptation to local circumstances is the first thing that expatriates learn. They find that local management is often less than enthusiastic in following dictates from head-quarters about HR practice and with good reason: it's been tried before with less than impressive consequences. An enabling kind of policy is another matter. Processes to improve coordination, and to transfer key technologies and know-how, are usually of great interest to local managers in multinationals but a substantial degree of adaptation to local labour markets, employment laws and cultural norms is essential to running their business. The centralising managers at head office who may try, for whatever reason, to standardise HR practices often become reconciled to the 'patchwork quilt' of compromises that remains after rounds of corporate restructuring.

The problem for many governments, and for trade unions and community groups, is that many multinational firms are only too keen to take advantage of lower labour costs and less demanding employment regulations. Globalisation has opened up huge opportunities for multinationals to hire capable workforces in developing countries at much lower costs. It is possible for powerful firms to push for productivity improvements in nearly all countries, including 'coercive comparisons' that threaten their workforces at home. Such strategies are often a source of ethical concerns, and are fuelling the growth of regional and global employment standards by which management behaviour can be judged. Multi-nationals are coming under close scrutiny for the legitimacy of their HR strategies, irrespective of how long or complex the value chain in which they are embedded. Their visibility on the High Streets and Main Streets of the wealthy world make them are an obvious place for unions and lobby groups to start when surfacing problems of labour exploitation that are deeply seated and in which local suppliers are often more heavily implicated than multinationals.

There is one final criterion that we should use to unpack the HR implications of MNCs: their role in, and impact on, employee development. The bonus-driven model of HRM is clearly important in multinational corporations, and financialisation may be sponsoring more of it, but the requirement to develop a cadre of managers capable of operating across boundaries means that their recruitment, development and career planning will often be superior to that of companies based only in one country. They are often highly desirable places for individual development, across hierarchical levels, across complex functions and across diverse societies. The evidence suggests that MNCs are, on average, better managed than their indigenous counterparts in a given market or location. In the UK, they produce a higher proportion of GDP than their numerical presence would predict. A heavy concentration of multinationals headquartered in a country is most likely a principal driver of that country's managerial and scientific capabilities. And an MNC sensitive to local cultures, learned, for example, through operating in China or India, can demonstrate a breadth of commercial understanding and cultural sensibility that others, operating only in their domestic market, have never gained.

12

Final thoughts: main themes and next steps

The purpose of this final chapter is twofold. First, we summarise and integrate our most important themes. The book has traversed numerous studies, examined a range of frameworks and theories and reached a set of important conclusions at the end of each chapter. We will not be repeating all of our conclusions, but what we will do in this chapter is underline the most important themes of the book as a whole. In so doing, we take the chance to offer our personal views on the trends we see in theory and practice. We then conclude with an important 'so what?' question: how can managers in firms improve the processes for developing HR strategy in their organisations to deal more effectively with the HR problems they face and the opportunities that HRM presents?

The main themes of this book

If we were to boil down the book's messages to a few key themes, what would they be? We think that seven major themes underpin the book:

Theme one: human resource strategy is an essential element in business strategy, not some kind of dubious appendage to it, and plays a critical role in organisational viability and relative performance.

Human resources belong to people, but they are critical for the survival and success of organisations. HRM is the process through which managers attempt to build a workforce with the kind of human resources their organisation needs and create the kind of human performances that will make it successful.

It is concerned with how work is organised and with how people are employed to do it. As such, HRM is an essential aspect of establishing, growing and maintaining a business, a function that has strategic significance in all organisations. HRM is also an essential aspect of attempts to restructure and renew organisations. 'HR strategy' is the term we use to describe the critical set of choices that managers make around how to build their workforce and how to manage it. A reasonably effective HR strategy is a necessary, though not a sufficient, condition of business survival or viability. In organisations that do survive, the quality of HR strategy has impacts on relative performance.

This theme has implications for the two business disciplines we bring together in this book: strategic management and HRM. In terms of strategic management, we take issue with anyone who thinks HRM lacks strategic significance. Improving the process of strategic management has everything to do with people: with who is attracted to the firm, with how they learn to work together and with the organisational culture they create over time. It involves making some critical decisions about 'talent', about the recruitment, development and retention of people, and it involves subtle forms of teamwork and cooperation, both within the management team and throughout the organisation. It contributes to the idiosyncrasies that can make an organisation a superior performer or a 'basket case'. This means that human resource management bears close study if we want to understand and improve the quality of strategic management in an organisation. Because it is so critical to organisational success, we take the view that greater attention should be paid to HR strategy within the theory of strategic management.

In terms of the academic study of HRM, we challenge approaches that focus analysis only on individual techniques or on claims about 'best practice'. The theory of HRM has been driven too much from a focus on individual HR practices, organised into silos (such as selection, remuneration or training) and largely missing out on an analysis of the quality of the employment relationship and its embeddedness in a particular context, as Legge (1978) argued long ago. The role of the academic study of strategic HRM is to 'connect the dots', identifying overall patterns in work and employment, including the factors that shape them in different contexts, and the ways in which they link to outcomes for organisations, workers and society. Strategic HRM should help researchers and practitioners to recognise models of HRM, to understand how they have evolved and the strategic tensions that characterise them, help them to measure their impacts and develop ways for how they might be improved.

Theme two: the goals of HRM are multidimensional and subject to strategic tensions.

If the first theme underlines the strategic significance of HRM, the second key lesson is that HRM's role should not be thought of only in terms of a single, profit-oriented 'bottom line'. To be sure, HRM's contribution to economic performance is critical. Managers, in practice, tend to make the kind of investments in employee pay and conditions that give them a chance of establishing or maintaining a profitable business, as Kaufman (2010) has emphasised. We wish to underscore, rather than minimise, the importance of the profit driver in management behaviour. Failure to understand its impact leads to inappropriate advocacy of 'best practice' and discredits the academic literature of HRM with practising managers. However, a good performance in HRM is *multi*dimensional, incorporating more than this. At the same time as they are concerned with the cost-effectiveness or profit-rationality of their approach to HRM, managers typically think about how to secure legitimacy in the societies in which the firm operates. Firms are embedded in societies.

That social legitimacy is an important goal in HRM has been emphasised in this book, consistent with institutional perspectives in organisational sociology and labour economics. As a baseline, we have argued that the ethical or social duty of firms is to employ people according to legal requirements and to work positively with important cultural norms for employee management. But it is well known that there are firms that fail to meet this standard and that try to 'fly under the radar'. Reaching the situation where the vast majority of firms operate legitimately in HRM is a major step forward in any society, improving outcomes for workers and communities and helping to protect firms themselves from exploitative forms of competition. As part of this, we have argued that it is important for firms to support international conventions on human rights, such as those that seek to eliminate child labour, human slavery, union suppression and various forms of discrimination. As the previous chapter indicates, we think that multinational companies need to set an example in fostering more legitimate practices, as several are trying to do in their response to the Rana Plaza disaster in Bangladesh. Multinational firms have major economic power and a positive use of it is to sponsor healthy change in the value chains in which they are embedded.

On top of cost-effectiveness and social legitimacy, there are other strategic goals that can be observed in HRM. Over time, successful firms embed significant elements of flexibility into their HRM to enable them to cope better with change and thus make profits in the future. They develop forms of human resource advantage, although they vary in the extent to which they are based on nurturing an elite group of employees or extend beyond the elite to a larger section of the workforce (and, if so, which section). The challenge of managing change should never be underestimated. The natural tendency in organisations is to focus on stabilising performance in the immediate context (the 'short-run'). The more this is done, the more difficult it is to generate a capacity to flex the organisation or perform well over the longer run. In the dynamic picture, we also observe management seeking to enhance its power to act. Much of this is rational because firms depend on having management teams that can coordinate stakeholders to achieve common ends and to react sensibly to change. However, too much emphasis on management power can undermine the scope for employee voice and thus threaten social legitimacy. Too much power concentrated in management hands can also lead to an overemphasis on management rewards, which has been contributing to the increasing disparity in income distribution in Anglophone societies.

This theme, then, underlines the fact that pursuing multiple goals in HRM inevitably involves grappling with a range of strategic tensions. Among the most important of these are the problems associated with labour scarcity and employee motivation, the tension between short-run productivity and long-run adaptability, the tension between corporate survival and employee security and the potential for conflict between managerial power and social legitimacy.

Theme three: while general principles can assist all managers to improve HRM, they typically adapt HR strategy to the firm's specific context and they are wise to do so.

A key part of the book's review of the theory of strategic HRM examines the debate between two perspectives: 'best fit' and 'best practice'. These are perspectives that can characterise both academics and practitioners. Advocates of best fit have emphasised the contingent nature of HRM, while advocates of best practice have gone in search of a universally superior set of HR practices. It is easy to challenge claims about 'best practice' by asking who stands to benefit from it (i.e. best for whom?) and by examining research on the actual distribution of HR practices and HR investments, which is not flattering to the best-practice case. However, it must be said that there are aspects of best practice in the micro domains of HRM that are widely recognised as valuable. When companies in an Anglophone country commit to a selection process, for example, they are well advised to avoid invalid predictors of performance, including asking candidates questions that don't relate to how they would do the job. There is also a role for identifying better HRM models within particular industry contexts, bearing in mind that such models will more likely be based on 'equifinality' (aiming to achieve similar performance outcomes) than on exact lists of HR practices.

Most importantly, in our view, there is a role for identifying general principles of HRM: desirable principles which, if applied, will bring about more effective management of people. It is possible to argue that, 'ceteris paribus' (other things being equal), all firms are better off when they pursue certain principles in HRM. Starting in Part 1, but then more fully in Part 2, of this book, we sought to identify principles of this nature, including principles around the strategic significance of HRM, the multidimensional nature of goals in HRM, the challenge of alignment in employment relationships and the social and political complexity of the 'black box' of HRM. One of these general principles is what we call the 'law of context' in HRM. This is the idea that managers inevitably adapt their HR strategies to their specific contexts, and they are wise to do so. Firms vary in their organisational characteristics, such as size, technologies and unionisation, and are embedded in industries and societies, which bring different conditions into play, such as different laws, cultural assumptions and labour markets. In any firm in which managers want to review their HR strategies, it is helpful to analyse the impact of a range of economic and social-political factors in the relevant context. We organised these on three levels: the societal, the industry and the organisational. Furthermore, we underlined the way in which the contingency perspective in HRM leads naturally into a more configurational or 'gestalt' perspective in which we understand businesses as interlocking sets of activities, incorporating linked choices in marketing, operations, finance and HRM. On top of this, we dedicated Part 3 of the book to analysing what we might call four 'mega-contexts': manufacturing, services, multidivisional firms and multinational firms. Each of these contexts is diverse, and we need some way of organising our understanding of HRM in them. This brings us to the next theme.

Theme four: models of HRM represent clusters of work and employment practices that vary within, and across, organisations.

Chapter 8 represented a transition in the book from talking about general principles to examining the contexts in which HRM takes place. To understand the shape of HRM in these contexts, we talked about 'models' of HRM, which are clusters of work and employment practices that have emerged for a particular group of workers. We talked about the craft model, originally developed by the medieval guilds, which were granted rights to control entry to a trade and its methods of work. This ancient model of HRM remains relevant today, wherever craftspeople retain a high level of control over their work practices and employment conditions, but industrialisation ushered in the industrial model of HRM. In this model, jobs were often low in skill, in scope and in control, and poor employment conditions fostered unionisation and government regulation. Our description of these models, and the sources we quoted, shows the importance of economic and social history to an understanding of patterns of HRM. Models for organising work and people arise and solidify in particular historical conditions as economies and societies change. Our story about models of HRM went on from there, moving into a description of high-involvement and outsourcing models of work in manufacturing and then into the service sector, where we highlighted scripted, informal, high-involvement, professional and expert models of HRM. From there, we took the story into multidivisional and multinational firms, where the issue becomes one of how corporate and transnational models of HRM are shaped. We saw here a tension between bonus-driven and development-oriented models of HRM, made more complex when firms operate across societies. Table 12.1 brings all this material together into a typology that summarises the book's understanding of different models of HRM. Here, we identify the key characteristics of each model, including common tensions associated with it, and comment briefly on its origins and typical context.

This typology is a way of summarising the huge variety we see in HRM. Its aim is to help researchers and practitioners identify which mix of models they are observing or experiencing in an organisation. It is possible to look at a supermarket, for example, and discern the outlines of a scripted model for the operating workforce and a salaried model for the managers. In a much larger and more diverse multidivisional firm, we need to look at various levels: this may reveal, for example, a development-oriented model for corporate executives and a range of approaches inside actual business units where there may be high-involvement models in those cases where higher product or service quality is being pursued and outsourcing models in others where cost reduction has become pressing. There may be various blends of the models shown in Table 12.1. A key function of this typology is to help managers ask themselves whether they have the appropriate mix of models of HRM for their environment and what they are trying to achieve in it. This is a big question in a multidivisional firm: do its models of HRM sit well with the goals and functions of each business unit and is the approach at corporate headquarters consistent with a healthy performance overall?

In this edition of *Strategy and Human Resource Management*, we have deliberately encouraged usage of the term 'model of HRM' or 'HRM model'. The notion of a model of HRM conveys the idea of a recognisable way of organising work and employing people but one that is never free of tensions. Each model has tensions that can be more or less severe in a particular case,

Table 12.1 Typology of models of HRM

Model of HRM	Characteristic features and tensions	Origins and typical context
Craft model	The artisan or craftworker exercises a high level of control over which techniques to use and how to use them. Craftworkers, collectively, have major influence over occupational entry (i.e. restrictive entry) and apprenticeship, leading to better wages or to self-employment.	Developed in the medieval era to foster productive crafts, such as masonry, carpentry, metal working and glass blowing, particularly in market towns and cities. Remains relevant in industrial and construction trades among more highly skilled workers.
Industrial model	Machine-paced, low-discretion jobs defined by managers or industrial engineers ('Taylorised jobs'). Work simplification and limited scope for personal development, creating motivational tensions. The breeding ground of trade union protest around issues of pay, safety and work intensification.	Developed in the nineteenth century and in the early decades of the twentieth century to enhance efficiency in factories. Reformed by governments and trade unions to pay better wages and meet higher standards of health and safety. Still prevalent in some manufacturing industries in developed countries and widespread in the developing world.
Salaried model	Jobs of higher responsibility, discretion, pay and security designed by managers for themselves and for white-collar specialists. Teamwork often important and career development actively fostered within the firm. A growing social concern about the skewing of rewards to the top.	The necessary corollary of the industrial model, which provides the decision-making structure and expertise that enables a large-scale factory to function. Now more generally applied across manufacturing and services, including an elite of executives on 'super salaries'.
Scripted model	The service equivalent of the industrial model, involving scripted interactions between front-line service workers and customers. Jobs are low in discretion and typically in pay. Surveillance is prevalent and there may be limited prospects for career development. Can bring order into the chaos of high-volume services, but stress and employee turnover are frequently high.	Developed by large-scale service firms offering standardised services (e.g. supermarkets, cinemas, call centres) to drive down costs and reduce heterogeneity in the service encounter. Designed to process large volumes of customers rapidly and consistently, enhancing profitability.

High-involvement model	Work organisation is reformed to break down 'Taylorism' to some extent. Employee empowerment, higher levels of skill and better incentives are core dimensions, but the impact on work intensity is likely to be variable. Managerial roles change to facilitate greater employee participation and this implies greater support from senior managers and HR specialists. The level of investment in HRM increases, and this raises questions around cost-effectiveness.	Exists in capital-intensive or high-tech firms where 'working smarter' is needed to meet competition. Also used in service firms targeting higher-quality market segments, as in higher-starred hotels and higher-quality air travel. A greater degree of empowerment enables workers to respond more effectively when service failures occur ('service recovery'), an issue of growing importance in a range of services.
Outsourcing model	The firm turns from employing its own staff to contracting out the work, which is outsourced to a specialist provider in the country of domicile or is offshored to a firm in another country. Which parts of the business are core and which parts can safely be outsourced is a difficult question because of social and technical interdependencies. The legitimacy of HR practices in the supply chain can be a cause of union and NGO protest.	Common in globalised manufacturing or service value chains where firms seek quantum improvements in labour cost or seek capabilities they no longer have on-shore. Regime competition occurs as governments try to attract forms of offshoring they consider desirable.
Informal model	Workers are managed personally by owners or supervisors without much use of formal policies or HR specialists. Trade unions are rare. Levels of employee turnover tend to be high, and firms may suffer from chronic problems of labour scarcity. Can provide a more trusting and flexible working environment when the owner fosters a climate of 'give-and-take' but can also provide a setting for exploitation of illegal and inexperienced workers.	Common in the early stages of industrialisation or business growth; remains common in family-owned businesses offering simple services and using personal networks to recruit.

Table 12.1 (Continued)

Model of HRM	Characteristic features and tensions	Origins and typical context
Professional/ expert models	Individuals are socialised into work practices through their higher education and in-house training. While lower-level work may be routinised, a high-involvement approach is adopted for complex or novel problems that demand a professional or expert judgement. High pay is possible for those who rise through the ranks or who develop a lucrative set of clients. However, greater pay comes with a higher workload, which can generate work–life imbalance. A target-driven, resource-constrained culture in the public sector, with the disruption of frequent restructuring, has impacts on stress, employee turnover and union protest.	Common in knowledge-intensive services, including among professionals such as lawyers and accountants and among less-regulated forms of knowledge work such as ICT; also common in those parts of the public sector that depend heavily on professional work (e.g. public health and education). As competition unfolds, routine or stand-ardised aspects of work may revert to efficiency-driven approaches, including outsourcing models of HRM, while problems demanding unusual or novel expertise remain within the professional/expert model.
Bonus-driven model	All multidivisional companies have ways of developing people, but the balance of emphasis in this model falls on monetary targets linked to performance-related pay. Can be liberating and highly rewarding for managers, but may drive greater outsourcing and a lower level of investment in long-run employee develop-ment. Under scrutiny in multinationals for its impacts on social legitimacy in the supply chain, fuelling the growth of employment standards by which management behaviour can be judged.	Essentially a variation of the salaried model occurring in multidivisional firms. SBUs are treated as separate enti-ties, which can be dispensed with when underperforming. Planning horizons are short and performance targets are monitored frequently, heightened by 'financialisation' and the growth of private-equity ownership. More common in the Anglo-American world where executives are heavily concerned with capital markets that seek higher rates of return.

| Development-oriented model | A second type of corporate model of HRM where the balance of emphasis falls more heavily on employee development, although bonuses are still likely to be important. In multinationals, incorporates greater attention to recruitment, development and career planning for internationally mobile managers and experts. Higher levels of investment in teams of HR specialists to support this. Multinationals can still be expected to be challenged on social legitimacy in their value chain. | Occurs in multidivisional firms aiming to develop core competences across business units and suppliers to foster innovation in products or processes. Places more emphasis on synergies through sharing know-how in networks. May be more typical in Japan and continental Europe. Prominent among multinationals that need to develop people who can traverse cultural and linguistic boundaries. |

something we have emphasised from Chapter 1. Another common term is 'HR system', which academics use to convey much the same idea (e.g. Lepak et al. 2006, Boxall, Ang and Bartram 2011). Writers using this term talk about HR strategy as a cluster of HR systems, as we have in previous editions. The problem we have encountered with this terminology, however, is that practitioners often use the term 'HR system' to refer to an IT system for handling HR data (i.e. an HR *information* system or HRIS). In our view, it is better to talk of models of HRM because people then recognise that we mean something much more significant about how people are managed and not simply a method of information processing.

Theme five: positive, high-quality idiosyncrasies in HRM can be sources of superior performance.

Although requirements for legitimacy in society and for 'table stakes' in particular industries make firms similar, managers inevitably put their own twists on models of HRM, and firms build a somewhat idiosyncratic pattern of human and social capital, as the resource-based view (RBV) of the firm indicates. There is always some degree of strategic choice available to managers, and particular personalities in leadership will inevitably put their own mark on HRM, as will the fact that, in any firm, a particular group of people is working together and learning as they go, developing their own practices and understandings in a somewhat unique culture. A key interest in this book has been on the question of what it is that can be competitively most valuable in HRM and how such sources of value can be built and defended, bearing in mind that what firms can achieve in building valuable resources is not solely within their control but depends on processes of resource development in the industries and societies in which they operate. The RBV argues that valuable, hard-to-imitate resources are built up over time as a result of critical choices ('path dependency') and thus become socially complex and causally ambiguous. The RBV and the dynamic capability perspective in strategic management present accounts of the firm's fortunes that are richly laced with *human* resource issues. This is seen in their emphasis on identifying the firm's core or distinctive competences, including human skill-sets, and their interest in the 'literati and numerati' of knowledge-intensive organisations (Teece 2011) and in how to foster organisational learning.

However, disentangling the role that HRM plays in competitive advantage is far from straightforward. Knowledge of HR policy or of individual HR techniques is hardly rare or particularly valuable. In fact, a lot of value can be destroyed through HRM, particularly when there are major disjunctures between managerial promises in policies and workplace realities in practice, which undermine employee trust, commitment and citizenship behaviours. The book's argument is that companies can acquire exceptional strengths in HRM when they attract and retain highly talented individuals (high-quality human capital) and combine their talents through highly positive organisational processes (powerful forms of social capital). Human resource advantage is greater when both these sources of value are present. This is much easier said than done and leads to the next two themes.

Theme six: the quality of alignment in its employment relationships affects the ability of an organisation to survive and build superior performances.

Constructing and maintaining a workforce depends on aligning the interests of the firm with those of workers, at least to a level that will enable sufficient numbers of people to be recruited and retained. This means that managers need an understanding of the employment relationship from the worker's perspective – and not simply from their own. This is the fundamental principle of interest alignment in HRM, which is concerned with issues of mutuality or reciprocity in employment relationships.

Current interest in the principle of alignment is associated with the notion of the 'talent management'. The more successful firms in the labour market are able to offer an interesting 'employment value proposition' (EVP), something that requires careful thought in firms or industries with attractiveness problems. However, having a strong EVP does not rule out problems of interest alignment. Organisations in which there are talent blockages, talent ghettos or chronic, unaddressed problems of human performance perform less effectively as a result of these issues.

To begin to address these challenges more effectively, managers need to develop an understanding of theories of employee well-being. This task has not been made easy by the enormous variety of academic theories on offer and the tendency of academics to specialise in a very limited part of it. We have reviewed this complex terrain and tried to emphasise some key principles. As a general rule, whether a job is working well for an individual depends on whether they see it as a meaningful use of their abilities: something that appeals to their vocational interests and that enables them to utilise their skills. Furthermore, there is a dynamic element to this because ambitious people seek greater avenues for personal fulfilment across their working life. Firms that cannot provide growth opportunities are likely to lose many of their more talented workers, and the more powerful forms of 'human capital advantage' will be beyond them. The intrinsic quality of any job can be assessed by analysing the particular blend of demands and resources that an individual, or an occupational group, is experiencing at work, including the pressures it generates. This can help to identify imbalances that undermine motivation, such as excessive forms of bureaucratic control or insufficient support from the line manager or work team. It can help to identify sources of excess stress or burnout. An understanding of how employees respond to extrinsic rewards is also essential because paid jobs are a form of social *and* economic exchange. Here, equity theory is very important: those who feel under-rewarded (in terms of pay and/or status) relative to their contribution, or who are experiencing a high degree of insecurity, are likely to search for better alternatives. Overall, theories of employee well-being are now very central in the study of strategic HRM, and the challenge facing academics is one of refining and better integrating them.

Theme seven: in any organisation where management wants to generate greater value through HRM, careful attention needs to be paid to the social process of HRM, to the 'black box' of links between HR policy and performance outcomes.

Let's assume that an organisation does have the mix of models of HRM it needs as its managers grapple with their external environment. Is HR strategy done and dusted, with nothing more to worry about? The answer is a resounding 'no'. The literature in strategic HRM has for several years been examining the fragile set of links between what is intended, what is enacted and what is perceived in HRM that lead on to employee attitudes and behaviours and thence to productive outcomes. Whatever the apparent 'content' of HRM, there are always 'process' issues in how it actually works. In a nutshell, this is the 'black box' problem, and theory in this area has something to offer managers in all organisations that want to create greater value through HRM. This includes large organisations that are well endowed with financial resources and teams of HR specialists but nonetheless have sources of untapped value because of the complex, multilayered nature of these interactions.

When some type of performance is seen as the dependent variable (e.g. productivity or quality), the fundamental building block is the AMO model of human performance, which argues that performance is a function of the individual's ability, motivation and opportunity to perform. The AMO model is simply an expression of the factors at play in any kind of human performance. The AMO variables are influenced by what the individual brings to the situation and by the situation in which they find themselves, including the firm's HR policies and practices and related variables in the production system and organisational context. The AMO model is an organising framework through which academics can test more specific theories, such as theories around human capital and skill utilisation, social exchange and organisational justice, and theories around the motivating potential of the intrinsic dimensions of work. Studies are needed that consider all three AMO variables and how they interact.

But analysis at the individual level is not enough. To understand the dynamics of the 'black box', we must conceptualise HRM as a social process in organisations, involving a range of actors who play a variety of roles. What senior managers want to achieve with a workforce, and how they envisage doing so, is the logical place to start in a social analysis of HRM. The extent to which senior managers form a coherent view of HRM and carry it through consistently is very variable. Greater coherence and consistency in HRM offer value to management, but they are regularly threatened by changing economic and socio-political circumstances, which lead to trade-offs within management and between organisational and employee interests, as occurred during the Global Financial Crisis and in the sovereign debt crises that followed it. A management team that respects employee voice in these conflictual situations, ensuring that there is a strong level of substantive, procedural and interpersonal justice, will negotiate these difficulties more effectively, building a reputation for integrity and doing less damage to the culture of the firm.

Research on the links between HRM and performance has increasingly recognised the crucial role of line managers in 'bringing HRM to life' and their impact on the well-being of their team members. Line managers write much of their own script in HRM irrespective of formal HR policies, something that is apparent in complex policy domains such as performance appraisal, which is heavily dependent on line manager enactment. This involves an array of skills and is an inherently political process, with much about it that can demotivate, as much as motivate, the employee and their line manager. It is increasingly appreciated that the pathway to improvement in HRM depends on how senior leaders and HR specialists develop, support and incentivise their line managers. Managing line managers more effectively helps to equip, and motivate them, to manage the workforce more effectively.

In any kind of large organisation, employees are receiving signals on various levels, with the potential for conflict among them and the potential for shifting philosophies, leaders and resources to destabilise trust. On top of this, research confirms that individuals can make quite different attributions about management's purposes in implementing what seem to be the same HR practices. Individual employees form their own perception of the psychological climate in their organisation but we can talk meaningfully of a social or organisational climate when they form a relatively common perception of management's intentions and actions. This, of course, can be positive or negative, with the more positive climates, in conjunction with good levels of human capital, leading to better levels of engagement and cooperation and thence to forms of competitive advantage. As labour process theorists remind us, it is important to avoid casting employees as acquiescent or passive conduits of HR strategy. Workers are independent agents who may assert their own identities and pursue their own interests in the workplace, helping to shape what performance means and how the organisation will achieve it.

Developing a 'more strategic approach' to HRM

These key themes lead to a final question: what can managers do about them? All firms have HR strategies but how can they be improved by those who want to create greater value through HRM, either dealing more effectively with problems or taking advantage of untapped potential? This is what some mean by taking a 'more strategic approach' to HRM. It implies better analysis of existing performance and better planning in HRM.

We believe that there is much to be gained from a review of the quality of HR strategy in the firm. Formal planning processes, when they involve the key line managers who manage the majority of staff, offer a way of surfacing informal learning about what does and does not work in the management of people. When designed competently, planning sessions provide a means for periodic review: they can be used both to make emergent learning explicit and to consider new threats and opportunities. The value to be gained does not lie solely in the capacity to improve the analytical abilities of the firm but also has a political dimension, something which is always present in strategic management. As Lam and Schaubroeck (1998) explain, planning processes can be used to bring together key constituencies in the firm, hammering out new compromises and building commitment for desirable change. This is obviously of great relevance to large firms, including multidivisional and multinational firms, but the principles we will discuss here are also relevant to smaller ones. Small firms do not use the level of formality seen in management processes in large firms and are typically at a resource and legitimacy disadvantage (they have fewer resources and are much less well known). However, their leaders can use proactive thinking and nimble responses in a way that is very hard to do in large organisations. What matters is that managers in all firms regularly take time to evaluate their HRM performance and to think ahead in terms of the threats they face and the opportunities they could grasp in HRM.

Drawing on research and historical learning, what can we say about how to improve the quality of strategic analysis and planning in HRM?

Strategic analysis and planning in HRM: the intellectual challenge

Strategic analysis in HRM calls for the scanning and interpretation of a complex environment and the measurement of performance as an employer. The context of the firm's HRM needs careful research, incorporating an understanding of changes in the economic and socio-political environment. Qualitative research, involving reading of academic and industry publications, plus interviews of well-informed people inside and outside the firm, can be very helpful in interpreting the context, including trends in product markets, technologies, labour markets, employment laws, social attitudes and demography. However, quantitative analysis is increasingly part of strategic review in HRM, and is affecting the skills needed by HR specialists. We think that strategic analysis in HRM can usefully be framed around five questions:

1. *The question of 'strategic fit': does the organisation have a set of HRM models that fits its environment, its goals and its configuration of activities?*

This is the logical place to start. It involves an assessment of whether the models of HRM evident in the firm fit the key factors in its economic and social environment and its wider strategies for addressing them. Using Table 12.1 as a starting place, does the organisation have an appropriate set of HRM models in place? Take, for example, the case of a software development company trying to 'go global' with an innovative set of products for a fast-growing international market. There is no 'dominant design' yet in the industry, and competitors are rapidly developing new software solutions. Customers are shifting their allegiances as they try out new product features and suppliers. This introduces uncertainty into the software development process and a need to respond quickly to changing customer preferences. Attracting skilled developers and building skills in customer interaction are essential. A high level of on-the-job problem-solving with colleagues is needed to share learning. The firm has its managers employed on a salaried model, as is typical, but is the workforce sub-contracted via an outsourcing model or is it employed in-house and, if so, on what basis? An outsourced model may appear cheaper but introduces problems with contracting and intellectual property (IP) as well as reducing response times, even though time zones can be used to good effect. The need to access advanced expertise while protecting IP, and maximise responsiveness to customers, suggests that an expert model of HRM operated in-house would be a better strategic fit.

This is a simple illustration, but it is the kind of question that needs to be faced in every business unit (and, potentially, every workplace), introducing quite a degree of complexity into the strategic review of HRM as firms become larger and more diverse. Clearly, there is an important role here for HR specialists working with key operating managers to understand which models of HRM are working well and which are sub-optimal. Poorly performing models are likely to be evident in ongoing problems with such business outcomes as productivity, quality and flexibility. Then, on top of this, there is the question of the relationship between, or among, models in a complex business or corporation. Misfit or tension can occur between models, as, for example, when waged workers on an industrial or scripted model complain about what they perceive as the excesses of a bonus-driven culture among corporate executives. Such forms of protest can create circumstances where executives are forced to justify themselves more fully and may lead to a situation where the mix of models in a firm is more closely scrutinised.

2. *The talent question: within any given model of HRM, can the firm recruit and retain the people it needs?*

This second question assumes that the answer to the first question is fundamentally acceptable: the broad fit of the firm's models of HRM with its environment and internal priorities is appropriate. The next stage involves asking whether the firm can attract and retain the kind of employees it needs *within* the models of HRM it has adopted. At this point, skills in HR measurement come more fully into play. Researchers are using surveys, frequently online, and techniques such as regression and structural equation modelling to build these sorts of models, which can help to make a case for adapting a model of HRM or changing the elements in it to achieve a better outcome in terms of organisational attractiveness (see, for example, Tan's (2008) analysis of what predicts commitment among a sample of Malaysian knowledge workers). Employers worried about their ability to recruit and retain are increasingly being advised to use ICT to make better use of 'workforce or HR analytics'.[1] A leading example of mining employee data in this way is Google, where HR executive, Laszlo Bock, has commented that 'we need to be able to measure, to find out what does and doesn't work at Google rather than just adopt best practices'.[2]

---

[1] See, for example, http://cahrs.ilr.cornell.edu/CentersofExcellence/data.aspx?n=HR%20 Analytics/Metrics; http://public.deloitte.com/media/analytics/3-minute-guide-to-work force-analytics.html, accessed 24/2/15.
[2] http://www.theatlantic.com/business/archive/2013/10/how-google-uses-data-to-build-a-better-worker/280347/, accessed 13/3/15.

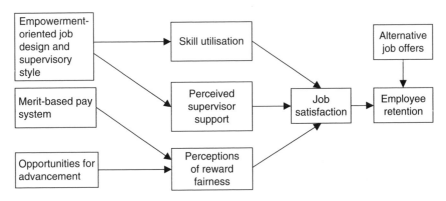

Figure 12.1   Drivers of job satisfaction and retention (a hypothetical model involving software developers within an expert model of HRM)

Taking our example forward, Figure 12.1 depicts the drivers of job satisfaction in our hypothetical software company. What the figure shows is the set of factors that drive the satisfaction and retention levels of the core group of software developers and how the intermediate or mediating factors involved (skill utilisation, perceived supervisor support and perceptions of reward fairness) can be tracked back to certain approaches to HR practices and management behaviour (in this case, empowerment-oriented job design and supervisory style, a merit-based pay system and opportunities for advancement). Problems with employee satisfaction can be expected to lead to higher levels of employee turnover, particularly if other employers are making more attractive offers. As the old saying goes, focusing on a leading indicator like job satisfaction helps to build a fence at the top of the cliff as opposed to providing an ambulance at the bottom. In this process, various drivers of employee satisfaction and retention can be tested and refined over time, leading to the identification of which ones have the greatest impact. The picture we have painted is, of course, conjectural and oversimplified. We have shown satisfaction as a dependent variable, but have not factored in other outcomes such as stress and work–life balance. In fact, we have left out various complexities in the predictors, mediators and moderating variables. All of these refinements can be added over time as managers enhance the quality of their workforce analytics.

3. *The performance question: is the model of HRM helping to deliver the kind of performance the firm needs?*

Our third question builds off the previous one, but looks at performance, or some critical aspect of it, as the dependent variable. HRM is always a contributor to performance, but how well is it doing so? What are its 'best shots' and what

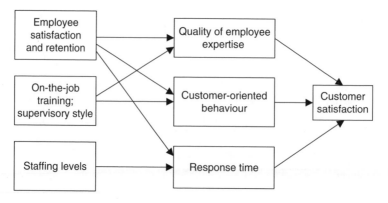

Figure 12.2 A hypothetical performance model (satisfaction with software services)

are its worst? In Figure 12.2, we continue the example from above and take levels of customer satisfaction as our dependent variable, aiming to relate HR variables and other performance drivers to it. This is the kind of exercise that researchers are increasingly arguing we need (for an interesting example, see Sergeant and Frenkel 2000). We choose customer satisfaction because it is a performance outcome that employees can directly influence in this organisation. It is both 'proximal' in this sense and consequential for the firm's ultimate success. The more customers are satisfied, the more the firm is likely to retain them, generating 'repeat business' and making the business more profitable and secure. In this case, our hypothetical surveys use a range of sources: we survey customers on their satisfaction and on their perceptions of customer-oriented behaviour, quality of expertise and response times, we survey employees on their attitudes and perceptions of HR practices and on the supervisory style of their managers, as before, and we use the firm's information system to track its staffing levels. What this hypothetical picture shows is that employee attitudes, on-the-job training and supervisory style are all important in improving the quality of expertise embedded in the product and driving customer-oriented behaviour, which influence how highly customers rate their experience. However, the firm's response times are also critical and these depend on good staffing levels. One of the obvious implications is that the firm needs to invest in a healthy level of staffing to meet customer demands in a timely way. Readers will see the AMO variables embedded in the mediators in the diagram (quality of expertise is an ability factor, customer-oriented behaviour is a motivational factor and response time is an opportunity factor). The kind of linkages depicted here can then be incorporated into broader approaches to measurement of business performance, such as the 'balanced scorecard' (Kaplan and Norton 1996, 2004, Guest 1997), which seeks to integrate indicators of people-related, operating, customer and financial performance.

Again, the diagram is oversimplified. We have not shown HR variables that dropped out of the analysis because they lacked predictive power, and we have not shown feedback loops or depicted a longitudinal approach to data gathering, which would be highly desirable if we are interested in establishing causality. We have not teased out more fully how and when variables are measured or whether qualitative methods, such as focus groups, could complement or improve on the survey approach. Issues of measurement are now treated at some length in the academic literature (e.g. Boselie, Dietz and Boon 2005, Wright et al. 2005, Paauwe 2009), where readers should look for greater guidance. The point, however, is that greater efforts to understand how variables in HRM affect the success of the business is an important step towards a more strategic approach to HRM, including which ones matter most, which ones are neutral, and which ones are having negative effects. This is now an important aspect of professional development for HR specialists and an ingredient in a more rigorous review of HRM in firms.

4. *The dynamic question: what economic and socio-political changes are likely to affect the firm's HR strategy and how should it prepare for them?*

The first three questions are all framed around the current context. Understanding this is critical and can lead to plans to generate greater value. However, as argued in Chapter 1, it is vital to accept that change is inevitable and that some preparation for the future is also crucial. We have not so far discussed the issue of the planning horizon but, as in all planning, this is important. Most HRM textbooks cover the techniques of short-run HR planning well, and companies typically find they need at least some of them. Some short-run planning is necessary just to stay afloat. Any type of recruitment, for example, involves some kind of thinking in advance about the firm's skill deficits and desirable types of candidate (even if this thinking becomes much sharper as the selection process unfolds). Where firms tend to be much weaker, however, is in the quality of their long-run HR planning (Gratton et al. 1999a, 1999b). Planning for the next three to five years (or beyond) is an important timeframe for considering how the organisation will improve its agility, including its capacity to renew its management and entrepreneurial capabilities, and how it will address challenges to its social legitimacy, such as increasing scrutiny of its performance in managing workforce diversity or employment relations in its supply chain. These are aspects of performance in HRM that cannot be improved simply by short-run planning and which may, in fact, be damaged by short-term actions.

A valuable approach in this context is scenario planning, which can be used to create readiness for a range of economic and socio-political futures. One thing that must be accepted about the future is that it is uncertain. As Anthony Giddens emphasised in the 1999 BBC Reith lectures on globalisation, we should 'expect the unexpected' and learn to manage risk.[3] In this context, Shell's multiple planning system is a celebrated case (de Geus 1988, Grant 1998). In the aftermath of the 1970s oil shocks, most oil companies in the 1980s planned for a scenario of permanently rising oil prices. Shell did this but also planned for significant price decreases, a scenario that was played out in early 1986 as oil prices fell from US$27 a barrel to US$17 in February and US$10 in April (and, we note, which played out again in 2014–15). As a result of the lateral thinking encouraged by its scenario planning, Shell was better prepared than other companies in the industry.

The process shown in Box 12.1 involves defining three business scenarios. One scenario is based on the most desirable circumstances. Such scenarios tend to assume that intelligent rivals do not exist and that the environment is generally benign, so it pays to define a second, more likely scenario in which there are competitive rivals and the environment has some surprises. Intelligent rivals inevitably place pressure on a firm's capacity to recruit and retain key people and build powerful forms of social capital. Finally, one can define a least desirable scenario in which there are major downturns or reversals in business fortunes. The bombing of the World Trade Center and the Pentagon in September 2001, and the Icelandic volcanic eruptions of 2010, should remind us that there are factors well beyond business control that can disrupt business performance.

It is then important to consider the HR implications of each of these scenarios and to broaden this out to consider wider stakeholder trends affecting HRM. This brings in questions around the supply of labour and the attitudes of the workforce, the strategies of rivals in the labour market and trends in employment regulation and social responsibility. Research by business planners and HR specialists, including better analysis of the firm's own HR data, can be used to identify key issues for HR strategy. This feeds into plans to meet long-run business needs and to cope with stakeholder trends. A major effort of this kind every three years or so can then be updated on an annual basis. Clearly, an exercise of this nature involves costs, including in management time, and is more likely to take place in a large firm. However, some level of thinking about how to prepare for an uncertain future is valuable in all firms.

---

[3] http://www.bbc.co.uk/programmes/p00gw9sl, accessed 20/2/15.

Box 12.1   An example of scenario-based HR planning

Step One: Identifying long-run business scenarios

- Identify the key rivals in your 'strategic group'.
- Identify three business scenarios that might be played out in the group over the next five years: (1) benign or most desirable scenario, (2) competitive or most likely scenario and (3) unstable or least desirable scenario.

Step Two: Assessing the firm's HR readiness

For each scenario, ask:

- What are the HR challenges posed by this scenario (e.g. challenges posed by inadequate social capital, by labour market competition or by the attitudes to the firm of current or potential employees)?
- What are our HR strengths to meet these challenges (e.g. existing depth of know-how in a key business area; strength of reputation as an employer)?
- What are our HR weaknesses in relation to these challenges (e.g. recruitment insufficiently focused on capabilities needed in the future; lack of employee development for future competitive needs; excessive turnover of core staff)?

Step Three: Identifying key stakeholder trends relating to HRM

Over the next five years, what are the likely trends in the following and what should the organisation do to prepare?

- Supply of labour and attitudes of the workforce. How might the quantity and quality of the labour pool change across the key occupational groups employed by the firm? What demographic and social attitudes can be anticipated (e.g. an ageing workforce)? How might the needs and aspirations of key employees differ from current needs and aspirations? What should the company do to prepare for these possible changes?
- HR strategies of key rivals. What are the threats they will most likely pose (e.g. 'poaching' of star employees)? What opportunities do they present (e.g. joint training initiatives)?
- Regulatory/responsibility changes. What new forms of regulation or employment standards, locally or internationally, could affect the company? What will our approach be to scrutiny of the social legitimacy of our value chain?

Box 12.1   (Continued)

Step Four: Planning HR strategies to meet long-run business needs and cope with stakeholder trends

- Focusing on the *most desirable* business scenario, list the key long-run HR research, review, policy or programme initiatives that must be taken for this scenario to become a reality and develop milestones for them over the next five years (e.g. a staged leadership development programme with an increasing annual budget; development of an annual employee attitude survey linked to customer surveying and jointly linked to annual business planning).
- Focusing on the *most likely* business scenario, identify how key HRM models should be improved to enhance readiness to cope with it.
- Focusing on the *least desirable* business scenario, identify how key HRM models should be improved to enhance readiness to cope with it.
- Identify HR initiatives that are (a) common across all scenarios, and (b) those that are unique and will require some development of flexible skills and processes in HRM.
- Identify the key priorities that should be pursued by the specialist HR function in supporting the organisation's HR strategy (e.g. development of a cadre of internationally capable managers; development of an international strategy for social legitimacy) and devise a plan for its roles, resourcing, relationships with line managers and reporting requirements.

5. The HR function question: how can HR departments contribute more strategically?

As shown in the final bullet point in Box 12.1, HR planning in large organisations inevitably leads to the question of how to manage the HR function so that it contributes more strategically. What should be its leading priorities or roles, at what level should it be resourced, how should it manage its relationships with line managers and how should it report its performance? As explained in Chapter 1, the strategy for managing the HR function is not the same as the organisation's workforce or HR strategy. However, how senior executives manage their HR specialists is a critical part of what it takes to improve HR strategy. In large organisations, the HR function can be complex, with multiple layers of specialists, both inside the organisation and networked with it externally. Debate about its focus and structure is ongoing among HR professionals and executives.[4] Building on the arguments in this book, we take the position that chief executives should expect their HR specialists to make a strategic contribution in three ways:

- *Distinctive expertise in the HR dimensions of business and corporate strategy*

HR directors need to understand the business and its performance metrics, but they are not employed as marketers, operations executives or accountants. Their strategic contribution rests on bringing something to the table that is different from the contributions of the people in these disciplines, something that is distinctively valuable to the organisation. This is their expertise in how to analyse and improve the HR dimensions of business and corporate strategy (the 'people logic' of the business), and it is here that CEOs should expect them to add value, including in the ways outline above;

- *The management and support of managers*

The organisation's HR specialists or consultants play key roles in the management of managers (Marginson et al. 1988, Hunt and Boxall 1998). They are critical to the process of building and renewing the management cadre and are vital to the ongoing process of supporting line managers to attract and successfully manage the workforce. This is not necessarily something for which they will always get direct credit, but it is critical to their role (Legge 1978);

- *Processes for employee voice and support*

At the same time as they are there to support managers, HR specialists have a special role to play in terms of promoting the legitimate treatment of the workforce and better alignment of its interests with those of management. This has long been recognised as part of the dualistic or paradoxical work of HR specialists (e.g. Watson 1977) and is something that employees continue to expect from them (e.g. O'Brien and Linehan 2014). While their ultimate loyalty is to management, HR specialists should add value by enhancing the organisation's processes for employee voice and helping it to manage the inevitable tensions and conflicts in employment relationships with integrity.

The pathway to achieving these outcomes, however, can involve a difficult process of professional development for HR specialists, including the

---

[4] See, for example, the collection of articles at http://www.cipd.co.uk/research/changing-hr-operating-models/, accessed 27/3/15.

development of skills in the financial analysis of HR programmes (Cascio and Boudreau 2010, Phillips and Phillips 2012). This is not needed where firms are simply required to comply with labour laws or demonstrate ethical treatment, such as actions to deal with sexual harassment (Phillips and Phillips 2012: 57–8). In these conditions, there is a moral or ethical case for responding irrespective of the financial outcomes. However, where they are seeking new investments that have major consequences and where alternative approaches have different costs and benefits, such as a new bonus system or a new programme for management development, HR specialists are increasingly asked to provide a 'business case' for their proposals. While they may have a deep understanding of the human relations principles associated with change in HRM, HR specialists are being tasked with justifying their plans for change with credible data rather than a set of assertions about 'best practice'.

Strategic analysis and planning in HRM: the political challenge

What we have discussed so far treats HR analysis and planning as an intellectual exercise, something benefiting from environmental scanning, interpretive insight and more rigorous measurement. This is true, but HR planning is also an inherently political process. To be successful, those driving it should aim to engage the key stakeholder groups involved in the management of people in the firm. In the broadest sense, stakeholder groups include shareholders, creditors, managers, employees, customers, suppliers, competitors, the local community, environmental interests and the state. In HR planning, however, the executives sponsoring the process need to focus on those stakeholder groups who are most affected by the quality of HRM in the firm. This means the process ought to be designed to consider the interests of the following:

> *Shareholders.* The views of those who own the firm need to be taken into account, particularly with the management of managers. In publicly listed companies, this is now very evident in the 'say on pay' laws in the UK, discussed in Chapter 5. There is also an important exposure for shareholders in companies where unions or watchdogs identify exploitative practices in the supply chain. Dismissing such criticisms because they relate to subcontractors is not something that will eliminate concerns in the news or social media, which can then connect to the High-Street reputation and employment standing of the firm. Annual reporting on corporate social performance, including HR issues, is now more common, creating opportunities for shareholders to respond directly or at shareholder meetings.

Senior and lower-level managers. The key issue here is to ensure that HR planning engages the entire management team. Senior managers need to use it to form and express their vision for managing people and to learn from the experiences of lower-level managers. As emphasised in this book, first-line managers manage the vast majority of people in any firm. Their responses and strategies are critical to shaping psychological contracts and the social climate of the firm and, thus, to the success of any major HR initiative. Their views can be canvassed in various ways. For example, all line managers might be surveyed on HR issues in the firm. Alternatively, or in addition, a representative group of line managers might be involved in the planning team. As part of their perspective, line managers should bring into the process an assessment of how other stakeholder groups, such as customers and competitors, are affected by the firm's models of HRM.

Employees themselves. It should be obvious that employees and potential recruits are 'clients' of HRM in the firm. Any HR planning process will be better if it allows for employee involvement. A common practice now in large firms is to conduct regular surveys of employee engagement. Some also use focus groups – smaller samples of staff in a facilitated discussion – to look more qualitatively at key issues. Strategic discussions can usefully be held with employee consultative committees and in partnership with trade unions. Data on how employees are reacting to HR policies and practices is fundamental to improving the quality of HR strategy in firms.

The state. Over time, governments play a key role in providing national forms of social capital. In the sense used here, this means the quantity and quality of the country's labour pool and its educational and social infrastructure. In exchange for access to these resources, governments require certain levels of compliance with labour regulations and anticipate employment opportunities for their citizens. At a minimum, the requirements of labour law ought always to influence the design of HR policy in firms. In the European Union, of course, this includes supra-national forms of regulation. For multinational firms, it includes a complex mix of questions around state regulation and employment standards in their value chain.

Clearly, only through dialogue among those centrally involved in managing people in the firm can the quality of HR planning be improved. As a general rule, the senior management team should drive HR planning (with the chief executive and top team leading but involving key line managers throughout the firm). HR specialists, where they exist, should *facilitate* the process and should contribute expertise in environmental scanning, contextual interpretation and workforce analytics, as we have just noted. Managers in other domains will typically want HR specialists to contribute their specialist expertise, but there is a fine line to be walked here. HR directors have an opportunity to show their distinctive skills and vision, but need to do so without creating the situation where HR planning is seen purely as their hobbyhorse or as something in their sectarian interest.

To be valuable, planning processes, in organisations of all sizes, should enhance strategic understanding and build strategic consensus. They should open up a fertile exchange within the organisation on its context, its past, its problems and its potential. Healthy involvement processes are critical to this. In badly run organisations, strategic planning is driven by the need to have certain planning rituals and to deliver a bureaucratic output (e.g. a set of reports containing targets and milestones). The process can sometimes be forced through cynically by the inner elite without any intention to listen to diverse views or face unpalatable truths. It is much better if haste and reporting pressure is de-emphasised and senior management leads a process that will allow people to share contrasting views in a safe environment.

Conclusions

Our message in this book is that HRM is an essential function in organisations, which depend on the human resources that belong to people. The importance of this should never be diminished. HRM is an indispensable aspect of what it takes to establish, grow, maintain and renew a business. While its contribution to economic or financial performance is critical, a good performance in HRM is multidimensional, incorporating issues around social legitimacy, organisational flexibility and managerial power. This complex set of goals introduces a range of conflicts and tensions, which managers in some firms handle more effectively than others. Our theoretical understanding of HRM benefits from an appreciation of general principles, but one of these is the fact that it is heavily shaped by its context, including a range of factors at societal, industry and organisational levels. Our ability to grapple with this environment is assisted by identifying some typical models or common patterns of HRM, ways in which work and employment practices coalesce for particular groups of workers in different contexts. Firms often incorporate several of these, and managers face the question as to whether they represent a good fit with the firm's environment, its goals and its internal configuration of activities. Within these general patterns, there is a multitude of variations engendered by the unique ways in which people arrive in a particular place and time and learn to work together. HRM is a double-edged sword: it offers both potential for greater value creation and a source of value destruction. Greater understanding of the drivers of employee well-being and of the interactions inside the 'black box' of HRM can enhance the quality of human and social capital in a firm. Practical improvement depends on processes that enhance strategic analysis and planning in HRM. This includes better skills in research and measurement and better engagement of the stakeholders involved. There are both intellectual challenges in taking a more strategic approach to HRM and political ones, as in strategic management generally.

References

Abernathy, W. and Utterback, J. (1978) 'Patterns of industrial innovation'. *Technology Review* 80(7): 40–7.

Adam, D., Purcell, J. and Hall, M. (2014) *Joint consultative committees under the Information and Consultation of Employees Regulations: A WERS analysis*. Research paper 04/14. London: Acas.

Adler, P. (1993) 'Time-and-motion regained'. *Harvard Business Review* January–February: 97–108.

Adler, P., Goldolftas, B. and Levine, D. (1999) 'Flexibility versus efficiency? A case study of model changeovers with Toyota production system'. *Organization Science* 10(1): 43–68.

Alpander, G., Carter, K. and Forsgren, R. (1990) 'Managerial issues and problem-solving in the formative years'. *Journal of Small Business Management* 28(2): 9–19.

Allen, J. and van der Velden, R. (2001) 'Educational mismatches versus skill mismatches: effects on wages, job satisfaction, and on-the-job search'. *Oxford Economic Papers* 3: 434–52.

Andrews, R. and Boyne, G. (2012) 'Structural change and public service performance: the impact of the reorganization process in English local government'. *Public Administration* 90(2): 297–312.

Appelbaum, E., Bailey, T., Berg, P. and Kalleberg, A. (2000) *Manufacturing Advantage: Why High-Performance Systems Pay Off*. Ithaca, NY: ILR Press.

Appelbaum, E. and Batt, R. (1994) *The New American Workplace*. Ithaca, NY: ILR Press.

Appelbaum, E., Batt, R. and Clark, I. (2013) 'Implications of financial capitalism for employment relations research: evidence of breach of trust and implicit contracts in private equity buyouts'. *British Journal of Industrial Relations* 51(3): 498–518.

Appelbaum, E., Bernhardt, A. and Murnane, R. (eds) (2003) *Low-Wage America: How Employers are Reshaping Opportunity in the Workplace*. New York: Russell Sage Foundation.

Aring, M. (2014) *Innovations in quality apprenticeships for high-skilled manufacturing jobs in the United States at BMW, Siemens, Volkswagen*. Geneva: International Labour Organization.

Armstrong, M. and Baron, A. (1995) *The Job Evaluation Handbook*. London: CIPD.

Aryee, S., Walumbwa, F., Seidu, E. and Otaye, L. (2012) 'Impact of high-performance work systems on individual- and branch-level performance: test of a multilevel model of intermediate linkages'. *Journal of Applied Psychology* 97(2): 287–300.

Atkinson, J. (1984) 'Manpower strategies for flexible organisations'. *Personnel Management* August: 28–31.

Aycan, Z. (2005) 'The interplay between cultural and institutional/structural contingencies in human resource management practices'. *International Journal of Human Resource Management* 16(7): 1083–1119.

Bach, S. (2011) 'A new era of public service employment relations? The challenges ahead'. *Acas Future of Workplace Relations discussion paper series*. London: Acas.

Bach, S. and Bordogna, L. (2013) 'Reframing public service employment relations: the impact of economic crisis on the new EU economic governance'. *European Journal of Industrial Relations* 19(4): 279–94.

Bach, S. and Kessler, I. (2012) *The Modernisation of the Public Services and Employee Relations*. Basingstoke: Palgrave

Bacon, N. and Blyton, P. (2001) 'High involvement work systems and job insecurity in the international iron and steel industry'. *Canadian Journal of Administrative Sciences* 18(1): 5–16.

Bacon, N., Wright, M. and Demina, N. (2004) 'Management buyouts and human resource management'. *British Journal of Industrial Relations* 42(2): 325–47.

Bacon, N., Wright, M., Demina, N., Bruining, H. and Boselie, P. (2008) 'The effects of private equity and buyouts in the UK and the Netherlands'. *Human Relations* 61(10): 1399–433.

Bacon, N., Wright, M., Scholes, L. and Meuleman, M. (2010) 'Assessing the impact of private equity on industrial relations in Europe'. *Human Relations* 63(9): 1343–70.

Baden-Fuller, C. (1995) 'Strategic innovation, corporate entrepreneurship and matching outside-in to inside-out approaches to strategy research'. *British Journal of Management* 6(S): 3–16.

Baden-Fuller, C. and Stopford, J. (1994) *Rejuvenating the Mature Business*. London: Routledge.

Baird, L. and Meshoulam, I. (1988) 'Managing two fits of strategic human resource management'. *Academy of Management Review* 13(1): 116–28.

Bakker, A. and Sanz-Vergel, A. (2013) 'Weekly work engagement and flourishing: the role of hindrance and challenge demands'. *Journal of Vocational Behavior* 83: 397–409.

Bakker, A., Van Veldhoven, M. and Xanthopoulou, D. (2010) 'Beyond the demand-control model: thriving on high job demands and resources'. *Journal of Personnel Psychology* 9(1): 3–16.

Baldamus, W. (1961) *Efficiency and Effort: An Analysis of Industrial Administration*. London: Tavistock.

Bamber, G., Stanton, P., Bartram, T. and Ballardie, R. (2014) 'Human resource management, lean processes and outcomes for employees: towards a research agenda'. *International Journal of Human Resource Management* 25(21): 2881–91.

Barney, J. (1991) 'Firm resources and sustained competitive advantage'. *Journal of Management* 17(1): 99–120.

Barney, J. (2000) 'Firm resources and sustained competitive advantage'. *Advances in Strategic Management* 17: 203–27.

Baron, R. and Kreps, D. (1999) *Strategic Human Resources: Frameworks for General Managers*. New York: Wiley.

Barr, P., Stimpert, J. and Huff, A. (1992) 'Cognitive change, strategic action, and organizational renewal'. *Strategic Management Journal* 13: 15–36.

Barrick, M., Mount, M. and Li, N. (2013) 'The theory of purposeful work behaviour: the role of personality, higher-order goals, and job characteristics'. *Academy of Management Review* 38(1): 132–53.

Baruch, Y. and Hind, P. (2000) 'Survivor syndrome – a management myth?' *Journal of Managerial Psychology* 15(1): 29–45.

Batt, R. (2000) 'Strategic segmentation in front-line services: matching customers, employees and human resource systems'. *International Journal of Human Resource Management* 11(3): 540–61.

Batt, R. (2002) 'Managing customer services: human resource practices, quit rates, and sales growth'. *Academy of Management Journal* 45: 587–97.

Batt, R. (2004) 'Who benefits from teams? Comparing workers, supervisors, and managers'. *Industrial Relations* 43(1): 183–212.

Batt, R. (2005) 'Organizational performance in services'. In Holman, D., Wall, T., Clegg, C., Sparrow, P. and Howard, A. (eds) *The Essentials of the New Workplace*. New York: Wiley.

Batt, R. (2007) 'Service strategies: marketing, operations and human resource practices'. In Boxall, P., Purcell, J. and Wright, P. (eds) *The Oxford Handbook of Human Resource Management*. Oxford: Oxford University Press.

Bauer, T. (2004) 'High performance workplace practices and job satisfaction: evidence from Europe'. Discussion Paper No. 1265, Institute for the Study of Labor (IZA).

Baumeister, A. and Bacharach, V. (2000) 'Early generic educational intervention has no enduring effect on intelligence and does not prevent mental retardation: the infant health and development program'. *Intelligence* 28(3): 161–92.

Becker, B. and Gerhart, B. (1996) 'The impact of human resource management on organizational performance: progress and practice'. *Academy of Management Journal* 39(4): 779–801.

Becker, B., Huselid, M., Pickus, P. S. and Spratt, M. F. (1997) 'HR as a source of shareholder value: research and recommendations'. *Human Resource Management* 36(1): 39–47.

Becker, T., Billings, R., Eveleth, D. and Gilbert, N. (1996) 'Foci and bases of employee commitment: implications for job performance'. *Academy of Management Journal* 39: 464–82.

Beer, M. (1997) 'The transformation of the human resource function: resolving the tension between a traditional administrative and a new strategic role'. *Human Resource Management* 36(1): 49–56.

Beer, M., Spector, B., Lawrence, P., Quinn Mills, D. and Walton, R. (1984) *Managing Human Assets*. New York: Free Press.

Belbin, M. (1981) *Management Teams: Why They Succeed or Fail*. Oxford: Butterworth-Heinemann.

Belbin, R. M. (1993) *Team Roles at Work*. Oxford: Butterworth-Heinemann.

Berggren, C. (1992) *The Volvo Experience: Alternatives to Lean Production in the Swedish Auto Industry*. London: Macmillan (now Palgrave Macmillan).

Bernard, A., Jensen, J. B. and Schott, P. (2006) 'Survival of the best fit: exposure to low-wage countries and the (uneven) growth of US manufacturing plants'. *Journal of International Economics* 68: 219–37.

Bevan, G. and Hood, C. (2006) 'What's measured is what matters: targets and gaming in the English public health care system'. *Public Administration* 84(3): 517–38.

Billett, S. (2006) 'Constituting the workplace curriculum'. *Journal of Curriculum Studies* 38(1): 31–48.

Black, S. and Lynch, L. (2001) 'How to compete: the impact of workplace practices and information technology on productivity'. *Review of Economics and Statistics* 83(3): 434–45.

Blasi, J. and Kruse, D. (2006) 'US high-performance work practices at century's end'. *Industrial Relations* 45(4): 547–78.

Blau, P. (1964) *Exchange and Power in Social Life*. New York: Wiley.

Blauner, R. (1964) *Alienation and Freedom: The Factory Worker and His Industry*. Chicago: University of Chicago Press.

Blumberg, M. and Pringle, C. (1982) 'The missing opportunity in organizational research: some implications for a theory of work performance'. *Academy of Management Review* 7(4): 560–9.

Blyton, P. and Turnbull, P. (2004) *The Dynamics of Employee Relations*. London: Palgrave Macmillan.

Boeker, W. (1989) 'Strategic change: the effects of founding and history'. *Academy of Management Journal* 32(3): 489–515.

Boselie, P., Dietz, G. and Boon, C. (2005) 'Commonalities and contradictions in HRM and performance research'. *Human Resource Management Journal* 15(3): 67–94.

Bosma, H. et al. (1997) 'Low job control and risk of coronary heart disease in Whitehall 11 (prospective cohort) study'. *British Medical Journal* 314: 558 (22 February).

Bosma, H. et al. (1998) 'Two alternative job stress models and the risk of coronary heart disease'. *American Journal of Public Health* 88(1): 68–74.

Bowen, D. and Ostroff, C. (2004) 'Understanding HRM-firm performance linkages: the role of the "strength" of the HRM system'. *Academy of Management Review* 29: 203–21.

Bowen, J. and Ford, R. (2002) 'Managing service organizations: does having a "thing" make a difference?' *Journal of Management* 28(30): 447–69.

Bowey, A. (1989) *Managing Salary and Wage Systems*. Aldershot: Gower.

Bowey, A. and Thorpe, R. (1986) *Payment Systems and Productivity*. Basingstoke: Macmillan (now Palgrave Macmillan).

Boxall, P. (1992) 'Strategic human resource management: beginnings of a new theoretical sophistication?' *Human Resource Management Journal* 2(3): 60–79.

Boxall, P. (1995) 'Building the theory of comparative HRM'. *Human Resource Management Journal* 5(5): 5–17.

Boxall, P. (1996) 'The strategic HRM debate and the resource-based view of the firm'. *Human Resource Management Journal* 6(3): 59–75.

Boxall, P. (1998) 'Achieving competitive advantage through human resource strategy: towards a theory of industry dynamics'. *Human Resource Management Review* 8(3): 265–88.

Boxall, P. (2003) 'HR Strategy and competitive advantage in the service sector'. *Human Resource Management Journal* 13(3): 5–20.

Boxall, P. (2007) 'The goals of HRM'. In Boxall, P., Purcell, J. and Wright, P. (eds) *The Oxford Handbook of Human Resource Management*. Oxford: Oxford University Press.

Boxall, P. (2013) 'Mutuality in the management of human resources: assessing the quality of alignment in employment relationships'. *Human Resource Management Journal* 23(1): 3–17.

Boxall, P., Ang, S. H. and Bartram, T. (2011) 'Analysing the "black box" of HRM: uncovering HR goals, mediators and outcomes in a standardized service environment'. *Journal of Management Studies* 48(7): 1504–32.

Boxall, P., Freeman, R. and Haynes, P. (2007) 'Conclusions: what workers say in the Anglo-American world'. In Freeman, R., Boxall, P. and Haynes, P. (eds) *What Workers Say: Employee Voice in the Anglo-American World*. Ithaca, NY: Cornell University Press.

Boxall, P. and Haynes, P. (1997) 'Strategy and trade union effectiveness in a neo-liberal environment'. *British Journal of Industrial Relations* 35(4): 567–91.

Boxall, P., Hutchison, A. and Wassenaar, B. (2015) 'How do high-involvement work processes influence employee outcomes?' An examination of the mediating roles of skill utilisation and intrinsic motivation'. *International Journal of Human Resource Management.* 26(13): 1737-52: 10.1080/09585192.2014.962070

Boxall, P. and Macky, K. (2009) 'Research and theory on high-performance work systems: progressing the high-involvement stream'. *Human Resource Management Journal* 19(1): 3–23.

Boxall, P. and Macky, K. (2014) 'High-involvement work processes, work intensification and employee well-being'. *Work, Employment and Society* 28(6): 963–84.

Boxall, P., Macky, K. and Rasmussen, E. (2003) 'Labour turnover and retention in New Zealand: the causes and consequences of leaving and staying with employers'. *Asia Pacific Journal of Human Resources* 41(2): 195–214.

Boxall, P. and Steeneveld, M. (1999) 'Human resource strategy and competitive advantage: a longitudinal study of engineering consultancies'. *Journal of Management Studies* 36(4): 443–63.

Boyer, K., Keong Leong, G., Ward, P. and Krajewski, L. (1997) 'Unlocking the potential of advanced manufacturing technologies'. *Journal of Operations Management* 15: 331–47.

Bozkurt, O. and Grugulis, I. (2011) 'Why retail work demands a closer look'. In Grugulis, I. and Bozkurt, O. (eds) *Retail Work*. Basingstoke: Palgrave Macmillan.

Bracker, J. (1980) 'The historical development of the strategic management concept'. *Academy of Management Review* 5(2): 219–24.

Braverman, H. (1974) *Labor and Monopoly Capital.* New York and London: Monthly Review Press.

Brewster, C., Sparrow, P., Vernon, G. and Houldsworth, L. (2011) *International Human Resource Management.* Third Edition. Wimbledon: CIPD.

Brewster, C., Wood, G. and Brookes, M. (2008) 'Similarity, isomorphism or duality? Recent survey evidence on human resource management policies of multinational corporations'. *British Journal of Management* 19: 320–42.

Broadbent, K. (2014) 'I'd rather work in a supermarket: privatization of home care in Japan'. *Work, Employment and Society* 28(5): 702–17.

Brown, C. and Reich, M. (1997) 'Micro-macro linkages in high-performance work systems'. *Organization Studies* 18(5): 765–81.

Brown, W. (2009) 'The influence of product markets on industrial relations'. In Blyton, P., Bacon, N., Fiorito, J. and Heery, E. (eds) *The Sage Handbook of Industrial Relations.* London: Sage.

Brynjolfsson, E. and Hitt, L. (2000) 'Beyond computation: information technology, organizational transformation and business performance'. *Journal of Economic Perspectives* 14(4): 23–48.

Bryson, A. (2004) *A Perfect Union? What Workers Want from Unions.* London: TUC.

Bryson, A., Charlwood, A. and Forth, J. (2006) 'Worker voice, managerial response and labour productivity: an empirical investigation'. *Industrial Relations Journal* 37(5): 438–55.

Bryson, A. and Freeman, R. (2007) 'What voice do British workers want?' In Freeman, R., Boxall, P. and Haynes, P. (eds) *What Workers Say: Employee Voice in the Anglo-American World.* Ithaca, NY: Cornell University Press.

Budd, J. and Zagelmeyer, S. (2010) 'Public policy and employee participation'. In Wilkinson, A., Golan, P., Marchington, M. and Lewin, D. (eds) *The Oxford Handbook of Participation in Organizations.* Oxford: Oxford University Press.

Buono, A. and Bowditch, J. (1989) *The Human Side of Mergers and Acquisitions.* San Francisco, CA: Jossey-Bass.

Buono, A., Bowditch, J. and Lewis III, J. (1985) 'When cultures collide: the anatomy of a merger'. *Human Relations* 53(5): 477–500.

Burawoy, M. (1979) *Manufacturing Consent.* Chicago: University of Chicago Press.

Burch, G. and Anderson, N. (2004) 'Measuring person-team fit: development and validation of the team selection inventor'. *Journal of Managerial Psychology* 19(4): 406–26.

Burgess, S. and Rees, H. (1998) 'A disaggregate analysis of the evolution of job tenure in Britain, 1975–1993'. *British Journal of Industrial Relations* 36(4): 629–55.

Buxton, J. (1998) *Ending the Mother War.* London: Macmillan (now Palgrave Macmillan).

Caldwell, R. (2008) 'HR business partner competency models: re-contextualising effectiveness'. *Human Resource Management Journal* 18(3): 275–94.

Campbell, D., Campbell, K. and Chia, H. (1998) 'Merit pay, performance appraisal, and individual motivation'. *Human Resource Management* 37(2): 131–46.

Campion, M. (1983) 'Personnel selection for physically demanding jobs: review and recommendations'. *Personnel Psychology* 36: 527–50.

Carroll, G. R. and Hannan, M. T. (eds) (1995) *Organizations in Industry: Strategy, Structure and Selection.* New York and Oxford: Oxford University Press.

Cartier, K. (1994) 'The transaction costs and benefits of the incomplete contract of employment'. *Cambridge Journal of Economics* 18: 181–96.

Cartwright, S. and Cooper, C. (1992) *Mergers and Acquisitions: The Human Factor.* Oxford: Butterworth-Heinemann.

Cascio, W. and Boudreau, J. (2010) *Investing in People: Financial Impact of Human Resource Initiatives.* Upper Saddle River, NJ: FT Press.

Chadwick, C., Way, S., Kerr, G. and Thacker, J. (2013) 'Boundary conditions of the high-investment human resource systems-small-firm labor productivity relationship'. *Personnel Psychology* 66: 311–43.

Challis, D., Samson, D. and Lawson, B. (2005) 'Impact of technological, organizational and human resource investments on employee and manufacturing performance: Australian and New Zealand evidence'. *International Journal of Production Research* 43(1): 81–107.

Chandler, A. (1962) *Strategy and Structure: Chapters in the History of Industrial Enterprise.* Cambridge, MA: MIT Press.

Chandler, A. (1977) *The Visible Hand: The Managerial Revolution in American Business.* Cambridge, MA: Harvard University Press.

Charlwood, A. and Terry, M. (2007) '21st-century models of employee representation: structures, processes and outcomes'. *Industrial Relations Journal* 38(4): 320–37.

Chênevert, D. and Tremblay, M. (2009) 'Fits in strategic human resource management and methodological challenge: empirical evidence of influence of empowerment and compensation practices on human resource performance in Canadian firms'. *International Journal of Human Resource Management* 20(4): 738–70.

Cherns, A. (1976) 'The principles of sociotechnical design'. *Human Relations* 29(8): 783–92.

Child, J. (1972) 'Organizational structure, environment and performance: the role of strategic choice'. *Sociology* 6(3): 1–22.

Child, J. (1997) 'Strategic choice in the analysis of action, structure, organizations and environment: retrospect and prospect'. *Organization Studies* 18(1): 43–76.

Child, J. and Smith, C. (1987) 'The context and process of organizational transformation: Cadbury Limited in its sector'. *Journal of Management Studies* 24(6): 564–93.

CIPD. (2014) *Putting Social Media to Work: Lessons from Employers.* http://www.cipd.co.uk/hr-resources/research/social-media-work-lessons-employers.aspx, accessed 24/7/14.

Clark, A. (2005) 'Your money or your life: changing job quality in OECD countries'. *British Journal of Industrial Relations* 43(3): 377–400.

Clegg, H. (1975) 'Pluralism in industrial relations'. *British Journal of Industrial Relations* 13(3): 309–16.

Clegg, H. (1994) *The History of British Trade Unions since 1889, Vol. III.* Oxford: Oxford University Press.

Clegg, S. and Haugaard, M. (2009) 'Introduction: why power is the central concept of the social sciences'. In Clegg, S. and Haugaard, M. (eds) *The Sage Handbook of Power.* Los Angeles: Sage.

Coff, R. (1997) 'Human assets and management dilemmas: coping with hazards on the road to resource-based theory'. *Academy of Management Review* 22(2): 374–402.

Coff, R. (1999) 'When competitive advantage doesn't lead to performance: the resource-based view and stakeholder bargaining power'. *Organization Science* 10(2): 119–33.

Collard, R. and Dale, B. (1989) 'Quality circles'. In Sisson, K. (ed) *Personnel Management in Britain.* Oxford: Blackwell.

Colli, A., Fernández Pérez, P. and Rose, M. (2003) 'National determinants of family firm development? Family firms in Britain, Spain, and Italy in the nineteenth and twentieth centuries'. *Enterprise and Society* 4: 28–64.

Colling, T. (1995) 'Experiencing turbulence: competition, strategic choice and the management of human resources in British Airways'. *Human Resource Management Journal* 5(5): 18–32.

Collings, D. and Mellahi, K. (2009) 'Strategic talent management: a review and research agenda'. *Human Resource Management Review* 19(4): 304–13.

Combs, J., Yongmei, L., Hall, A. and Ketchen, D. (2006) 'How much do high-performance work practices matter? A meta-analysis of their effects on organizational performance'. *Personnel Psychology* 59: 501–28.

Conyon, M., Girma, S., Thompson, S. and Wright, P. (2001) 'Do hostile mergers destroy jobs?' *Journal of Economic Behavior and Organization* 45: 427–40.

Cooke, F. L. (2006) 'Modeling an HR shared services center: experience of an MNC in the United Kingdom'. *Human Resource Management* 45(2): 211–27.

Cooke, F. L. (2014) 'Chinese multinational firms in Asia and Africa: relationships with institutional actors and patterns of HRM practices'. *Human Resource Management* 53(6): 877–96.

Cooke, W. (2001) 'The effects of labor costs and workplace constraints on foreign direct investment among highly industrialised countries'. *International Journal of Human Resource Management* 12(5): 697–716.

Cooke, W. (2007a) 'Integrating human resource and technological capabilities: the influence of global business strategies on workplace strategy choices'. *Industrial Relations* 46(2): 241–70.

Cooke, W. (2007b) 'Multinational companies and global human resource strategy'. In Boxall, P., Purcell, J. and Wright, P. (eds) *The Oxford Handbook of Human Resource Management*. Oxford: Oxford University Press.

Cordery, J. and Parker, S. (2007) 'Work organization'. In Boxall, P., Purcell, J. and Wright, P. (eds) *The Oxford Handbook of Human Resource Management*. Oxford: Oxford University Press.

Cox, A., Zagelmeyer, S. and Marchington, M. (2006) 'Embedding employee involvement and participation at work'. *Human Resource Management Journal* 16(3): 250–67.

Cribb, J., Disney, R. and Sibieta, L. (2014) 'The public sector workforce: past, present and future'. *IFS Briefing Note BN145*. London: Institute for Fiscal Studies.

Crichton, A. (1968) *Personnel Management in Context*. London: Batsford.

Cronshaw, M., Davis, E. and Kay, J. (1994) 'On being stuck in the middle or good food costs less at Sainsbury's'. *British Journal of Management* 5(1): 19–32.

Croucher, R. and Cotton, E. (2009) *Global Union Global Business: Global Union Federations and International Business*. London: Middlesex University Press.

Cullinane, S.-J., Bosak, J., Flood, P. and Demerouti, E. (2013) 'Job design under lean manufacturing and its impact on employee outcomes'. *Organizational Psychology Review* 3(1): 41–61.

Currie, G., Koteyko, N. and Nerlich, B. (2009) 'The dynamics of professions and development of new roles in public service organizations: the case of modern matrons in the English NHS'. *Public Administration* 87(2): 295–311.

Cyert, R. and March, J. (1956) 'Organizational factors in the theory of oligopoly'. *Quarterly Journal of Economics* 70(1): 44–64.

Cyert, R. and March, J. (1963) *A Behavioral Theory of the Firm*. Englewood Cliffs, NJ: Prentice Hall.

Danford, A., Durbin, S., Richardson, M., Tailby, S. and Stewart, P. (2009) '"Everybody's talking about me": the dynamics of information disclosure and consultation in high-skilled workplaces in the UK'. *Human Resource Management Journal* 19(4): 337–54.

Danford, A., Richardson, M., Stewart, P., Tailby, S. and Upchurch, M. (2004) 'High performance work systems and workplace partnership: a case study of aerospace workers'. *New Technology, Work and Employment* 19(1): 14–29.

Das, A. and Narasimhan, R. (2001) 'Process-technology fit and its implications for manufacturing performance'. *Journal of Operations Management* 19: 521–40.

Datta, D. and Grant, J. (1990) 'Relationships between types of acquisition, the autonomy given to the acquired firm, and acquisition success: an empirical study'. *Journal of Management* 16: 29–44.

Deane, P. (1969) *The First Industrial Revolution*. Cambridge: Cambridge University Press.

Deci, E. and Ryan, R. (2000) 'The "what" and "why" of goal pursuits: human needs and the self-determination of behavior'. *Psychological Inquiry* 11(4): 227–68.

Deery, S., Iverson, R. and Walsh, J. (2002) 'Work relationships in telephone call centers: understanding emotional exhaustion and employee withdrawal'. *Journal of Management Studies* 39(4): 471–97.

De Geus, A. (1988) 'Planning as learning'. *Harvard Business Review* March–April: 70–4.

Delaney, J., Lewin, D. and Ichniowski, C. (1989) *Human Resource Policies and Practices in American firms*. Washington, DC: U.S. Government Printing Office.

Delbridge, R. (2007) 'HRM and contemporary manufacturing'. In Boxall, P., Purcell, J. and Wright, P. (eds) *The Oxford Handbook of Human Resource Management*. Oxford: Oxford University Press.

Delbridge, R. and Whitfield, K. (2001) 'Employee perceptions of job influence and organizational participation'. *Industrial Relations* 40(3): 472–88.

Delery, J. and Doty, D. (1996) 'Modes of theorizing in strategic human resource management: tests of universalistic, contingency, and configurational performance predictions'. *Academy of Management Journal* 39(4): 802–35.

De Menezes, L., Wood, S. and Gelade, G. (2010) 'The integration of human resource and operation management practices and its link with performance: a longitudinal latent class study'. *Journal of Operations Management* 28(6): 455–71.

Demerouti, E., Bakker, A., Nachreiner, F. and Schaufeli, W. (2001) 'The job demands-resources model of burnout'. *Journal of Applied Psychology* 86: 499–512.

Deming, W. E. (1982) *Out of the Crisis*. Boston: MIT Press.

De Treville, S. and Antonakis, J. (2006) 'Could lean production job design be intrinsically motivating? Contextual, configurational, and levels-of-analysis issues'. *Journal of Operations Management* 24: 99–123.

Dierickx, I. and Cool, K. (1989) 'Asset stock accumulation and sustainability of competitive advantage'. *Management Science* 35(12): 1504–14.

DiMaggio, P. and Powell, W. (1983) 'The iron cage revisited: institutional isomorphism and collective rationality in organizational fields'. *American Sociological Review* 48(2): 147–60.

DiMaggio, P. and Powell, W. (1991) *The New Institutionalism in Organizational Analysis*. Chicago: University of Chicago Press.

Doeringer, P., Lorenz, E. and Terkla, D. (2003) 'The adoption of high-performance management: lessons from Japanese multinationals in the West'. *Cambridge Journal of Economics* 27: 265–86.

Doeringer, P. and Piore, M. (1971) *Internal Labor Markets and Manpower Analysis*. Lexington, MA: Heath.

Donaldson, T. and Preston, L. (1995) 'The stakeholder theory of the corporation: concepts, evidence, and implications'. *Academy of Management Review* 20(1): 65–91.

Doorewaard, H. and Meihuizen, H. (2000) 'Strategic performance options in professional service organisations'. *Human Resource Management Journal* 10(2): 39–57.

Dore, R. (2008) 'Financialization of the global economy'. *Industrial and Corporate Change* 17: 1097–1112.

Dowling, P. J., Festing, M, and Eagle, A. (2013) *International Human Resource Management*. Sixth Edition. London: Cengage Learning.

Drahokoupil, J. (2014) 'Decision-making in multinational corporations: key issues in international business strategy'. *Transfer* 20(2): 199–215.

Dunning, J. and Lundan, S. (2008) *Multinational Enterprises and the Global Economy*. Cheltenham: Edward Elgar.

Dyer, L. (1984) 'Studying human resource strategy'. *Industrial Relations* 23(2): 156–69.

Dyer, L. and Holder, G. (1988) 'A strategic perspective of human resource management'. In Dyer, L. (ed) *Human Resource Management: Evolving Roles and Responsibilities*. Washington, DC: Bureau of National Affairs.

Dyer, L. and Reeves, T. (1995) 'Human resource strategies and firm performance: what do we know and where do we need to go?' *International Journal of Human Resource Management* 6(3): 656–70.

Dyer, L. and Shafer, R. (1999) 'Creating organizational agility: implications for strategic human resource management'. In Wright, P., Dyer, L., Boudreau, J. and Milkovich, G. (eds) *Research in Personnel and Human Resource Management (Supplement 4: Strategic Human Resources Management in the Twenty-First Century)*. Stamford, CT and London: JAI Press.

Eaton, S. (2000) 'Beyond "unloving care": linking human resource management and patient care quality in nursing homes'. *International Journal of Human Resource Management* 11(3): 591–616.

Edwards, M. (2010) 'An integrative review of employer branding and OB theory'. *Personnel Review* 39(1): 5–23.

Edwards, P. and Ram, M. (2006) 'Surviving on the margins of the economy: working relationships in small, low-wage firms'. *Journal of Management Studies* 43(4): 895–916.

Edwards, P., Sánchez-Mangas, R., Tregaskis, O., Lévesque, C., McDonnell, A. and Quintanilla, J. (2013) 'Human resource management practices in the multinational company: a test of system, societal, and dominance effects'. *Industrial and Labor Relations Review* 66(3): 588–617.

Edwards, P. and Wright, M. (2001) 'High-involvement work systems and performance outcomes: the strength of variable, contingent and context-bound relationships'. *International Journal of Human Resource Management* 12(4): 568–85.

Edwards, T. and Kuruvilla, S. (2005) 'International HRM: national business systems, organizational politics and the international division of labour in MNCs'. *International Journal of Human Resource Management* 16(1): 1–21.

Edwards, T., Marginson, P. and Ferner, A. (2013) 'Multinational companies in crossnational context: integration, differentiation, and the interactions between MNCs and nation states'. *Industrial and Labor Relations Review* 66(3): 547–87.

Edwards, T. and Rees, C. (2006) *International Human Resource Management: Globalization, National Systems and Multinational Companies.* Harlow: Pearson Education.

Edwards, T. and Walsh, J. (2009) 'Foreign ownership and industrial relations'. In Brown, W., Bryson, A., Forth, J. and Whitfield, K. (eds) *The Evolution of the Modern Workplace.* Cambridge: Cambridge University Press.

Eilbert, H. (1959) 'The development of personnel management in the United States'. *Business History Review* 33: 345–64.

Eisenhardt, K. and Bird Schoonhovern, C. (1990) 'Organizational growth: linking founding team, strategy, environment, and growth among US semiconductor ventures, 1978–1988'. *Administrative Science Quarterly* 35(3): 504–29.

Eisenberger, R., Huntingdon, R., Hutchison, S. and Sowa, D. (1986) 'Perceived organizational support'. *Journal of Applied Psychology* 79: 617–26.

Eisenhardt, K. and Zbaracki, M. (1992) 'Strategic decision making'. *Strategic Management Journal* 13: 17–37.

Eliassen, K. and Sitter, N. (2008) *Understanding Public Management.* London: Sage.

Eurofound. (2012) *Work Organisation and Innovation.* Luxembourg: Publications Office of the European Union.

Evans, C., Harvey, G. and Turnbull, P. (2012) 'When partnerships don't match up: an evaluation of labour-management partnerships in the automotive components and civil aviation industries'. *Human Resource Management Journal* 22(1): 60–75.

Evans, P. and Genadry, N. (1999) 'A duality-based perspective for strategic human resource management'. In Wright, P., Dyer, L., Boudreau, J. and Milkovich, G. (eds) *Research in Personnel and Human Resources Management (Supplement 4: Strategic Human Resources Management in the Twenty-First Century).* Stamford, CT and London: JAI Press.

Evans, P., Pucik, V. and Barsoux, J.-L. (2002) *The Global Challenge: Frameworks for International Human Resource Management.* New York: McGraw-Hill.

Eysenck, H. (1953) *Uses and Abuses of Psychology.* London: Penguin.

Fabling, R. and Grimes, A. (2010) 'HR practices and New Zealand firm performance: what matters and who does it?' *International Journal of Human Resource Management* 21(4): 488–508.

Farndale, E. and Pauuwe, J. (2007) 'Uncovering competitive and institutional drivers of HRM practice in multinational corporations'. *Human Resource Management Journal* 17(4): 355–75.

Farndale, E., Van Ruiten, J., Kelliher, C. and Hope-Hailey, V. (2011) 'The influence of perceived employee voice on organizational commitment: an exchange perspective'. *Human Resource Management* 50(1): 113–29.

Farrell, D. (2005) 'Offshoring: value creation through economic change'. *Journal of Management Studies* 42(3): 675–83.

Feldman, E. (2014) 'Legacy divestitures: motives and implications'. *Organization Science* 25(3): 815–32.

Felstead, A., Fuller, A., Jewson, N. and Unwin, L. (2009) *Improving Working as Learning*. London: Routledge.

Felstead, A., Gallie, D., Green, F. and Zhou, Y. (2010) 'Employee involvement, the quality of training and the learning environment: an individual level analysis'. *International Journal of Human Resource Management* 21(10): 1667–88.

Fenton-O'Creevy, M. (1998) 'Employee involvement and the middle manager: evidence from a survey of organizations'. *Journal of Organizational Behavior* 19(1): 67–84.

Ferner, A., Bélanger, J., Tregaskis, O., Morley, M. and Quintanilla, J. (2013) 'U.S. multinationals and the control of subsidiary employment policies'. *Industrial and Labor Relations Review* 66(3): 645–69.

Ferris, G., Arthur, M., Kaplan, D., Harrell-Cook, G. and Frink, D. (1998) 'Toward a social context theory of the human resource management-organization effectiveness relationship'. *Human Resource Management Review* 8(3): 235–64.

Fisher, M. and Ferlie, E. (2013) 'Resisting hybridization between modes of clinical risk management: contradiction, contest and the production of intractable conflict'. *Accounting, Organization and Society* 38(1): 30–49.

Flanders, A. (1970) *Management and Unions*. London: Faber.

Fletcher, A., Guthrie, J., Steane, P., Roos, G. and Pike, S. (2003) 'Mapping stakeholder perceptions for a third sector organisation'. *Journal of Intellectual Capital* 4(4): 505–27.

Folger, R. (2005) 'Justice and employment: moral retribution as a contra-subjugation tendency'. In Coyle-Shapiro, J., Shore, L., Taylor, M., Tetrick, L. (eds) *The Employment Relationship: Examining Psychological and Contextual Perspectives*. Oxford: Oxford University Press.

Folger, R. and Cropanzano, R. (1998) *Organizational Justice and Human Resource Management*. Thousand Oaks, CA: Sage.

Forth, J., Bewley, H. and Bryson, A. (2006) *Small and Medium-Sized Enterprises: Findings from the 2004 Workplace Employment Relations Survey*. London: Department of Trade and Industry.

Foster, R. (1986) *Innovation: The Attacker's Advantage*. New York: Summit.

Fox, A. (1974) *Beyond Contract: Work, Power and Trust Relations*. London: Faber and Faber.

Francis, R. (2013) *Report of the Mid Staffordshire NHS Foundation Trust Public Inquiry*. London: Department of Health.

Freeman, J. (1995) 'Business strategy from the population level'. In Montgomery, C. (ed) *Resource-Based and Evolutionary Theories of the Firm: Towards a Synthesis*. Boston: Kluwer.

Freeman, J. and Boeker, W. (1984) 'The ecological analysis of business strategy'. *California Management Review* 26(3): 73–86.

Freeman, R. (2007) 'Can the US clear the market for representation and participation?' In Freeman, R., Boxall, P. and Haynes, P. (eds) *What Workers Say: Employee Voice in the Anglo-American World*. Ithaca, NY: Cornell University Press.

Freeman, R., Boxall, P. and Haynes, P. (eds) (2007) *What Workers Say: Employee Voice in the Anglo-American World*. Ithaca, NY: Cornell University Press.

Frenkel, S. (2000) 'Introduction: service work and its implications for HRM'. *International Journal of Human Resource Management* 11(3): 469–76.

Frenkel, S., Tam, M., Korczynski, M. and Shire, K. (1998) 'Beyond bureaucracy? Work organization in call centres'. *International Journal of Human Resource Management* 9(6): 957–79.

Frese, M. and Zapf, D. (1994). 'Action as the core of work psychology: a German approach'. In Dunnette, M., Triandis, H. and Hough, L. (eds) *Handbook of Industrial and Organizational Psychology*, Vol. 4., 2nd ed. Palo Alto, CA: Consulting Psychologists Press.

Froud, J. and Williams, K. (2007) 'Private equity and the culture of value extraction'. *New Political Economy* 12(3): 405–20.

Fuchs, S. and Edwards, M. (2012) 'Predicting pro-change behaviour: the role of perceived organizational justice and organizational identification'. *Human Resource Management Journal* 22(1): 39–59.

Gallie, D. (ed) (2007) *Employment Regimes and the Quality of Work*. Oxford: Oxford University Press.

Gallie, D. (2013) 'Direct participation and the quality of work'. *Human Relations* 66(4): 453–73.

Gallie, D. and Zhou, Y. (2013) 'Job control, work intensity, and work stress'. In Gallie, D. (ed) *Economic Crisis, Quality of Work, and Social Integration*. Oxford: Oxford University Press.

Gallie, D., Zhou, Y., Felstead, A. and Green, F. (2012) 'Teamwork, skill development and employee welfare'. *British Journal of Industrial Relations* 50(1): 23–46.

Gamble, J. (2010) 'Transferring organisational practices and the dynamics of hybridisation: Japanese retail multinationals in China'. *Journal of Management Studies* 47(4): 705–33.

Geare, A. (1977) 'The field of study of industrial relations'. *Journal of Industrial Relations* 19(3): 274–85.

Geare, A., Edgar, F. and Deng, M. (2006) 'Implementation and consumption of HRM: stakeholder differences'. *Research and Practice in Human Resource Management* 14(2): 34–48.

Geary, J. (2007) 'Employee voice in the Irish workplace'. In Freeman, R., Boxall, P. and Haynes, P. (eds) *What Workers Say: Employee Voice in the Anglo-American World*. Ithaca, NY: Cornell University Press.

Gereffi, G. (1995) 'Global production systems and third world development'. In Stallings, B. (ed) *Global Change, Regional Response: The New International Context of Development*. Cambridge: Cambridge University Press.

Gereffi, G. and Frederick, S. (2010) 'The global apparel value chain: challenges and opportunities for developing countries'. Policy Research Working Paper 5281, The World Bank.

Gereffi, G., Humphrey, J. and Sturgeon, T. (2005) 'The governance of global value chains'. *Review of International Political Economy* 12(1): 78–104.

Gersick, C. (1991) 'Revolutionary change theories: a multilevel exploration of the punctuated equilibrium paradigm'. *Academy of Management Review* 16(1): 10–36.

Ghemawat, P. and Costa, J. E. (1993) 'The organizational tension between static and dynamic efficiency'. *Strategic Management Journal* 14: 59–73.

Giangreco, A. and Peccei, R. (2005) 'The nature and antecedents of middle manager resistance to change: evidence from an Italian context'. *International Journal of Human Resource Management* 16(10): 1812–29.

Gilbert, J. and Boxall, P. (2009) 'The management of managers: challenges in a small economy'. *Journal of European Industrial Training* 33(4): 323–40.

Gilligan, C. (1982) *In a Different Voice: Psychological Theory and Women's Development*. Cambridge, MA: Harvard University Press.

Gitell, J. (2009) *High Performance Health Care*. New York: McGraw Hill.

Gitell, J. and Bamber, G. (2010) 'High- and low-road strategies for competing on costs and their implications for employment relations: international studies in the airline industry'. *International Journal of Human Resource Management* 21(2): 165–79.

Gitell, J., Seidner, R. and Wimbush, J. (2010) 'A relational model of how high performance work systems work'. *Organization Science* 21(2): 299–311.

Godard, J. (1991) 'The progressive HRM paradigm: a theoretical and empirical re-examination'. *Relations Industrielles* 46(2): 378–400.

Godard, J. (2001) 'Beyond the high-performance paradigm? An analysis of variation in Canadian managerial perceptions of reform programme effectiveness'. *British Journal of Industrial Relations* 39(1): 25–52.

Godard, J. (2004) 'A critical assessment of the high-performance paradigm'. *British Journal of Industrial Relations* 42(2): 349–78.

Godard, J. and Delaney, J. (2000) 'Reflections on the "high performance" paradigm's implications for industrial relations as a field'. *Industrial and Labor Relations Review* 53(3): 482–502.

Goergen, M., O'Sullivan, N. and Wood, G. (2011) 'Private equity takeovers and employment in the UK: some empirical evidence'. *Corporate Governance: An International Review* 19(3): 259–75.

Goergen, M., O'Sullivan, N. and Wood, G. (2014) 'The consequences of private equity acquisitions for employees: new evidence on the impact on wages, employment and productivity'. *Human Resource Management Journal* 24(2): 145–58.

Gohler, G. (2009) '"Power to" and "power over"'. In Clegg, S. and Haugaard, M. (eds) *The Sage Handbook of Power*. Los Angeles: Sage.

Gokhale, J., Groshen, E. and Neumark, D. (1995) 'Do hostile takeovers reduce extramarginal wage payments?' *Review of Economics and Statistics* 77: 470–85.

Gooderham, P., Morley, M., Brewster, C. and Mayrhofer, W. (2004) 'Human resource management: a universal concept?' In Brewster, C., Mayrhofer, W. and Morley, M. (eds) *Human Resource Management in Europe: Evidence of Convergence?* Oxford: Elsevier.

Gooderham, P., Nordhaug, O. and Ringdal, K. (1999) 'Institutional and rational determinants of organizational practices: human resource management in European firms'. *Administrative Science Quarterly* 44: 507–31.

Goold, M. and Campbell, A. (1987) *Strategies and Styles: The Role of the Centre in Managing Diversified Corporations*. Oxford: Blackwell.

Goold, M., Campbell, A. and Alexander, M. (1994) *Corporate-Level Strategy: Creating Value in the Multibusiness Company*. New York: Wiley.

Gordon, G. and DiTomaso, N. (1992) 'Predicting corporate performance from organizational climate'. *Journal of Management Studies* 26(6): 783–98.

Gospel, H. (1973) 'An approach to a theory of the firm in industrial relations'. *British Journal of Industrial Relations* 11(2): 211–28.

Gottschalg, O. and Zollo, M. (2007) 'Interest alignment and competitive advantage'. *Academy of Management Review* 32(2): 418–37.

Gouldner, A. (1960) 'The norm of reciprocity: a preliminary statement'. *American Sociological Review* 25: 161–78.

Gould-Williams, J. (2007) 'HR practices, organizational climate and employee outcomes: evaluating social exchange relationships in local government'. *International Journal of Human Resource Management* 18(9): 1627–47.

Grant, D. (1999) 'HRM, rhetoric and the psychological contract: a case of "easier said than done"'. *International Journal of Human Resource Management* 10(2): 327–50.

Grant, R. (1991) 'The resource-based theory of competitive advantage: implications for strategy formulation'. *California Management Review* 33(2): 114–35.

Grant, R. (1998) *Contemporary Strategy Analysis*. Third Edition. Oxford: Blackwell.

Grant, R. (2010) *Contemporary Strategy Analysis*. Seventh Edition. Hoboken, NJ: John Wiley & Sons.

Gratton, L., Hope-Hailey, V., Stiles, P. and Truss, C. (1999a) 'Linking individual performance to business strategy: the people process model'. *Human Resource Management* 38(1): 17–31.

Gratton, L., Hope-Hailey, V., Stiles, P. and Truss, C. (1999b) *Strategic Human Resource Management: Corporate Rhetoric and Human Reality*. Oxford: Oxford University Press.

Green, A., Atfiel, G., Adam, D. and Staniewicz, T. (2013) *Determinants of the Composition of the Workforce in the Low Skilled Sectors of the UK Economy*. Lot 2: Qualitative Research – Final Report, Warwick Institute for Employment Research.

Green, F. (2006) *Demanding Work: The Paradox of Job Quality in the Affluent Economy*. Princeton, NJ: Princeton University Press.

Green, F. (2008) 'Leeway for the loyal: a model of employee discretion'. *British Journal of Industrial Relations* 46(1): 1–32.

Greener, I. (2013) *Public Management*. Second Edition. Basingstoke: Palgrave

Greer, I. and Hauptmeier, M. (forthcoming) 'Management whipsawing: the staging of labor competition under globalization'. *Industrial and Labor Relations Review.*

Griffeth, R., Hom, P. and Gaertner, S. (2000) 'A meta-analysis of the antecedents and correlates of employee turnover: update, moderator tests, and research implications for the next millennium'. *Journal of Management* 26(3): 563–88.

Guest, D. (1995) 'Human resource management, trade unions and industrial relations'. In Storey, J. (ed) *Human Resource Management: A Critical Text*. London: Routledge.

Guest, D. (1997) 'Human resource management and performance: a review and research agenda'. *International Journal of Human Resource Management* 8(3): 263–76.

Guest, D. (1998) 'Is the psychological contract worth taking seriously?' *Journal of Organizational Behavior* 19: 649–64.

Guest, D. (2007) 'Human resource management and the worker: towards a new psychological contract?' In Boxall, P., Purcell, J. and Wright, P. (eds) *The Oxford Handbook of Human Resource Management*. Oxford: Oxford University Press.

Guest, D. and Bryson, A. (2009) 'From industrial relations to human resource management: the changing role of the personnel function'. In Brown, W., Bryson, A., Forth, J. and Whitfield, K. (eds) *The Evolution of the Modern Workplace*. Cambridge: Cambridge University Press.

Guthrie, J. (2007) 'Remuneration: pay effects at work'. In Boxall, P., Purcell, J. and Wright, P. (eds) *The Oxford Handbook of Human Resource Management*. Oxford: Oxford University Press.

Guy, F. (2003) 'High-involvement work practices and employee bargaining power'. *Employee Relations* 25(5): 453–69.

Hackman, J. R. and Oldham, G. R. (1980) *Work Redesign*. Reading, MA: Addison-Wesley.

Halbesleben, J., Harvey, J. and Bolino, M. (2009) 'Too engaged? A conservation of resources view of the relationship between work engagement and work interference with family'. *Journal of Applied Psychology* 94(6): 1452–65.

Hall, M. and Purcell, J. (2012) *Consultation at Work: Regulation and Practice*. Oxford: Oxford University Press.

Hall, R. (1993) 'A framework linking intangible resources and capabilities to sustainable competitive advantage'. *Strategic Management Journal* 14: 607–18.

Hambrick, D. (1987) 'The top management team: key to strategic success'. *California Management Review* 30(1): 88–108.

Hambrick, D. (1995) 'Fragmentation and the other problems CEOs have with their top management teams'. *California Management Review* 37(3): 110–27.

Hamel, G. and Prahalad, C. (1993) 'Strategy as stretch and leverage'. *Harvard Business Review* 71(2): 75–84.

Hamel, G. and Prahalad, C. (1994) *Competing for the Future*. Boston: Harvard Business School Press.

Hamori, M., Bonet, R. and Cappelli, P. (2011) 'How organizations obtain the human capital they need'. In Burton-Jones, A. and Spender, J.-C. (eds) *The Oxford Handbook of Human Capital*. Oxford: Oxford University Press.

Hannan, M. (1995) 'Labor unions'. In Carroll, G. and Hannan, M. (eds) *Organizations in Industry: Strategy, Structure and Selection*. Oxford and New York: Oxford University Press.

Harley, B., Sargent, L. and Allen, B. (2010) 'Employee responses to "high-performance work system" practices: an empirical test of the disciplined worker thesis'. *Work, Employment and Society* 24(4): 740–60.

Harney, B. and Jordan, C. (2008) 'Unlocking the black box: line managers and HRM-performance in a call centre context'. *International Journal of Productivity and Performance Measurement* 57(4): 275–96.

Harvey, G. and Turnbull, P. (2010) 'On the go: walking the high-road at a low cost airline'. *International Journal of Human Resource Management* 21(2): 230–41.

Haspeslagh, P. and Jemison, D. (1991) *Managing Acquisitions: Creating Value through Corporate Renewal*. New York: Free Press.

Haworth, N. and Hughes, S. (2003) 'International political economy and industrial relations'. *British Journal of Industrial Relations* 41(4): 665–82.

Hayes, R. and Pisano, G. (1996) 'Manufacturing strategy: at the intersection of two paradigm shifts'. *Production and Operations Management* 5(1): 25–41.

Haynes, P. and Allen, M. (2000) 'Partnership as union strategy: a preliminary evaluation'. *Employee Relations* 23(2): 164–87.

Haynes, P. and Fryer, G. (2000) 'Human resources, service quality and performance: a case study'. *International Journal of Contemporary Hospitality Management* 12(4): 240–8.

Hebdon, R. and Kirkpatrick, I. (2005) 'Changes in the organization of public services and their effects on employment relations'. In Ackroyd, A., Batt, R., Thompson, P. and Tolbert, P. (eds) *The Oxford Handbook of Work and Organisations*. Oxford: Oxford University Press.

Hedley, B. (1977) 'Strategy and the business portfolio'. *Long Range Planning* 10(1): 9–15.

Hedlund, G. (1994) 'A model of knowledge management and the N-Form corporation'. *Strategic Management Journal* 15: 73–90.

Henderson, R. (1995) 'Of life cycles real and imaginary: the unexpectedly long old age of optical lithography'. *Research Policy* 24: 631–43.

Hendry, C., Arthur, M. and Jones, A. (1995) *Strategy through People*. London and New York: Routledge.

Heracleous, L. and Wirtz, J. (2009) 'Strategy and organization at Singapore Airlines: achieving sustainable advantage through dual strategy'. *Journal of Air Transport Management* 15: 274–9.

Herzberg, F. (1968) 'One more time: How do you motivate employees?' *Harvard Business Review* January–February: 53–63.

Hill, C. and Jones, T. (1992) 'Stakeholder-agency theory'. *Journal of Management Studies* 29(2): 131–54.

Hill, S. (1991) 'Why quality circles failed but total quality management might succeed'. *British Journal of Industrial Relations* 29(4): 541–68.

Hird, M., Marsh, C. and Sparrow, P. (2009) 'HR delivery systems: re-engineered or over engineered?' Centre for Performance-led HR, Lancaster University Management School.

Hochschild, A. (1986) *The Managed Heart: Commercialization of Human Feeling*. Berkeley, CA: University of California Press.

Hofstede, G. (1980) *Culture's Consequences: International Differences in Work-Related Values*. Thousand Oaks, CA: Sage.

Hofstede, G. (1983) 'The cultural relativity of organizational practices and theories'. *Journal of International Business Studies* 14(2): 73–89.

Hofstede, G. and Bond, M. H. (1988) 'The Confucius connection: from cultural roots to economic growth'. *Organizational Dynamics* 16: 5–21.

Holden, R. (2011) 'Lean thinking in emergency departments: a critical review. *Annals of Emergency Medicine* 57(3): 265–78.

Holland, J. (1973) *Making Vocational Choices: A Theory of Careers*. Englewood Cliffs, NJ: Prentice-Hall.

Hom, P., Tsui, A., Wu, J., Lee, T., Zhang, A., Fu, P. and Lan, L. (2009) 'Explaining employment relationships with social exchange and job embeddedness'. *Journal of Applied Psychology* 94(2): 277–97.

Hood, C. (2006) 'Gaming in target world: the targets approach to managing British public services'. *Public Administration Review* 66: 515–21.

Hoopes, D., Madsen, T. and Walker, G. (2003) 'Guest editors' introduction to the special issue: why is there a resource-based view? Toward a theory of competitive heterogeneity'. *Strategic Management Journal* 24: 889–902.

Hope-Hailey, V., Gratton, L., McGovern, P., Stiles, P. and Truss, C. (1997) 'A chameleon function? HRM in the '90s'. *Human Resource Management Journal* 7(3): 5–18.

Horwitz, F., Heng, C. and Quazi, H. (2003) 'Finders, keepers? Attracting, motivating and retaining knowledge workers'. *Human Resource Management Journal* 13(4): 23–34.

Hubbard, N. (1999) *Acquisition Strategy and Implementation*. Basingstoke: Macmillan (now Palgrave Macmillan).

Hubbard, N. and Purcell, J. (2001) 'Managing employee expectations during acquisitions'. *Human Resource Management Journal* 11(2): 17–33.

Huber, V. and Fuller, S. (1998) 'Performance appraisal'. In Poole, M. and Warner, M. (eds) *The IEBM Handbook of Human Resource Management*. London: Thomson Business Press.

Hughes, J. (2008) 'The high-performance paradigm: a review and evaluation'. Learning as Work Research Paper, No. 16, Learning as Work Team, Cardiff School of Social Sciences, Cardiff University.

Hughes, S. (2002) 'Coming in from the cold: labour, the ILO and the international labour standards regime'. In Wilkinson, R. and Hughes, S. (eds) *Global Governance: Critical Perspectives*. London: Routledge.

Hughes, S. (2005) 'The International Labour Organisation'. *New Political Economy* 10(3): 413–25.

Hunt, J. and Boxall, P. (1998) 'Are top human resource specialists "strategic partners"? Self-perceptions of a corporate elite'. *International Journal of Human Resource Management* 9(5): 767–81.

Hunt, S. (1995) 'The resource-advantage theory of competition'. *Journal of Management Inquiry* 4(4): 317–22.

Hunt, S. (2000) *A General Theory of Competition*. Thousand Oaks, CA: Sage.

Hunter, J. and Hunter, R. (1984) 'Validity and utility of alternate predictors of job performance'. *Psychological Bulletin* 96: 72–98.

Hunter, J., Schmidt, F. and Judiesch, M. (1990) 'Individual differences in output variability as a function of job complexity'. *Journal of Applied Psychology* 75(1): 28–42.

Hunter, J., Schmidt, F., Rauschenberger, J. and Jayne, M. (2000) 'Intelligence, motivation, and job performance'. In Cooper, C. and Locke, E. (eds) *Industrial and Organizational Psychology*. Oxford: Blackwell.

Hunter, L. (2000) 'What determines job quality in nursing homes?' *Industrial and Labor Relations Review* 53(3): 463–81.

Huselid, M. (1995) 'The impact of human resource management practices on turnover, productivity, and corporate financial performance'. *Academy of Management Journal* 38: 635–72.

Huselid, M., Becker, B. and Beatty, R. (2005) *The Workforce Scorecard: Managing Human Capital to Execute Strategy*. Boston: Harvard Business School Press.

Hutchinson, S. and Purcell, J. (2011) 'Managing ward managers for roles in HRM in the NHS: overworked and under-resourced'. *Human Resource Management Journal* 20(4): 357–74.

Hyman, R. (1987) 'Strategy or structure? Capital, labour and control'. *Work, Employment and Society* 1(1): 25–55.

Ichniowski, C. and Shaw, K. (1999) 'The effects of human resource management systems on economic performance: an international comparison of US and Japanese plants'. *Management Science* 45(5): 704–21.

Ichniowski, C., Shaw, K. and Prennushi, G. (1997) 'The effects of human resource management practices on productivity: a study of steel finishing lines'. *American Economic Review* 87(3): 291–313.

Inkson, K. (2008) 'Are humans resources?' *Career Development International* 13(3): 270–9.

Isenberg, D. J. (1984) 'How senior managers think'. *Harvard Business Review* November–December: 81–90.

Jackson, S. and Schuler, R. (1995) 'Understanding human resource management in the context of organizations and their environments'. *Annual Review of Psychology* 46: 237–64.

Jacoby, S. (1984) 'The development of internal labor markets in American manufacturing firms'. In Osterman, P. (ed) *Internal Labor Markets*. Cambridge, MA: MIT Press.

Jacoby, S. (2004) *Employing Bureaucracy: Managers, Unions, and the Transformation of Work in the 20th Century*. Mahwah, NJ: Lawrence Erlbaum.

Jacoby, S. (2005) *The Embedded Corporation: Corporate Governance and Employment Relations in Japan and the United States*. Princeton, NJ: Princeton University Press.

James, L. A. and James, L. R. (1989) 'Integrating work environment perceptions: explorations into the measurement of meaning'. *Journal of Applied Psychology* 74(5): 739–51.

James, L. R., Choi, C., Ko, C.-H., McNeil, P., Minton, M., Wright, M. and Kim, K. (2008) 'Organizational and psychological climate: a review of theory and research'. *European Journal of Work and Organizational Psychology* 17(1): 5–32.

Janis, I. (1972) *Victims of Groupthink*. Boston: Houghton Mifflin.

Jany-Catrice, F., Gadrey, N. and Pernod, M. (2005) 'Employment systems in labour-intensive activities: the case of retailing in France'. In Bazen, S., Lucifora, C. and Salverda, W. (eds) *Job Quality and Employer Behaviour*. Basingstoke and New York: Palgrave Macmillan.

Jarzabkowski, P. and Balogun, J. (2009) 'The practice and process of delivering integration through strategic planning'. *Journal of Management Studies* 46(8): 1255–88.

Jayaram, J., Droge, C. and Vickery, S. (1999) 'The impact of human resource management practices on manufacturing performance'. *Journal of Operations Management* 18: 1–20.

Jensen, M. (1989) 'The eclipse of the public corporation'. *Harvard Business Review* September–October: 61–74.

Jensen, M. and Meckling, W. (1976) 'Theory of the firm: managerial behavior, agency costs and ownership structure'. *Journal of Financial Economics* 3: 305–60.

Jensen, P. and Pedersen, T. (2011) 'The economic geography of offshoring: the fit between activities and local context'. *Journal of Management Studies* 48(2): 352–72.

Jiang, K., Lepak, D., Hu, J. and Baer, J. (2012) 'How does human resource management influence organizational outcomes? A meta-analytic investigation of mediating mechanisms'. *Academy of Management Journal* 55(6): 1264–94.

Jiang, K., Takeuchi, R. and Lepak, D. (2013) 'Where do we go from here? New perspectives on the black box in strategic human resource management research'. *Journal of Management Studies* 50(8): 1448–80.

Jones, G. (2005) *Renewing Unilever: Transformation and Tradition*. Oxford: Oxford University Press.

Jones, S. (1994) 'The origins of the factory system in Great Britain: technology, transaction costs or exploitation?' In Kirby, M. and. Rose, M. (eds) *Business Enterprise in Modern Britain*. London: Routledge.

Judge, T., Higgins, C., Thoresen, C. and Barrick, M. (1999) 'The big five personality traits, general mental ability, and career success across the life span'. *Personnel Psychology* 52: 621–52.

Juravich, T. and Hilgert, J. (1999) 'UNITE's victory at Richmark: community-based union organizing in communities of color'. *Labor Studies Journal* 24(1): 27–41.

Kalleberg, A. (2011) *Good Jobs, Bad Jobs: The Rise of Polarized and Precarious Employment Systems in the United States, 1970s-2000s*. New York: Russell Sage Foundation.

Kalleberg, A., Marsden, P., Reynolds, J. and Knoke, D. (2006) 'Beyond profit? Sectoral differences in high-performance work practices'. *Work and Occupations* 33(3): 271–302.

Kamoche, K. (1996) 'Strategic human resource management within a resource-capability view of the firm'. *Journal of Management Studies* 33(2): 213–33.

Kaplan, R. and Norton, D. (1996) *The Balanced Scorecard: Translating Strategy into Action*. Boston: Harvard Business School Press.

Kaplan, R. and Norton, D. (2001) *The Strategy-Focused Organization*. Boston: Harvard Business School Press.

Kaplan, R. and Norton, D. (2004) *Strategy Maps: Converting Intangible Assets into Tangible Outcomes*. Boston: Harvard Business School Press.

Karasek, R. (1979) 'Job demands, job decision latitude, and mental strain: implications for job redesign'. *Administrative Science Quarterly* 24: 285–308.

Karasek, R. and Theorell, T. (1990) *Healthy Work: Stress, Productivity, and the Reconstruction of Working Life*. New York: Basic Books.

Katz, H. and Darbishire, O. (2000) *Converging Divergences: Worldwide Changes in Employment Systems*. Ithaca, NY: Cornell University Press.

Kaufman, B. (2004) 'Prospects for union growth in the United States in the early 21st century'. In Verma, A. and Kochan, T. (eds) *Unions in the 21st Century*. Basingstoke and New York: Palgrave Macmillan.

Kaufman, B. (2010) 'SHRM theory in the post-Huselid era: why it is fundamentally misspecified'. *Industrial Relations* 49(2): 286–313.

Kaufman, B. and Miller, B. (2011) 'The firm's choice of HRM practices: economics meets strategic human resource management'. *Industrial and Labor Relations Review* 64(3): 526–57.

Kay, J. (1993) *Foundations of Corporate Success*. Oxford: Oxford University Press.

Kaysen, C. (1960) 'The corporation: how much power? What scope?' In Mason, E. (ed) *The Corporation in Modern Society*. Cambridge: Harvard University Press.

Keenoy, T. (1992) 'Constructing control'. In Hartley, J. and Stephenson, G. (eds) *Employment Relations: The Psychology of Influence and Control at Work*. Oxford: Blackwell.

Kelly, J. (1998) *Rethinking Industrial Relations: Mobilization, Collectivism and Long Waves*. London: Routledge.

Kenney, M., Goe, W., Contreras, O., Romero, J. and Bustos, M. (1998) 'Learning factories or reproduction factories? Labor-management relations in the Japanese consumer electronics maquiladoras in Mexico'. *Work and Occupations* 25(3): 269–304.

Kessler, I. (1998) 'Payment systems'. In Poole, M. and Warner, M. (eds) *The IEBM Handbook of Human Resource Management*. London: Thomson Business Press.

Kessler, I. (2015) 'Exploring the relationship between human resource management and organizational performance in the healthcare sector'. *Oxford Handbooks Online*, April. DOI:10.1093/oxfordhb/9780199935406.013.13

Kessler, I., Heron, P. and Dopson, S. (2012) *Valuing Healthcare Assistants*. Oxford: Oxford University Press.

Kessler, I. and Purcell, J. (1992) 'Performance-related pay: objectives and application'. *Human Resource Management Journal* 2(3): 16–33.

Kessler, I. and Purcell, J. (1996) 'The value of joint working parties'. *Work, Employment and Society* 10(4): 663–82.

Kets de Vries, M. and Miller, D. (1984) *The Neurotic Organization*. San Francisco, CA: Jossey-Bass.

Kilgour, J. (2008) 'Job evaluation revisited: the point factor method'. *Compensation and Benefits Review* 40(4): 37–48.

King, A. and Zeithaml, C. (2001) 'Competencies and firm performance: examining the causal ambiguity paradox'. *Strategic Management Journal* 22: 75–99.

Kintana, M., Alonso, A. and Olaverri, C. (2006) 'High-performance work systems and firms' operational performance: the moderating role of technology'. *International Journal of Human Resource Management* 17(1): 70–85.

Knox, A. and Walsh, J. (2005) 'Organisational flexibility and HRM in the hotel industry: evidence from Australia'. *Human Resource Management Journal* 15(1): 57–75.

Kochan, T. (2007) 'Social legitimacy of the human resource management profession: a U.S. perspective'. In Boxall, P., Purcell, J. and Wright, P. (eds) *The Oxford Handbook of Human Resource Management*. Oxford: Oxford University Press.

Kossek, E. and Pichler, S. (2007) 'EEO and the management of diversity'. In Boxall, P., Purcell, J. and Wright, P. (eds) *The Oxford Handbook of Human Resource Management*. Oxford: Oxford University Press.

Kostova, T. and Zaheer, S. (1999) 'Organizational legitimacy under conditions of complexity: the case of the multinational enterprise'. *Academy of Management Review* 24(1): 64–81.

Korczynski, M. (2001) 'The contradictions of service work: call centre as customer-oriented bureaucracy'. In Sturdy, A., Grugulis, I. and Willmott, H. (eds) *Customer Service: Empowerment and Entrapment*. Basingstoke: Palgrave Macmillan.

Koukoulaki, T. (2014) 'The impact of lean production on musculoskeletal and psychosocial risks: an examination of sociotechnical trends over 20 years'. *Applied Ergonomics* 45: 198–212.

KPMG. (1999) 'Unlocking shareholder value: the key to success'. In *Mergers and Acquisitions: A Global Research Report*. London: KPMG.

Krugman, P. (1997) *Pop Internationalism*. Cambridge, MA: MIT Press.

Kuvaas, B. and Dysik, A. (2009) 'Perceived investment in employee development, intrinsic motivation and work performance'. *Human Resource Management Journal* 19(3): 217–36.

Lacey, R. (1986) *Ford: The Men and the Machine*. London: Heinemann.

Lam, S. and Schaubroeck, J. (1998) 'Integrating HR planning and organisational strategy'. *Human Resource Management Journal* 8(3): 5–19.

Lakhani, T., Kuruvilla, S. and Avgar, A. (2013) 'From the firm to the network: global value chains and employment relations theory'. *British Journal of Industrial Relations* 51(3): 440–72.

Langfred, C. (2005) 'Autonomy and performance in teams: the multilevel moderating effect of task interdependence'. *Journal of Management* 31: 513–29.

Lanvin, B. and Evans, P. (2013) *The Global Talent Competitiveness Index*. Insead: Singapore.

Lashley, C. (1998) 'Matching the management of human resources to service operations'. *International Journal of Contemporary Hospitality Management* 10(1): 24–33.

Latham, G. and Latham, S. (2000) 'Overlooking theory and research in performance appraisal at one's peril: much done, more to do'. In Cooper, C. and Locke, E. (eds) *Industrial and Organizational Psychology*. Oxford: Blackwell.

Latham, G., Sulsky, L. and MacDonald, H. (2007) 'Performance management'. In Boxall, P., Purcell, J. and Wright, P. (eds) *The Oxford Handbook of Human Resource Management*. Oxford: Oxford University Press.

Lawler, E. (1986) *High-Involvement Management*. San Francisco, CA: Jossey-Bass.

Lazear, E. (1999) 'Personnel economics: past lessons and future directions'. *Journal of Labor Economics* 17(2): 199–236.

Leana, C. and Van Buren, H. (1999) 'Organizational social capital and employment practices'. *Academy of Management Review* 24(3): 538–55.

Lee-Kelley, L., Blackman, D. and Hurst, J. (2007) 'An exploration of the relationship between learning organisations and the retention of knowledge workers'. *The Learning Organization* 14(3): 204–21.

Lees, S. (1997) 'HRM and the legitimacy market'. *International Journal of Human Resource Management* 8(2): 226–43.

Legge, K. (1978) *Power, Innovation, and Problem-Solving in Personnel Management*. London: McGraw-Hill.

Legge, K. (1995) *Human Resource Management: Rhetorics and Realities*. Basingstoke: Macmillan (now Palgrave Macmillan).

Legge, K. (2005) *Human Resource Management: Rhetorics and Realities*. Basingstoke and New York: Palgrave Macmillan.

Lengnick-Hall, M. and Lengnick-Hall, C. (2005) 'International human resource management research and social network/social capital theory'. In Bjorkman, I. and Stahl, G. (eds) *Handbook of Research into International HRM*. Cheltenham: Edward Elgar.

Léonard, D., Pulignano, V., Lamare, R. and Edwards, T. (2014) 'Multinational corporations as political players' *Transfer* 20(2): 171–82.

Leonard-Barton, D. (1992) 'Core capabilities and core rigidities: a paradox in managing new product development'. *Strategic Management Journal* 13: 111–25.

Leonard-Barton, D. (1998) *Wellsprings of Knowledge: Building and Sustaining the Sources of Innovation*. Boston: Harvard Business School Press.

Lepak, D., Liao, H., Chung, Y. and Harden, E. (2006) 'A conceptual review of human resource management systems in strategic human resource management research'. *Research in Personnel and Human Resources Management* 25: 217–71.

Lepak, D. and Snell, S. (1999) 'The strategic management of human capital: determinants and implications of different relationships'. *Academy of Management Review* 24(1): 1–18.

Lepak, D. and Snell, S. (2007) 'Employment sub-systems and the "HR architecture"'. In Boxall, P., Purcell, J. and Wright, P. (eds) *The Oxford Handbook of Human Resource Management*. Oxford: Oxford University Press.

Lepine, J., Lepine, M. and Jackson, C. (2004) 'Challenge and hindrance stress: relationships with exhaustion, motivation to learn, and learning performance'. *Journal of Applied Psychology* 89(5): 883–91.

Levinson, D. (1978) *The Seasons of a Man's Life*. New York: Knopf.

Levinson, D. and Levinson, J. (1996) *The Seasons of a Woman's Life*. New York: Knopf.

Liden, R., Bauer, T. and Erdogan, B. (2004) 'The role of leader-member exchange in the dynamic relationship between employer and employee: implications for employee socialization, leaders, and organizations'. In Coyle-Shapiro, J., Shore, L., Taylor, S. and Tetrick, L. (eds) *The Employment Relationship: Examining Psychological and Contextual Perspectives*. Oxford: Oxford University Press.

Littler, C. (1982) *The Development of the Labour Process in Capitalist Societies: A Comparative Study of the Transformation of Work Organization in Britain, Japan, and the USA*. London: Heinemann.

Lockett, A., Thompson, S. and Morgenstern, U. (2009) 'The development of the resource-based view of the firm: a critical appraisal'. *International Journal of Management Reviews* 11(1): 9–28.

Longenecker, C., Sims, H. and Gioia, D. (1987) 'Behind the mask: the politics of employee appraisal'. *Academy of Management Executive* 1(3): 183–93.

Lorenz, E. and Valeyre, A. (2005) 'Organisational innovation, human resource management and labour market structure: a comparison of the EU-15'. *Journal of Industrial Relations* 47(4): 424–42.

Lovas, B. and Ghoshal, S. (2000) 'Strategy as guided evolution'. *Strategic Management Journal* 21: 875–96.

Lovelock, C., Patterson, P. and Walker, R. (2007) *Services Marketing*. Fourth Edition. Sydney: Pearson Education Australia.

Lovelock, C., Patterson, P. and Wirtz, J. (2010) *Services Marketing: An Asia-Pacific and Australian Perspective*. Fifth Edition. Sydney: Pearson Australia.

Mabey, C. (2008) 'Management development and firm performance in Germany, Norway, Spain and the UK'. *Journal of International Business Studies* 39: 1327–42.

MacDuffie, J. (1995) 'Human resource bundles and manufacturing performance: organizational logic and flexible production systems in the world auto industry'. *Industrial and Labor Relations Review* 48(2): 197–221.

Macky, K. and Boxall, P. (2007) 'The relationship between high-performance work practices and employee attitudes: an investigation of additive and interaction effects'. *International Journal of Human Resource Management* 18(4): 537–67.

Maguire, S. and Phillips, N. (2008) '"Citibankers" at Citigroup: a study of the loss of institutional trust after a merger'. *Journal of Management Studies* 45(2): 372–401.

Mahoney, J. and Pandian, J. (1992) 'The resource-based view within the conversation of strategic management'. *Strategic Management Journal* 13(5): 363–80.

March, J. (1962) 'The business firm as a political coalition'. *The Journal of Politics* 24(4): 662–78.

March, J. and Simon, H. (1958) *Organizations*. New York: Wiley.

Marchington, M. (1989) 'Joint consultation in practice'. In Sisson, K. (ed) *Personnel Management in Britain*. Oxford: Blackwell.

Marchington, M. (1995) 'Involvement and participation'. In Storey, J. (ed) *Human Resource Management: A Critical Text*. London: Routledge.

Marchington, M., Carroll, M. and Boxall, P. (2003) 'Labour scarcity and the survival of small firms: a resource-based view of the road haulage industry'. *Human Resource Management Journal* 13(4): 3–22.

Marchington, M. and Grugulis, I. (2000) '"Best practice" human resource management: perfect opportunity or dangerous illusion?' *International Journal of Human Resource Management* 11(6): 1104–24.

Marginson, P., Edwards, P., Martin, R., Purcell, J. and Sisson, K. (1988) *Beyond the Workplace. Managing Industrial Relations in the Multi-Establishment Enterprise*. Oxford: Blackwell.

Marginson, P. and Meardi, G. (2010) 'Multinational companies: transforming national industrial relations?' In Colling, T. and Terry, M. (eds) *Industrial Relations: Theory and Practice*. Chichester: John Wiley and Sons.

Marshall, V. and Wood, R. (2000) 'The dynamics of effective performance appraisal: an integrated model'. *Asia Pacific Journal of Human Resources* 38(3): 62–90.

Marsick, V. and Watkins, K. (1990) *Informal and Incidental Learning in the Workplace*. London and New York: Routledge.

Martin, J. (1992) *Cultures and Organizations: Three Perspectives*. New York: Oxford University Press.

Martínez Lucio, M. and Stuart, M. (2004) 'Swimming against the tide: social partnership, mutual gains and the revival of "tired" HRM'. *International Journal of Human Resource Management* 15(2): 410–24.

Marx, K. (1990) [1867] *Capital, Volume I*. Ben Fowkes (trans). London: Penguin Books.

Maslach, C. and Jackson, S. (1984) 'Burnout in organizational settings'. *Applied Social Psychology Annual* 5: 133–53.

Maslow, A. (1970) *Motivation and Personality*. New York: Harper and Row.

McBride, J. (2008) 'The limits of high performance work systems in unionised craft-based work settings'. *New Technology, Work and Employment* 23(3): 213–28.

McGee, J. (2003) 'Strategic groups: theory and practice'. In Faulkner, D. and Campbell, A. (eds) *The Oxford Handbook of Strategy*. Oxford: Oxford University Press.

McGovern, P., Gratton, L., Hope-Hailey, V., Stiles, P. and Truss, C. (1997) 'Human resource management on the line?' *Human Resource Management Journal* 7(4): 12–29.

McKay, P., Avery, D. and Morris, M. (2009) 'A tale of two climates: diversity climate from subordinates' and managers' perspectives and their role in store unit performance'. *Personnel Psychology* 62: 767–91.

McKinsey & Company. (2012) *Manufacturing the Future: the Next Era of Global Growth and Innovation*. http://www.mckinsey.com/insights/manufacturing/the_future_of_manufacturing, accessed 25/10/14.

McLaughlin, K., Osborne, P. and Ferlie, E. (2002) *New Public Management: Current Trends and Future Prospects*. London: Routledge.

McMillan, J. (1992) *Games, Strategies and Managers*. Oxford and New York: Oxford University Press.

McWilliams, A. and Smart, D. (1995) 'The resource-based view of the firm: does it go far enough in shedding the assumptions of the S-C-P paradigm?' *Journal of Management Inquiry* 4(4): 309–16.

Meyer, A., Tsui, A. S. and Hinings, C. R. (1993) 'Configurational approaches to organizational analysis'. *Academy of Management Journal* 36(6): 1175–95.

Meyer, S. (1981) *The Five Dollar Day: Labor Management and Social Control in the Ford Motor Company 1908–1921*. Albany, NY: State University of New York Press.

Michailova, S. (2002) 'When common sense becomes uncommon: participation and empowerment in Russian companies with Western participation'. *Journal of World Business* 37: 180–7.

Michie, J. and Sheehan, M. (2005) 'Business strategy, human resources, labour market flexibility and competitive advantage'. *International Journal of Human Resource Management* 16(3): 445–64.

Milkovich, G., Newman, J. and Gerhart, B. (2013) *Compensation*. Boston: McGraw Hill.

Miller, D. (1981) 'Toward a new contingency approach: the search for organizational gestalts'. *Journal of Management Studies* 18(1): 1–26.

Miller, D. (1992) 'Generic strategies; classification, combination and context'. *Advances in Strategic Management* 8: 391–408.

Miller, D. and Friesen, P. (1980) 'Momentum and revolution in organizational adaptation'. *Academy of Management Journal* 23(4): 591–614.

Miller, D. and Shamsie, J. (1992) 'The resource-based view of the firm in two environments: the Hollywood film studios from 1936 to 1965'. *Academy of Management Journal* 39(3): 519–43.

Miller, D. and Shamsie, J. (1996) 'The resource-based view of the firm in two environments: the Hollywood film studios from 1936 to 1965'. *Academy of Management Journal* 39(3): 519–43.

Millward, N., Bryson, A. and Forth, J. (2000) *All Change at Work: British Employment Relations 1980–1998 as Portrayed by the Workplace Industrial Relations Survey Series*. London: Routledge.

Mintzberg, H. (1978) 'Patterns in strategy formation'. *Management Science* 24(9): 934–48.

Mintzberg, H. (1990) 'The design school: reconsidering the basic premises of strategic management'. *Strategic Management Journal* 11(3): 171–95.

Mintzberg, H. (1994) 'Rethinking strategic planning part 1: pitfalls and fallacies'. *Long Range Planning* 27(3): 12–21.

Morgan, G. (1997) *Images of Organization*. Thousand Oaks, CA: Sage.

Morgan, G. (2005) 'Understanding multinational corporations'. In Ackroyd, A., Batt, R., Thompson, P. and Tolbert, P. (eds) *The Oxford Handbook of Work and Organisations*. Oxford: Oxford University Press.

Morgan, G. (2014) 'Financialization and the multinational company'. *Transfer: European Review of Labour and Research* 20(2): 183–97.

Morgeson, F. and Humphrey, S. (2006) 'The work design questionnaire (WDQ): developing and validating a comprehensive measure for assessing job design and the nature of work'. *Journal of Applied Psychology* 91(6): 1321–39.

Morris, J., Wilkinson, B. and Gamble, J. (2009) 'Strategic international human resource management or the "bottom line"? The cases of electronics and garments commodity chains in China'. *International Journal of Human Resource Management* 20(2): 348–71.

Morrison, D., Cordery, J., Girardi, A. and Payne, R. (2005) 'Job design, opportunities for skill utilization, and intrinsic job satisfaction'. *European Journal of Work and Organizational Psychology* 14(1): 59–79.

Mueller, D. (1997) 'First-mover advantages and path dependence'. *International Journal of Industrial Organization* 15(6): 827–50.

Mueller, F. (1996) 'Human resources as strategic assets; an evolutionary resource-based theory'. *Journal of Management Studies* 33(6): 757–85.

Mueller, F. and Purcell, J. (1992) 'The Europeanization of manufacturing and the decentralisation of bargaining: multinational management strategies in the European automobile industry'. *International Journal of Human Resource Management* 3(2): 15–35.

Murphy, K. and Cleveland, J. (1991) *Performance Appraisal: An Organizational Perspective*. Boston: Allyn and Bacon.

Murray, A. (1988) 'A contingency view of Porter's "generic strategies"'. *Academy of Management Review* 13(3): 390–400.

Murray, G., Jalette, P., Bélanger, J. and Lévesque, C. (2014) 'The "hollowing out" of the national subsidiary in multinational companies: is it happening, does it matter, what are the strategic consequences?' *Transfer* 20(2): 217–36.

Nahapiet, J. and Ghoshal, A. (1998) 'Social capital, intellectual capital and the organizational advantage'. *Academy of Management Review* 23(2): 242–66.

Nelson, R. (1991) 'Why do firms differ, and how does it matter?' *Strategic Management Journal* 12: 61–74.

Newbert, S. (2007) 'Empirical research on the resource-based view of the firm: an assessment and suggestions for future research'. *Strategic Management Journal* 28: 121–46.

Newman, K. and Nollen, S. (1996) 'Culture and congruence: the fit between management practices and national culture'. *Journal of International Business Studies* 27(4): 753–79.

Niepce, W. and Molleman, E. (1998) 'Work design issues in lean production from a socio-technical systems perspective: Neo-Taylorism or the next step in sociotechnical design?' *Human Relations* 51: 3, 259–74.

Nishii, L., Lepak, D. and Schneider, B. (2008) 'Employee attributions of the "why" of HR practices: their effects on employee attitudes and behaviors, and customer satisfaction'. *Personnel Psychology* 61: 503–45.

Nissen, B. (2000) 'Living wage campaigns from a "social movement" perspective: the Miami case'. *Labor Studies Journal* 25(3): 29–50.

Norburn, D. and Birley, S. (1988) 'The top management team and corporate performance'. *Strategic Management Journal* 9: 225–37.

O'Brien, E. and Linehan, C. (2014) 'A balancing act: emotional challenges in the HR role'. *Journal of Management Studies* 51(8): 1257–85.

O'Brien, G. (1982) 'The relative contribution of perceived skill-utilization and other perceived job attributes to the prediction of job satisfaction: a cross-validation study'. *Human Relations* 35(3): 219–37.

O'Brien, G. (1983) 'Skill-utilization, skill-variety and the job characteristics model'. *Australian Journal of Psychology* 35(3): 461–8.

Odiorne, G. (1985) *Strategic Management of Human Resources*. San Francisco, CA: Jossey-Bass.

Ogbonna, E. and Harris, L. (1998) 'Managing culture: compliance or genuine change?' *British Journal of Management* 9(4): 273–89.

Ohmae, K. (1985) *Triad Power: The Coming Shape of Global Competition*. New York: Free Press.

Ohno, T. (1988) *Just-in-Time: For Today and Tomorrow*. Cambridge, MA: Productivity Press.

Oliver, N. and Wilkinson, B. (1988) *The Japanization of British Industry*. Oxford: Basil Blackwell.

O'Neill, G. (1995) 'Linking pay to performance: conflicting views and conflicting evidence'. *Asia Pacific Journal of Human Resources* 33(2): 20–35.

Ono, T., Lafortune, G. and Schoenstein, M. (2013) 'Health workforce planning in OECD countries: a review of 26 projection models from 18 countries'. OECD Health Working Papers, No. 62, OECD Publishing. http://dx.doi.org/10.1787/5k44t787zcwb-en

Organ, D. (1988) *Organizational Citizenship Behavior: The Good Soldier Syndrome*. Lexington, MA: Lexington Books.

Orlitzky, M. (2007) 'Recruitment strategy'. In Boxall, P., Purcell, J. and Wright, P. (eds) *The Oxford Handbook of Human Resource Management*. Oxford: Oxford University Press.

Ortega, J. (2009) 'Why do employers give discretion? Family versus performance concerns'. *Industrial Relations* 48(1): 1–26.

Osterman, P. (1987) 'Choice of employment systems in internal labor markets'. *Industrial Relations* 26(1): 46–67.

Osterman, P. (2001) 'Employers in the low-wage/low-skill labor market'. In Kazis, R. and Miller, M. (eds) *Low-Wage Workers in the New Economy*. Washington, DC: The Urban Institute Press.

Ouchi, W. (1980) 'Markets, bureaucracies and clans'. *Administrative Science Quarterly* 25: 129–41.

Paauwe, J. (2009) 'HRM and performance: achievements, methodological issues and prospects'. *Journal of Management Studies* 46: 129–42.

Paauwe, J. and Boselie, P. (2003) 'Challenging "strategic HRM" and the relevance of the institutional setting'. *Human Resource Management Journal* 13(3): 56–70.

Paauwe, J. and Boselie, P. (2007) 'Human resource management and societal embeddedness'. In Boxall, P., Purcell, J. and Wright, P. (eds) *The Oxford Handbook of Human Resource Management*. Oxford: Oxford University Press.

Parker, S. (2003) 'Longitudinal effects of lean production on employee outcomes and the mediating role of work characteristics'. *Journal of Applied Psychology* 88(4): 620–34.

Parker, S. (2014) 'Beyond motivation: job and work design for development, health, ambidexterity, and more'. *Annual Review of Psychology* 65: 661–91.

Pascale, R. (1985) 'The paradox of "corporate culture": reconciling ourselves to socialization'. *California Management Review* 27(2): 26–41.

Peccei, R. and Rosenthal, P. (2001) 'Delivering customer-oriented behaviour through empowerment: an empirical test of HRM assumptions'. *Journal of Management Studies* 38: 831–57.

Penrose, E. (1959) *The Theory of the Growth of the Firm*. Oxford: Blackwell.

Peter, L. J. and Hull, R. (1969) *The Peter Principle: Why Things Always Go Wrong*. New York: William Morrow and Company.

Peteraf, M. and Shanley, M. (1997) 'Getting to know you: a theory of strategic group identity'. *Strategic Management Journal* 18(S): 165–86.

Pfeffer, J. (1998) *The Human Equation: Building Profits by Putting People First*. Boston: Harvard Business School Press.

Pfeffer, J. and Salancik, G. R. (1978) *The External Control of Organizations: A Resource Dependence Perspective*. New York: Harper and Row.

Phillips, J. and Phillips, P. (2012) *Proving the Value of HR: How and Why to Measure ROI*. Alexandria, Virginia: Society for Human Resource Management.

Pil, F. and MacDuffie, J. (1996) 'The adoption of high involvement work practices'. *Industrial Relations* 35(3): 423–55.

Pinfield, L. and Berner, M. (1994) 'Employment systems: toward a coherent conceptualisation of internal labour markets'. In Ferris, G. (ed) *Research in Personnel and Human Resources Management*. Stamford, CT and London: JAI Press.

Piore, M. and Sabel, C. (1984) *The Second Industrial Divide: Prospects for Prosperity*. New York: Basic Books.

Pirenne, H. (1937) *Economic and Social History of Medieval Europe*. New York: Harvest Books.

Poell, R. (2014) 'Workplace learning theories and practices'. In Walton, R. and Valentin, C. (eds) *Human Resource Development: Practices and Orthodoxies*. Basingstoke: Palgrave Macmillan.

Polanyi, M. (1962) *Personal Knowledge*. New York: Harper.

Poole, M. (1986) *Industrial Relations: Origins and Patterns of National Diversity*. London: Routledge.

Poole, M. (1990) 'Editorial: human resource management in an international perspective'. *International Journal of Human Resource Management* 1(1): 1–15.

Porter, M. (1980) *Competitive Strategy*. New York: Free Press.

Porter, M. (1985) *Competitive Advantage: Creating and Sustaining Superior Performance*. New York: Free Press.

Porter, M. (1990) *The Competitive Advantage of Nations*. London: Macmillan (now Palgrave Macmillan).

Porter, M. (1991) 'Towards a dynamic theory of strategy'. *Strategic Management Journal* 12(S): 95–117.

Porter, M. and Siggelkow, N. (2008) 'Contextuality within activity systems and sustainability of competitive advantage'. *Academy of Management Perspectives* 22(2): 34–56.

Poutsma, E., Ligthart, P. and Veersma, U. (2006) 'The diffusion of calculative and collaborative HRM practices in European firms'. *Industrial Relations* 45(4): 513–46.

Price, R. (2011) 'Technological change, work re-organization and retail workers' skills in production-oriented supermarket departments'. In Grugulis, I. and Bozkurt, O. (eds) *Retail Work*. Basingstoke: Palgrave Macmillan.

Priem, R. and Butler, J. (2001) 'Is the resource-based "view" a useful perspective for strategic management research?' *Academy of Management Review* 26(1): 22–40.

Purcell, J. (1989) 'The impact of corporate strategy on human resource management'. In Storey, J. (ed) *New Perspectives on Human Resource Management*. London: Routledge.

Purcell, J. (1996) 'Contingent workers and human resource strategy: rediscovering the core/periphery dimension'. *Journal of Professional HRM* 5: 16–23.

Purcell, J. (1999) 'The search for "best practice" and "best fit": chimera or cul-de-sac?' *Human Resource Management Journal* 9(3): 26–41.

Purcell, J. (2014a) 'Employee voice and engagement'. In Truss, C., Delbridge, R., Alfes, K., Shantz, A. and Soane, E. (eds) *Employee Engagement in Theory and Practice*. London: Routledge.

Purcell, J. (2014b) 'Disengaging from engagement'. Provocation series paper. *Human Resource Management Journal* 24(3): 241–54.

Purcell, J. and Ahlstrand, B. (1994) *Human Resource Management in the Multidivisional Company*. Oxford: Oxford University Press.

Purcell, J. and Georgiadis, K. (2007) 'Why should employers bother with worker voice?' In Freeman, R., Boxall, P. and Haynes, P. (eds) *What Workers Say: Employee Voice in the Anglo-American World*. Ithaca, NY: Cornell University Press.

Purcell, J. and Hall, M. (2012) 'Voice and participation in the modern workplace: challenges and prospects'. *Future of Workplace Relations Discussion Paper*. London: Acas.

Purcell, J. and Hutchinson, S. (2007) 'Front-line managers as agents in the HRM-performance causal chain: theory, analysis and evidence'. *Human Resource Management Journal* 17(1): 3–20.

Purcell, J. and Kinnie, N. (2007) 'HRM and business performance'. In Boxall, P., Purcell, J. and Wright, P. (eds) *The Oxford Handbook of Human Resource Management*. Oxford: Oxford University Press.

Purcell, J., Kinnie, N., Swart, J., Rayton, B. and Hutchinson, S. (2009) *People Management and Performance*. London: Routledge.

Ramsay, H. (1977) 'Cycles of control: worker participation in sociological and historical perspective'. *Sociology* 11(3): 481–506.

Radnor, Z., Holweg, H. and Waring, J. (2012) 'Lean in healthcare: the unfilled promise?' *Social Science and Medicine* 74: 364–71.

Rayton, B., Dodge, T. and D'Analeze, G. (2012) *The Evidence, Employee Engagement Task Force 'Nailing the Evidence' Workgroup*. Engage for Success, http:/www.engageforsuccess.org/wp-content/uploads/2012/09/The-Evidence.pdf, accessed 24/7/2014.

Reed, R. and DeFillippi, R. (1990) 'Causal ambiguity, barriers to imitation, and sustainable competitive advantage'. *Academy of Management Review* 15(1): 88–102.

Rees, C. and Edwards, T. (2009) 'Management strategy and HR in international mergers: choice, constraint and pragmatism'. *Human Resource Management Journal* 19(1): 24–39.

Reynolds, P. (1987) 'New firms: societal contribution versus survival potential'. *Journal of Business Venturing* 2: 231–46.

Riisgaard, L. and Hammer, N. (2011) 'Prospects for labour in global value chain chains: labour standards in the cut flower and Banana Industries'. *British Journal of Industrial Relations* 49(1): 168–90.

Riordan, M. and Hoddeson, L. (1997) *Crystal Fire: The Birth of the Information Age*. New York: Norton.

Robertson, I. and Cooper, C. (2011) *Well-Being: Productivity and Happiness at Work.* Basingstoke: Palgrave Macmillan.

Robinson, S. (1996) 'Trust and the breach of the psychological contract'. *Administrative Science Quarterly* 41(4): 574–99.

Rock, M. (1984) *Handbook of Wage and Salary Administration.* New York: McGraw-Hill.

Rondeau, K. and Wagner, T. (2001) 'Impact of human resource management on nursing home performance'. *Health Services Management Research* 14: 192–202.

Roos, G. (2012) *Manufacturing into the Future.* Adelaide Thinker in Residence 2010-11. http://www.thinkers.sa.gov.au/roosreport/, accessed 13/11/14.

Rose, M. (1994) 'Job satisfaction, job skills, and personal skills'. In Penn, R., Rose, M. and Rubery, J. (eds) *Skill and Occupational Change.* Oxford: Oxford University Press.

Rose, M. (2000) 'Work attitudes in the expanding occupations'. In Purcell, K. (ed) *Changing Boundaries in Employment.* Bristol: Bristol Academic Press.

Rose, M. (2003) 'Good deal, bad deal? Job satisfaction in occupations'. *Work, Employment and Society* 17(3): 503–30.

Rosenthal, P. (2004) 'Management control as an employee resource: the case of front-line service workers'. *Journal of Management Studies* 41(4): 601–22.

Rosenthal, P., Hill, S. and Peccei, R. (1997) 'Checking out service: evaluating excellence, HRM and TQM in retailing'. *Work, Employment and Society* 11(3): 481–503.

Rousseau, D. (1995) *Psychological Contracts in Organizations.* Thousand Oaks, CA: Sage.

Rowlinson, M. (1997) *Organisations and Institutions: Perspectives in Economics and Sociology.* London: Macmillan (now Palgrave Macmillan).

Rubery, J. (1994) 'Internal and external labour markets: towards an integrated analysis'. In Rubery, J. and Wilkinson, F. (eds) *Employer Strategy and the Labour Market.* Oxford: Oxford University Press.

Rucci, A., Kirn, S. and Quinn, R. (1998) 'The employee-customer-profit chain at Sears'. *Harvard Business Review* 76(1): 82–97.

Rumelt, R. (1987) 'Theory, strategy and entrepreneurship'. In Teece, D. (ed) *The Competitive Challenge.* New York: Harper and Row.

Sako, M. (1998) 'The nature and impact of employee "voice" in the European car components industry'. *Human Resource Management Journal* 8(2): 6–13.

Saks, A. (2006) 'Antecedents and consequences of engagement'. *Journal of Managerial Psychology* 21(7): 600–19.

Samuel, P. and Bacon, N. (2010) 'The contents of partnership agreements in Britain 1990-2007'. *Work, Employment and Society* 24(3): 430–48.

Sanders, J., Dorenbosch, L., Grundemann, R. and Blonk, R. (2011) 'Sustaining the work ability and work motivation of lower-educated older workers: Directions for work redesign'. *Management Revue* 22(2): 132–50.

Saunders, M. and Thornhill, A. (2003) 'Organisational justice, trust and the management of change: an exploration'. *Personnel Review* 32(3): 360–75.

Schaufeli, W. (2014) 'What is engagement?' In Truss, C., Delbridge, R., Alfes, K., Shantz, A. and Soane, E. (eds) *Employee Engagement in Theory and Practice.* London: Routledge.

Schleifer, A. and Summers, L. (1988) 'Breach of trust in hostile takeovers'. In Auerbach, A. (ed) *Corporate Takeovers: Causes and Consequences.* Cambridge, MA: National Bureau of Economic Research.

Schmidt, J. (ed) (2002) *Making Mergers Work: the Strategic Importance of People.* Alexandria: Towers Perrin/SHRM Foundation.

Schmitt, N. and Kim, B. (2007) 'Selection decision making'. In Boxall, P., Purcell, J. and Wright, P. (eds) *The Oxford Handbook of Human Resource Management.* Oxford: Oxford University Press.

Schnaars, S. (1994) *Managing Imitation Strategies.* Basingstoke and New York: Macmillan (now Palgrave Macmillan).

Schuler, R. and Jackson, S. (1987) 'Linking competitive strategies and human resource management practices'. *Academy of Management Executive* 1(3): 207–19.

Schumpeter, J. (1950) *Capitalism, Socialism and Democracy*. New York: Harper and Row.

Schwartz, H. and Davis, S. (1981) 'Matching corporate culture and business strategy'. *Organizational Dynamics* 60: 30–48.

Scott, W. (2008) *Institutions and Organizations: Ideas and Interests*. Third Edition. Los Angeles: Sage.

Segal-Horn, S. (2003) 'Strategy in service organisations'. In Faulkner, D. and Campbell, A. (eds) *The Oxford Handbook of Strategy*. Oxford: Oxford University Press.

Seifert, A. (2008) 'Global employee information and consultation procedures in worldwide enterprises'. *International Journal of Comparative Labour Law and Industrial Relations* 24: 327–37.

Sergeant, A. and Frenkel, S. (2000) 'When do customer contact employees satisfy customers?' *Journal of Service Research* 3(1): 18–34.

Shah, R. and Ward, P. (2003) 'Lean manufacturing: context, practice bundles, and performance'. *Journal of Operations Management* 21: 129–49.

Shibata, H. (2008) 'The transfer of Japanese work practices to plants in Thailand'. *International Journal of Human Resource Management* 19(2): 330–45.

Shore, L., Tetrick, L., Taylor, S., Coyle-Shapiro, J., Liden, R., McLean Parks, J., Wolfe Morrison, E., Porter, L., Robinson, S., Roehling, M., Rousseau, D., Schalk, R., Tsui, A. and Van Dyne, L. (2004) 'The employee–organization relationship: a timely concept in a period of transition'. *Research in Personnel and Human Resources Management* 23: 291–370.

Short, J., Payne, G. and Ketchen, D. (2008) 'Research on organizational configurations: past accomplishments and future challenges'. *Journal of Management* 34(6): 1053–79.

Siebert, W. and Zubanov, N. (2009) 'Searching for the optimal level of employee turnover: a study of a large UK retail organization'. *Academy of Management Journal* 52(2): 294–313.

Siegrist, J. (1996) 'Adverse health effects of high-effort/low-reward conditions'. *Journal of Occupational Health Psychology* 1(1): 27–41.

Simon, H. (1947) *Administrative Behavior*. New York: Free Press.

Simon, H. (1985) 'Human nature in politics: the dialogue of psychology with political science'. *American Political Science Review* 79(2): 293–304.

Sisson, K. (1993) 'In search of HRM'. *British Journal of Industrial Relations* 31(2): 201–10.

Sisson, K. (2000) *Direct Participation and the Modernisation of Work Organisation*. Dublin: European Foundation for the Improvement of Living and Working Conditions.

Sisson, K. and Purcell, J. (2010) 'Management: caught between competing views'. In Colling, T. and Terry, M. (eds) *Industrial Relations Theory and Practice*. Third Edition. Chichester: Wiley.

Smale, A. (2008) 'Foreign subsidiary perspectives on the mechanisms of global HRM integration'. *Human Resource Management Journal* 18(2): 135–53.

Smith, A. (1776) *An Inquiry into the Nature and Causes of the Wealth of Nations*. London: W. Strahan.

Smith, P. (2004) 'Nations, cultures and individuals: new perspectives and old dilemmas'. *Journal of Cross-Cultural Psychology* 35(1): 6–12.

Snape, E. and Redman, T. (2010) 'HRM Practices, organizational citizenship behaviour, and performance: a multi-level analysis'. *Journal of Management Studies* 47(7): 1219–47.

Snape, E., Redman, T. and Wilkinson, A. (1993) 'Human resource management in building societies: making the transformation?' *Human Resource Management Journal* 3(3): 44–61.

Snell, S. and Dean, J. (1992) 'Integrated manufacturing and human resources management: a human capital perspective'. *Academy of Management Journal* 35(3): 467–504.

Snell, S., Youndt, M. and Wright, P. (1996) 'Establishing a framework for research in strategic human resource management: merging resource theory and organizational learning'. *Research in Personnel and Human Resources Management* 14: 61–90.

Soane, E., Shantz, A., Alfes, K., Truss, C., Rees, C. and Gatenby, M. (2013) 'The association of meaningfulness, well-being, and engagement with absenteeism: a moderated mediation model'. *Human Resource Management* 52(3): 441–56.

Soderberg, A.-M. and Vaara, E. (eds) (2003) *Mergers Across Borders: People, Cultures and Politics.* Copenhagen: Copenhagen University Press.

Solar, P. (2006) 'Shipping and economic development in nineteenth century Ireland'. *Economic History Review* 59(4): 717–42.

Sparrow, P. and Braun, W. (2007) 'Human resource strategy in international context'. In Harris, M. (ed) *Handbook of Research in International Human Resource Management.* Mahwah, NJ: Lawrence Erlbaum.

Sparrow, P., Brewster, C., Harris, H. (2004) *Globalizing Human Resource Management.* London and New York: Routledge.

Spender, J.-C. (1989) *Industry Recipes.* Oxford: Blackwell.

Spender, J.-C. (2014) *Business Strategy: Managing Uncertainty, Opportunity, and Enterprise.* Oxford: Oxford University Press.

Sprigg, C., Jackson, P. and Parker, S. (2000) 'Production teamworking: the importance of interdependence and autonomy for employee strain and satisfaction'. *Human Relations* 53(11): 1519–43.

Standing, G. (2011) *The Precariat: The New Dangerous Class.* London: Bloomsbury

Stansfield, S., Fuhrer, R., Shipley, M. and Marmot, M. (1999) 'Work characteristics predict psychiatric disorder: prospective results from the Whitehall II study'. *Occupational and Environmental Medicine* 56: 302–7.

Steedman, H. and Wagner, K. (1989) 'Productivity, machinery and skills: clothing manufacture in Britain and Germany'. *National Institute Economic Review* May: 40–57.

Sterling, A. and Boxall, P. (2013) 'Lean production, employee learning and workplace outcomes: a case analysis through the ability-motivation-opportunity framework'. *Human Resource Management Journal* 23(3): 227–40.

Stiglitz, J. (2010) *Freefall: Free Markets and the Sinking of the Global Economy.* London: Allen Lane.

Storey, D. (1985) 'The problems facing new firms'. *Journal of Management Studies* 22(3): 327–45.

Streeck, W. (1987) 'The uncertainties of management in the management of uncertainty: employers, labour relations and industrial adjustment in the 1980s'. *Work, Employment and Society* 1(3): 281–308.

Suchman, M. (1995) 'Managing legitimacy: strategic and institutional approaches'. *Academy of Management Review* 20(3): 571–610.

Sun, L.-Y., Aryee, S. and Law, K. (2007) 'High-performance human resource practices, citizenship behaviour, and organizational performance: a relational perspective'. *Academy of Management Journal* 50(3): 558–77.

Swart, J. (2007) 'HRM and knowledge workers'. In Boxall, P., Purcell, J. and Wright, P. (eds) *The Oxford Handbook of Human Resource Management.* Oxford: Oxford University Press.

Swart, J. and Kinnie, N. (2003) 'Sharing knowledge in knowledge-intensive firms'. *Human Resource Management Journal* 13(2): 60–75.

Tailby, S. (2012) 'Public service restructuring in the UK: the case of the English National Health Service'. *Industrial Relations Journal* 43(5): 448–64.

Tailby, S. and Winchester, D. (2000) 'Management and trade unions: towards social partnership?' In Bach, S. and Sisson, K. (eds) *Personnel Management: A Comprehensive Guide to Theory and Practice.* Oxford: Blackwell

Takeuchi, R., Lepak, D., Wang, H. and Takeuchi, K. (2007) 'An empirical examination of the mechanisms mediating between high-performance work systems and the performance of Japanese organisations'. *Journal of Applied Psychology* 92(4): 1069–83.

Tan, F. M. (2008) 'Organisational support as the mediator of career-related HRM practices and affective commitment: evidence from knowledge workers in Malaysia'. *Research and Practice in Human Resource Management* 16(2): 8–24.

Tattersall, I. (2012) *Masters of the Planet: The Search for our Human Origins.* New York: Palgrave Macmillan.

Tayeb, M. (1995) 'The competitive advantage of nations: the role of HRM and its socio-cultural context'. *International Journal of Human Resource Management* 6(3): 588–605.

Taylor, F. W. (1911) *Principles of Scientific Management*. New York and London: Harper and Brothers.

Taylor, M. and Collins, C. (2000) 'Organizational recruitment: enhancing the intersection of research and practice'. In Cooper, C. and Locke, E. (eds) *Industrial and Organizational Psychology*. Oxford: Blackwell.

Teece, D. (2011) *Dynamic Capabilities and Strategic Management*. Oxford: Oxford University Press.

Teece, D., Pisano, G. and Shuen, A. (1997) 'Dynamic capabilities and strategic management'. *Strategic Management Journal* 18(7): 509–33.

Theodore, N. et al. (2012) 'Under the radar: tracking the violation of labour standards in low-wage industries in the US'. In Warhurst, C., Carre, F., Findlay, P. and Tilly, C. (eds) *Are Bad Jobs Inevitable?* Basingstoke: Palgrave Macmillan, 208–23.

Thompson, P. (2003) 'Disconnected capitalism: or why employers can't keep their side of the bargain'. *Work, Employment and Society* 17(2): 359–78.

Thompson, P. (2011) 'The trouble with HRM'. *Human Resource Management Journal* 21(4): 355–67.

Thompson, P. and Harley, B. (2007) 'HRM and the worker: labor process perspectives'. In Boxall, P., Purcell, J. and Wright, P. (eds) *The Oxford Handbook of Human Resource Management*. Oxford: Oxford University Press.

Toh, S., Morgeson, F. and Campion, M. (2008) 'Human resource configurations: investigating fit with the organizational context'. *Journal of Applied Psychology* 93(4): 864–82.

Trevor, C., Gerhart, B. and Boudreau, J. (1997) 'Voluntary turnover and job performance: curvilinearity and the moderating influences of salary growth and promotions'. *Journal of Applied Psychology* 82: 44–61.

Trist, E. and Bamforth, K. (1951) 'Some social and psychological consequences of the long-wall method of coal-getting'. *Human Relations* 4: 3–38.

Trompenaars, F. and Hampden-Turner, C. (1997) *Riding the Waves of Culture: Understanding Cultural Diversity in Business*. London: Nicholas Brealey.

Tuchman, B. (1996) *The March of Folly: From Troy to Vietnam*. London: Papermac.

Tushman, M., Newman, W. and Romanelli, E. (1986) 'Convergence and upheaval: managing the unsteady pace of organizational evolution'. *California Management Review* 29(1): 29–44.

Tyler, T. and Blader, S. (2003) 'The group engagement model: procedural justice, social identity, and cooperative behaviour'. *Personality and Social Psychology Review* 7(4): 349–61.

Uhl-Bien, M., Graen, G. and Scandura, L. (2000) 'Indicators of leader–member exchange (LMX) for strategic human resource management systems'. *Research in Personnel and Human Resources Management* 18: 137–85.

UK Commission for Employment and Skills. (2012) *Sector Skills Insights: Advanced Manufacturing*. UKCES. https://www.gov.uk/government/publications/manufacturing-sector-skills-insights, accessed 11/11/14.

Ulrich, D. (1998) 'A new mandate for human resources'. *Harvard Business Review* January–February: 123–34.

UNCTAD. (2007) 'The universe of the largest transnational corporations'. *United Nations Conference on Trade and Development*. New York and Geneva: United Nations.

UNCTAD. (2013) *World Investment Report 2013. Global Value Chains: Investment and Trade for Development*. New York and Geneva: United Nations.

Utterback, J. (1994) *Mastering the Dynamics of Innovation*. Boston: Harvard Business School Press.

Vandenberg, R. J., Richardson, H. A. and Eastman, L. J. (1999) 'The impact of high involvement work processes on organizational effectiveness: a second-order latent variable approach'. *Group & Organization Management* 24(3): 300–39.

Van Engen, M., Vinkenburg, C. and Dikkers, J. (2012) 'Sustainability in combining career and care: challenging normative beliefs about parenting'. *Journal of Social Issues* 68(4): 645–64.

Van Iddekinge, C., Roth, P., Putka, D. and Lanivich, S. (2011) 'Are you interested? A meta-analysis of relations between vocational interests and employee performance and turnover'. *Journal of Applied Psychology* 96(6): 1167–94.

van Wanrooy, B., Bewley, H., Bryson, A., Forth, J., Freeth, S., Stokes, L. and Wood, S. (2013) *Employment Relations in the Shadow of Recession: Findings from the 2011 Workplace Employment Relations Study.* Basingstoke: Palgrave.

Veliyath, R. and Srinavasan, T. (1995) 'Gestalt approaches to assessing strategic coalignment: a conceptual integration'. *British Journal of Management* 6(3): 205–19.

Vidal, M. (2007) 'Manufacturing empowerment? "Employee involvement" in the labour process after Fordism'. *Socio-Economic Review* 5(2): 197–232.

Volberda, J. (1998) *Building the Flexible Firm: How to Remain Competitive.* New York: Oxford University Press.

Vroom, V. (1964) *Work and Motivation,* New York: Wiley.

Waddington, J. and Kerr, A. (2009) 'Transforming a trade union? An assessment of the introduction of an organizing campaign'. *British Journal of Industrial Relations* 47(1): 27–54.

Wall, T., Corbett, M., Martin, R., Clegg, C. and Jackson, P. (1990) 'Advanced manufacturing technology, work design and performance: a change study'. *Journal of Applied Psychology* 75(6): 691–7.

Wall, T., Jackson, P. and Davids, K. (1992) 'Operator work design and robotics system performance'. *Journal of Applied Psychology* 77(3): 353–62.

Walshe, K. (2010) 'Reorganisation of the NHS in England'. *BMJ* 341: c3843.

Walton, R., Cutcher-Gershenfeld, J. and McKersie, R. (1994) *Strategic Negotiations: A Theory of Change in Labor–Management Relations.* Boston: Harvard Business School Press.

Warner, M. (1998) 'Taylor, Frederick Winslow (1856–1915)'. In Poole, M. and Warner, M. (eds) *The IEBM Handbook of Human Resource Management.* London: Thompson Business Press.

Warr, P. (2007) *Work, Happiness, and Unhappiness.* London: Lawrence Erlbaum.

Watson, T. (1977) *The Personnel Managers.* London: Routledge.

Watson, T. (1986) *Management, Organization and Employment Strategy: New Directions in Theory and Practice.* London: Routledge.

Watson, T. (2005) 'Organizations, strategies and human resourcing'. In Leopold, J., Harris, L. and Watson, T. (eds) *The Strategic Managing of Human Resources.* Harlow: Pearson Education.

Watson, T. (2007) 'Organization theory and HRM'. In Boxall, P., Purcell, J. and Wright, P. (eds) *The Oxford Handbook of Human Resource Management.* Oxford: Oxford University Press.

Webb, S. and Webb, B. (1902) *Industrial Democracy.* London: Longman.

Wernerfelt, B. (1984) 'A resource-based view of the firm'. *Strategic Management Journal* 5(2): 171–80.

West, G. and DeCastro, J. (2001) 'The Achilles heel of firm strategy: resource weaknesses and distinctive inadequacies'. *Journal of Management Studies* 38(3): 417–42.

West, M., Dawson, J., Admasachew, L. and Topakas, A. (2011) *NHS Staff Management and Health Service Quality: Results from the NHS Staff Survey and Related Data.* London: Department of Health. http://www.dh.gov.uk/en/Publicationsandstatistics/index.htm, accessed 14/6/2014.

West, M., Guthrie, J., Dawson, J., Borrill, C. and Carter, M. (2006) 'Reducing patient mortality in hospitals: the role of HRM'. *Journal of Organizational Behaviour* 27(7): 983–1002.

Westcott, M. (2009) 'Private equity in Australia'. *Journal of Industrial Relations* 51(4): 529–42.

Wever, K. (1995) *Negotiating Competitiveness: Employment Relations and Organizational Innovation in Germany and the United States*. Boston, MA: Harvard Business School Press.

Whittington, R. (1993) *What Is Strategy – And Does It Matter?* London: Routledge.

Whittington, R. and Mayer, M. (2000) *The European Corporation: Strategy, Structure and Social Science*. Oxford: Oxford University Press.

Wilkinson, A. and Willmott, H. (1995) *Making Quality Critical: New Perspectives on Organisational Change*. London: Routledge.

Wilkinson, B., Gamble, J., Humphrey, J., Morris, J. and Anthony, D. (2001) 'The new international division of labour in Asian electronics: work organization and human resources in Japan and Malaysia'. *Journal of Management Studies* 38(50): 675–95.

Williams, J. (1992) 'How sustainable is your competitive advantage?' *California Management Review* 34(3): 29–51.

Willman, P., Bryson, A. and Gomez, R. (2007) 'The long goodbye: new establishments and the fall in union voice in Britain'. *International Journal of Human Resource Management* 18: 1318–34

Williamson, O. (1964) *The Economics of Discretionary Behavior: Managerial Objectives in a Theory of the Firm*. Englewood Cliffs, NJ: Prentice Hall.

Williamson, O. (1970) *Corporate Control and Business Behavior*. Englewood Cliffs, NJ: Prentice-Hall.

Williamson, O. (1981) 'The modern corporation: origins, evolution, attributes. *Journal of Economic Literature* 19(4): 1537–68.

Windolf, P. (1986) 'Recruitment, selection, and internal labour markets in Britain and Germany'. *Organization Studies* 7(3): 235–54.

Winterton, J. (1994) 'Social and technological characteristics of coal-face work: a temporal and spatial analysis'. *Human Relations* 47(1): 89–118.

Winterton, J. (2007) 'Training, development and competence'. In Boxall, P., Purcell, J. and Wright, P. (eds) *The Oxford Handbook of Human Resource Management*. Oxford: Oxford University Press.

Womack, J., Jones, D. and Roos, D. (1990) *The Machine that Changed the World: The Triumph of Lean Production*. New York: Rawson Macmillan.

Wood, G. and Wright, M. (2009) 'Private equity: a review and synthesis'. *International Journal of Management Reviews* 11(4): 361–80.

Wood, S. (1996) 'High commitment management and payment systems'. *Journal of Management Studies* 33(1): 53–77.

Wood, S. and Bryson, A. (2009) 'High involvement management'. In Brown, W., Bryson, A., Forth, J. and Whitfield, K. (eds) *The Evolution of the Modern Workplace*. Cambridge: Cambridge University Press.

Wright, M., Amess, K., Weir, C. and Girma, S. (2009) 'Private equity and corporate governance: retrospect and prospect'. *Corporate Governance: An International Review* 17(3): 353–75.

Wright, P. and Gardner, T. (2004) 'The human resource – firm performance relationship: methodological and theoretical challenges'. In Holman, D., Wall, T., Clegg, C., Sparrow, P. and Howard, A. (eds) *The New Workplace: A Guide to the Human Impact of Modern Work Practices*. London: John Wiley.

Wright, P., Gardner, T., Moynihan, L. and Allen, M. (2005) 'The relationship between HR practices and firm performance: examining causal order'. *Personnel Psychology* 58(2): 409–46.

Wright, P., McMahan, G. and McWilliams, A. (1994) 'Human resources and sustained competitive advantage: a resource-based perspective'. *International Journal of Human Resource Management* 5(2): 301–26.

Wright, P. and Nishii, L. (2013) 'Strategic HRM and organizational behaviour: integrating multiple levels of analysis'. In Paauwe, J., Guest, D., Wright, P. (eds) *Human Resource Management and Performance: Achievements and Challenges*. Oxford: Wiley-Blackwell.

Wright, P. and Snell, S. (1998) 'Toward a unifying framework for exploring fit and flexibility in strategic human resource management'. *Academy of Management Review* 23(4): 756–72.

Wrzesniewski, A. and Dutton, J. (2001) 'Crafting a job: revisioning employees as active crafters of their work'. *Academy of Management Review* 26(2): 179–201.

Youndt, M., Snell, S., Dean, J. and Lepak, D. (1996) 'Human resource management, manufacturing strategy, and firm performance'. *Academy of Management Journal* 39(4): 836–66.

Zatzick, C. and Iverson, R. (2006) 'High-involvement management and workforce reduction: competitive advantage or disadvantage?' *Academy of Management Journal* 49(5): 999–1015.

Zatzick, C., Moliterno, T. and Fang, T. (2012) 'Strategic (mis)fit: the implementation of TQM in manufacturing organizations'. *Strategic Management Journal* 33: 1321–30.

Zoghi, C. and Mohr, R. (2011). 'The decentralization of decision making and employee involvement within the workplace: evidence from four establishment datasets'. *British Journal of Industrial Relations* 49: 688–716.

Author index

Abernathy, W., 43
Adam, D., 134, 140, 141, 142
Adler, P., 21, 198
Ahlstrand, B., 7, 148, 233
Alexander, M., 90, 229, 269, 270
Allen, B., 171
Allen, J., 117
Allen, M., 138
Alonso, A., 66
Alpander, G., 36
Anderson, N., 52
Andrews, R., 227
Ang, S., 27, 162, 174, 207, 284
Antonakis, J., 197, 199
Appelbaum, E., 23, 66, 133,155, 160,
    188, 189, 234, 235, 238, 239, 245
Aring, M., 195
Armstrong, M., 124, 126
Arthur, M., 18
Aryee, S., 67, 204
Atkinson, J., 10, 11, 107
Avery, D., 170
Avgar, A., 252
Aycan, Z., 62

Bach, S., 139, 216, 217, 218, 219, 220,
    222
Bacharach, V., 157
Bacon, N., 138, 164, 237
Baden-Fuller, C., 44, 84
Baird, L., 68, 162
Bakker, A., 116, 120, 199
Baldamus, W., 123

Balogun, J., 32
Bamber, G., 38, 39, 202
Bamforth, K., 134, 187
Barney, J., 37, 83, 84, 85, 86, 87, 88,
    89, 96
Baron, A., 124, 126
Baron, R., 60, 99, 100, 163
Barr, P., 47, 49
Barrick, M., 156, 157, 160, 162
Barsoux, J.-L., 256, 257, 262, 268, 269
Bartram, T., 27, 162, 174, 207, 284
Baruch, Y., 249
Batt, R., 24, 66, 70, 151, 167, 188, 203,
    207, 209, 211, 234, 235, 238, 239,
    245
Bauer, T., 119, 167
Baumeister, A., 157
Beatty, R., 7, 26, 110
Becker, B., 7, 26, 76, 80, 110, 163
Becker, T., 167
Beer, M., 58, 59, 60, 168
Belbin, M., 47, 53
Belbin, R., 53
Berggren, C., 187
Bernard, A., 192
Berner, M., 27, 186
Bernhardt, A., 23, 66
Bevan, G., 223
Bewley, H., 139
Billett, S., 111
Bird Schoonhovern, C., 42
Birley, S., 52
Black, S., 190

Blackman, D., 214, 215
Blader, S., 145
Blasi, J., 77
Blau, P., 16, 159
Blauner, R., 9, 181, 184, 190
Blumberg, M., 155
Blyton, P., 20, 39, 164
Boeker, W., 42, 51
Bolino, M., 122
Bond, M., 62, 65
Bonet, R., 108
Boon, C., 155, 293
Bordonga, L., 219, 220
Boselie, P., 13, 61, 155, 242, 293
Bosma, H., 120
Boudreau, J., 75, 110, 126, 174, 298
Bowditch, J., 244, 246
Bowen, D., 162, 170, 171, 203, 204, 207
Bowey, A., 123, 125, 129
Boxall, P., 4, 5, 8, 9, 12, 14, 18, 19, 27,
    34, 40, 52, 58, 66, 76, 84, 94, 97,
    98, 102, 106, 107, 112, 115, 118,
    119, 122, 137, 138, 139, 144, 148,
    159, 160, 162, 166, 167, 174, 189,
    197, 199, 205, 207, 208, 209, 213,
    284, 297
Boyer, K., 190
Boyne, G., 227
Bozkurt, O., 206, 207
Bracker, J., 33
Braun, W., 271
Braverman, H., 20, 171, 183
Brewster, C., 28, 262
Broadbent, K., 218
Brookes, M., 262
Brown, C., 21
Brown, W., 138
Brynjolfsson, E., 190
Bryson, A., 119, 137, 139, 145, 146,
    253, 265,
Budd, J., 142
Buono, A., 244, 246
Burawoy, M., 20, 171, 183
Burch, G., 52

Burgess, S., 118
Butler, J., 89
Buxton, J., 118

Caldwell, R., 168
Campbell, A., 90, 229, 240, 269, 270
Campbell, D., 127
Campbell, K., 127
Campion, M., 77, 157
Cappelli, P., 108
Carroll, G., 11, 38, 42, 43, 44
Carroll, M., 18, 106, 208
Carter, K., 36
Cartier, K., 19
Cartwright, S., 246
Cascio, W., 110, 174, 298
Chadwick, C., 70
Challis, D., 190
Chandler, A., 183, 186, 197, 230
Charlwood, A., 138, 146
Chênevert, D., 70, 71
Cherns, A., 134, 158
Chia, H., 127
Chicha, M.-T., 125
Child, J., 39, 41, 46, 47, 49, 50
CIPD, 139, 141
Clark, A., 122
Clark, I., 234, 235, 238, 239, 245
Clegg, H., 20, 22, 184
Clegg, S., 16
Cleveland, J., 113
Coff, R., 86, 97
Collard, R., 144
Colli, A., 208
Colling, T., 8
Collings, D., 104, 110, 112, 116
Collins, C., 106
Combs, J., 76, 77
Conyon, M., 245
Cooke, F., 66, 167, 253, 269
Cooke, W., 15, 23, 63, 65, 193, 265
Cool, K., 83
Cooper, C., 122, 246
Cordery, J., 183, 207

Costa, J., 41
Cotton, E., 253, 267
Cox, A., 140
Cribb, J., 220
Crichton, A., 74, 111
Cronshaw, M., 69
Cropanzano, R., 20, 145, 247
Croucher, R., 253, 267
Cullinane, S., 199, 201
Currie, G., 225
Cutcher-Gershenfeld, J., 164
Cyert, R., 8, 50

D'Analeze, G., 146
Dale, B., 144
Danford, A., 144, 198
Darbishire, O., 66
Das, A., 35, 71
Datta, D., 244
Davids, K., 190
Davis, E., 69
Davis, S., 248
De Geus, A., 294
De Menezes, L., 87, 112, 198
De Treville, S., 197, 199
Dean, J., 66
Deane, P., 182
DeCastro, J., 91
Deci, E., 119, 121
Deery, S., 207
DeFillippi, R., 37, 86, 89
Delaney, J., 9, 76
Delbridge, R., 145, 198
Delery, J., 71, 74, 78
Demerouti, E., 120, 199
Demina, N., 237
Deming, W. E., 188
Deng, M., 169
Dierickx, I., 83
Dietz, G., 155, 293
Dikkers, J., 118
DiMaggio, P., 13, 38, 61
Disney, R., 220
DiTomaso, N., 166

Dodge, T., 146
Doeringer, P., 63, 80, 185
Donaldson, T., 15, 40, 50
Doorewaard, H., 214
Dopson, S., 219
Dore, R., 234
Doty, D., 71, 74, 78
Dowling, P., 28, 262, 268
Drahokoupil, J., 257
Droge, C., 71
Dunning, J., 254, 255, 256, 257
Dutton, J., 171
Dyer, L., 11, 26, 60, 76
Dysik, A., 158, 160

Eagle, A., 28, 262, 268
Eastman, L., 189
Eaton, S., 67
Edgar, F., 169
Edwards, M., 106, 247
Edwards, P., 14, 19, 20, 80, 106, 140,
    209, 262
Edwards, T., 65, 255, 256, 264
Eilbert, H., 74
Eisenberger, R., 159
Eisenhardt, K., 47, 49
Eliassen, K., 217
Erdogan, B., 167
Eurofound, 164
Evans, C., 138
Evans, P., 18, 104, 164, 256, 257, 262,
    268, 269
Eysenck, H., 74, 108

Fabling, R., 66, 77
Fang, T., 71
Farndale, E., 142, 265
Farrell, D., 206
Feldman, E., 229, 243, 244
Felstead, A., 111, 112, 160
Fenton-O'Creevy, M., 167
Ferlie, E., 217, 222
Fernández-Pérez, P., 208
Ferner, A., 256, 263, 264

Ferris, G., 161, 166
Festing, M., 28, 262, 268
Fisher, M., 222
Flanders, A., 22, 134, 144, 185
Fletcher, A., 223
Folger, R., 20, 145, 247
Ford, R., 203, 204, 207
Forsgren, R., 36
Forth, J., 139, 145, 146, 253
Foster, R., 43, 44
Fox, A., 136, 183, 186
Francis, R., 224
Frederick, S., 191, 193
Freeman, J., 32, 36, 42
Freeman, R., 23, 66, 137, 139, 146
Frenkel, S., 203, 207, 208, 292
Frese, M., 156
Friesen, P., 41, 44
Froud, J., 234, 236
Fryer, G., 211
Fuchs, S., 247
Fuller, S., 113

Gadrey, N., 9
Gaertner, S., 122
Gallie, D., 111, 119, 215
Gamble, J., 63, 64, 262, 263
Gardner, T., 155
Geare, A., 9, 169
Geary, J., 263
Gelade, G., 87, 112, 198
Genadry, N., 18, 164
Georgiadis, K., 138, 145, 146
Gereffi, G., 191, 193, 252, 258
Gerhart, B., 75, 76, 80, 123, 126
Gersick, C., 42
Ghemawat, P., 41
Ghoshal, A., 5, 98
Ghoshal, S., 88
Giangreco, A., 147
Gilbert, J., 19
Gilligan, C., 118
Gioia, D., 51, 113, 114
Gitell, J., 38, 39, 161, 224

Godard, J., 9, 71, 77, 78
Goergen, M., 236, 237, 238, 239, 248
Gohler, G., 16
Gokhale, J., 245
Goldoftas, B., 21
Gomez, R., 137, 139
Gooderham, P., 61
Goold, M., 90, 229, 240, 269, 270
Gordon, G., 166
Gospel, H., 15
Gottschalg, O., 89
Gouldner, A., 159
Gould-Williams, J., 159
Graen, G., 149, 167
Grant, D., 21, 97, 165, 171
Grant, J., 244
Grant, R., 32, 96, 242, 294
Gratton, L., 7, 293
Green, A., 208, 209
Green, F., 134, 215
Greener, I., 217, 219, 221, 222, 223
Greer, I., 265
Griffeth, R., 122
Grimes, A., 66, 77
Groshen, E., 245
Grugulis, I., 8, 73, 206, 207
Guest, D., 20, 149, 155, 159, 166, 265, 292
Guthrie, J., 124, 127
Guy, F., 207

Hackman, R., 119, 121, 160, 187
Halbesleben, J., 122
Hall, M., 134, 137, 140, 141, 142, 143, 146, 152, 170
Hall, R., 85, 96
Hambrick, D., 47, 52
Hamel, G., 34, 90, 91, 93, 94
Hammer, N., 257, 259, 267
Hamori, M., 108
Hampden-Turner, C., 63, 78
Hannan, M., 11, 22, 38, 42, 43, 44, 184
Harley, B., 20, 119, 162, 171
Harney, B., 208

Harris, L., 151
Harvey, G., 38, 39, 138
Harvey, J., 122
Haspeslagh, P., 248
Haugaard, M., 16
Hauptmeier, M., 265
Haworth, N., 136
Hayes, R., 12
Haynes, P., 66, 137, 138, 139, 148, 211
Hebdon, R., 217, 218, 220, 222
Hedley, B., 233
Hedlund, G., 97, 240, 242
Henderson, R., 43
Hendry, C., 18
Heng, C., 214, 215
Heracleous, L., 211
Herzberg, F., 187
Hilgert, J., 23
Hill, C., 40, 50
Hill, S., 144, 151, 197
Hind, P., 249
Hinings, C., 40
Hird, M., 269
Hitt, L., 190
Hochschild, A., 207
Hoddeson, L., 88
Hofstede, G., 14, 62, 63, 65, 78
Holden, R., 225
Holder, G., 60
Holland, J., 116
Holweg, H., 225
Hom, P., 122, 159
Hood, C., 222, 223
Hoopes, D., 86
Hope-Hailey, V., 167
Horwitz, F., 214, 215
Hubbard, N., 245, 247, 248
Huber, V., 113
Huff, A., 47, 49
Hughes, J., 198
Hughes, S., 24, 136
Hull, R., 109
Humphrey, J., 258
Humphrey, S., 158

Hunt, J., 52, 297
Hunt, S., 12, 35, 37, 47, 85, 96
Hunter, J., 47, 98, 108, 113, 156
Hunter, L., 67
Hunter, R., 156
Hurst, J., 214, 215
Huselid, M., 7, 26, 76, 77, 110
Hutchinson, S., 111, 167, 168, 174, 208, 222
Hutchison, A., 189
Hyman, J., 22, 171

Ichniowski, C., 76, 78, 80, 145
Inkson, K., 4
Isenberg, D., 47
Iverson, R., 164, 170, 207

Jackson, C., 121
Jackson, P., 190, 191
Jackson, S., 61, 68, 69, 70, 109, 157
Jacoby, S., 185, 186, 241
James, L. A., 169
James, L. R., 169, 170
Janis, I., 51
Jany-Catrice, F., 9
Jarzabkowski, P., 32
Jayaram, J., 71
Jemison, D., 248
Jensen, J., 192
Jensen, M., 16, 235
Jensen, P., 194
Jiang, K., 155, 158, 161
Jones, A., 18
Jones, D., 188, 197
Jones, G., 269, 270
Jones, S., 182
Jones, T., 40, 50
Jordan, C., 208
Judge, T., 156
Judiesch, M., 47, 98, 108
Juravich, T., 23

Kalleberg, A., 66, 123
Kamoche, K., 86

Kaplan, R., 33, 41, 90, 292
Karasek, R., 120, 184
Katz, H., 66
Kaufman, B., 8, 18, 61, 71, 77, 78, 147, 184, 276
Kay, J., 69, 98
Kaysen, C., 8
Keenoy, T., 19
Kelly, J., 20
Kenney, M., 64
Keron, P., 219
Kerr, A., 220
Kessler, I., 127, 128, 139, 145, 216, 217, 218, 219, 220, 222, 225
Ketchen, D., 71
Kets de Vries, M., 114
Kilgour, J., 124, 126
Kim, B., 74
King, A., 89
Kinnie, N., 98, 155, 172
Kintana, M., 66
Kirkpatrick, I., 217, 218, 220, 222
Kirn, S., 212
Knox, A., 67
Kochan, T., 73
Korczynski, M., 207
Kossek, E., 14, 80
Kostova, T., 14
Koteyko, N., 225
Koukoulaki, T., 200
KPMG, 245
Kreps, D., 60, 99, 100, 163
Krugman, P., 191
Kruse, D., 77
Kuruvilla, S., 65, 252
Kuvaas, B., 158, 160

Lacey, R., 184
Lafortune, G., 105
Lakhani, T., 252, 258
Lam, S., 288
Langfred, C., 191
Lanvin, B., 18, 104
Lashley, C., 67
Latham, G., 74, 79, 113

Latham, S., 113
Law, K., 67
Lawler, E., 133, 188, 189
Lawson, B., 190
Lazear, E., 16, 126, 127
Leana, C., 5
Lee-Kelley, L., 214, 215
Lees, S., 14
Legge, K., 7, 8, 72, 97, 165, 275, 297
Lengnick-Hall, C., 270
Lengnick-Hall, M., 270
Léonard, D., 252, 257
Leonard-Barton, D., 44, 87, 91, 92, 93, 94, 100, 101, 244
Lepak, D., 27, 98, 99, 100, 112, 161, 169, 170, 284
Lepine, J., 121
Lepine, M., 121
Levine, D., 21
Levinson, D., 117, 118
Levinson, J., 118
Lewin, D., 76
Lewis III, J., 244
Li, A., 156, 157
Liden, R., 167
Ligthart, P., 139
Linehan, C., 7, 297
Littler, C., 171, 183
Lockett, A., 83
Longenecker, C., 51, 113, 114
Lorenz, E., 63, 64, 80, 198
Lovas, B., 88
Lovelock, C., 35, 203, 204
Lundan, S., 254, 255, 256, 257
Lynch, L., 190

Mabey, C., 268, 269
MacDonald, H., 74, 79, 113
MacDuffie, J., 162, 164, 187, 191, 248
Macky, K., 76, 139, 144, 159, 166, 167
Madsen, T., 86
Maguire, S., 246
Mahoney, J., 83
March, J., 8, 50, 115

Marchington, M., 8, 18, 73, 106, 140, 144, 208, 209
Marginson, P., 52, 253, 256, 263, 264, 297
Marsh, C., 269
Marshall, V., 113, 114
Marsick, V., 111
Martin, J., 151
Martínez-Lucio, M., 138
Marx, K., 4
Maslach, C., 109, 157
Maslow, A., 4
Mayer, M., 242
McBride, J., 119, 162, 171, 172
McGee, J., 65
McGovern, P., 167, 241
McKay, P., 170
McKersie, R., 164
McKinsey & Company, 179, 194, 195, 196, 198
McLaughlin, K., 217
McMahan, G., 88, 97
McMillan, J., 51
McWilliams, A., 88, 89, 97
Meardi, G., 253, 263
Meckling, W., 16, 235
Meihuizen, H., 214
Mellahi, K., 104, 110, 112, 116
Meshoulam, I., 68, 162
Meyer, A., 40
Meyer, S., 183
Michailova, S., 63
Michie, J., 70, 71
Milkovich, G., 123
Miller, B., 8, 18, 71, 78, 147
Miller, D., 40, 41, 44, 69, 84, 114
Millward, N., 145, 253
Mintzberg, H., 32, 33, 39, 46
Mohr, R., 133
Moliterno, T., 71
Molleman, E., 197
Morgan, G., 161, 182, 252, 260
Morgenstern, U., 83
Morgeson, F., 77, 158
Morris, J., 64

Morris, M., 170
Morrison, D., 160
Mount, M., 156, 157, 160, 162
Mueller, D., 42, 43, 46
Mueller, F., 88, 89, 96, 265
Murnane, R., 23, 66
Murphy, K., 113
Murray, A., 69
Murray, G., 257

Nahapiet, J., 5, 98
Narasimhan, R., 35, 71
Nelson, R., 40, 83
Nerlich, B., 225
Neumark, D., 245
Newbert, S., 83
Newman, J., 123
Newman, K., 63
Newman, W., 41
Niepce, W., 197
Nishii, L., 169, 172
Nissen, B., 23
Nollen, S., 63
Norburn, D., 52
Nordhaug, O., 61
Norton, D., 33, 41, 90, 292

O' Sullivan, N., 236, 237, 238, 239, 248
O'Brien, E., 7, 297
O'Brien, G., 117
O'Neill, G., 127
Odiorne, G., 107
Ogbonna, E., 151
Ohmae, K., 253
Ohno, T., 188
Olaverri, C., 66
Oldham, G., 119, 121, 160, 187
Oliver, C., 188, 198
Ono, T., 105
Organ, D., 158
Orlitzky, M., 106
Ortega, J., 209
Osborne, P., 217
Osterman, P., 9, 10, 21, 27, 185, 186, 206, 208

Ostroff, C., 162, 170, 171
Ouchi, W., 59

Paauwe, J., 13, 61, 242, 265, 293
Pandian, J., 83
Parker, S., 121, 183, 184, 191, 198, 207
Pascale, R., 34
Patterson, P., 35, 203, 204
Payne, G., 71
Peccei, R., 147, 151, 162, 163, 174, 212
Pedersen, T., 194
Penrose, E., 82, 83, 96
Pernod, M., 9
Peter, L. J., 109
Peteraf, M., 67
Pfeffer, J., 40, 50, 75
Phillips, J., 298
Phillips, N., 246
Phillips, P., 298
Pichler, S., 14, 80
Pil, F., 164, 191, 248
Pinfield, L., 27, 186
Piore, M., 185, 188
Pirenne, H., 181
Pisano, G., 12, 94
Poell, R., 111
Polanyi, M., 97
Poole, M., 8, 58
Porter, M., 12, 36, 37, 38, 40, 41, 46, 65,
    67, 68, 69, 71, 76, 83, 84, 102
Poutsma, E., 139
Powell, W., 13, 38
Prahalad, C., 34, 90, 91, 93, 94
Prennushi, G., 145
Preston, L., 15, 40, 50
Price, R., 206
Priem, R., 89
Pringle, C., 155
Pucik, V., 256, 257, 262, 268, 269
Purcell, J., 7, 16, 71, 76, 98, 99, 111,128,
    129, 134, 137, 138, 140, 141, 142,
    143, 145, 146, 147, 148, 152, 155,
    167, 168, 170, 172, 174, 208, 222,
    224, 231, 233, 241, 245, 248, 265

Quazi, H., 214, 215
Quinn, R., 212

Radnor, Z., 225
Ram, M., 14, 19, 20, 106, 140, 209
Ramsay, H., 136
Rayton, B., 146
Redman, T., 8, 160
Reed, R., 37, 86, 89
Rees, C., 255, 264
Rees, H., 118
Reeves, T., 76
Reich, M., 21
Reynolds, P., 35
Richardson, H., 189
Riisgaard, L., 257, 259, 267
Ringdal, K., 61
Riordan, M., 88
Robertson, I., 122
Robinson, S., 246
Rock, M., 124
Romanelli, E., 41
Rondeau, K., 225
Roos, D., 188
Roos, G., 195, 197
Rose, M., 117, 119, 122, 123, 208
Rosenthal, P., 151, 162, 163, 174, 208,
    212
Rousseau, D., 20, 50, 163
Rowlinson, M., 51
Rubery, J., 18, 36
Rucci, A., 212
Rumelt, R., 86
Ryan, R., 119, 121

Sabel, C., 188
Sako, M., 146
Saks, A., 145
Salancik, G., 40, 50
Samson, D., 190
Samuel, P., 138
Sanders, J., 121
Sanz-Vergel, A., 116
Sargent, L., 171

Saunders, M., 145
Scandura, L., 149, 167
Schaubroeck, J., 288
Schaufeli, W., 120, 121, 122
Schleifer, A., 245
Schmidt, F., 47, 98, 108
Schmidt, J., 245
Schmitt, N., 74
Schnaars, S., 42
Schneider, B., 169
Schoenstein, M., 105
Schott, P., 192
Schuler, R., 61, 68, 69, 70
Schumpeter, J., 38, 41, 86
Schwartz, H., 248
Scott, W., 13, 14, 61
Segal-Horn, S., 202, 203, 204
Seidner, R., 161
Seifert, A., 266
Sergeant, A., 292
Shafer, R., 11
Shah, R., 197, 198
Shamsie, J., 84
Shanley, M., 67
Shaw, K., 78, 80, 145
Sheehan, M., 70, 71
Shibata, H., 64
Shore, L., 159
Short, J., 71
Shuen, A., 94
Sibieta, L., 220
Siebert, W., 9, 204
Siegrist, J., 123
Siggelkow, N., 36, 71
Simon, H., 47, 115
Sims, H., 51, 113, 114
Sisson, K., 16, 146, 208, 241
Sitter, N., 217
Smale, A., 259, 263
Smart, D., 89
Smith, A., 182
Smith, C., 50
Smith, P., 75
Snape, E., 8, 160

Snell, S., 21, 44, 66, 98, 99, 100, 112
Soane, E., 159
Soderberg, A., 245
Solar, P., 191
Sparrow, P., 269, 271
Spender, J-C., 34, 47, 65
Sprigg, C., 191
Srinavasan, T., 40
Standing, G., 123
Stansfield, S., 120
Steedman, H., 25, 71
Steeneveld, M., 5, 94, 97, 213
Sterling, A., 112, 160, 197, 199
Stiglitz, J., 16, 128
Stimpert, J., 47, 49
Stopford, J., 44
Storey, D., 18
Streeck, W., 10
Stuart, M., 138
Sturgeon, T., 258
Suchman, M., 14
Sulsky, L., 74, 79, 113
Summers, L., 245
Sun, L-Y., 67
Swart, J., 98, 212, 214

Tailby, S., 138, 219
Takeuchi, R., 159, 161
Tan, F., 290
Tattersall, I., 180
Tayeb, M., 79
Taylor, F., 183
Taylor, M., 106
Teece, D., 5, 35, 36, 37, 42, 43, 71, 87,
    94, 95, 96, 97, 101, 195, 284
Terkla, D., 63, 64, 80
Terry, M., 138
Theodore, N., 149
Theorell, T., 120, 184
Thompson, P., 20, 119, 162, 171, 234,
    235, 239, 240, 241, 243
Thompson, S., 83
Thornhill, A., 145
Thorpe, R., 129

Toh, S., 77
Tremblay, M., 70, 71
Trevor, C., 75, 126
Trist, E., 134, 187
Trompenaars, F., 63, 78
Tsui, A., 40
Tuchman, B., 51
Turnbull, P., 20, 38, 39, 138
Tushman, M., 41
Tyler, T., 145

Uhl-Bien, M., 149, 167
Ulrich, D., 168
UNCTAD, 252
Utterback, J., 43

Vaara, E., 245
Valeyre, A., 198
Van Buren, H., 5
Van der Velden, R., 117
Van Engen, M., 118
Van Iddekinge, C., 116, 157
Van Veldhoven, M., 120, 199
van Wanrooy, B., 8, 107, 113, 123, 134,
    137, 139, 140, 141, 142, 146, 169,
    223, 228, 241
Vandenberg, R., 189
Veersma, U., 139
Veliyath, R., 40
Vickery, S., 71
Vidal, M., 198
Vinkenburg, C., 118
Volberda, J., 242
Vroom, V., 155

Waddington, J., 220
Wagner, K., 25, 71
Wagner, T., 225
Walker, G., 86
Walker, R., 35
Wall, T., 190
Walsh, J., 67, 207, 256
Walshe, K., 227
Walton, R., 164

Ward, P., 197, 198
Waring, J., 225
Warner, M., 183
Warr, P., 75
Wassenaar, B., 189
Watkins, K., 111
Watson, T., 6, 20, 36, 81, 182,
    187, 297
Way, S., 70
Webb, B., 19
Webb, S., 19
Wernerfelt, B., 83, 84, 85, 87
West, G., 91
West, M., 224, 225
Westcott, M., 238
Wever, K., 25
Whitfield, K., 145
Whittington, R., 32, 242
Wilkinson, A., 8, 188, 197
Wilkinson, B., 64, 188, 198
Williams, J., 8, 16, 46, 50
Williamson, O., 8, 16, 50, 232
Willman, P., 137, 139
Willmott, H., 188, 197
Wimbush, J., 161
Winchester, D., 138
Windolf, P., 18, 106
Winterton, J., 25, 64, 134, 187, 196
Wirtz, J., 203, 204, 211
Womack, J., 188, 197
Wood, G., 236, 237, 238, 239, 248, 262
Wood, R., 113, 114
Wood, S., 87, 112, 127, 128, 198, 265
Wright, M., 80, 234, 235, 236,
    237, 238
Wright, P., 21, 44, 88, 97, 155, 172, 293
Wrzesniewski, A., 171

Xanthopoulou, D., 120, 199

Youndt, M., 44, 74, 80

Zagelmeyer, S., 140, 142
Zaheer, S., 14

Zapf, D., 156
Zatzick, C., 71, 164, 170
Zbaracki, M., 47, 49
Zeithaml, C., 89

Zhou, Y., 215
Zoghi, C., 133
Zollo, M., 89
Zubanov, N., 9, 204

Subject index

ability, *see* employee ability
absenteeism, 146, 162, 209
acquisitions, *see* mergers and acquisitions
adult life-cycle theory, 117–8
ageing workforce, 295
agency theory, 16, 51, 235
agility, *see* organisational agility
Air Products, 99
airline industry, 38–9, 210
alignment principle, 89, 104–31,
    285–6, *see also* mutuality
AMO framework/model, 155–61,
    172–3, 175, 182, 189, 286, 292
analytical HRM, xi
apparel industry, *see* clothing
    manufacturing industry
Apple Computer, 42–3, 213
apprenticeships, 181
appropriability, 86
assembly line, 184, 197, 207
asset specificity, 87
attitude surveys, 76, 296
automobile industry, 93, 164, 184, 195,
    210, 254
autonomous work groups, 187, 189
autonomy, *see* employee control,
    employee involvement,
    management power
Aviva, 203

balanced scorecard, 90, 292–3
banking and finance sector, 16,
    76, 93, 125, 128–9, *see also*
    financialisation

bargaining model, 20, *see also* effort-
    reward balance
barriers to imitation, 37–8, 85–90,
    102–3
Bay of Pigs, 51
benchmarking, 265
best-fit school, 57–81, 277–8
best-practice school, 57–81, 277–8
black box problem, 26, 154–76, 190,
    278, 286–7
black hole firms, 149
Bleak House model of HRM, 208
BMW, 194–5
bonus-driven model of HRM, 240–3,
    268–73, 282, *see also* pay
bossnapping, 13
Boston Consulting Group (BCG)
    matrix, 233–4
bounded rationality, 47
British Oxygen, 99
buddy systems, 111
bundling, 162–3
bureaucratic HRM, 43–4, 59, 66, 125,
    139–40, 185–6, 200, 208, 217,
    224, 286
burnout, 108–9, 122
business case, 298
business models, 9, 27, 37, 39, 71, 195,
    209
business strategy, *see* strategy
buyouts, 237–9

C&NW, 49
Cadbury, 50, 253

call-centre industry, 70–1, 150, 207–8, 259, 280

Canon, 90

capabilities, *see* competences, dynamic capabilities

capital markets, 231, 234–6, 239–43, 250

career development, *see* talent management

careerists, 50–1

causal ambiguity, 89–90, 92,103

change management, 21–2, 42–6, 147, 162, 223, 239, 248, 265, 276–7

Chaparral Steel, 92, 101

chief executives, *see* management

chronic underachievers, 108–9, 117

clan model of HRM, 59

clothing manufacturing industry, 266, *see also* Rana Plaza

cognition, 47–9

coherence, 162–4, 179, 175, 287

collective bargaining, 22–4, 61, 132, 134–5, 137–8, 143, 185, 218, 221, 264, 266–7, 271

collectivism, 62

command-and-control style, 149

commitment-oriented HRM, 98–100, 107, 127–8

compensation, *see* pay

competences
core, 44, 90–1
distinctive, 90
enabling, 93
supplemental, 93
see also dynamic capabilities

competitive advantage
sustained, 12, 37–9, 54, 82, 85, 88, 94, 284–5, 288
temporary, 12, 37
see also parenting advantage

competitive disadvantage, 97, 103, 188

competitive parity, 96

competitive strategy, *see* strategy

compliance, 7, 14–15, 17, 61, 144, 221, 225, 268, 299

configurational perspective, 40, 71, 278

conglomerates, 232–3

consistency, 60, 162–4, 166, *see also* internal fit

consultative committees/forums, 134–6, 140–3, *see also* employee voice

context, *see* law of context, best-fit school, industry fit, organisational fit, societal fit

contingency perspective, 58, 67–72, 82, 154, 278

control, *see* employee control, employee involvement, labour power, management power

core/periphery models of HRM, 99–103, 204, *see also* HR architecture

corporate social responsibility, 15, 194, *see also* social legitimacy

corporate strategy, *see* strategy

cost-effectiveness, 8–10, 77–8, 101, 193, 276

cost-oriented HRM, 69–71, 100, 194

craft model of HRM, 181, 280

culture
national, 14, 62–5, 74–5, 262–6
organisational/workplace, 84, 114, 166, 244–9

cycles of control, 136

decent work agenda, 23–4

demand-control-support (DCS) model, 120, *see also* job strain

de-skilling, 182–4

development-oriented model of HRM, 240–3, 250, 268–73, 283

difficult conversations, 113

disconnected capitalism, 235

discretion, *see* employee control, employee involvement, high-involvement model of HRM

discretionary effort, 160, *see also* employee motivation

discrimination, 14, 24, 80, 276
distinctive inadequacies, 91
diversification, 229–30
diversity climate, 170–1
division of labour, 182
divisionalised companies, *see*
    multidivisional firms
dominant coalition, 46
dominant designs, 43
downsizing, 6, 240, 243–50
dynamic capabilities, 94–6
Dyson, 11–2, 26, 101–2, 254

education sector, 25, 64–5, 102, 196,
    216–8, 221, 223, 282, 299
effort-reward balance, 123, 286, *see*
    also equity theory, organisational
    justice
emotional labour, 207
employee
    ability, 155–7
    attitudes, 159, 169–76, 174, *see*
        also employee attributions,
        motivation, perceptions
    attributions, 169, 176, 287
    control, 119, 133, 160, *see also*
        employee involvement
    engagement, 120–1, 159, 173–4
    growth, 116–9
    interests, 116–31
    involvement, 132–3, 139, 147–8,
        160, 164, 189–91, 237
    motivation, 19–21, 116–31, 155–61
    perceptions, 20, 81, 107, 144–6, 151,
        155, 159–60, 169–76
    performance, 107–10, 112–5,
        155–61
    resistance, 20–21, 147, 172–3, 225,
        246, *see also* labour process
        theory, trade unions
    rights, 132, 144, 149, 154
    turnover, *see* labour turnover
    well-being, 115–31, 199–200, 223–7,
        237–9, 246–9, 285–6

voice, 132–53, *see also* consultative
    committees/forums, trade unions
employer
    branding, 106, 215
    of choice, 15, 100
employment
    ethics, 14–5, 153, 267, 298, *see also*
        social legitimacy
    practices, 6, 64
    regulation, 15, 61, 272, 294, *see also*
        employee rights, social legitimacy
    relationship, 20, 104, 115, 117, 119,
        130, 137, 154, 159–60, 169, 275,
        278, 285, 297
    security, 75, 107, 116, 122–3, 138,
        164, 185, 235, 247, 270
    value proposition, 106
empowerment, *see* high-involvement
    model of HRM
engagement, *see* employee engagement
entrepreneurship, 37, 42
Equal Employment Opportunity
    (EEO), 14–5
equifinality, 78, 80, 277
equity theory, 20, 123–131, 286, *see*
    also organisational justice
establishment context/phase, 42
ethics, *see* employment ethics
European Union, 132, 257, 299
executive search, 52–3
experience curve, 42
expert model of HRM, 213–6, 282
expressivism, 119, 130
external equity, *see* equity theory
external fit, 68, *see also* industry fit,
    organisational fit, societal fit
extrinsic motivators, *see* employee
    motivation

factory system, 181–4
Fairchild Semiconductor, 88
fairness, *see* equity theory,
    organisational justice
family firms, 208–9

fast followers, 42
financial control, 240–1, 249
financialisation, 16–7, 101, 234–6,
    260–1, 268
funding strategy, 35
first-line managers, *see* management
flexibility, *see* organisational agility,
    organisational flexibility
focus strategy, 68, 76
footwear manufacturing industry, 192
forcing and fostering, 164
Ford, Henry, 183–4
Fordism, 183–5, 198
front-line managers, *see* management
functional equivalence, *see* equifinality
functional flexibility, 11

gender
    and career patterns, 118
    and work-life balance, 215
    neutrality in pay, 125
General Electric, 32, 242
General Motors, 188, 230, 265
gestalt perspective, 40, 71, 278
global financial crisis, 10, 16, 18, 22,
    36, 73, 93, 123, 129, 219, 236
global value chains, 252, 257–60
globalisation, 191–5, 201, 242, 272,
    294
goals of HRM, *see* human resource
    management
governments, *see* employment
    regulation, regime advantage,
    social legitimacy, societal fit
Great Depression, 184, 191
groupthink, 51

harmonisation, 100
Harvard framework, 58–60
headhunting, 52
health sector, 18–9, 105, 157, 161, 216,
    218, 223–4, 227
high-commitment management, *see*
    commitment-oriented HRM

high-involvement model of HRM, 133,
    164, 188–91, 198, 200, 211–2,
    214, 281
high-performance work systems, 75–8,
    189
high potentials, 108–9, 112, 126, 271
high-road models, 38, 70
Hollywood film studios, 84
homo economicus, 47
honey traps, 114, 124, 131
horizontal fit, *see* internal fit
hotel industry, 67, 71, 209–11, 281
HR analytics, 290–1
HR-function strategy, 26, 28, 168,
    296–8, *see also* HR specialists
HR planning, 289–301
HR policy, 60, 80, 96–7, 103, 156,
    163–4, 167, 169, 173, 263,
    286–7
HR practices, 57–81, 96–7, 162–3,
    168–9, 173, 263, 277, 291–2
HR specialists
    and employee voice, 146
    and the black box, 172–3
    in multinationals, 269
    roles of, 7, 28, 52, 296–300
    see also HR-function strategy
HR strategy
    and the HR function, 26–8, 168
    and the resource-based view,
        82–103
    corporate, 27–8, 228–50
    defined, 25–30
    in manufacturing, 179–201
    in multidivisional firms, 228–50
    in multinational firms, 251–73
    in services, 202–27
    see also human resource
        management, strategic HRM
HR systems, 162, 284, *see* human
    resource management–typology
    of models
human capital, 5–6, 97–8, 105–115,
    158, 174, 215, 227, 285, 287–8

human capital advantage, 12, 97, 104, 131, 285
Human Relations Movement, 187
human resource advantage, 12–13, 17, 29, 98, 101–2, 276, 285
human resource architecture, 98–100
human resource management
    analytical approach to, xi
    defined, 5–7, 28, 35
    goals of, 7–17, 29–30, 275–7
    principles of, xi, 79–81, 278
    strategic tensions and problems in, 17–25, 29–30, 275–7
    typology of models, 278–84
human resources
    defined, 3–5
    in the RBV, 83–5, 96–103
    see also human capital

IBM, 42–3, 62, 255
imitation, 42–3
individualism, 62, 75, 152
industrial democracy, see consultative committees/forums, employee voice
industrial model of HRM, 27, 184–6, 200, 280
Industrial Revolution, 181–4
industry
    analysis, 46
    clusters, 102
    evolution, 42–5, 53–4
    fit, 65–7, 278
    recipes, 65
informal model of HRM, 208–9, 281
Information and Consultation of Employees (ICE) regulations, 140
information technology, 46, 93, 190, 259, 271, see also internet
inimitability, see barriers to imitation
innovation, 11, 27, 38, 42–4, 59, 64, 69–70, 77, 95, 147, 149, 170, 189, 233, 242, 250, 259
institutional perspective/theory, 13–14, 61, 276

Intel, 43
intellectual capital, see human capital
intelligence, 156–7
interdependence, 99–100, 127
interest alignment, see alignment principle
internal equity, see equity theory, organisational justice
internal fit, 60, 162–5, 175, see also coherence, consistency
internal labour markets (ILMs), 185–6, 200
international division of labour, 64–5
international HRM, 28, 62, 65
International Labour Organization (ILO), 23–4, 132, 135–6
internet, 34, 36, 38, 45, 86, 93, 95, 191, 257
intrapreneurship, 42
intrinsic motivators, see employee motivation
Investors in People (IiP), 15

Japanese management, 63–4, 78–9, 187–8, 197, 200, 241–2, 262
job
    analysis, 124
    characteristics theory, 119–20, 160
    complexity, 108
    crafting, 171
    demands-resources model, 120–1, 199, 201
    enrichment, 119, 187, 189
    evaluation, 124–5
    quality, 115–31
    satisfaction, see employee attitudes, employee well-being
    security, see employment security
    simplification, 182
    strain, 120
joint consultative committees, see consultative committees/forums, employee voice
joint working parties, 145

justice, *see* organisational justice
just-in-time (JIT), 197

key value generators, 50
know-how, *see* employee ability
knowledge
   -based view (KBV), 90–1
   explicit, 97
   -intensive services, 212–6
   management, 94
   tacit, 97
   workers, 212–6

labour
   costs, 9, 26, 65, 138, 192–3
   hoarding, 21
   law, *see* employment regulation
   markets, 18–9, 61–2
   power, 4, 50, 136
   process theory, 20, 119, 171, 176
   scarcity, 18–9, 105–6
   surpluses, 107
   turnover, 21, 96–7, 118, 187, 207,
      209, 218, 246, 258, 280–2, 291
law firms, 203
law of context, 81, 179, 278, 262–6
lay-offs, *see* downsizing
leader-member exchange (LMX),
   149, 167
leadership, 5, 44, 53, 62–3, 84, 151,
   166, 233, 240, 284, 296, *see also*
   management
lean production, *see* production
learning, 111, 118–20, 154, 189, 199,
   215, 247–9, 284, 288
learning factories, 64
legal compliance, *see* compliance
legislation, *see* employment regulation
legitimacy, *see* social legitimacy
life-cycle theory, *see* adult life-cycle
   theory, industry evolution,
   organisational life-cycle
long-run agility, *see* organisational
   agility
low-road models, 38, 70

management
   accounting, 186
   consultancy, 149
   development, 52–3, 112, 268–71
   front-line, 7, 113, 144–5, 149,
      166–8, 173, 176, 250, 264, 287–8,
      296–7, 299
   middle, 24, 89, 147, 149, 167
   of managers, 52–3
   power, 15–17, 132–53, 235, 241,
      277, 300
   style in employee relations, 148–53
   top/senior, 34, 88, 95–6, 149, 161,
      163, 166, 172–3, 222, 228
manufacturing
   advanced/capital-intensive/high-tech,
      9, 66, 190, 195–6, 203, 210, 281
   HR strategy in, 179–201
   labour-intensive/low-tech, 66,
      192–3, 195, 201
   lean, 87, 111–2, 196–201
   types of, 180–3, 187–8, 190, 195, 197
marginal performers, 108–9, 117
market model of HRM, 59
marketing, 24, 31, 35, 37, 40, 44, 51,
   54, 71, 83, 106, 172, 230, 278
mass production, *see* production
mature context/phase, 43–4
mediating processes, 158
mental models, 48–9
mergers and acquisitions, 243–50, 264
Microsoft, 41
migrant labour, 9, 179, 208
mining industry, 106
monopolies, 83, 213
motivation, *see* employee motivation
motorcycle industry, 188
multidivisional firms, 228–50
multinational firms, 251–73
mutuality, 39, 115–6, 130, 159, *see also*
   alignment principle

nation states, *see* employment
   regulation, social legitimacy,
   societal fit

national culture, *see* culture
neo-liberalism, 152
networked organisation (N-form), 242–3
new public management, 217–27
newspaper industry, 45
non-substitutability, *see* barriers to imitation
NUMMI (Toyota–GM plant), 198–9

offshoring model of HRM, 192–5, 254, 281
oil shocks, 294
oligopolies, 46, 50, 83
operations management/strategy, 31, 35–6, 54, 71, 101, 103, 172, *see also* production
opportunity to perform, 155–60, 175, 286
organisational
  agility, 10–11, 26, 145, 293
  citizenship behaviours, 158
  climate, *see* social climate
  culture, *see* culture
  fit, 67–72, 278
  flexibility, 10–11, 17, 21–2, 276
  justice, 20–1, 145, 159, 247, 250, 286, *see also* equity theory
  life-cycle, 68
  performance, 154–76, 286–8, *see also* competitive advantage, viability
  politics, 49–51
  process advantage, 98, *see also* social capital
  survival, *see* viability
outsourcing model of HRM, 99, 192–5, 281

parenting advantage, 41, 229–34, 249, 270
partnerships, 213
path dependency, 87, 92
Pax Victoriana, 191

pay
  as a motivator, 122–31
  equity, 123–30
  executive, 17, 73, 129
  performance-related, 126–30
perceived organisational support, 145, 159–60, 175
perfect competition, 83
performance appraisal, 112–5
performance equation, *see* AMO framework/model
performance management, 130, 217–8, 221–4, 227, 269
performance-related pay, *see* pay
personal growth, 116–20, 131, 214
personality, 157
personnel management, x–xi, 59, 72
perverse incentives, 128–31
Peter Principle, 109
pivotal positions, 110
poaching, 19
politics, *see* organisational politics
power, *see* labour power, management power
power distance, 62, 140
powerholic personality, 114
precariat, 123
private equity, 234–9, 249–50
privatisation, 218
production
  batch, 181
  continuous flow, 183–4
  craft, 180–1
  lean, 87, 111–2, 188, 196–201, 225
  mass, 181–4, 187–8, 197
  systems, 35, 156–9, 165, 172, 188, 190, 197–9, 201, 286
productivity, 9, 38, 49, 63, 76, 92, 99, 126–7, 138, 146, 190, 227, 235–9, 249, 272, 277, 290
professional model of HRM, 213–6, 221–27, 282
provisioning motive, 122

psychological
climate, 169–70, 176
contract, 20–1, 163, 165–6
public sector, 216–27
punctuated equilibrium, 41–2

quality circles, 144, *see also* total
quality management

Rana Plaza, 23, 267–8
rater bias, 113
reciprocity, *see* alignment
principle, mutuality, perceived
organisational support
recruitment and selection, 105–8
redundancies, *see* downsizing
regime advantage, 256, 271
regulation, *see* employment
regulation
remuneration, *see* pay
renewal context/phase, 44–5
reproduction factories, 64
research methods, 174–5, 290–1
resource-based view (RBV), 82–91, 93,
96, 98, 102, 284
resource-dependence theory, 50
resource mobility barriers, 88
rest-home industry, 67
retail sector, 9, 106–7, 206, 238
reward systems, *see* pay
rhetoric versus reality, 165–6, 176
Rock Island, 49

Safelite, 126
salaried model of HRM, 27, 186–7,
200, 280
scenario planning, 294–6
Schumpeterian shocks, 37–8, 86, 103
Scientific Management, 183–4, *see also*
Taylorism
S-curve, 43–5
Sears, 21
scripted model of HRM, 207–8, 226,
280

selection, *see* recruitment and
selection
self-actualisation, 4
self-determination theory, 119
self-management, 4–5
self-managing teams, *see* autonomous
work groups
semi-conductor industry, 88, 195
service-profit chain, 212
services
characteristics of, 66, 202–4
differentiated, 209–10
knowledge-intensive, 212–6
public sector, 216–27
standardised and simple, 205–6
Shell, 294
Shockley Semiconductor, 88
short-run responsiveness, 10–11,
see also organisational flexibility
sit by Nellie, 111
skill utilisation, 116–7
small firms, 18, 106,139–40, 208–9
social
capital, 5–6, 98, 158, 270–1
climate, 21, 170–1, 176
complexity, 87–8, 92
context theory, 161, 176
exchange, 159
legitimacy, 13–15, 132–53, 186,
193–4, 266–8
media, 139, 141
order, 22, 102, 144
partners, 61
support, 121
societal fit, 25, 61–65, 262–6, 278
socio-technical work systems, 134,
187
solid citizens, 108–9
Sony, 90
specialisation, *see* Scientific
Management, Taylorism
stakeholder perspective, 40, 50
standardisation, 163, 198, 217
star employees, 108–9

states, *see* employment regulation, social legitimacy, societal fit
steel industry, 78, 168
STEM subjects, 196
strain, *see* job strain
strategic business units (SBUs), 90, 232
strategic choice perspective, 39–41
strategic fit, 289–90
strategic groups, 66–7, 79, 202, 295
strategic HRM
  academic study of, xi, 275
  and sustained competitive advantage, 82–103
  best fit *versus* best practice in, 57-81
  see also HR strategy, human resource management
strategic management process, 46–54, 275
strategic planning, 32, 39, 46, 289–301
strategic problems, 31–41, 53–4
strategy
  and the life-cycle of firms, 41–46
  and the resource-based view, 82–90
  business, 40, 60, 61, 72, 83, 274
  competitive, 40, 68–71, 76, 83–4
  corporate, 41, 229–34, 242
  defined, 31–41, 53–4
  emergent, 39
  see also strategic management process, strategic planning, strategic problems
stress, 120, 173–4, 190, 200, 207–8, *see also* job strain, work intensification
strikes, 20–2, 50, 162, 220, 267, *see also* employee resistance, worker activism
success trap, 49
succession planning, 112
super-salaries, 17, *see also* bonus-driven model of HRM, pay
survival, *see* viability
survivor syndrome, 249
sustained competitive advantage, *see* competitive advantage

sweetheart unionism, 150–1
synergy, 241–2, 250

table stakes, 34–6, 54, 93–4, 284
takeovers, *see* mergers and acquisitions
talent
  blockages, 109–10
  ghettos, 110
  management, 104–31, 158, 195–6, 214, 285
  spirals, 110
Taylorism, 183–5, 200, *see also* Scientific Management
team-building, 52–3
teamwork, 6, 12, 48, 53, 64, 88, 90, 112, 164, 187, 191, 214, 223–5, 275
technology, *see* information technology, manufacturing
telecommunications industry, 70
time-and-motion study, *see* Scientific Management, Taylorism
time orientation, 62
total quality management (TQM), 71, 197
town hall meetings, 134
Toyota production system, 188, 197–8
trade unions
  and industrial model, 184–6
  and management style, 148–51
  and 'partnership' agreements, 138
  bargaining with, 134–7
  history of, 22–3, 137–9, 184–5
  in the public sector, 137, 139, 220
trade-offs, 18–30, 277
training and development, 110–2
transnational corporations, *see* multinational firms
trucking industry, 18
trust in management, 145, 148–51, 153, 171, 176

uncertainty avoidance, 62
Unilever, 269–71
union avoidance, 241, 263

unions, *see* trade unions
unique timing and learning, 87–8
United Nations (UN), 23
universalism, *see* best-practice school
upper echelons, 52

vertical fit, *see* external fit
vertical integration, 230, 242
viability, 8–10, 29, 34–7, 39, 107, 109,
    221, 238, 274–5
vocational
   education and training (VET), 25
   interests, 116
voice, *see* employee voice
Volvo, 187

wage-work bargain, *see* effort-reward
    balance
war for talent, 18, *see also* talent
    management
well-being, *see* employee well-being
whanau interviewing, 78
whipsawing, 265
women, *see* gender

work
   in manufacturing, 180–201
   in services, 202–27
   intensification, 164, 183, 198
   -life balance, 4–5, 122, 215
   mechanistic model of, 183
   practices/processes, 6, 64
workaholism, 122
worker activism, 171–2, *see also*
    employee resistance, strikes
workforce
   analytics, 290–1
   differentiation, 112, *see also* core/
    periphery models of HRM, HR
    architecture
   performance, 154–76, 286–8
   quality, 107–110
   strategy, 26, 28, *see also* HR strategy
workplace culture, *see* organisational
    culture
works councils, *see* consultative
    committees/forums

zero-hours contracts, 10, 204